TV Creators

The Television Series │ Robert J. Thompson, Series Editor

television series

TV creators

CONVERSATIONS WITH
AMERICA'S TOP PRODUCERS
OF TELEVISION DRAMA
VOLUME TWO

James L. Longworth, Jr.

Syracuse University Press

The Library of Congress has cataloged volume 1 as follows

Library of Congress Cataloging-in-Publication Data

Longworth, James L., 1954–
    TV creators : conversations with America's top
producers of television drama / James L. Longworth,
Jr.— 1st ed.
        p. cm. — (The Television series)
    Includes bibliographical references and index.
    ISBN 0-8156-2874-9 (alk. paper)—
    ISBN 0-8156-0652-4 (pbk.: alk. paper)
    1. Motion picture producers and directors—
United States—Interviews. I. Series.

PN1998.2 .L64 2000
791.45'0232'092273—dc21

                                                00-039476

    ISBN 0-8156-2953-2 (cl.)
    ISBN 0-8156-0702-4 (pbk.)

Manufactured in the United States of America

"Everyone who is breathing has a story that they want to tell. You can write a diary, you can write an essay, or a poem. Or you can write a short story, a play, or a movie, or a television show. I think it takes a certain amount of courage to start writing that story. And then it takes even more courage to finish the story."

—TOM FONTANA, award-winning writer/producer, *St. Elsewhere; Homicide: Life on the Street; Oz*

This book is dedicated to storytellers past, present, and future.

Television, the scorned stepchild of drama, may well be the basic theater of our century.

—PADDY CHAYEFSKY, writer

A bad show is never that bad when it gets good ratings.

—MICHAEL DANN
former programming executive for CBS

Born on March 11, 1954, in Winston-Salem, North Carolina, Jim Longworth displayed an early talent for writing and broadcasting. As a student at R. J. Reynolds High School, he became one of the youngest announcers for commercial station WSJS Radio, and while attending the University of North Carolina at Greensboro, Longworth learned all facets of television production at the campus studio. After graduating he followed a career path in commercial television that included jobs ranging from camera operator to hosting and producing a live, daily talk show.

In 1980 Longworth and his wife, Joanne, founded a television production company that today specializes in production and distribution of documentaries and public-affairs programming. Longworth has written articles for *TV Guide, Western Clippings,* and *Columbia House RE-TV.*

Jim is a voting member of the Academy of Television Arts and Sciences and serves as a judge for the Prime Time Emmys. In November of 2000 he produced and moderated "Women in Drama" for the Academy, which featured Tyne Daly, Amy Brenneman, Lorraine Toussaint, Annie Potts, Melina Kanakaredes, Dixie Carter, Kathleen Quinlan, and Sela Ward, along with showrunners John Masius, Marshall Herskovitz, Barbara Hall, Paul Haggis, and Nancy Miller.

Longworth has written, produced, and directed hundreds of TV programs and public-service announcements, including one that helped win passage of the nation's first significant handgun legislation. He also produced a public-service announcement that documented the link between animal abuse by children and the violent crimes they later commit as adults.

Jim's first book, *TV Creators: Conversations with America's Top Producers of Television Drama* (volume one), was published in November of 2000. He is currently developing several teleplays.

contents

Illustrations

Preface

AS moving day neared for the outgoing Clinton administration, a stack of bumper stickers could be found in the office of exiting U.S. Surgeon General Dr. David Satcher (*Broadcasting & Cable*, January 8, 2001). Deliberately printed with numerous misspellings and distributed by TV-Free America, the stickers proclaimed, "Surgoen Generel's Warnig: Telivison Promots Iliteracy."

All over the country, conservative organizations, congressmen, and so-called proponents of a family-friendly agenda raged against TV as a corrupting influence. An Annenberg Public Policy Center study added fuel to the fire, pointing out that nearly 60 percent of children have TV sets in their bedrooms and that nine out of ten parents could not actually identify the age ratings for the programs their kids watched (*Time*, July 17, 2000). Activists like Joan Anderson, author of *Getting Unplugged*, urged her readers to break the TV habit, saying, "TV is not a member of our family; it's a stranger. Would you let a stranger into your child's bedroom?" (*Time*, January 1, 2001)

However, such sentiment was not a modern-day phenomenon. In March of 1985, *Harper's Magazine* quipped, "Disparaging television has long been a favorite national pastime—second in popularity only to watching it." TV—you can't live with it, and you just can't seem to turn it off. What is a media-addicted society to do?

The fact is, there *are* a lot of bad programs on television, mostly in the form of reality/game shows, where contestants will do almost anything for money, and in daytime talk shows, where guests will *say* just about anything for a chance at their fifteen minutes of fame (and a free haircut back home). There are plenty of bad news programs as well, all of which are eager to capitalize on and sensationalize other people's faults and tragedies. And then there are bad sitcoms, where, like thick gravy poured over spoiled meat, laugh tracks are used to cover up inferior writing. *Frasier, Becker,* and *Everybody Loves Raymond* are the exceptions, but even they struggle to maintain originality. That leaves dramas, which for the most part have historically been excellent, regardless of form or era. Certainly *Apple's Way*, for example, was not as well crafted as *The Waltons,* and *Deep Space Nine* was not as engaging as its parent series *Star Trek.* But even mediocre dramas were and continue to have more thought-provoking content and redeeming value than do most sitcoms, especially those produced over the past decade.

Anti-TV groups, though, like to take aim at dramas, claiming that partial nudity, occasional profanity, and on-screen violence are responsible for every sex crime and school shooting in America. In truth, TV dramas are not guilty of anything except trying to entertain, inspire, and educate. At a 1989 gathering of the now-defunct Viewers for Quality Television, the late NBC president Brandon Tartikoff said, "A quality show is one in which the people who are crafting it are really working at the height of their powers. Their intention is not to do what has been done before, but to try to establish some new territory, a new horizon for whatever kind of show that they're doing" (*The Story of Viewers for Quality Television*).

This second volume, as did its predecessor, seeks to recognize men and women who are, as Tartikoff said, "at the height of their powers," and who continue to establish "new territory." These are the creators, producers, writers, and showrunners of quality television drama who are still active in the new millennium and whose personal stories are as inspiring as the teleplays they bring us each week.

As was pointed out in volume one of this series, TV creators are a generally underappreciated lot and few have achieved widespread notoriety outside of Hollywood. Stuart Kaminsky in his book *Writing for Television* reminded us that, "Fame is an unlikely result of writing for television. How many television writers can you name?" Of course, an increasing number of books and magazine articles are helping to shed light on the brilliant artists whose work usually remains in the shadow of those who perform it. TV creators themselves are beginning to feel a sense of fraternity in this new age of drama. In an April 2001 episode of *The Sopranos*, Meadow Soprano is introduced to an entertainment attorney who, she is told, "represents Dick Wolf." "The sportscaster?" she asks. "No," replies her friend, "The producer of *Law & Order* and *New York Undercover*." "Oh," says Meadow, "I loved that show." Meanwhile, *Once and Again* co-creator Marshall Herskovitz pressed his partner Ed Zwick into acting duty, giving Zwick newfound recognition. Most viewers still did not know Ed as an Emmy-winning writer and Oscar-winning producer, but they did come to respect him as a psychiatrist. Hey, it's progress.

But the twelve producers featured in this second installment of *TV Creators* have more in common than just being underappreciated. Most have come from humble beginnings to achieve great financial success and critical acclaim. Some began their career as playwrights (Sorkin, Campbell, and Haggis), others as novelists (Hall and Huggins). Several cut their teeth writing sitcoms (Hall, Haggis, Whedon, and Williamson), while others started out as actors (Spelling, Sorkin, Campbell). Most are baby boomers, and two (Spelling and Huggins) are TV pioneers whose careers have spanned six decades. All of them had mentors who were instrumental in nurturing and encouraging their talents, and all of them, without exception, are white.

In reviewing the first volume of *TV Creators*, Irv Letofsky of *The Hollywood Reporter* criticized my failure to include any African American producers. Had Letofsky been better informed about the industry he was assigned to cover, he would have known that, at the time of publication, there *were* no black TV creators of weekly drama series. Paris Barclay, who co-created with Steven Bochco the short-lived *City of Angels*, was scheduled for inclusion in this edition, but later called to cancel on advice from his attorney. Barclay had departed the series, and the split from Bochco was, apparently, none too amicable. The sad truth is, there remains a dearth of African American writers, producers, and showrunners in television drama. In fact, "dearth" may not be a strong enough word. As of this writing, there is still not one black creator/writer/showrunner at the helm of a weekly network drama series.

For now, though, we can at least be grateful that network programming chiefs are still willing to invest time and money in quality dramas, and that is no small commitment, given the rising pressure to develop more economical nonfiction programming. After all, not every drama produced by the twelve individuals in this book is a top-ten show. Some do not even win their time period. And by the time this book goes to press, some shows will have been canceled. But all of the dramas written about here and all of the creators examined within these pages have made and continue to make a lasting contribution to our culture.

Ed Zwick told me that I was the James Boswell for TV creators. He called me some other things too, but that is a matter for litigation. Nevertheless, as I reflected on my newfound moniker, I was flattered. If this series of books can, in any small way, help to bring more widespread understanding of and attention to the talented individuals who toil behind the scenes (producing the equivalent of a motion picture every two weeks), then perhaps being Boswell to their collective Samuel Johnson is not such a bad way to be remembered.

Acknowledgments

FOr some reason, I have always liked to write, and for that I have many people to thank who encouraged me along the way. My earliest memories are of drawing dirty pictures on the living room wall. I was only four years old, so I do not recall what captions accompanied my pornographic art, but I do remember being punished. The lesson I learned was that my First Amendment rights apply everywhere except in the living room. Wall writing not withstanding, my parents were always very supportive of my creative endeavors, and for that I am grateful. By age six, I started composing love ballads, which I used to refer to as "sad songs" because, while singing them for my family, I would always cry at my own lyrics. In elementary school, I won the Freedom Foundation Award for my essay, "Why I Love America." The judges of that prestigious contest had no idea that I had once "done time" sitting in the corner for violating community standards of decency.

While working my way through college, I signed on with WFMY-TV in Greensboro, North Carolina, ostensibly to run studio camera and to clean up "accidents" left by nervous children in attendance at our afternoon kiddie show. But thanks to program director Jack Markham, I was given an opportunity to write, shoot, produce, and host documentaries. I also served a tour of duty in news, where one of Walter Cronkite's top writers, Rabun Matthews, harnessed my energy and made sure I did not embarrass him too often. And I spent time at an ad agency, where Janet Merritt turned me into a pretty decent copywriter. Over the past thirty years I have written everything from commercials to documentaries to magazine articles, and now, to this second in a series of books. To all those mentioned, your mentoring was much appreciated and has not been forgotten.

Of course, I am particularly grateful to the twelve TV creators who spent some of their precious little free time with me and to their executive assistants and confidants who kept track of schedules and appointments. Special thanks to Laura Brew, Lauren Carpenter, Mark Dube, Marcie Gold, Diego Guttierrez, Renate Kamer, Laurie Lieser, Steve Lyons, Patty Sachs, Dianne Salzberg, Gian Sardar, and Ken Thompson.

I was also extremely fortunate to be able to call upon some industry heavyweights to help with my research. Particular thanks go to Garth Ancier,

Jerry Bruckheimer, Stephen J. Cannell, Susanne Daniels, Les Moonves, and my buddy Don Ohlmeyer.

Thanks also to some of television's most underappreciated taskmasters. Beth Haiken at CBS, Curt King at NBC, Laura Sharp at Warner Brothers Television, Michael Kurinsky at Industry Entertainment, and the WB's Cathy Schaper and Keith Marder all made sure that I had photos and tapes at my disposal and that I would not go to jail for using them.

A special salute to my trusted friends Robert O'Donnell and Melissa Brown at the Academy of Television Arts & Sciences for their support when I produced and moderated "Women In Drama.' Because of their hard work, the event, which featured more than a dozen of Hollywood's elite, went off without a hitch; as a result, I was able to include input from our panelists in this book.

A belated thanks to John Fruehwirth, director of Syracuse University Press, who held my hand (figuratively speaking) during the editing of my first book. His instruction allowed me to do a better job of construction the second time around. Thanks are in order to other members of the Syracuse University Press team as well, including Amy Farranto and series editor Robert Thompson. Bob is the person who roped me into publishing *TV Creators*, so if you do not like what I have written, blame him. Thanks also go to Pelican Street Studio for their creative design.

Thanks are long overdue to my pal Dan Seaman, who helped me sharpen my forensic skills in college and today remains a touchstone.

I also want to thank my sister Linda, whose phone calls always came at just the right time and whose words of support never failed to lift my spirits.

And, kudos to my wife, Joanne, for the life journey she has embarked upon with me. Our road along the way has been rocky at times, but, as *X-Files* agent Dana Scully said to her partner Fox Mulder, "I wouldn't change a day. Well, maybe that Fluke Man thing. I could have lived without that just fine." We all encounter our own kind of Fluke Man in life, but he's always easier to defeat when you have the support of someone you love.

Finally, my thanks to you, the reader, for agreeing to invest your time and money in these pages. I only hope that you have as much fun reading our interviews as I had conducting them.

Introduction

Game-show producers willing to do almost anything for the sake of ratings. Hollywood being charged with gender, age, and racial discrimination. Congress trying to encroach on the creative process. Unions fighting for more money. Affiliates battling networks. Consumers reluctant to purchase expensive new technology. And a handful of corporations trying to own everything we watch. These events happened in: (a) the 1950s, (b) the 1960s, (c) the 1970s, (d) the 1980s, (e) the 1990s, (f) the 2000s, or (g) all of the above. The answer is "(g) all of the above," proving that in television as in life, the more things change the more they stay the same.

In the 1950s Senator Joseph McCarthy ran roughshod over the entertainment industry, trying to remove the "red menace" from Hollywood. In 2001 Senator Joseph Lieberman and others continued their crusade to remove the sex-and-violence menace from the airwaves.

In the 1950s the producers of *Twenty One* prompted contestants in order to guarantee a dramatic outcome. In 2001 the producer of *Survivor: The Australian Outback* was accused by a contestant of influencing the outcome of the previous year's contest.

In the 1960s, '70s, and '90s the NAACP accused Hollywood of "white washing" and Congress appointed commissions to study the problem. In the new millennium, the NAACP was still demanding racial diversity both in front of and behind the cameras.

In the early 1960s industry insiders were surprised that consumers did not immediately embrace color TV. Today, television technologists are baffled about why consumers will not invest upwards of five thousand dollars for a high-definition television.

In 1988 a strike by the Writers Guild crippled the television industry, and in 2001 that same group teetered on a repeat performance.

In the 1990s networks and their affiliates went to war over compensation issues, and in 2001 a consortium of TV stations fought attempts by the webs to increase ownership caps and interfere with local programming choices.

In the 1970s independent studios complained of networks having an ownership stake in and control over distribution of programming. By 2001 independent producers and studios were almost extinct due to mega-mergers that had put control of the industry in the hands of just a few companies.

It seems that we in the television industry continue to fight the same battles and raise the same concerns nearly every decade, and for the most part we seldom achieve resolution or win lasting reform.

One exception is the increasing presence of women in drama. Until 1999 fewer than thirty prime-time dramas had ever starred a woman in the title or lead role. In 1962 Bette Davis pondered openly why there were no lady lawyers on TV. Now, thanks to the revolution of '99, women in drama are more prominent than in any time during our history; and that, unlike racial disparities or battles over program control or high-definition TV, represents a substantive change for the better.

Nevertheless, the battles and issues that continue to rage affect how we watch; when we watch; and who produces, writes, and stars in *what* we watch. What follows is an overview of some major developments in the television industry during the opening years of the new millennium.

THE NEW AGE OF DRAMA

According to Nielsen Media research, eight of the top ten prime-time programs in the 1996–97 season were comedies (*Time*, March 12, 2001). In fact, throughout the 1990s prime time was inundated with sitcoms, most of which had "sit" but very little "com." At one point in the decade, NBC flooded its schedule with comedies, much to the chagrin of former west-coast president Don Ohlmeyer. "The biggest mistake we ever made at NBC was going to eighteen comedies," he said. "That's what started our decline, and we went there because people started getting greedy, and the sales department wanted to sell eighteen comedies, and the programming department wanted to announce that they were the first entity that had ever had eighteen comedies on the air. I finally just gave up, and when I left the meeting I said, 'If everybody wants to do it, fine.' But I put up a sign in my office, and it's still there, which says, 'Delusional.' It's got the date of the decision that May. It was a 'delusional' decision [to do that many comedies], and that's what started the decline."

During that "delusional" comedy blitz, however, *Law & Order, Touched by an Angel, NYPD Blue,* and *ER* were born into and survived the '90s, but they were the exceptions to the rule. It was not until they were joined in January of 1999 by *Providence* that the drama genre began its new age. Since then, networks and cable alike have jumped on the drama bandwagon and have, in many cases, done so with women as the lead drivers.

The Age of Drama had only been up and running a short time, though, when it was challenged by so-called realty/game shows. Multiple weekly broadcasts of *Who Wants to Be a Millionaire*, along with *Survivor, Big Brother, Temptation Island*, and others, skewed the Nielsens so that hour dramas struggled to maintain their rightful audience shares. But like a patient investor during a bear market, dramas held on and began to catch a break. By 2001, *Millionaire*'s demographics started to age and, in some instances, actually helped fictional hour shows find an audience. *JAG*, for example, benefitted from channel-surfing viewers who had grown weary of *Millionaire*. Meanwhile, *Survivor: The Australian Outback* elevated its schedulemate *CSI: Crime Scene Investigation* to a regular spot in the top ten—at one point even helping the crime show to reach number two.

Concurrently, cable channels were either entering the drama-series arena or stepping up their involvement with it. Lifetime continued to hit home runs by adding *Strong Medicine* and *The Division* to its Sunday-night powerhouse lineup, which included veteran *Any Day Now*. The Sci-Fi channel, USA, and TNT continued to build upon their drama fare, and even Court TV entered the fray with reruns of *Profiler* and *The Rockford Files*. But the biggest story on cable was with pay TV. Showtime and HBO had already become well established with groundbreaking made-for-TV movies, but 2001 brought a paradigm shift in the industry with the success of *The Sopranos*. David Chase's two-hour season opener pulled in more than eleven million viewers, beating all other network and cable shows in its time period. As the Associated Press's David Bauder pointed out, "That's remarkable since HBO, a pay cable service with just thirty-three million subscribers, is only in about one third the homes of the broadcast networks." *The Sopranos* also helped to diminish the 2001 Oscar telecast, whose ratings were the lowest since 1997.

Once again HBO, which also had *Oz* in its stable, was raising the bar for dramatic television, causing everyone else to develop more innovative hour shows. To better compete in the drama genre, networks and cable even reached out to men who had made their reputations in big-screen motion pictures. Joining TV veterans Ed Zwick, Marshall Herskovitz, and Barry Levinson (who had already tested the small-screen waters with *thirtysomething, Once and Again*, and *Homicide: Life on the Street*) were more big names, including James *"Titanic"* Cameron (Fox's *Dark Angel*), Paul *"Quiz Show"* Attanasio (ABC's *Gideon's Crossing*), and Sydney *"The Verdict"* Lumet (A&E's *100 Centre*

Street), all of whom crossed over into TV in the new millennium. Clearly, the once-mighty barriers between the two industries of film and television had come tumbling down, and TV was much the richer for it. For all practical purposes, these big-screen "defections," coupled with Chase's mob hit on the Oscars, signaled the end to a bifurcated creative community that had been apart for entirely too long.

REALITY GAMES

Television has always been a medium of contests, with programmers competing for scripts, talent, ratings, advertisers, and awards. It is understandable, then, that as the new millennium got under way, networks tried to win at their game by *playing* games. ABC's *Who Wants to Be a Millionaire* started the trend in 1999 and became so popular that by 2000 the network began airing it four times per week. Even in the 1950s and '60s, when game shows were prime-time staples, they appeared only weekly. But ABC milked its newfound treasure to the max, and initially the unprecedented strategy paid off. Aging demographics and strong competition from dramas, however, would eventually erode some of *Millionaire*'s strength.

Fox's *Who Wants to Marry a Millionaire*, on the other hand, died a quick and embarrassing death when one lucky couple refused to consummate their short-lived marriage and the bride fulfilled her desire for a normal life by posing nude in *Playboy*. Then, after a brief respite from the genre, the network offered up *Temptation Island*, where supposedly betrothed couples would spend time with attractive strangers on a romantic island as a test of fidelity. Later one couple revealed they were only along for the media exposure and another confessed to already having had a child together. Following the first episode, Fox sponsors Quaker Oats and Best Buy pulled their ads, and at least one station (WRAZ, Raleigh) refused to air the seduction series.

There were other entries into the reality sweepstakes, including ABC's *The Mole* and UPN's *Chains of Love*. The latter, from the producers of *Big Brother*, literally chained five people together for four days. What does *that* say about TV and the proverbial weakest link?

The king of the reality series, though, was *Survivor*. The first edition premiered in the summer of 2000 and registered huge wins over mostly rerun TV. The show took place on an island, and contestants were divided into tribes. It was the contestants' job to compete and connive until, after several months of rigorous backbiting, all but one participant had been "voted off" by the others. America caught *Survivor* fever, so much so that, in an unprecedented move, competing networks helped CBS to promote its groundbreaking series. Both NBC's and ABC's morning shows produced regular *Survivor* segments—this from a group of networks who had refused to cooperate on how to cover the 2000 presidential debates! Knight Ridder's Kinney Littlefield referred to this practice as "corporate incest," where *Good Morning America, Today,* and *The Early Show* treated reality/games "as if it were real news and not a shill" (August 26, 2000). Cross-promotional assistance had occurred before, of course, but not at that level. *Who Wants to Be a Millionaire,* for example, conducted periodic celebrity matches where stars from CBS and NBC would appear. But that intramural love fest was partially checked when the show's demos started greying. NBC refused to let *The West Wing* star Martin Sheen appear as scheduled, and CBS's Les Moonves, who was already benefitting from cross-network *Survivor* hype, issued a similar order to his troops, "Don't help the enemy" (*Variety,* October 23, 2000). Perhaps *Survivor* did not need any help in the promotion department, but it did suffer some public-relations setbacks. Nearly a year after the first installment, one of the losing contestants (Stacey Stillman) sued producer Mark Burnett for interfering in the process by urging her removal early on. *Survivor: The Australian Outback* followed in the fall of 2001 and it too was fraught with controversy, including the accidental burning of one contestant and the senseless slaughter of a pig by another.Despite protests by animal-rights activists, *Survivor: The Australian Outback* proved to be as popular as its predecessor. CBS late-night king David Letterman was particularly critical of the animal slaughter and took every opportunity to take potshots at the series as well as at his boss, Les Moonves. I asked Moonves for his thoughts on the "reality" trend and its potential threat to hour dramas. "It is never our intention, now or in the future, to have more than an hour or so of reality programming on the schedule," Moonves said. "I think it is a great addition to have in the mix, great dramas, great comedies, a few good news magazines, a few good movies, and some reality. I think it only strengthens dramas. The addition of *Survivor* to our schedule means there will be one less drama, but that would have been our weakest drama, and this way, it will just increase the quality of these. Now, is there some danger when you look at a show like *Millionaire* that is on four nights a week? Absolutely. Too much of anything is no good for this business. I've said to my agent friends, 'Guys, we're all in this business together. We're all going to sink or swim together. Don't overreach how greedy you get.' In success there's plenty for everybody, but don't make it so the news magazines and the game shows look so much more attractive economically that the accountants at the networks start saying, 'Gee, why are you even doing a drama? Just put on another news magazine.'"

As usual, Moonves's assessment and predictions were right on target, and his confidence grew tremendously following a validating call from his idol. "Walter Cronkite called me after the first *Survivor* and said, 'You know Les, I thought you were crazy when you put that show on. I wondered what was happening to our network. But you had the vision and courage, and you're bringing the luster back to CBS.' I gotta tell you, I almost broke down," Moonves said. "Getting that call from Walter gave me goose bumps." Sure enough, *Survivor* strengthened the network and even helped to catapult one drama (*CSI*) into a mega-hit after it had been scheduled to follow the popular tribe tripe.

Meanwhile, over at NBC former programming chief Garth Ancier was fired for admirably *not* having developed any reality shows. In July of 2000 at a Critics Association meeting Ancier's then-boss, Scott Sassa, went so far as to apologize for the Peacock's lack of "realty." Kudos to Ancier for his resolve in refusing to lower the bar.

But we should be clear about one thing. Though billed as "reality" programming, these and other similar shows had little to do with reality. They are "game" shows, pure and simple, where contestants compete for a cash prize. To say they are anything else does a disservice to the handful of true reality programs that came into their own in the new millennium. For sheer, unrehearsed, unprompted drama, HBO was, again, a genre leader with its *Taxi Cab Confessions*, and ABC's *Hopkins 24/7* proved that a real hospital docudrama could outperform a fictional one. *Hopkins 24/7* was a six-part series that followed medical cases and the lives of the patients and doctors involved in treatment. The second installment actually beat an *ER* repeat in the ratings.

Whether or not the realty/game craze will endure is anyone's guess, but the Academy of Television Arts & Sciences (ATAS) did its part by legitimizing the new genre. Beginning in the fall of 2001, two new Emmy categories were established for "Outstanding Nonfiction Programming," with one designated for *Survivor*-type shows and the other for more traditional gamers, like *Millionaire*.

Clearly the New-Age trend in reality/games had an impact on TV dramas, both good and bad. As was noted earlier, in some cases these contest shows actually buoyed other network programming, but they also undeniably took up air time that could have been devoted to quality hour dramas.

Writers and actors threatening to strike in 2001 were increasingly worried about this trend. David Kelley, on the other hand, saw a silver lining in the cloud formed by nonfiction, "I think one upside from all this reality programming is that you're going to see stronger writing staffs on the live action programming. I do have the strongest stable of writers with me that I have ever had" (*The Hollywood Reporter*, August 1–7, 2000). And, in an interview with this author, former NBC executive Garth Ancier (now executive vice president of programming for Turner Broadcasting) echoed Kelley's sentiments, "I actually think there's going to be plenty of work for everyone who's talented." But Ancier himself was saddled with one game that took a *lot* of work away from a *lot* of talented people in the drama genre. In what will go down in history as the mother of all programming mishaps, NBC in 2000 made a deal (against Ancier's advice) with Vince McMahon's World Wrestling Federation for a 50 percent ownership stake in the newly formed XFL (short for "Extreme Football League"). Put simply, the XFL was faux football, complete with wrestling-style announcers (including Minnesota Governor Jesse "the Body" Ventura), scantily clad cheerleaders, and the promise of on-field body contact that would make the NFL look like a Pop Warner contest. In order to accommodate the deal, NBC jettisoned its entire Saturday-night drama line-up consisting of *Profiler*, *Pretender*, and *The Others*, all of which comprised a "Thrillogy" that was attractive to advertisers. NBC's Bob Wright had put out the word that he wanted the XFL to "get the young men on Saturday nights" (*TV Guide*, February 2001). But XFL not only did *not* hold on to young males, it also lost just about everyone else in the process. Fox sports analyst Keith Olbermann quipped, "If the ratings go any lower, the announcers will be able to address the viewer by his first name" (*TV Guide*, March 24, 2001). Olbermann should have been a psychic instead of a sports broadcaster. The XFL (which premiered on February 3) lost 75 percent of its audience by the second weekend, and by mid-March had become the lowest-rated show in the history of prime-time television with a 1.6 rating. By April the discarded drama thrillogy was looking pretty good.

Whether real games or fake ones, the networks' obsession with nonfictional programming had significantly altered the broadcast landscape. And with few exceptions (like the XFL), the networks turned a tidy profit by producing shows that did not require the services of—or payment to—"above the line" artists. Thirty years ago when a network wanted to experiment with alternative programming the result was a one-man show by Hal Holbrook as Mark Twain. But in 2001 we are treated to chained humans and pig slaughters. The late Fred Friendly, former president of CBS, once remarked, "Commercial television makes so much money doing its worst, that it cannot afford to do its best" (*The Quotable Writer*). As students of television drama, we can only hope that the realty/game trend abates or at least improves, and that networks will be encouraged to spend more of their money developing the next *The West Wing* instead of rushing to broadcast something much less expensive to produce, like *Temptation Island*. The question is, will the current corporate structures that control our airwaves be so inclined.

VERTICAL INTEGRATION

Not long ago "vertical integration" simply meant that a network ordered a crossover between two shows or a spin-off of one to another. Andy Griffith and Sheldon Leonard did it in the 1960s with *Gomer Pyle* and *Mayberry R.F.D.*, and in the 1970s Norman Lear created new shows from characters who had appeared on an existing series. In the late '80s, CBS paired up *Murder, She Wrote* with *Magnum P.I.* NBC had success in the '90s by teaming *Law & Order* with *Homicide: Life on the Street* for several two-hour specials, and then allowed *Profiler* and *Pretender* to meet before showing both of them the door. Even now, the drama crossover is not a lost art. In 2001 David Kelley, Paul Attanasio, and ABC combined forces to present a shared story line between *The Practice* and *Gideon's Crossing*.

But today the term "vertical integration" has an entirely different meaning and carries with it an enormous impact on television in general and on hour dramas in particular. In the 1990s NBC was swallowed up by General Electric, ABC and Lifetime were purchased by Disney, and CBS became a Viacom property. Meanwhile, Rupert Murdoch created his own corporate empire (NewsCorp), which included Fox, the FX Network, and, later, a financial stake in Viacom's UPN. Then in January of 2001 vertical integration moved to another level, when America On Line (AOL) and Time Warner Cable tied the knot, forever changing the relationship between programming and delivery systems. The AOL/TW stable included HBO, the WB network, and Warner Brothers Television, which supplied dramas to CBS (*The Fugitive*) and NBC (*ER*). It also included the former Turner Broadcasting family of CNN, TBS, and TNT, the latter of which had stepped up its efforts to develop original movies and series.

The AOL/TW marriage was particularly chilling to those who feared a monopoly in the works. Disney, for example, had opposed the merger, having already been burned once when Time Warner pulled all ABC affiliate stations from its cable systems nationwide following a dispute over carriage rates. But for creators, writers, and producers of television drama, the real threat of vertical integration was its concentration of virtually unregulated power in the hands of just a few individuals. In the 1970s small studios had successfully lobbied Congress to enact "FinSyn," which limited network ownership of programs and prohibited their financial interest in syndication of the same. But FinSyn was repealed in the 1990s, and that, coupled with the rise in mega-mergers, made small, independent studios who specialized in dramas almost extinct. Aaron Spelling, for example, was rolled into the Viacom Paramount family. Others, like Stephen Cannell, got out of the hour business all together. Moreover, with networks now in control of program delivery and with corporate siblings to synergize with, the development of television dramas became inexorably linked with their delivery. In other words, Disney-owned ABC began to prefer purchasing and broadcasting programs from subsidiary production house Touchstone, while CBS looked to make deals with Paramount, and so forth. In fact, by 2000 every major network except NBC was corporately aligned with a major content supplier. The Peacock countered by building a relationship with Studios USA, using Dick Wolf's *Law & Order* franchise as the foundation.

Of course, networks' search for control over their products was not a new phenomenon. As William Hawes points out in his book *Live Television Drama*, Bill Paley had decided in the late 1940s that "CBS, not the sponsors, theatrical producers, or ad agencies should produce our programs." What Paley could not have known, though, is that, fifty years later, vertically integrated webs would have the potential to stifle independent creativity, thus limiting the available product pool. Cannell's solution for insuring an honest exchange and unlimited supply of quality product is for Congress to reinstate FinSyn. Former NBC chief Don Ohlmeyer, however, disagrees with the premise that today's corporate ownership arrangements are, per se, a barrier to the discovery of great programming. "I hear all these excuses from different people, whether it's guys who don't have shows on the air, or minority writers, or elderly writers," Ohlmeyer said. "In all the years I've been around television, I've never seen a great show not get made. You sit there week after week and hear shitty pitches. Month after month you read shitty scripts. And when something comes along, do you honestly believe that all four networks are so stupid that they would miss it? Just ask yourself. All four networks plus HBO and Showtime, and all of these other channels that can produce an original show, do you honestly believe that a good show is not going to get made because of vertical integration? It's a nice excuse in the abstract, OK? But it's an excuse, nonetheless." In defending vertical integration, Stephen McPherson, vice president of Touchstone, told *Variety*'s Josef Adalian, "When you have the same people who are programming [a web] investing in creating assets, that helps to shape a smooth pipeline to getting a show on the air" (January 15, 2001).

However, "smooth" does not exactly describe the crosstown bitterness that ensued as a result of vertically driven program negotiations. Throughout most of 2001, for example, a battle raged between Fox and the WB over which web would have *Buffy the Vampire Slayer* on its schedule in 2002. *Buffy* had always aired on the WB, but the show was, after all, produced by 20th Century Fox. Fox wanted to produce, own, *and* broadcast *Buffy* and was willing to pay handsomely for that right. Eventually, the show moved to UPN, a weblet partially owned by Fox parent Newscorp. One way or the other, the WB was "outfoxed" by vertical integration. Meanwhile, Fox was under siege by a host of producers and actors who believed they were victims of vertically integrated program sales. Steven Bochco, for example, sued Fox for underselling *NYPD Blue* reruns to the FX Channel without first seeking what he believed would have been higher bids from other, non-Newscorp outlets. NBC even came under fire for playing vertical favorites. Both Dick Wolf (*Law and Order: Criminal Intent*) and John Wells accused the Peacock of saving the coveted 10 P.M. time slots for net-owned programs. (Wells's *Third Watch* was moved to 9 P.M.) Such squabbles may have been just the tip of the iceberg, and the prospect of putting synergy above all else worried even those who supported vertical integration. McPherson told Joe Schlosser (*Broadcasting & Cable*) "The day a studio takes a show off a rival network and onto its own, will be a dark day in Hollywood" (March 12, 2001).

And lest we forget, there would be no networks to vertically integrate were it not for local station affiliates. But as the new millennium dawned, TV station owners were none too pleased with their prime-time providers. In March of 2001 the Network Affiliated Station Alliance (NASA), which represents more than 600 ABC, CBS, and NBC stations, asked the FCC to launch a formal investigation into abuse of power by the webs. NASA alleged that networks were using the threat of losing an affiliation as a means of preventing local stations from preempting the web's programming, and, in some cases, attempting to manipulate and subvert the sale of a station and subsequent transfer of its license.

With several owned and operated stations (O&O's) in the networks' stables and satellite delivery systems already in place, it is possible that affiliates as we know them will soon become moot to the strong, vertically integrated webs. If that happens, privately owned TV stations will have to find a way to succeed based on their own ingenuity and a commitment to locally produced programming, rather than being reliant upon network fare. TV stations, like independent studios, were feeling the full effects of vertical integration in the opening years of this century, but they were not the only ones displeased with network policies.

DIVERSITY

It is perhaps ironic that, while networks were enthusiastically embracing integration of business units, they were slow to integrate just about anything else. The 1999–2000 television season was labeled by some as a "whitewash" because of the shortage of African American leads in prime time. A Screen Actors Guild study found that, although blacks comprised 25 percent of moviegoers, for example, they were cast in only 14 percent of TV and film roles in 1999 (SAG report 2001). The numbers were worse for behind-the-scenes talent, where only 3.5 percent of Writers Guild members were African American (*People*, April 2, 2001), and in 1999, hours worked by black directors in taped TV programs fell to 2.4 percent, the lowest since 1990 (*The Hollywood Reporter*, December 11, 2000).

NAACP President Kweisi Mfume threatened a boycott unless networks agreed to make substantive and immediate changes. Some producers scrambled to add African American actors to an already-established white cast, but Mfume was not satisfied. Then in February 2000 the NAACP reached agreements with ABC, CBS, Fox, and NBC, with all four networks promising reform. NBC began a diversity program that required every series that reached its second season to hire a new minority writer. But Mfume continued to dangle the threat of boycott over the heads of the webs. Unlike the previous fall, the 2000–2001 schedule included several prominent black actors in leading dramatic roles, including Andre Braugher (ABC's *Gideon's Crossing*), Mykelti Williamson (CBS's *The Fugitive*), and Chi McBride (Fox's *Boston Public*). Still, some critics pointed to these as cosmetic changes. In his book *Prime Time Blues*, Donald Bogle pointed out that, although Eric LaSalle was the star of a workplace drama (NBC's *ER*), "We never see his character go out with a few African American friends, nor do we learn what it is like for him to lead two lives."

The National Hispanic Media Coalition joined in the debate and aligned with the NAACP in an effort "to make TV truly inclusive" (*Associated Press*, November 18, 2000). Dennis Leoni, creator of Showtime's *Resurrection Boulevard*, remarked, "The disappointing thing about the broadcast networks is that there's nothing broad about their casting" (*EMMY Magazine*). Leoni was justified in his concern. According to the 2000 Census, the U.S. Hispanic population has grown 58 percent in ten years, yet only 2 percent of characters on TV are Latino (*Time*, May 28, 2001). The Screen Actors Guild (SAG) report in 1999 showed that Latinos had been cast in only 4.4 percent of TV and film roles combined, with Asian Americans in 2.2 percent, and Native Americans in 0.2 percent. Emotions were running high, and networks and producers were under a racial microscope.

Following a January 2001 episode of *Law & Order*, NBC issued an apology to the National Puerto Rican Coalition for what that group charged was an unflattering portrayal of Puerto Ricans and promised not to rerun the show later in the season. Executive producer Dick Wolf blasted NBC for its reaction, saying, "The network has caved in to the demands of a special interest group, and I am extremely disappointed with their decision . . . I think it sets an extremely dangerous precedent" (*The Hollywood Reporter*, January 6, 2001). Ironically, Wolf, who was providing much-needed employment for scores of Latino actors, was put on the hot seat for providing much-needed jobs to scores of Latino actors. In October of 2001, NBC bought the Telemundo Network and found a way to attract 35 million Hispanic viewers *without Law and Order.*

Working on another front, Mfume began calling on Congress to reinstate "FinSyn," which, when enacted in 1971, limited ownership of programs by networks and denied them the rights to domestic syndication. Mfume believed, as did Stephen Cannell, that a return to those regulations would create a "safe harbor for independent producers" (*The Hollywood Reporter*, March 2001).

Earlier, the NAACP's Debbie Liu had admitted that the diversity problem was moving in the right direction but warned, "given the appalling lack of progress of every network to measurably further opportunities for Asian Pacific Americans, Latinos, and Native Americans, we have a long, long way to go" (*Broadcasting & Cable*, November 20, 2000).

Meanwhile, Nancy Miller, creator of the civil-rights drama *Any Day Now*, whose show had done more to promote racial understanding than any other series in history, was speaking out for another minority: women.

Asked if television was gender blind, Miller said, "No." Her remarks, raised during the Academy of Television Arts & Sciences's "Women in Drama" event (November 2, 2000), were in reaction to a comment made by CBS chief Les Moonves to this author during an earlier interview. Said Moonves, "I think America, and certainly television, is now totally gender blind. Probably 75 percent of the vice presidents who work for me are women."

Moonves had reason to be optimistic and proud. Under his leadership women had made advances both in the front office and on the air. Following NBC's success with *Providence* in January 1999, CBS saw an opportunity to re-energize its women's demographics. *Judging Amy* and *Family Law* were introduced in the fall of 1999 and, together with shows like ABC's *Once and Again*, paved the way for a new era of women in drama.

But Nancy Miller's reluctance to believe that Hollywood had become gender blind was understandable. According to SAG data released in 2000 (for 1998–99), females were still earning less than males and were still occupying fewer lead roles than men. And while Miller, Barbara Hall, Brenda Hampton, and Martha Williamson had reached the pinnacle of their profession, they, as women showrunners of TV drama, were still in a distinct minority. The good news is that, in the new century, the number of women in lead roles was increasing. Where dramas are concerned, those roles were empowered and substantive. No longer restricted to housework and secretarial jobs, female characters in the New Age of Drama were now lawyers, judges, and vampire slayers. Women in drama were also beginning to look more healthy and less anorexic, sending a signal to young girls that "too thin is *not* in" for the new millennium. Sela Ward (*Sisters, Once and Again*) and Lorraine Toussaint (*Any Day Now*), speaking at the ATAS's "Women in Drama" event, commented on the new trend toward healthier bodies. Said Ward, "What young women are trying to aspire to [trying to emulate a superthin model] truly doesn't exist." Toussaint added, "Women have been brainwashed by one standard of beauty." Lorraine advised young women to "Celebrate your bodies, no matter what they look like."

Increasingly, what women in drama were "looking like" was *successful*. The Lifetime channel, with its trio of *Any Day Now, The Division*, and *Strong Medicine*, broke all previous records for viewership and, for the first time in its seventeen-year history, was the number-one cable network in prime time for the month of January 2001. (*TV Guide*)

It is also important to note that the new siege of women in drama had not been led by teenagers. Kathleen Quinlan, Annie Potts, Sela Ward, and Bonnie Bedalia are in their mid to late forties, while Tyne Daly and Dixie Carter are in their fifties and sixties respectively. But while older actresses had become more in demand, older writers apparently, had not.

In October of 2000 the Associated Press reported that two dozen television writers filed a federal lawsuit seeking more than two hundred million dollars in damages for alleged age discrimination by the major networks, producers, and talent agencies. Among the plaintiffs were Emmy-winning scribe Tracy Kennan Wynn, who wrote *The Autobiography of Miss Jane Pittman.* Said the fifty-five-year-old Wynn, "All of a sudden, everything stopped. I stopped getting phone calls. My agent stopped getting phone calls. The notion that only young people can write for young people is specious" (*Associated Press*, October 27, 2000).

To paraphrase both Liu and Miller: women, African Americans, Asians, Latinos, Native Americans, and the elderly still have a long, long way to go, and clearly there is a higher probability of equity the more that disenfranchised persons ascend to positions of authority within the network structure. But if the debate over diversity has taught us anything it is that, when it comes to television, there is really only one color that matters: *green.*

SPONSORED DRAMAS

While networks struggled to make their front offices and programs look more like America, advertisers were hard at work ensuring that prime-time content, regardless of who starred in it, would be more wholesome.

The Family Friendly Programming Forum was founded in 1999 by forty-three national advertisers who agreed to donate one million dollars per year for development of family-oriented scripts. The WB was the first web to receive FFPF funds, and by November 2000 CBS and ABC had joined the campaign. There is, of course, precedent for advertiser involvement in the development of programming. In the 1950s most prime-time shows were owned at least in part by sponsors and advertising agencies. Even in the new millennium, Hallmark continues to provide sponsor support beyond just the placement of thirty-second commercials.

But in the fall of 2000 sponsors and producers ventured into new territory. Following the film industry's lead, television experimented with on-screen product endorsement in exchange for big bucks. In July the WB launched a teen drama, *The Young Americans,* which was supported by twenty-five million dollars from Coca-Cola. In return, the producer, Steven Antin, assured his benefactor that the cast would be seen drinking Coca-Cola in every episode. ABC, meanwhile, cut a deal with Johnson & Johnson to sponsor a commercial-free premiere of the medical drama *Gideon's Crossing.* While Johnson & Johnson made no request for on-screen endorsements, it is likely that a close examination of Andre Braugher's gauze pads would reveal a politically correct product placement.

As of this writing, the Family Friendly Programming Forum is still committed to script development. The Coca-Cola experiment, on the other hand, showed little prospect of becoming standard operating procedure for network dramas, at least for now. But while product endorsements may come and go, television could count on one reoccurring phenomenon: politics.

GOVERNMENT ENCROACHMENT

To some producers, even mutually beneficial advertiser support can conjure up images of interference, so it is not surprising that any mention whatsoever of *government* involvement sets off alarms all over Hollywood. It is a controversy that is as old as the televison industry itself.

Having learned about Congressional intrusions from filmmakers operating under the watchful eye of the Hays Office, TV networks established their own departments of Standards and Practices to help monitor potentially objectionable material and adhere to the Code of Television Standards as set forth by the National Association of Radio and Television Broadcasters. Louis Chunovic, in his book *One Foot on the Floor,* reminds us that the first indication of Congressional censorship was from the Gathers Committee, which mandated a raising of necklines on the dresses of TV actresses. Throughout the 1950s, sex was on the mind of most politicians (take that any way you wish). Though the arrival of Lucille Ball's baby was much heralded in the press and awaited by fans, CBS forbade her producers from using the word "pregnant" in any of their scripts. In the early 1960s on-screen married couples were still sleeping in separate beds, and in the '70s, while sleeping arrangements had long since been resolved, other issues had not. Producer Earl Hamner told Robert Alley (*The Producer's Medium*) of an incident that occurred on *The Waltons.* "We wanted to do an episode which involved Mary Ellen's first period. It was written by a woman, Joanne Lee, and was very sensitively done . . . there was nothing clinical. CBS did not prohibit us from showing it, but Bob Wood said, 'We would prefer you did not.'"

But society in the post-Vietnam, post-Woodstock, post-Watergate '70s had come of age and was seeking answers as it became more permissive toward, and tolerant of, various sexual behaviors. Hal Holbrook and Martin Sheen portrayed homosexual lovers in *That Certain Summer* (1972), and Movies of the Week became a proving ground for pushing the sexual envelope, focusing on issues ranging from rape to prostitution. Just when we thought we had seen and heard everything on network television, along came *NYPD Blue*. Created by Steven Bochco in the Bill Clinton '90s, the producer kept ABC and its affiliates on edge with a regular display of naked behinds and anatomically laced profanities.

In 2001 the Henry J. Kaiser Foundation released a report that tracked sex on TV. The report stated that in the 1998–99 season, 67 percent of prime-time shows featured sexual content, and a year later that number had risen to 75 percent. (*Broadcasting & Cable*, February 12, 2001) We had come a long way since Lucy's immaculate conception and censorship of cleavage.

As for violence, television was replete with it in the 1950s. Hardly a half hour went by without a villain being shot by a cop or a western marshal. But as the peace-and-love '60s set in, networks showed fewer and fewer on-screen demises. Both *Gunsmoke* and *Bonanza*, for example, became almost devoid of overt violence in their final years despite the fact that nearly everyone in both casts carried a six shooter. The 1970s was also the decade of the TV detective, but, again, bloodshed was minimized. Joe Mannix, though wounded repeatedly, was, like some indestructible cartoon character, usually back on his feet for more action by the next scene.

It is important to note, too, that most TV creators are loathe to have Congress or conservative groups lump sex with violence when debating content controls. After all, the two concepts are, in theory, polar opposites. Sexual acts are generally portrayed as expressions of love, whereas shootings, beatings, and murders are always expressions of violence. Still, every decade or so politicians hold hearings, call press conferences, and announce the formation of commissions in order to root out the evil tandem of sex and violence from the public airwaves. For the most part, political fervor eventually dies down and reforms are put on the back burner until the next election cycle. But the issue of TV content and its possible effect on societal violence escalated following the tragic massacre at Columbine High School in 1999. Congress stepped up its attacks on Hollywood and used the rise in school shootings as a platform for cleaning up television once and for all. Brenda Hampton, producer of the WB's *7th Heaven*, indicated that television is not responsible for such real-life tragedies, saying, "The most annoying thing to me is we still refuse to talk about the one thing that caused those shootings, and that is mental illness . . . it's much easier to assign blame because we'd all feel better about having solved the problem" (*TV Creators*, volume one).

But during the post-Columbine period, a host of senators, including Joseph Lieberman (Al Gore's running mate in the 2000 presidential election), continued to play the blame game with television as the target. At one point Lieberman even proposed tying broadcasters' license renewal to the type of content that they aired. Then, in February of 2001, Senator Ernest Hollings of South Carolina raised the stakes as well as the rhetoric by floating "safe harbor" legislation. Claiming that voluntary restraints had been ineffective in helping to stem the tide of youth violence, Hollings proposed that networks be prohibited from airing indecent programs before ten P.M. Said the senator, "We know from studies that there is more violence on television during prime time, during 'sweeps weeks,' and even on weekend afternoons. Why? Because violence sells, and money talks, and no amount of self regulation and no amount of antitrust exemptions is going to change the profit incentive" (*The Hollywood Reporter*, February 16, 2001).

Clearly, politicians were still lamenting the failure of their earlier attempts to encroach on TV content. On June 26, 2000, the Associated Press reported that only two in five parents owned a V-chip or other similar device designed to block out objectionable material on TV, and that only 50 percent of owners had activated them. Moreover, according to a 1999 study by the National Institute on Media and the Family, although 81 percent of all parents said they were concerned about the amount of violence their children watched on television, less than 60 percent had bothered to establish rules about TV viewing. In any event, as Brenda Hampton had proffered, neither technology nor Hollywood was to blame for school shootings or teen suicides, so it was particularly frightening to think that the U.S. Senate's "Safe Harbor" legislation might open the door for arbitrary interpretation of what is or is *not* decent. In April of 2001, the FCC released its long-awaited guidelines for decency, and while artists worry about political fallout, there is no indication that witch hunts are forthcoming. In fact, the television industry sighed a breath of relief when newly elected President George W. Bush appointed Secretary of State Colin Powell's son Michael to head the FCC. The younger Powell told *TV Guide*, "There's a lot of garbage on TV, and a lot of things children shouldn't be seeing, but I don't think my government is my nanny. It's up to viewers, not government to do something" (March 31, 2001).

TECHNOLOGY

While Michael Powell may have been opposed to government interference in program content, neither he nor anyone else at the FCC was willing to adopt a laissez faire approach to other broadcasting-related matters. After all, the licensing and use of frequencies, broad-band spectrums, and new communications technology falls well within the FCC's purview. But consumer acceptance of new technology cannot always be legislated or mandated. Throughout the 1990s broadcasters heralded the arrival of high-definition television, and by the fall of 2000 the major networks were at least partially on board, with CBS and its tech partner Panasonic leading the way by broadcasting seventeen prime-time shows in HDTV. Despite a government-imposed deadline for conversion to digital by 2006, many local broadcasters were dragging their feet, and consumers were reluctant to invest thousands of dollars in a TV set that showed only a smattering of programs produced using the new technology. In volume one of *TV Creators*, the point was made that HDTV could not improve bad programs. In January 2001 PAX Net founder Bud Paxson echoed that view, telling *Broadcasting & Cable* magazine, "Larry King will not look better in HDTV." Clearly, no matter what deadlines are imposed for conversion, the transition to digital will continue to be a rocky and costly road to traverse.

Meanwhile, though DirecTV was ordered by the courts to appease TV stations by carrying local signals, other providers of high-tech delivery systems were, to use an election-night phrase, waiting for the final returns. For example, industry experts predicted that the new millennium would usher in a fully integrated use of television and the Internet. Deborah McAdams and Ken Kerschbaumer reported "Streaming techies predicted that within five years, television and computers would be one in the same" (*Broadcasting & Cable*). But as with HDTV, the fact that a certain technology is readily available does not mean it will be readily embraced. A Pew Internet study released in the fall of 2000 (*Associated Press*, September 22, 2000) offered tech moguls some sobering news. Of the homes equipped with computers and connected to the Internet, nearly 60 percent said they had no plans to go online. Ouch! Then there are the set-top box manufacturers, who could not have been encouraged by Fred Dressler's comment at the 2000 Western Cable Show. The Time Warner Cable executive announced, "There are a lot of people in America who don't want boxes on top of their TV sets, whether digital or analog" (*Broadcasting & Cable*).

Despite the delays in implementation and discouraging data from the Pew poll, however, digital communications will eventually take hold in the heartland. In the meantime, networks are finding new and innovative ways to link their prime-time programming to fans who have already become accustomed to and reliant upon the Internet. In 2000 ABC's *Drew Carey Show* was simulcast via the Internet, and a year later NBC enticed viewers of the *Saturday Night Movie* to go online and compete for a hundred thousand dollar cash prize. Moreover, network-owned web sites themselves were restructured, as CBS's Les Moonves said, to "make sure that the symbiotic relationship between broadcast and online will be explored and exploited to the fullest extent" (*Broadcasting & Cable*, February 19, 2001).

The Internet was also being used for archival and nostalgic purposes. SpecTV.com, a private company, launched a service in 2000 that allowed online users to view failed television pilots. Again, though, as most Americans waited for more affordable, accessible, quality video-on-demand from their computers, TV creators were discovering new markets for their products, thanks to technology. In the summer of 2000, for example, Legacy Interactive released an interactive CD-ROM drama titled *Code Blue*, starring *7th Heaven*'s Stephen Collins and other top-flight actors. A former *ER* writer penned the one hundred and twelve page script, which featured the largest SAG cast ever assembled for a computer game. Of course, the size of the cast is moot if the actors are on strike, and for the first two years of the new millennium unions kept the industry in an uproar.

THE GUILDED AGE

Politics was the rage in 2000, with America split between George Bush and Al Gore. The network news divisions contributed to the fervor and the furor by miscalling the Florida vote not once, but twice. In the end, Gore won the national popular vote and Bush captured the Electoral College, leaving voters in a quandary over the absence of a leader with a mandate. Not so in Hollywood. As the new century began, tinseltown had two strong leaders at the helm of its two most powerful unions: William Daniels (*St. Elsewhere*) helmed the Screen Actors Guild (SAG) and John Wells (*ER*) led the Writers Guild of America (WGA). No matter what side of the debate you were on, there was no doubt that the two hospital-drama veterans were deeply committed to protecting not their own wealth but the financial security of their rank-and-file members.

Daniels kicked off the strike season in 2000 when his guild picketed production of broadcast commercials. At issue was a pay dispute with national advertisers who depended on SAG members to voiceover and perform in their TV and radio spots. The strike ended peaceably in early 2001, just in time for the rhetoric to heat up between the WGA and the Alliance of Motion Picture and Television Producers (AMPTP).

Among the scribes' concerns were residual payments and the "film by" credit usually only claimed by directors. If the WGA struck, SAG and AFTRA (with a combined membership of 140,000) would surely honor it. Wells was resolute, though professionally conflicted, having to wear a producer's hat part of the day and a writer's hat the other.

Although portrayed as a hardliner, SAG president Daniels, who had lived through the devastating writers' strike of 1988, was careful not to fuel the strife with incendiary rhetoric. Daniels pointed out, "There doesn't have to be a strike for actors and performers to receive a fair deal and an equitable share of the income being created directly through their work" (*The Hollywood Reporter*, January 16, 2001). Daniels, like other Hollywood vets, knew what was at stake. According to Jack Kyser, chief economist for the Los Angeles County Economic Development Corporation, a strike by both writers and actors would have cost the local economy as much as two billion dollars per month. (*The Hollywood Reporter*, March 20, 2001)

Networks and studios had no intention of getting caught with their program pants down and began "strike-piling" material in anticipation of a summer 2001 walkout. In a letter sent to 11,000 WGA members, Wells urged his colleagues not to comply with or participate in the additional work orders. But some, like writer/producer Dick Wolf, refused to bite the hands that fed his *Law & Order* franchise (NBC and USA). Wolf's team set to work and stored up additional episodes like a prewinter squirrel hoarding nuts. Meanwhile, Fox announced that it had eighty-three half hours of comedy and twenty-six hours of dramas in the can. ABC was dusting off theatrical films, and CBS was preparing to expand its news magazines, something networks did during the strike of 1988. *That* work stoppage gave birth to CBS's *48 Hours* and ABC's *Prime Time Live*. Of course, another plus for the networks was vertical integration itself. As was previously mentioned, all of the major webs (except NBC) were owned by content suppliers and buoyed by new-found corporate synergy. Translation? The networks were in a much stronger position to weather a strike in 2001 than they had been in 1988.

Drama King Wolf warned all parties, "This has to be settled, or we're looking at the end of television as we know it" (*Variety*, September 11, 2000). Fortunately, a strike was averted and nobody had to find out if Wolf's prediction would have come true.

While no group got everything it wanted, at least one organization was pleased with the resolution. The Academy of Television Arts & Sciences had planned to postpone its September 2001 Emmy telecast for fear that no SAG members would cross the WGA's picket line, which would have left viewers without any celebrities to view. Fortunately the Emmys went forward, but with some important changes in place.

THE EMMY AWARDS

In addition to creating two new categories to accommodate the "reality/game" craze of 2001, the Academy also turned an experimental project into a permanent fixture. Until 2000 the ATAS had adhered to a judging process that dated back to Rod Serling's (*The Twilight Zone*) tenure as president of the organization forty years earlier. The system had required judges to hole up in a Los Angeles meeting place (usually a hotel) for a weekend to screen Emmy entries. That system eliminated many active members from participating in the judicial process due to busy work schedules and an unwillingness to sacrifice two days in a darkened, smoke-filled room. The result was decades of "comfort-zone" voting, in which the same shows and stars always seemed favored to win, while more nonconformist programming and performers were overlooked. *The Andy Griffith Show* was a perennial top ten and even ended its run in 1968 finishing number one in the Nielsens. Yet because it was a rural comedy, neither it (nor its star) was ever recognized by the Academy judges. The quirky *St. Elsewhere,* which was named by *TV Guide* as the best drama series of all time, never won an Emmy for outstanding drama over its entire six-year run. Even *The Sopranos* was overlooked in its freshman year in favor of the David Kelley juggernaut.

So in the fall of 2000 the Academy took a bold step by allowing at-home judging. Some media critics blasted the ATAS's decision, predicting that at-home review would promote corrupted voting. They reasoned that there was no way to monitor whether or not the new livingroom judges would watch all of the tapes as required before marking their ballots.

Having served as one of the first at-home judges, I can attest to how well the new system worked. While I cannot speak for my fellow adjudicators, I am sure that we all took the Academy rules to heart and watched every entry as instructed. I only found one fault with the process, and that had nothing to do with at-home versus Los Angeles viewing. My concern was with one drama producer who submitted an entry that was atypical of his normal weekly output. Instead of offering judges a sampling of a typical multi-story-line episode, he submitted a one-theme story line. Taken separately, it was more powerful than any of the other competing drama series' entries, but I was being asked to vote on outstanding "series," not outstanding "episode." For that reason, I believe the Academy should consider adding a "best episode" category, similar to the method used to distinguish between Grammys in "Best Single" and "Best Album" categories.

Unquestionably, though, the grand experiment in democracy succeeded. New shows and new faces picked up awards, and hundreds of ATAS members participated in the process who otherwise would have been left out. Now, if only the Academy would invent a category for "Best Book About TV," the system would be perfect.

CONCLUSION

The new millennium launched a new age for drama and opened up more opportunities for creators, actors, technicians, and viewers than ever before. Direct broadcast satellite users could select programs from hundreds of sources, and Hollywood's creative community could apply its craft to any number of nontraditional delivery systems ranging from multiple pay-cable channels to streaming video projects via the Internet. True, the networks had become in-house oriented, but for every Disney/ABC there were ten other outlets providing opportunities for above-the-line artists.

In 1983 legendary studio boss and network programming executive Grant Tinker complained to Todd Gitlin about a diluted talent pool in TV, saying, "Nobody's setting out to make shit, but there are just so many Jim Brookses and Allen Burnses. Television would be wonderful if it were only on Wednesday night" (*Inside Prime Time*). Well, two decades later television *is* wonderful on Wednesday nights, with NBC alone boasting *The West Wing* and *Law & Order* back to back. But almost every night has great dramas if you just know where to look. As for availability of talent, there are definitely more TV creators than ever before, but the good news is they now have a larger and much more diverse arena in which to compete. That makes for great entertainment as we, the viewers, stand on the sidelines and judge for ourselves which programs best suit our tastes. As long as the delivery systems do not shrink or become too monopolistic, and as long as Congress stays out of our TV sets, we will continue to enjoy many more "Wednesday nights" in the future.

Producer Profiles

Donald Bellisario was born to immigrant parents in a small, Pennsylvania mining town just five years before America entered World War II. The global conflict had a great impact on young Don, who would go on to serve in the Marines and later integrate military themes into many of his televison programs.

Bellisario honed his writing skills while working as a newspaper reporter, then learned how to write and produce for television while he was employed at an advertising agency. After moving to Hollywood and working on hit series such as *Baa Baa Black Sheep*, Don created a number of dramas on his own, including *Airwolf*, *Quantum Leap*, and *Magnum P.I.* His hit show *JAG*, which deals with military lawyers, originated on NBC in 1995 then moved to CBS a year later, where it has enjoyed enormous success ever since.

A native Floridian and graduate of Florida State University, clifton campbell began his career as a playwright in Chicago, where he was then recruited to write for the highly touted NBC period drama *Crime Story*. In fact, crime writing became a staple for Campbell, whose series credits include *21 Jump Street*, *Moloney*, and *Wiseguy*, the latter of which netted Campbell both Golden Globe and Emmy nominations. Clifton is best known, however, for his work on *Profiler*, a weekly suspense thriller that pitted a female agent against the killers she studied.

Even as a child, Glenn Gordon Caron was in awe of good dialogue. He studied the banter in *I Spy* and *Butch Cassidy and the Sundance Kid*, and later incorporated that style of writing into his own films and television shows.

Although he continues to write and direct motion pictures, Glenn is best known for his work on the small screen, having cut his teeth on *Remington Steele* before creating his signature series, *Moonlighting*. The genre-busting "dramedy" starring Cybill Shepherd and a then-unknown Bruce Willis netted sixteen Emmy nominations in its second season. After a decade's absence from TV, Caron returned in 1999 to create *Now and Again* for CBS. He followed that in 2001 with *When I Grow Up* for Fox.

Paul Haggis, a native of Canada, began writing and producing plays in a little community theater built by his father. Paul's first foray into television was as a cartoon scribe, then he graduated to the writing staffs of a number of TV series including *The Facts of Life* and *thirtysomething*.

Returning to his Canadian roots, Haggis created the quirky drama *Due South*, about a Mountie transplanted to the United States. He also created the critically acclaimed crime series *EZ Streets*, and the David Caruso vehicle *Michael Hayes*. In 1999 Paul was one of several producers who helped usher in a new era of dramas starring women in the lead role. *Family Law* is Haggis's biggest commercial success to date and has become a solid performer for CBS.

Born in Chatham, Virginia, Barbara Hall is an accomplished novelist, having written more than a half-dozen books. She is also a television veteran, with experience on such shows as *Newhart*, *I'll Fly Away*, *Northern Exposure*, and *Chicago Hope*.

An outspoken advocate for women in television, Hall is one of just a handful of female showrunners in series drama. She is the executive producer of the highly acclaimed *Judging Amy*, whose co-creator, Amy Brenneman, is also the star.

Roy Huggins is a television legend, having created drama series in six different decades. He began his career as a mystery writer, then went on to pen screenplays for Columbia. He joined Warner Brothers Television in the mid-1950s and helped to change the face of TV drama, creating such shows as *Maverick* and *77 Sunset Strip*.

Huggins also created the award-winning private-eye series, *The Rockford Files* with his old *Maverick* star, James Garner, in the lead. But it is his 1962 masterpiece, *The Fugitive*, for which Roy is best known. Its two-hour series finale was the highest-rated episode in television history up to that time, and it would later spawn two motion-picture incarnations. In 2000 *The Fugitive* came full circle, making its return to TV nearly forty years after the original Huggins show had premiered.

Like millions of television viewers, John McNamara is a huge fan of *The Fugitive* and a great admirer of Roy Huggins. But in 2000 John turned his affection into a series revival, using many of the same stories and plot twists from the original show.

McNamara was born in Ann Arbor, Michigan, and his earliest attempts at writing included entering and winning a short-story competition. His early television credits include the offbeat western *The Adventures of Brisco County, Jr.*, the dark drama *Profit*, and *Lois & Clark*, an updated take on the Superman saga. Today, John has a long-term deal with Warner Brothers Television.

Aaron Sorkin grew up in Scarsdale, New York, but he might as well have been born on Broadway. Trips to the theater were a regular occurrence for young Sorkin, who was enthralled by the words and music of the Great White Way. After graduating Syracuse University, Aaron struggled as an actor and playwright until he forsook the former for the latter and focused his attention solely on writing. His first big hit was *A Few Good Men*, which enjoyed a long run in New York before being developed into a major motion picture. He then wrote a screenplay for *The American President*, which catapulted him into the "A" list of Hollywood writers.

Against the advice of friends, Sorkin put a booming film career on hold and made the leap to television, creating *Sports Night* for ABC. But it was *The West Wing* that sealed Aaron's place in television history. The political drama, inspired by many of his unused story lines written for *The American President*, won over record numbers of viewers and in its second season also won every major industry award, including an Emmy for outstanding drama series.

Nearly forty years before Aaron Sorkin put on the greasepaint, another Aaron was making his way to Hollywood to take a stab at acting. Born in Texas, **Aaron Spelling** came from a poor family, but it was the prejudice against his ethnic heritage that was most difficult for him to endure. Thanks to a supportive teacher and two loving parents, Spelling was encouraged to pursue a career in writing. At first he made ends meet by picking up acting jobs, but by the late 1950s he had settled into writing for television, beginning with mentor Dick Powell's *Zane Grey Theater*. Spelling's first sole creation was *Johnny Ringo* in 1959, and he went on to produce more than sixty TV series.

Among his biggest hits were *Charlie's Angels*, *The Love Boat*, *Fantasy Island*, *Starsky & Hutch*, *Family*, and *Dynasty*. And just when media critics thought it was time for Aaron to hang up his pipe, the old master reinvented television drama with the high school series *Beverly Hills 90210*. Throughout the 1990s and well into the new century, Spelling unleashed a string of youth and family-oriented dramas, including *7th Heaven*, *Melrose Place*, and the acclaimed civil-rights show *Any Day Now*.

JOSS whedon experienced bullying and isolation as a youth, but as an adult he found a way to exorcize his childhood demons by creating a TV series about an empowered girl who protects her school against the ultimate bullies: vampires. Joss was schooled both in England and America and has a rare ability to identify with, then write about, conflicted underdog characters. His hit shows *Buffy the Vampire Slayer* and its spin-off *Angel* are filled with humor, something Whedon came by naturally. Both his father and grandfather wrote television comedy, and Joss himself began his TV career writing for the sitcom *Roseanne*. In 2000 Whedon was nominated for an Emmy for his nearly dialogue-free *Buffy the Vampire Slayer* episode titled "Hush."

Martha williamson also began her TV career by writing comedy, but she was uncomfortable with the genre and crossed over into drama. A musician at heart, Williamson is an accomplished singer who performed often during her stay at Williams College. She also has an abiding love for and faith in God, which in 1994 led CBS to call upon her to refurbish a troubled drama pilot about angels. Martha put her faith-based stamp on the show, and *Touched by an Angel* was born.

In the late 1990s Williamson expanded the focus of the series from simply helping individuals in trouble to awakening viewers to various international issues and crises. Episodes dealing with human rights and sociopolitical struggles gained widespread media attention, making Martha a highly sought-after speaker whose opinions and insights are regarded even in the halls of Congress.

No one can go from being a hotel tram operator to being the creator of the most-watched TV drama of the new millennium. No one except Anthony zuiker, that is. Born in Chicago, then transplanted to Las Vegas, young Anthony learned about life in the fast lane, growing up in a city that never sleeps. He had two great loves: gambling and writing. In his pursuit for the latter he would write anything for anyone; whether it was an ad campaign or foreign-language instruction books, Zuiker lived for writing. Then after circulating several film scripts around Hollywood, he caught the eye of movie mogul Jerry Bruckheimer, who was expanding into television. Asked for series ideas, Zuiker responded with *CSI: Crime Scene Investigation*, a groundbreaking look at criminal forensics and the rest, as they say, is history.

TV creators

AARON SORKIN | Lyricist

Aaron Sorkin. COURTESY OF AARON SORKIN.

TELEVISION CREDITS

1998–2000	*Sports Night* (ABC)
1999–	*The West Wing* (NBC)

MW MW MW

If it's true that you cannot make a silk purse out of a sow's ear, then someone forgot to tell Aaron Sorkin. Each week when preparing a new script for his hit show, *The West Wing,* he takes such deadly dry topics as the census or budget negotiations and manages to turn them into high drama. This might seem an impossible task for most writers, but Sorkin is *not* most writers. While others may construct stories, plot twists, and character profiles that must then be transposed into conversation, Aaron already thinks in the language of dialogue. His is a rare gift, and prime-time is a better place for it.

But lest we attempt to label his talent by genre, one has only to watch an episode of *The West Wing* or tapes of *Sports Night* to know that Aaron Sorkin is also a master of intellectual, comic banter in the tradition of Garson Kanin, Neil Simon, and Larry Gelbart. It should, therefore, come as no surprise that his writing has been primarily influenced by live theater. Aaron's dialogue has a lyrical quality to it, as if he were writing a scene for the Schubert instead of a television show for NBC. And that's OK with those of us who cannot afford tickets to a Broadway show. We can just stay home and witness great theater for free every Wednesday night at nine. *The West Wing* director Tommy Schlamme told the *Hollywood Reporter,* "Aaron gives us the music with his ideas, and the cast creates this magnificent orchestra."

Aaron is clearly in love with words, and we, in turn, are in love with how those words affect us.

Aaron Sorkin was born in Manhattan in 1960 into a loving and supportive family, which includes an older brother and sister. His mother is a retired schoolteacher who still tutors students in English as a second language. His father is a copyright attorney for Time Warner. With both parents having made their living by spinning words, Aaron early on developed an appreciation for the power of language.

The Sorkins moved to Scarsdale, New York, when Aaron was eight years old. Several years later, he experienced his first brush with presidential politics.

SORKIN: Nixon was running for re-election in 1972, and I was not particularly politically active at all. Not many eleven year olds are. (*Both laugh.*) But I had a crush on a girl named Jenny Lavin, who was in my sixth-grade class. She was working at the local McGovern headquarters after school, and I thought it would be a pretty good idea if I did too.

Longworth: So all this was about sex?

SORKIN: It *always* is. (*Laughs.*) So I went down there and stuffed envelopes, and there was a weekend where they asked us all to go to White Plains. The Nixon motorcade was going to be going through there, and we were going to be holding up our McGovern signs. I was holding up one of our McGovern signs on a two by four, and I don't remember what it said, but I'm sure it was nothing more incendiary than, "McGovern for President." And as the Nixon motorcade was going by, a hundred-and-forty-three-year-old woman (*laughs*), who was shorter than I was, came up from behind me, grabbed this sign out of my hand, whacked me over the head with it, threw it on the ground, and stomped on it. And so, where I fell in the political spectrum was pretty much forged in steel at that point. (*Both laugh.*) I'm pretty sure that everything I've written has, in some way, been an effort to get back at that woman. (*Both laugh.*)

When he was not chasing girls or being hit with placards, young Aaron enjoyed watching television. His favorite programs included *F-Troop, The Monkees, The Partridge Family, The Mary Tyler Moore Show,* and *M*A*S*H*. But, again, it was live theater that had the most profound impact on Aaron's life and future career.

SORKIN: My parents took me to the theater a lot. And, again, neither of them is in show business, or theater people. It's just when they were young, that's what they did. They went to the theater just as a matter of habit, and they kept all of the playbills. Afterward, one or both of them would write a little note on the cover, the date, the occasion, you know, like an anniversary or birthday, and they would write down what they thought of the play. They kept the playbills in a little box in this cabinet in the living room, and I would all the time just get down in the floor, open up the cabinet, drag out this box, and play with the playbills. I can remember the smell of them, and I would memorize the cast of every one of these great plays. And then they would take me to the theater on Thanksgiving, or Christmas Eve, we would go on birthdays, things like that.

Longworth: So it became special to attend the theater.

SORKIN: It became very special [to] my developmental understanding of things. By age fourteen I had a clear memory of having gone to plays for a while.

But Sorkin's earliest memory of the theater came as a result of his friendship with the family of a famous actor.

SORKIN: While we were living in Manhattan, I went to this sort of artsy, private school in Greenwich Village called The Little Red School House on

Bleeker Street. One of my classmates was the daughter of the actor Hershel Bernardi [*Peter Gunn*]. Hershel had replaced Zero Mostel in *Fiddler on the Roof* on Broadway, and I was six or seven years old, and not really aware of all this. But the Bernardis had kids the same age as all the kids in my family, so we sort of each had a companion in each of our grades. On Saturdays my parents would drop us off at the Bernardis' place, and every once in a while their nanny would park us back stage at the Imperial Theater where *Fiddler* was playing. My first [play] that I ever saw was from back stage.

Longworth: So, growing up, your "sand box" was the Imperial Theater?

SORKIN: It was. I mean, I don't remember a lot from being little, but I have a real memory standing there backstage in puzzlement watching a guy in profile and having no idea who he was facing or who he was singing to, or who was out there watching him sing, [Aaron vocalizes with expert precision] "Wonder of wonders, miracle of miracles." And I think, "What's going on here?" But from that point on, when my parents would take me to plays, it was just huge for me, and all I wanted to do was see it again and talk about it all the way home in the car. It wasn't until I was fourteen watching *Pippin*, of all things, that it occurred to me that people up there doing that, were doing that for a living. They weren't magical people from a magical land. That was their *job*, just like my father went to his job, and my mother went to hers.

Aaron's love of plays eventually led him to Syracuse University where he majored in, what else, theater. After college, he returned to the Big Apple to seek his fortune.

SORKIN: I was living in a tiny studio apartment on the East Side for fifty dollars a week . . . I'm twenty-two, I've come to New York . . . to begin my life as a struggling actor the way everybody else does when they get out of acting school. And I'm working a series of survival jobs. You take whatever you can, bar tending, bussing tables, driving a cab, handing out leaflets dressed up as a moose at the South Street sea port. (*Both laugh.*)

Longworth: Oh yeah, everybody does that! (*Both laugh.*) Are you sure that blow on the head with the Nixon placard didn't—

SORKIN: (*Laughs.*) By the way, I *had* my standards. When I got hired for the moose job, they wanted me to speak as the moose. The leaflet I was handing out was for the sportsman's show at the Javits Center. And it turns out the sportsman's show wasn't for baseball, football, and basketball. It was for hunting. And I felt horrible that I was going to play this sweet moose, sending people over to buy guns to shoot me with. So I told them that I wouldn't speak because I was a moot moose, I mean, a mute moose. (*Both laugh.*)

Then, in what must be the most ironic twist of fate in the annals of show biz, Sorkin stumbled onto a talent that would eventually lead him to television, only because he could not *watch* television. "One Friday, a friend of mine from high school who was a struggling journalist went out of town with his girlfriend [now his wife]. He had his grandfather's old typewriter with him, and didn't want to have to schlepp it out of town with him. So he asked me to keep this typewriter for him over the weekend. It was a semiautomatic typewriter, that is to say, you plugged it in and the keys were electric, but it had a manual return. So it was one of those Friday nights like you only have in New York. It was terrible. You feel like everyone in the world has been invited to a party that you didn't get invited to. Everybody is out doing something fun. It was raining, I didn't have a dollar in my pocket, and the TV didn't work. And literally, all there was to do was [mess with] this typewriter. I don't know what happened, but I put a piece of paper in the typewriter, and wrote dialogue for the first time."

And it would not be the last. Sorkin went on to pen *A Few Good Men*, which began as a successful Broadway play before it morphed into a blockbuster film. *The American President* followed, and suddenly Sorkin was a hot property. Along the way, he also worked on *The Rock* for friend and producer Jerry Bruckheimer, who said of Sorkin, "Aaron is one of a kind. He's a brilliant writer. In Hollywood he's in the top one percent as far as writing, both for features and for television. He's so gifted, and I want to work with gifted people because it makes me look good." ABC then picked up Sorkin's first TV series, *Sports Night,* a dramedy inspired by ESPN. Aaron became a huge fan of the jock network when he was pulling all-nighters while writing *The American President*. As he told *Emmy Magazine*, "[ESPN's] *Sports Center* kept me company. After a while it became more than background music. I believed it was the best written, best produced show on television, fiction or non. And just like Holden Caulfield, I wanted to be able to hang out with these people."

But Sorkin's first foray into the small screen was fraught with problems. Before *Sports Night* premiered in the fall of 1998, ABC forced him to tape before a live audience *and* to add a laugh track to augment the real laughs. Sorkin complied, but told *Entertainment Weekly*'s Joe Flynt that he would not insert a laugh track "where the audience didn't laugh" (September 25, 1998).

Sports Night was both admired and admonished, sometimes by the same publications. For example, *TV Guide* went on the attack at the outset, saying, "the show spends only half of its running time being funny, and just as often turns serious, with drama that ranges from the poignant to the preachy"

(September 12, 1998). But two years later, the magazine awarded *Sports Night* a cover story (March 11, 2000), titled, "The Best Show You're Not Watching," with Matt Roush describing it as "Not quite comedy, not quite drama, and certainly not about sports." Roush's inability to place a precise label on the show foreshadowed its ultimate demise. In that same article ABC's Stu Bloomberg commented, "research indicates viewers still can't figure it out. . . . how sad that it has to fit into one category or another."

Sorkin might have been schooled in presidential politics, but television politics was a new arena for him. In addition to acquiescing to the laugh track, Sorkin had to endure network sniping about *Sports Night*'s poor ratings. Even so, the show was attracting eleven million viewers weekly, prompting Sorkin to write a life-imitates-art-imitates-life episode about consultants interfering with the fictional *Sports Night* staff, one of whom remarks "Anyone who can't make money on *Sports Night* should get out of the moneymaking business."

Sorkin had already had success in the theater, so it must have been surreal to have a TV network gripe about eleven million viewers, or, to put it another way, ten times more people than saw *A Few Good Men* during its entire run on Broadway. "I still feel like I'm writing a play and Tommy Schlamme [producer/director of *The West Wing*] turns it into a television show" (*TV Guide,* March 11, 2000).

Sports Night's problems mounted, but not just because of ABC's displeasure. In the fall of 1999, Sorkin began to spread his considerable talents too thin. With John Wells (*ER*) and NBC finally willing to take a chance on *The West Wing,* Sorkin was suddenly writing and producing two prime-time programs for two different networks every week. "Ordinarily I finish a *Sports Night* script by Sunday night," he told *Entertainment Weekly.* "[The cast] reads it Monday morning, we rehearse Monday and Tuesday, and we shoot on Wednesday, Thursday, and Friday. I write *The West Wing* while they shoot" (February 25, 2000).

True, David Kelley had maintained a similarly frenetic schedule while writing and producing *The Practice* and *Ally McBeal,* but Kelley had been accustomed to the pressures of television since the days of *L.A. Law.* Sorkin, on the other hand, was used to working in film and theater, where deadlines were not as crucial. But whatever the reasons—whether lack of network promotion, poor time slot, writing burn-out, or all of the above—*Sports Night* was on the way out. It had premiered as the sixth-highest-rated new show in 1998, but its eleven million viewers now translated into a sixty-sixth–place finish. ABC pulled the plug in the spring of 2000. HBO and Showtime both made offers to pick up the series, but Sorkin declined, instead focusing his full attention on *The West Wing*. Garth Ancier, former president of NBC, later observed, "I think Aaron and David Kelley are probably the only two writers who can literally craft a show from whole cloth in their head. Thankfully, Aaron has not divided his time as much as David has, and I think that's why the quality of *The West Wing* is generally better than the quality of David's shows."

The White House–based drama was a hit almost from day one. It remains number one among viewers who earn $75,000 or more, and it is number one with viewers who have home access to the Internet. (Source: A.C. Nielsen) Unlike the criticism leveled at the fictional *Sports Night* consultant, somebody at NBC obviously knew how to make money with *The West Wing*. A bona fide commercial hit, *The West Wing* is also a critical success, having swept every major award since 2000 including nine Emmys and the prestigious Peabody Award. Ever the principled artist, Sorkin even spurned one of the show's honors. In August 2000 during taping of the Family Television Awards on CBS, *The West Wing*'s Allison Janney's comments in support of the striking Screen Actors' Guild were cut from the final broadcast. Sorkin promptly returned his award for best drama series.

Thus, the new millennium was off to a bittersweet start for the boy wonder. *Sports Night* and its canned laughter were canned, while *The West Wing* was riding a wave of unprecedented popularity. Sorkin was named to *Entertainment Weekly*'s list of the most powerful people in show business (he ranked number sixty-two) and as one of television's top ten MVPs by *TV Guide*. As icing on the cake, Warner Brothers Television signed Sorkin to a long-term development deal worth sixteen million dollars.

At the end of the first season, a team of home-grown terrorists opened fire on the entire *The West Wing* bunch, and viewers were left with the most compelling cliffhanger since J.R.'s late-night encounter with Kristen. Prior to the shooting scenario, *The West Wing* was averaging between thirteen and fifteen million viewers per week. But the two-hour second-season opener pulled in twenty-five million viewers. Everyone survived the assassins' bullets with life, limb, awards, and wallets in good shape.

Once again Sorkin had managed the impossible. He had written a left-leaning political drama without putting people to sleep or alienating half of the country. Of course, there have been critics. Conservative Texas Congressman Tom DeLay blasted *The West Wing* as having "disdain for religious faith"

(*Time*, May 15, 2000). Sorkin responded, calling DeLay's criticism a "cheap shot [against] a violence-free series that idealizes public service." DeLay later admitted that he had never actually watched *The West Wing*. Most Washington insiders *had* watched, though. Clinton Secretary of State Madeline Albright called Sorkin's episode about India–Pakistan relations "the best exposition of foreign policy on TV" (*Time*, May 15, 2000). *Time* magazine itself proclaimed, "*The West Wing* has become our national civics lesson."

Meanwhile, *The West Wing* has won over viewers of almost every political and religious persuasion. It is a show that uplifts the human spirit by giving us a president who is honest, intelligent, and passionate about his beliefs along with a staff that, despite its political leanings, will go to the mat for anyone. That feel-good appeal also has won over skeptics in the television industry. In 1999, *Entertainment Weekly*'s Ken Tucker wrote, "*The West Wing* could collapse under the weight of its own sappiness" (October 22). But by the second season, he proclaimed it "The Show of the Year." *TV Guide* called it "The ultimate work place drama," while the Peabody committee noted it was a show "about ideas and ideals." John Wells summed up the collective sentiment accurately for *Newsweek*, "I think there's a tremendous pent up desire in this country to believe in our leaders" (September 6, 1999). On that point Republicans, Democrats, and Nielsens could all agree. Adds *The West Wing* consultant and former White House Press Secretary Dee Dee Myers, "The show has the potential the longer it's on the air to recast what people think about politics" {*Written By*, November 2000).

But despite all of the high praise, both Sorkin and his series remain well grounded. "I'm not a journalist. My obligation isn't to tell the truth. My obligation is to captivate you for however long I've asked for your attention." (*Brill's Content*, March 2000.)

Still, it is appropriate that a young man so skilled in shaping dramatic dialogue is having such an impact on shaping the national dialogue. Because of that, he will likely captivate us for a long, long time to come.

I first spoke with Aaron Sorkin prior to the start of his second season on *The West Wing*.

Longworth: I want to begin by going back to your starving-artist period. Specifically, what happened between the time you discovered the old typewriter and when you became a superstar?

SORKIN: I spent hours there tapping away at that typewriter, and then the next morning I invited two actor friends of mine over. One of them is on *Sports Night*. We went to Syracuse together. I said listen, I've written this thing.

Can you come over and read it out loud with me. We're going to read the parts out loud, and tell me if I've done anything here. My recollection is that there wasn't even enough money for photo copies, so we sat on the floor with the pages between us. We looked over at each other and read it out loud, and it *sounded* really good. It was honest-to-God dialogue, and it really moved.

Longworth: What was it?

SORKIN: It was the first play I ever wrote. It was called *Removing All Doubt*. It was from a Mark Twain quote, "'Tis better to remain silent and be thought a fool, than to open your mouth and remove all doubt." The play was about fifteen or twenty pages, and we must have read it through three times. It was a real page turner. And these two guys, Tim [Timothy Davis Reed] and Darren were incredibly encouraging, saying "This is terrific. That's writing! Write more!" And it was that day, sort of my first daytime of being a writer (because I had started the night before), the question started to creep up: "This is great dialogue, but what's happening in the *story* exactly?" So it was day one of being a writer that I realized what my Achilles' heel was going to be. I then continued writing *Removing All Doubt* for over the course of two years. I would then get to the end, and go back to the beginning. And nearly every other Wednesday I would invite friends over to the apartment and then friends of the friends, for a seven-character play, and we would read all the parts, and I would remember, in my head, I'm *still* an actor now. Twenty-two years of thinking of yourself that way doesn't go away over night, [so] I was reading the lead role, and writing it for myself. And the play starts to get sent out and agents were really interested in it. Producers started to read it, and there began to be these stage readings of the play, which had become very well attended, so the word got out there. I was working at the Neil Simon Theater on 52nd Street, and at the time, *Brighton Beach Memoirs* was playing. And, one of the actors in the play named Mark Nelson who would later be in the original cast of *A Few Good Men*, told me that when he came into the show, Matthew Broderick was *leaving* the show, and the last thing Matthew said to Mark was "Hey listen, I want to give you a heads up on something. The bartender at the balcony bar is a really good playwright." (*Both laugh.*) "You should go talk to him." (*Laughs.*) But, believe it or not, before I ever got the play produced I already had legal problems. (*Laughs.*)

Longworth: From Mark Twain? Do you see dead people?

SORKIN: Not from Mark Twain at all. There was a big-time Broadway producer named Zeb Buckman who wanted to option the play. We had a meeting and I thought this was the most fantastic thing in the world. And the very next day I got a call from his next in command, a woman named Victoria Lang, who very casually said, "Listen Aaron, I think I'm the person to produce this play, not Zeb. I've been working in Zeb's office for years, so I'm going to produce the play, OK?" And I say, "Ah, sure, as long as somebody's producing the play." And that was the beginning of the end. (*Laughs.*) Zeb fired the woman, and put an injunction on production of the play. It's still in my drawer, and, by the way, thank God for that as well, because now I look back at it, and it's like every playwright's first play, you know? It was about twentysomethings sort of struggling in their world.

Longworth: Well if you are murdered tomorrow, will somebody take that play out of the drawer and make money off of it?

SORKIN: Oh, please God let them not. Go do the four-hundred-page version of *The American President* instead. (*Both laugh.*)

Longworth: So we are still in the wilderness years and now, you write *A Few Good Men* on spec.

SORKIN: Yeah. I'm still a bartender now. *Removing All Doubt* is kind of in the drawer. By the way, an important thing that happened during *Removing All Doubt,* my sister, Lt. JG Deborah Sorkin, United States Navy, calls me and says, "Aaron, you're never going to believe where I'm going tomorrow. I'm going to our base in Guantanamo Bay, Cuba. Ten Marines have broken into the barracks room with a platoon mate of theirs, and they nearly killed the guy, and they're claiming they did it 'cause they were following an order'." And I said, "Debbie, those guys sound horrible. You should just go down there and fry them, or hang them or something." And she said, "I would, but I'm defending them." (*Both laugh.*)

Longworth: Did you hit her over the head with a placard at that point?

SORKIN: Well I started to think about that. I thought, "Gee, I'm twenty-five going on twenty-six now. And I'm still working as a bartender, and I like that I've gotten myself an agent. And I like that the stage readings of the plays are going on. But it's time now to do a play. I want to write something, I want it to be done. And then eventually, I'd like to make a living doing this." Movies and television were never a part of my world. I *went* to movies, I *watched* plenty of television, I just didn't think of them the same way I thought of plays. So it didn't occur to me that the way to break in as a writer was to try and get a staff position on a TV show. It never, ever occurred to me. What *did* occur to me was that there are any number of one-act play festivals in New York, which are very well attended and the reviewers come. Of course, a thousand people a year submit their plays to these festivals. Later I read an article in the *New York Times*, a piece that tickled me. Alan Alda was directing and starring in a movie called *Sweet Liberty.*

Longworth: I loved that movie.

SORKIN: I liked that movie too. The whole movie was shot on Long Island. In fact, I think in the Hamptons. And in this movie, they described a moment. They're going for a very difficult, long exterior shot. They're shooting something six-hundred feet away, and Michael Caine needs to show up on horseback, and it needs to take place right at magic hour, just as the sun is going down below the horizon. So there isn't a big window of opportunity to get the shot. You pretty much got one, two, *maybe* three takes, tops, and you're cooked, and you've got to try it again the next day. And the article was about how Alan Alda really *is* as nice a guy as everyone says he is, and that the only time this reporter saw him lose it, was trying to get this shot. They had it lined up perfectly, and it was all ready to go, and from out of nowhere, a cow walks into the shot way off into the distance. And Alda starts screaming, "Cow! Get out of the shot!" When the DP leans over and says, "You know Alan, don't worry about it, we can matt it out in post." So Alan yells out "Alright cow, stay where you are, you're fine!" And they got the shot. And reading that article I wrote a one-act play called *Hidden in the Picture,* about a director trying to get that shot. It's in a volume called *The Best Short Plays of the Eighties,* and it was done by this one-act play festival, and I was in it.

Longworth: What part did you play?

SORKIN: I played the writer of the movie, and Nathan Lane played the director. It was on a bill with three other one-act plays, one of which was a new Harvey Fierstein play. Harvey was very hot coming off of *Torch Song Trilogy,* so all the first-string critics showed up, and the next day in the *New York Times* was a review that basically said "A new Harvey Fierstein one-act opened last night, but the story is this guy Aaron Sorkin who wrote *Hidden in the Picture.*" So I got some attention for that. It all of a sudden became important to me, rather than *star* in the play, I wanted to find the best actor I could to play the part. I was really very much becoming the playwright, and not the guy who works in front of the audience. And so I was really done acting. I would do the play again with Timothy Busfield, who is now in *The West Wing* and was in *A Few Good Men* on Broadway for a while, but that was the last time I acted. As soon as I had written the one-act, I went to *A Few Good Men* immediately. I wrote one draft, and then a second draft. Gave it to my agent, who said, "Gee this is terrific. I'm going to send it to our west coast office right away. They're going to be able to get you a job, a staff position on a TV show."

And I said, "That sounds great, but what about doing a play?" And he said, "Well it's a huge cast, twenty-two characters. It's so big the only place you could do it is on Broadway. Broadway isn't going to do a play by a twenty-six, twenty-seven-year-old playwright that nobody's ever heard of. It's not going to happen." And that night, he happened to be speaking to the development person for David Brown, the film producer for Zanuck-Brown, who had just finished doing *The Verdict*. And this person was saying that David had such a great time doing *The Verdict* that he wanted to do another courtroom drama, and did my agent know of any? (*Both laugh.*) And that was the ball game.

Longworth: In *A Few Good Men*, Joanne, upon meeting Caffey for the first time, says,"I expected someone older." As a wunderkind, do you ever get that reaction in Hollywood?

SORKIN: Yeah, it's funny you should say that. You're actually the first person who has asked me if I get that question, and it's something that comes up a lot, which is to say people who haven't met me expect me to be much older than I am. And just because of the things I have written about and in the style in which I've written.

Longworth: You write "older."

SORKIN: I seem to. There are certain days I find that troubling. And yet, I oughtn't find anything troubling, you know what I'm saying? I enjoy what I write, and I'm able to make a living from it.

Longworth: How does it hamstring you?

SORKIN: It's not so much that it hamstrings me. I sometimes feel like when I see the work of writers my age writing very specifically about either my generation or Bohemia, if you will, I feel personally connected to both those things. And yet I never write about them. I write kind of the way that Preston Sturges might.

Longworth: I know this is not a book about film, and not to belabor the discussion about *A Few Good Men*, but it really seemed to me that the Tom Cruise character, Caffey, is almost Aaron Sorkin in a way. There were references to his father having been a lawyer, and your father and brother were lawyers.

SORKIN: Right, I would say even more than specifics like that. A lot of the people that I'll write—whether it's Caffey in *A Few Good Men*, Andrew Sheppard in *The American President*, or any of the characters in *The West Wing*—that often times, specifically with Caffey, what we'll meet is a nice enough guy. In other words, we're not telling the story of a bad guy becoming good. He's a likeable guy who's just not living up to his potential who has yet to be challenged by something and risk something in a kind of selfless act. In Caffey, we discover that he is a brilliant plea bargainer, that he dispenses with things easily and quickly, and that he is as Demi Moore's character, Joanne Galloway, says, "You're just going to kind of lay low for three years until you can get out of the Navy and get a real job." And the emotional arc of the thing is watching the character go from a guy who refers to the military and their "bozo code of honor," and ends up saying very righteously to Jessup, "Don't call me son; I'm a lawyer and an officer in the United States Navy."

Longworth: The other question is, what the heck do *you* know about the military?

SORKIN: Certainly nothing before my sister joined up, which was an unusual event in our family. I don't come from a military family. My father served in World War II, but my sister, after she graduated from law school, decided she wanted to spend a few years in the Judge Advocate General's corp to get trial experience. And I had stupidly, up to that point, felt that anybody who would join the military must love killing [and be] sort of a jarhead with a falsely narrow and bigoted view. So I got to meet some of the people she was working with, and hear about some of the things that they were doing, and *why* they would join the military, and I thought, "My opinion is dumb, it's wrong, it's stupid." I wanted to then write about people who were serving in the military who I liked.

Longworth: Don Bellisario [creator of *Magnum P.I.* and *JAG*] made the point to me one day about the prejudice that existed in Hollywood against anyone who tried to produce pro-military dramas on television.

SORKIN: By the way, the impression has existed even [in film], because I did the play on Broadway and then came out to California for my first meeting with Rob Reiner, who was to direct this film. It was really in the first couple of hours of the meeting that my heart sank down to my ankles because we were talking about the two defendants, Dawson and Downey, and I was talking about them in the most complimentary terms. And Rob was saying (*Aaron imitates Reiner in a shouting voice*) "They joined the Marines, they've got to like killing." And I was afraid he was going to have a heart attack, because he kind of turns red and sweat starts pouring off his forehead. And I thought, "Oh boy, we're going to make *A Few Good Men* and it's not going to be a valentine to the service?" (*Both laugh.*)

Longworth: Jumping ahead for a moment to *The West Wing*. Earlier you talked about the Caffey-like, or Aaron-like, person who seems to pop up in all of your work. The overachieving, competent guy. It seems like you've got the characters molded to where they all sort of fit that pattern—fast talking, getting things done, being very committed to their beliefs.

SORKIN: Well one of the nice things about writing, and for me there are many, but one of the nice things is I'm allowed to present the version of myself which I could present if I'm given [time] to rewrite. If I'm given time alone in my room (*laughs*) to consider things. If I'm allowed to decide what everybody else says in addition to what I say. And so it's not unusual that you would find a much better, highly polished version of myself.

Longworth: With some people I interview, they are essentially, at the core, the same person they were when they were five years old. They liked to write then, and they like to write now, and so forth. You're still who you were as a kid, a real lyricist in terms of being able to hear voices and words, but in a way you're very different, too.

SORKIN: Yeah, that's very well put. Well there *is* an interesting thing in terms of being able to hear voices and words. The way I am the same is that, growing up, the thing that most influenced me, and was the most important to me becoming a writer as an adult, was that I absolutely loved the sound of language. I was always surrounded by smart people, people who I really believed were considerably smarter than I was.

Longworth: Is that why you agreed to spend time with *me* today?

SORKIN: (*Laughs.*)

Longworth: He laughs disdainfully.

SORKIN: Hardly. There's a story that perhaps can illustrate this, which is that I'm Jewish but never had any religious training, I never went to Hebrew school. And in my family, the boys, on their thirteenth birthday, had a big party. There wasn't a bar mitzvah even though I think we called it one. It was just big party. Well I'm in seventh grade, I was twelve, about to be thirteen, and nearly every Saturday you're going to a friend's bar mitzvah. My love for all things theatrical was really starting to be developed, *and* I loved the service, and I loved the fact that the bar mitzvah boy got to be the star. You went up there, and there was this great recitation in another language, and there were costumes and an audience.

Longworth: Great theater.

SORKIN: It *was* great theater, and temples are theaters. And I decided I had made a huge mistake, that I really *did* want to be bar mitzvahed—so I called a local rabbi and said, "I'm turning thirteen in six weeks, and I'd like you to teach me the Torah so I can be bar mitzvahed." And he said, "I can't teach you the Torah in six weeks; it would take years." And I said, "No, you don't understand, you don't have to actually teach it to me. I have a really good ear. If you just say it in a tape recorder, I can learn it phonetically." And he explained to me that I was missing the point of the experience. (*Both laugh.*) And what I think that illustrates is that with, say, *The West Wing*, and, frankly, everything that I write, I'm not interested in reality as much as I'm interested in the *appearance* of reality. It doesn't matter to me. I don't understand when a movie or show is coming out, that the production will boast, "We did this incredible research! We're using the exact same pencils they used." That doesn't get you anywhere on film; that's just something you can say to Jay Leno. It's silly and you're sending your prop person on a fool's errand. On the other hand if you can do something or say something where the audience believes, "God, those people know what they're talking about, then that's good. I'm looking behind the scenes at something. I'm getting to see what happens in the two minutes before and after CNN." I need words, I need phrases that *sound* like an intelligence briefing, that *sound* like something that would happen in the situation room. I need names of guns and terminology of things. There are a couple of times in *A Few Good Men,* there are a couple of times in *The American President,* there are several times on *The West Wing,* and many, many times on *Sports Night,* by the way, in the control room I make up entire phrases, just because I am imitating in a sort of refined gibberish the *sound* of a studio control room, the *sond* of a situation room, the *sound* of a press briefing, the *sound* of sports. I don't know if you watch *Sports Night* or not, but in the control room, there'll be entire pages of meaningless things, like, "Count me in four from the rollback, I need the box set on two." It absolutely means nothing, but the viewer, frankly, is going to think it's authentic. Much more authentic than if I had them say something that the viewer understood, because the viewer's not going to believe that what goes on in a big-time control room is anything they could understand.

Longworth: Some of the critics who are really in your corner on *The West Wing* have angered political journalists with reviews like, "Sorkin's dialogue is so on the money that the American people are going to learn more about issues than they would from looking at *The Nightly News* or reading *The Times.*" Some dyed-in-the-wool political journalists have gotten pissed about that.

SORKIN: And I get that, by the way, and *nobody* should be getting their news from *The West Wing.* Nobody should be getting their information from *The West Wing.* People should be entertained by *The West Wing.* I'll add to that, though, I don't play it fast and loose with anything that's important. I'm talking about if I have a throwaway line where I just need the end of a conversation to sound like something's important. It is just a bridge from one place to the next. It's the *sound* of the White House, the *sound* of people who know what they're talking about.

Longworth: Your rare ability to hear and then process sounds drove the rabbi crazy. Does that also create a problem with your writers in the sense that you're so involved, often creating dialogue at the last minute, that you've effectively relegated them to a helping role rather than to one of actually writing? Wouldn't that tend to drive them nuts?

SORKIN: Yeah, I bet I do, on *both* shows, by the way. But there is a staff here [on *The West Wing*] of very dedicated, very talented writers who do not get to open the throttle. I know [that] a lot of people who create shows will write the pilot, they'll kind of write the next couple of episodes, and then they'll slowly step back into more of a supervisory role once people get the idea of the show, and then they'll take the staff's scripts and start to run them through their own typewriter, and then after the first season, it won't even be *that* anymore. And the fact is, and I don't mean to insult anybody when I say this, I'm not a producer. I'm not a television producer. I'm a writer, which is to say that my interest is not in empire building. "Oh great, I got *this* show successfully launched, now let me do my next one." Although I know appearances can be deceiving, because I did two shows back to back, one season to the next, but what I love doing is writing.

Longworth: So why even *hire* writers in the first place?

SORKIN: Well, that's a good question and a perfectly fair question. You know the fact is that, as the season went on, I think that the writers discovered the way they can best help the show. They're all very smart people and they're all very into the show. [They'll be] writing a two- or three-page memo to me on a subject, like "Here's three pages on proportional response, pro and con, and here's why the response *should* be proportional, and here's why we should wipe the sons of bitches off the face of the earth." And I'll say, "Gee, this is great, and now there's a story to be gotten from this." And then I'll write it, because that's what I like doing. Now the real question is, why don't those writers then say "Aaron, I love the show, and I wish you all the luck in the world, but I'm a writer and I want to write too, so I'm going to go someplace else." And the fact that they don't do that frankly makes me emotional (*laughs*), that they stick around anyway.

Longworth: Well then since you like to have a hand in everything, let's talk about burn-out. At one point you were writing two shows simultaneously, and there were even critics who opined that *Sports Night* was suffering because you were focused on *The West Wing*. Now we don't have to get into the criticism too deeply but . . .

SORKIN: You can if you want.

Longworth: OK. Is that criticism valid? Can one thing suffer when you're working on two things at once? And, if so, why did you do it?

SORKIN: It can be true, and it can be true for a couple of reasons. One is the obvious. There are only so many hours in the week. *Sports Night* was a seven-day-a-week job to begin with, generally Monday through Thursday. As soon as the table read was done on Monday with *Sports Night*, I'd spend the next four days agonizing because I didn't have any ideas for next week. And, Friday, finally push comes to shove and you've got to write something, and I started to get excited about what I was thinking, and, by Sunday night, the script is done and it goes on the table Monday, and you start all over again. So you get tired. You are constantly living in fear because you have to write the next one, and you don't have any ideas for it, and you want it to be good. But the real problem is this: doing two shows at once, writing two shows at once is probably not something I'll ever do again, and I wouldn't recommend it to anybody. For one thing, just emotionally, you constantly feel like you're cheating on your wife. You always feel a little bit dirty. You badly want each cast and each crew and each network to really know how you feel inside, which is that you love this show and you are completely dedicated to this show. And the appearance is otherwise, that your focus is split somehow. Disney and Warner Brothers, where we do the two shows, are separated by about three-quarters of a mile. And I always feel like I have a secret family someplace else. *The West Wing* group wasn't bothered too much by *Sports Night* because they've never known a world without *Sports Night*. *Sports Night*, though, is just like the older kid, and you've just brought this new baby home from the hospital, so it was a little tough there. But mostly the biggest trouble is this, when I'm back to page one, I've turned in a script, and, now, you're still looking at an empty piece of paper again. The process is one of walking around, driving around, you'll turn music on, you'll talk to yourself, and something will strike you as funny or emotional, gripping, or frightening, anything. Just one little kernel of a thing, and that's where you start. I need a scene that will get me to that point. I need a scene to put that great joke in. Once I have that scene, I think, "How did I *get* to that scene?" You're working crabwise a lot. And the tough thing about two shows is that when that thing *does* hit you, the piece of music comes on, and you think "I want to write a scene that ends with *this* song coming in 'cause that will be really effective," then where are you going to put it?

Sports Night or *The West Wing?* In other words, where is the engine headed toward? And that's very hard, and that, by the way, was really where the *Sports Night* staff was extremely helpful this year. I no longer this year could afford the Monday-through-Thursday kind of pacing around, thinking about what I was going to start writing on Friday. Come Friday, oftentimes they would say, "Here's what *we* were thinking of. How about something like this?" And I'd say "Nah," and they'd say "How about something like *this?*" And we'd get the discussion going, so I really wasn't by myself this year.

Longworth: You've written plays and television shows. A playwright can afford to get writer's block, but in television you don't have that luxury because of deadlines. Do you ever hit an impasse, and what do you do to snap out of it in order to make deadline?

SORKIN: Well, you said it. First of all, when I began writing *A Few Good Men,* and I guess it was the last thing I wrote on spec (in other words, the last thing I hadn't already been hired to write with an expectation at the end of it). I was supporting myself by bartending in Broadway Theaters, and when you do that, you're tending bar from 7:30 to 8:00, or from 1:30 to 2:00 if it's a matinee, during what's called the "walk-in," when people are coming in, and for fifteen minutes at intermission. And you're [working] on your script during the first act. I wrote *A Few Good Men* on cocktail napkins, mostly during the first act of *La Caux Au Fol* at the Palace Theater. I would come home with my pockets stuffed with cocktail napkins, dump them out on the table, and start writing. I took all of the time that I wanted and wrote many, many drafts of *A Few Good Men.*

Longworth: Do you still have the napkins?

SORKIN: Wouldn't it be great if I still did? (*Laughs.*) But I don't. And back then I always said, "I feel like I don't write, I rewrite." And it was really true. I would just write pages and pages and pages of dialogue, with very little plot. Plot is something I've never been particularly comfortable with. I'm not a natural storyteller. I wasn't the kid around the campfire saying, "I got a million of them." I wasn't that guy. It's really just the sound of dialogue, so that plot follows the dialogue for me.

Longworth: You're a lyricist.

SORKIN: Well put. So I'd write these pages of crackling dialogue, and then on page nineteen, I'd say OK *this* is interesting. So I've now got to go back to page one and set this up. Things would get written that way. Well then, when I came out to do the movie, that was going to be *it* for me. I was going to do the film adaptation of *A Few Good Men,* and go back to New York and write my next play. I'm pretty sure that the Writers Guild contract, from the day of the initial payment till the day the first draft is due, is twelve weeks after that, or something, but with *The American President* and *A Few Good Men*, I think I probably took close to two years on just those first drafts, just rewriting, and rewriting, and rewriting. So one day it's about three o'clock and it's not going well, and I pick up the phone and I call Rob Reiner, who's not just the director, he's the producer and one of the owners of the studio. And I say "Hey Rob, it's not going well. I know I said it was going to be in next week, but it's going to be a couple more weeks after that." You cannot do that in television, cannot, cannot, cannot. The script's got to be on the table *that* day or you're holding up a network. So, both *Sports Night* and *The West Wing*, we *shoot* my first draft, and that is perilous, to say the least.

Longworth: Is there ever a moment where you're running onto the set to rewrite words just before they come out of Rob Lowe's mouth?

SORKIN: Yeah, not as much as you might think, but, yes. Specifically with Rob Lowe, I just did that about twenty minutes ago. I went over there and added a little thing. But, yes.

Longworth: We don't usually get into discussions about technical matters, but let me ask you about photography on *The West Wing*. Now, that's shot with a single camera, right?

SORKIN: Oh yeah, just like a movie.

Longworth: OK, let's say you had four cameras. Wouldn't postproduction take less time?

SORKIN: Yeah, that's a question people ask a lot, and without getting too technical about it, and by the way, I *couldn't* get too technical with you, because it's all I can do to master a Kodak Instamatic. (*Both laugh.*) I am not a filmmaker. But I can tell you this. Just like in movies, lighting is terribly specific to the exact shot that you're doing. Every once in a while we're doing a scene, which, for whatever reason, we're actually able to use two cameras, but most of the time the scene is only lit for one camera angle, and if you tried to light it for two you'd blow the lighting for one of them. So it is a painstaking process. One of my early mentors, to use a pretentious word, was the writer William Goldman, who told me that my first day on a movie set, my first day on *A Few Good Men*, was going to be the most exciting day of my life, and the most boring days of my life were going to be every day that followed. (*Both laugh.*) And basically, watching a movie get made, or watching *The West Wing* get made, as much as I love it, it moves in increments of inches, and most of the time you're waiting for large equipment to be moved from here to there.

Longworth: Last question about the writing of *The West Wing*. From where do you get the story ideas? Real situations, real news headlines?

SORKIN: Sometimes. With *The West Wing* I like to *not* grab things from the front page, because it'll begin to seem like a Movie of the Week, like something disposable. Also, the front page does the front page better than we can do it, the actual drama that's going on. On the other hand, you can find an item on page twenty-three and usually, sometimes stories don't come to you full blown. I mean, it's a sentence that we think was funny, or gets you thinking about something. I was reading an article probably a year ago about some diplomatic confirmations that were being held up in the Senate. I don't know if you remember, but Clinton wanted to appoint an ambassador to Luxembourg.

Longworth: Yeah, and Jesse Helms held it up.

SORKIN: Jesse Helms was *very* upset about it because the man was gay. So not only was he holding up *this* confirmation, he was holding up several others as well, including the president's nominee for Ambassador to the Federated States of Micronesia. (*Laughs.*) And there was just something that struck me. And, by the way, if you don't know, the Federated States of Micronesia is a country of one hundred and seven tiny islands in the Pacific. It's got a population of about forty-two. And there was just something that struck me funny about choosing an ambassador for that. I just wanted to *use* that. I had to look at a globe; I wasn't even sure where the place was. And so, I'll rip that out and stick it in a file of miscellaneous *The West Wing* ideas, and nearly every week, when I have nothing, I'll go through that and think, "Is there anything here?" Since the first day of the season I've been talking to the staff about the Federated States of Micronesia. Same thing with any number of items. Also, three of the staffers have considerable Washington experience: Dee Dee Myers, who was Clinton's first press secretary; Pat Caddell, who ran Jimmy Carter's campaign; and Lawrence O'Donnell, who was Chief of Staff for the Senate Finance Committee.

Longworth: Do they keep you honest?

SORKIN: They keep me honest and they keep me excited. (*Laughs.*)

Longworth: Do you rely on them to argue specific points of the issues related to a particular topic?

SORKIN: What I look for in the three of them, and for that matter the others who are on the staff, too, about a half a dozen people, I'm aware that we're all pretty much coming from the same political place, though in the case of Pat and Dee Dee and Lawrence, their political opinions are much more sophisticated than the rest of us. And I will often write them a memo saying,

"First just tell me what you think, then tell me what the really smart person in the room who disagrees with you is going to say," because they have all had these arguments with smart people. In *A Few Good Men*, the scene that people seem to remember is where Nicholson is on the stand. I think one of the reasons that scene works the way it does is that, even though he is admitting the fact that he contributed to this kid's death and certainly covered it up, at the end of his "You can't *handle* the truth" scene, I think we're all thinking, "That made a certain amount of sense to me" in a frightening way. Boy, when you can hit *that* note, you're really fine.

Longworth: You spoke earlier of how there's a little bit of you in all your characters, so let's look at Leo in *The West Wing* and his problem with drugs. Was that story line based on you and your experience and, if so, is it realistic in terms of how you felt when faced with a similar situation?

SORKIN: There's certainly a little bit because I'm a recovering addict. Now again, I generally don't start with a big idea. I start with something very small that I find interesting, and I look for a story where that will fit nicely. With Leo it was this. There are AA meetings going on all over the world, twenty-four hours a day. I guarantee you that within five miles of you there's one happening right now. And you don't need a ticket, you don't need a reservation, nobody checks your ID. You walk in the door and sit down. There are a few exceptions. Commercial airline pilots have private, secret AA meetings for obvious reasons. Judges have their own AA meetings. Surgeons have their own AA meetings, very secret for obvious reasons. So it occurred to me that if there were these secret AA meetings, from either drug or alcohol abuse, is it not possible that *somewhere* deep in the basement of government, late at night in Washington, D.C., is an AA meeting for government officials so high profile that they couldn't possibly go to a regular AA meeting?

Longworth: Do you know if your assumption is accurate?

SORKIN: I have no idea, but again, the *appearance* of reality is more important to me. I would say this: I would be really surprised if there weren't. I have to believe that, with the five hundred and forty-five Congressmen and Senators, with all the agency directors, and with all these people who work in the White House, there have got to be a bunch of people there who are recovering alcoholics, and it wouldn't shock me at all if there *were* such a meeting.

Longworth: Leaving *The West Wing* for a moment, let's talk about the television industry. Your friend Jerry Bruckheimer now has a hit show on CBS, *CSI*. In the old days, producer/director/writers like Bruckheimer, James

Cameron [*Dark Angel*], or Paul Attanasio [*Gideon's Crossing*] would never consider doing a TV show.

SORKIN: I'm really glad you mentioned Paul; I'm so psyched that he's "hoppin' in the pool." (*Laughs.*) I really like him a lot. Paul is really the writer in Hollywood who I'd like to be.

Longworth: But why the big change in attitude? I know there's quite a lot of money to be made in television at the producing level, but there are a lot of risks, too.

SORKIN: There's a lot of money, but none of the people you just named need much money. I think that the walls are down. I don't think there is any prejudice toward television as a medium anymore. I think it's kind of the "Wild, Wild West" out there. And given that, there aren't, and I'm going to walk the plank now, there aren't that many great television shows out there. I think that a great writer like Paul, I think a great producer like Jerry, and by the way, you left out Steven Spielberg. Talk about a guy who doesn't need money or attention. (*Laughs.*) There's simply a feeling, just like there was with me on *Sports Night* and *The West Wing*, it wasn't a matter of "Gee I want to do a television show, let me think of an idea," it was "I got an idea, it's not a movie, it's not a play, what this is, is episodic, it's a television series. Let me try that."

Longworth: OK, but television has always been episodic in nature, so why are we all of the sudden seeing a stampede of filmmakers to TV?

SORKIN: I don't think television is a second-class citizen anymore. When I started to do *Sports Night*, I must tell you I was a little concerned. I think there were some people around me who were a little concerned, but didn't really want to say it. Some of them *did* say it. There was a concern that I had a very healthy feature career going, and that it would somehow be cheapened or tarnished by doing television. And it's not for me to say, but I don't think that's happened. That's what I mean by the walls have come down. I think that, particularly for writers, they watch what David Milch does, they watch what Bochco does, they watch what Kelley does. It's possible that some of them even watch what I do. And they think, "You know, there's good writing happening on television." By the way, television is built for writers. If you're the creator, you're the boss. You would do well not to go into work with that attitude, but you're the boss. It's also immediate gratification. When I'm writing a screenplay, and I write a joke, I'm not going to hear the laugh for another year and a half. The script I write today is going to be on film next week and on television two weeks after that.

Longworth: And sometimes you *never* hear the laugh.

SORKIN: And sometimes you never hear the laugh. (*Both laugh.*)

Longworth: Let's talk for a moment about the differences between television and feature films. Even if *A Few Good Men* opens opposite *Star Wars*, people are eventually going to see it, if not that week then later, either in the theater or on home video, but they'll see it. In other words it may take time for people to find you, but that's OK. Legend has it that a network executive told you that *Sports Night*'s "ten million viewers just doesn't cut it." Today everything in TV is more and more about ratings and less and less about quality. Example *Who Wants to Be a Millionaire* and reality shows, which are directly or indirectly having a negative impact on writers and producers of drama.

SORKIN: Nothing is good about *Who Wants to Be a Millionaire* except for the people doing *Who Wants to Be a Millionaire*.

Longworth: So my rather protracted question is, perhaps not just about the differences in the two mediums specifically, but the state of television in general these days as it relates to your craft. Does it concern you?

SORKIN: Yeah it *does* concern me because I'm so personally involved with it now. First I wanted to mention, just in terms of television versus movies, the other great advantage to television is, if you're doing a film, you work very hard on it for several years. Long before photography starts, you're there writing the script and going nuts. And then you shoot the film and you cut the film and you *open* the film. And if your movie is a big, big, blockbuster, smash hit, you are part of the public consciousness for maybe three weeks. If you're not [a smash hit], you are stillborn. We work just as hard at *The West Wing* and we remain part of the public consciousness each and every week.

Longworth: That has to be gratifying.

SORKIN: It's extremely gratifying. I like it very much. And by the way, one of the things, and I'll answer your other question, but one of the things that we *haven't* talked about that's also nice about the writing of the show is that you get to do mostly "middles." You don't have to do so much beginning and end. It's an ongoing story. It feels to me like chapters in a great Dickens novel that just keeps going. But as far as the state of television, I think that network television is still a little bit rocked back on its heels from the huge impact of cable. It cannot be underestimated how cable has changed television. From the days (and the days seem like yesterday) when there were just three networks, and now there are nine thousand things that you can watch, and it's changed things in this way. First of all, the talent pool of writers is spread extremely thin. We're getting into a touchy area, but we were talking about the writing staff before. If there was someone on the staff who could write *The West Wing*, they wouldn't be working for me. They'd have their own show. In the old days, when there weren't that many shows, someone who is a showrunner now would have been a low-level staff writer and would work their way up, and it would take several years.

Longworth: It's like what's happened in major league baseball ever since expansion.

SORKIN: Exactly. It has diluted the pitching. It's exactly like that. Except imagine, instead of two new teams being added or four new teams, there were fifty new teams being added, or a hundred new teams being added. You and I would be the backup shortstop for a major league baseball team at this point. So there is that.

Longworth: OK, but back to the network guy who told you that ten million viewers doesn't cut it in television. I'm thinking, "Why not?"

SORKIN: Yeah, every once in a while you're going to get an *ER* or a *Seinfeld* that's going to get thirty million people, but it's only going to happen every once in a while. And it seems to me that network television has got to change the economics of TV so that you can make a living from ten million people watching your show. That's the only choice left. Now obviously it's possible. Cable does it. I was able to ask Gary Shandling last year, "Did HBO ever really care how many people were watching your show?" And, by the way, *The Larry Sanders Show*, one of the best shows that's been on television in a long, long time, was one of the lowest-rated shows on *cable*, not just on television. And he said no, they never really cared how many people were watching the show, just how much public acclaim it got. Remember, on network television your customers aren't the audience; your customers are the advertisers. The audience isn't paying for anything. On HBO there *are* no advertisers. You're dealing with subscription. And on HBO you've got *this* many Emmy awards, you've got Gary Shandling on the cover of *The New Yorker*, that kind of thing, people are buying subscriptions. Now interestingly, *The Sopranos*'s audience in its second season rose 60 percent from its first season, which is whopping by anybody's standards. Young men, and I'm talking about fourteen year olds, they lost *them* apparently because their attention spans aren't sufficient to bridge the hiatus (*laughs*) to get from one season to the next, and they found something else. And I asked Chris Albrecht, the head of HBO, "Why do you care if you lost them? They already bought HBO?" And he said, "they are the demographic most likely to disconnect." And I forgot, yeah, people turn off HBO, too.

Longworth: Since we're on the subject of audiences, the people who watch *The West Wing* are not fourteen-year-old boys, and yet your viewers are part of an overall populace that boasts the lowest voter turnout in American history. Now all of the sudden *The West Wing* is becoming more and more popular. I know you said that you don't want people getting their news from your show, but can you deny that you may have had an impact on re-energizing voters to the political process?

SORKIN: I like the sound of that, don't get me wrong. And I think it's terrific. But let's return to the economics for a second, and to the demographics that watches *The West Wing*. The demographics that watches *The West Wing* is awfully similar to the demographics that watches *Sports Night*. What's really similar is the demographic that won't watch either.

Longworth: Meaning?

SORKIN: Very young people, young boys mostly. But both shows "Index" very well, as they say. What does that mean? It means that the incomes and education level of both audiences are extremely high. And here's what I'm getting at. In the *New York Times* when you advertise for a play, when we took out space to advertise for *A Few Good Men*, the rates don't depend on the size of space or the location of the ad. They depend on what you're advertising. Nobody pays more for advertising space in the *New York Times* than plays—nobody. Movies pay less, supermarkets pay less, financial institutions pay less, Saks Fifth Avenue pays less. Everybody pays less for ad space than plays. Why? Because theatergoers read the *New York Times* and *only* the *New York Times*. The *New York Times* has us by the back of the neck. We have to advertise in the *New York Times*. You have no other place to advertise [for a play] so they can squeeze us. I believe, without getting too snooty about it, that Mercedes-Benz and Nokia, and companies like that, frankly don't have that many places on television that they can advertise that make sense for them. And I think that's the way to compensate for the fact that the total number of eyes looking at the television may be lower than they are for *Dharma and Greg*. Mercedes needs to be charged for the fact that they can't advertise on *Dharma and Greg*, they can only advertise on *The West Wing*. There are other shows, too, but in other words, television needs to take the *New York Times*'s attitude. We know we've got a show here that is not going to appeal to as large a mass as *Who Wants to Be a Millionaire*, but it's going to appeal to a very specific group of people, and it's a group of people that certain advertisers have a difficult time locating on television. Well, we've brought them right to you! Here are ten million potential Mercedes-Benz buyers. We're going to have to charge you for it, because we don't have fifteen million people, we only have ten. And I think that that's the way to deal with a show like *The West Wing*.

Longworth: According to your model, then, you should be able to charge more for thirty seconds than they do in *ER*.

SORKIN: Absolutely. Actually *ER* is an example of a different thing, which I would charge more money for. By far the most valuable television time to a movie company is Thursday night at ten o'clock. Movies open on Friday. Their audience is watching television Thursday night at ten o'clock.

Longworth: You're in the wrong business. You should be in advertising.

SORKIN: (*Laughs.*) By the way I am not pulling these things out of thin air. I am surrounded by smart people. They tell me these things. Anyway, we've gotten off topic.

Longworth: That's OK. Since we spoke of *ER*, I am reminded of a story that has been circulated about the first meeting between you and John Wells. It was at a great little spot called the Pino Bistro on Ventura Boulevard where the two of you talked about doing *The West Wing*. Is it true that you showed up not knowing what you were going to pitch?

SORKIN: I'm very dumb about meetings. Meetings are sort of how Hollywood runs. Everybody has meetings, and there seems to be the appearance that something is going on. And so, I've never taken them seriously. My parents grew up in the Depression, and just like you find with people of that era, no matter how well they've come out of the Depression (and both my parents came out of it very well), they never lose the fear that it can all go away. So they . . . don't like to waste things, all of which is commendable, and it was the same thing with me. Honestly, no matter how well you're doing, when your agent calls you and says "So and so would like to have a meeting with you," frankly you're so happy that so and so has heard of you and likes your work, there's no way you're going to say, "Gee I'm happy about that, but I've got nothing to tell you." You're never going to do that. So I had this meeting set up with John Wells, and I thought it was going to be a shmoozy meeting, like "hey, one of these days we'll get together, and that would be great." And the night before the meeting a few friends were over for dinner. And one of them, a writer, Aquiva Goulson, was in my office and saw *The American President* poster, and said, "You know, this would make a great television series." And I said "Don't be ridiculous. I don't want to cheapen the movie by doing a television series. I'm done with that." And I went in to lunch the next day, and somehow just as soon as I saw that it wasn't just John, it was me and John and like six agents, I realized, "Gee, this isn't going to be a shmoozy meeting where we say 'Let's get together someday.' He's expecting me to pitch something, and he's an impressive guy. I like this guy, and I don't want to waste his time." And it suddenly hit me that there were so many things I had wanted to do in *The American President*. My first draft of *The American President* was close to four hundred pages long. And the reason was that I had gotten really caught up in many other stories. Te story between the president and Annette Benning was just one of many stories that were going on.

Longworth: So even then it was somewhat episodic in your mind?

SORKIN: Very episodic in my mind. You could go forty or fifty pages in that first draft without seeing either Michael Douglas or Annette Benning in them. Scenes just about Michael J Fox, Anna Dever Smith, David Paymer, or any of those guys. I turned in the four hundred-page draft and Rob said, "Well, you've definitely got a movie here, but I think you got to shave away everything but the romance between the president and Sidney." And so always in my mind I had these other stories that I didn't tell, none of which I've told yet on *The West Wing*. (*Laughs.*) But I did say to John [Wells], "I'd like to do a show about senior staffers at the White House, not about the president, but about the staff." And I began to tell some of the stories from that *American President* [draft], some of the things George Stefanopolis had told me when I was at the White House. So I began to describe my vision for the show. And John said, "That's great, let's do it." Now again, before *A Few Good Men*, I was used to never actually *doing* anything. You sit around your apartment with your friends and dream of stuff. "Yes, we'll put on a show, we'll get a barn," that kind of thing. It's never gonna happen, but that's OK, you talk about it anyway, because somebody's got a six-pack of beer, and we're in our twenties, and we're struggling artists, and we *should* be talking about it. It didn't occur to me that when John Wells said "Let's do it," and I said "OK," that we're doing a TV show *now!* (*Both laugh.*) And that's how it happened.

Longworth: But as everyone now knows, *The West Wing* just about didn't get on the air, and was in fact delayed because of the real drama that was being played out in the headlines over President Clinton and his sex scandal.

SORKIN: That's right. It was supposed to debut at the exact same time as *Sports Night,* so I consider that whole delay a real blessing, a real blessing. But there were two reasons. Even before the drama in the White House, I remember I turned in the pilot script before we knew who Monica Lewinski was. Back then everything was run by Don Ohlmeyer and Warren Littlefield.

They were lukewarm at best about the idea of a Washington show on TV. Washington shows, political dramas, are anathema on television.

Longworth: So you felt they were taking the safe view.

SORKIN: Yes. But John is the person who could really fill you in on these details. John swings a pretty big bat at NBC, obviously.

Longworth: So he strong-armed the network?

SORKIN: Pressured them. At one point I think CBS was coming along saying, "We'll give you thirteen episodes on the air." I think that NBC started to hear the footsteps. And then when Monica Lewinski came along, we knew we would have to lay out at least a year if it ever got on the air at all. Don Ohlmeyer and Warren Littlefield were replaced by Scott Sassa and Garth Ancier, who read the script right away, picked up the phone, said, "We love the show, we're doing the show." And that's when we all came to work.

Longworth: Are you surprised at how well *The West Wing* has performed? I mean, as good as it is, it could still have been a sixtieth-ranked show. Instead, it usually wins its time period during a normal week.

SORKIN: I'm so delighted. First of all, in terms of surprise, again, that same part of my brain is saying, "I wonder if this is the last job I'll have?" (*Laughs.*) I'm always surprised when anyone but my immediate family watches anything that I do. But in this particular case, after a year of *Sports Night* I felt like, "All right, if there are ten million people who want to come out for this kind of writing, then, that's OK." For me, where I cut my teeth, if you got seventy-five people into a church basement in Soho on Friday night, that meant you were sold out. You were thrilled. Ten million people is very satisfying. And it's a number so large, it's beyond comprehension to me. I don't know what ten million people look like. When we began this conversation talking about being the same now as when we were younger, back in the days when I was holding that McGovern sign, I also have a real distinct memory of feeling kind of sorry for Richard Nixon because I didn't think anybody was going to vote for him. That's how little I understood the rest of the people living in the country. And it wasn't just that I was a little kid. In 1984 I was already one year out of college. Ronald Reagan won re-election by one of the biggest landslides in history, and I was not acquainted with a single person who voted for him. I began thinking, "*I'm* the rest of the people who live in the country. We're not all the same. Everyone is different." And so, while I was never really bumming that *Sports Night* wasn't faring well in the ratings, I never believed, and I don't think anyone ever believed, that it was because the show wasn't good. I think people believed it was because the show wasn't like other things that were on television. In terms of the critical praise, and all the award nominations, and things like that, my ego was very satisfied that, essentially, this is the price you pay for snob appeal, that you're also not going to be particularly popular. And so with *The West Wing* I just assumed that we were in for more of the same and girded myself for what happens to you when your show isn't doing well in the ratings, which is to say you get a lot of notes from the network telling you what they want you to do. They want you to do more of this and less of that. Could you bring in this? Could you do that? Girding myself for low morale among the cast, which I thought was going to be sad because we had started with such great spirits. Now the fact that this show is popular with audiences has, well, I've never exhaled quite so loudly in my life. (*Laughs.*)

Longworth: How about interference from Standards and Practices. Any problems on *The West Wing?*

SORKIN: Not nearly as much as you'd think, though some of them have been very funny.

Longworth: Such as?

SORKIN: You cannot say "Goddam" on television. (*Laughs.*) You simply can't. You can't take the Lord's name in vain. You will forgive me, but we will be able to say, "mother fucker" on network television before we'll be able to say "Goddam." (*Both laugh.*) And it's too bad, because, just rhythmically, "Goddam" and "Jesus Christ," I wish I could have them once in a while. One of the things that hasn't happened yet, but I think it's just because I haven't tripped the wire yet, is this. I was nervous about NBC being owned by General Electric, a company that, as you know, doesn't just make its money from lightbulbs and refrigerators. They are a huge, huge, huge military contractor. A giant military contractor. If I said the wrong thing about the B-1 Bomber. If I just did a joke like, "Dammit, the lights went out on the dashboard of the bomber," that there might be some trouble. Now I haven't heard a word about any of that, but like I said, it may just be because I haven't tested them.

Longworth: But back to bad language. You could use it on HBO.

SORKIN: Particularly a show like *The West Wing,* you and I only get to view the president on CNN, on television, at speeches, conventions, public forums. We have never seen the president say "fuck." And that's a behind-the-scenes thing. But I would never move *The West Wing* from NBC. NBC has simply been too good to us. Too supportive, too helpful. They like the show too much. They've created a paradise for us here.

Longworth: But you're saying the show could be better on HBO? Or just different?

SORKIN: I'm saying it would be a little different on HBO, and, by the way, there are plenty of people out there, plenty of them who would be turned off by the use of that kind of language. And so you give a little, and you get a little. There's no doubt that the show would be watched by fewer people on HBO, just because everything is watched by fewer people on HBO. I'm perfectly happy with *The West Wing* right where it is. I hope we stay where we are. I don't anticipate that the Thursday ten o'clock slot is going to open up any time soon (*both laugh*), but when it does, I hope NBC knows we're happy to move to that.

Longworth: Are you having fun now?

SORKIN: I couldn't have more fun. Yes, I am. It's so hard, it's terrifying. But it's so much fun. It's so rewarding.

Longworth: And will you run for office?

SORKIN: You don't want me. (*Laughs.*)

Longworth: Why not? What would be the worst thing about having you in office?

SORKIN: Well, I don't really *know* anything. (*Both laugh.*)

Longworth: That would be kind of a problem, wouldn't it?

SORKIN: (*Laughs.*) Yes.

Longworth: Earlier you said that performers were not magical people, that they were just doing a job. I can't help but sense that with you, an actor turned writer, there's still a lot of magic.

SORKIN: Of course. There's a tremendous amount of magic, and the magic never went away for me.

ROY | Television
HUGGINS | Maverick

Roy Huggins. COURTESY OF ROY HUGGINS.

TELEVISION CREDITS

1955–56	*King's Row* (ABC)
1955–63	*Cheyenne* (ABC)
1956–57	*Conflict* (ABC)

1957–60	*Colt .45* (ABC)
1957–62	*Maverick* (ABC)
1958–64	*77 Sunset Strip* (ABC)
1962–71	*The Virginian* (NBC)
1963–67	*The Fugitive* (ABC)
1963–65	*Kraft Suspense Theater* (NBC)
1965–68	*Run for Your Life* (NBC)
1968–69	*The Outsider* (NBC)
1969–72	*The Lawyers* (NBC, part of *The Bold Ones*)
1971–73	*Alias Smith and Jones* (ABC)
1972–73	*Cool Million* (NBC)
1973–74	*Toma* (ABC)
1974–80	*The Rockford Files* (NBC)
1975–78	*Baretta* (ABC)
1976	*City of Angels* (NBC)
1984	*Blue Thunder* (ABC)
1984–91	*Hunter* (NBC)
2000–2001	*The Fugitive* (CBS)

〰〰 〰〰 〰〰

Ask Roy Huggins to explain how he became a writer, and he will tell you it was by accident. Ask him how he became a legendary producer whose dramas always met with success, and you will get the same answer. According to Roy, life is just a series of accidents, each one building upon the other to complete a full canvas. He also employs this approach when constructing television scripts, in which one scene gives way to the next-most-interesting thing that occurs. John Shanahan, creator of the remedial reading program *Hooked on Phonics,* observed that "success is an accident . . . well placed." The truth is that Roy Huggins is successful because he is a disciplined professional who possesses a healthy sense of skepticism and an undaunted spirit of individuality. He is a true maverick who manipulates accidents by setting them in motion, or, at the very least, by assuring that they are "well placed." Moreover, by leveraging those so-called accidents to his advantage, Huggins is able to swim upstream and across the current, where less "accident"-prone men would have drowned. There is no doubt that, had Roy been a musical composer instead of a producer, he, not Paul Anka, would have written *My Way.*

Stephen Cannell, one of the most prolific producers of drama in the history of television, worked for Roy and can testify to the Huggins method. "Roy is still one of the most creative guys in town, even at his age," Cannell says. "He has rules for how things should be done that he believes in desperately, and is loathe to abandon. And, they tend to be really good rules."

While Roy applies his own rules to structure and process and demands that they be followed, he has made his reputation by *breaking* rules, especially those set down by people and institutions with whom he disagrees.

As a young man he broke the rules of convention by studying the teachings of socialism, then broke with the Communist party when Russia signed the Nazi pact. He later testified before Congress, but broke Joe McCarthy's rules for upholding the Hollywood blacklist system.

Roy broke the rules of live-to-tape production by shooting TV dramas as telefilms. He also broke the rules of the sacred TV western by creating an antihero. He broke the rules of prime-time by introducing a lead character who eluded and outsmarted the law. He broke the rules of network programming by inventing the ninety-minute Movie of the Week, and he broke the rules of format by proving that a ninety-minute western series could land in the top ten. Roy even proved that a seasoned rule breaker could capitalize on previously broken rules by making something new out of something old.

John McNamara, executive producer of *The Fugitive* revival, in describing the show's hero (Dr. Richard Kimble) said, "He wants to stay, but he has to run." McNamara might just as well have been describing Roy Huggins. Moving from one project to another, Huggins has created, produced, written, and directed dramas in six decades, rivaling Aaron Spelling for longevity in the production of [network] one-hour series. And, like the classic western antihero, Roy was never willing to be tied down for very long, always looking to ride off to another challenge, but changing the landscape in the process. "Roy has redesigned the medium of television," said Stephen Cannell. "It's easy enough to go along and just do the next series, like *Friends,* but it's a lot harder to redefine the medium, because you have a lot of things going against you."

In reviewing Huggins's revival of *The Fugitive,* Ken Tucker explained the show's evergreen appeal. "Who among us hasn't been accused of something—albeit on a much smaller scale, usually a sin of omission or commission—from which we wished we could escape?" (*Entertainment Weekly,* October 13, 2000) During his long career, Huggins has, himself, on occasion been accused, derided, and doubted, but, in the end, just like Dr. Kimble, has always been vindicated.

Stephen Cannell, speaking of his mentor, said, "He was my godfather in the business. He was my greatest teacher. Everything that I do know and feel about doing television has its roots in Roy." The roots of the television industry itself run to Roy. It is an industry that began by breaking rules, being innovative, and defying boundaries, but that periodically needed Roy to remind it how to stay fresh. While producing *Maverick*, Huggins issued a ten-point guide for his writers to follow. Among them was, "clichés give comfort, so please live in discomfort." Now in his late eighties, Roy is still challenging the industry not to get too comfortable.

Roy the maverick was born in 1914 in Littelle, Washington. His father was a lumberman, and his mother was a housewife until she was widowed, when she opened a series of beauty salons. Roy was the baby of his family, which included brother Jack and two sisters, Eva and Mavourneen (mispronounced by young Roy as "Marvel"). Although neither parent was creatively inclined, Roy attributes his talents to the heritage of his ancestors. "I used to think it was an Irish characteristic, because my grandmother was born in Ireland, and they [the Irish] like to think of themselves as bards, poets."

Roy briefly attended the University of Oregon, then journeyed to Los Angeles, where he enrolled in UCLA and obtained a degree in political science. Two years of graduate school followed. But his scholarly, poli-sci fascination with socialism ended when the Communists signed a pact with Nazi Germany in 1939. During World War II Roy served as Special Representative in Charge of Recruitment for the National War Agency, covering the areas of southern California, Arizona, and Nevada. But his office did very little recruiting after 1943, so, tied to a desk job with plenty of time on his hands, Huggins, a fan of Raymond Chandler, decided to write a book. "I found that it was almost impossible to write a mystery novel and not sell it, unless you just could not write at all," he says. "So I wrote a mystery novel, and sold it." The luck of the Irish was with him, and Roy sold his book, *Double Take*, to Columbia. Said Huggins, "I was an accidental writer. I wrote a movie accidentally." Roy would go on to write other novels, including *Lovely Lady, Pity Me*, which was a forerunner to *The Fugitive*.

In 1951 Roy was blacklisted by Senator Joseph McCarthy's House Un-American Activities Committee (HUAC) for having once belonged to the Communist Party. In the meantime, Huggins's screenplay for *Hangman's Knot* was a hot property in Hollywood, so the maverick writer set out to challenge

HUAC. Knowing that the purchase of a script did not by itself constitute employment, Roy devised a way to actually be hired by a studio even though he was blacklisted. "Warner offered me $25,000 for the script alone, but I took the offer from Columbia for $17,000 because it included being *hired* as the director of the picture."

In 1952 Roy was called to appear before the House Un-American Activities Committee to reveal names of communists in the entertainment industry. Knowing that HUAC admitted it already had the names, and fully aware that refusing to cooperate carried serious consequences, Roy complied. "I had a wife and two kids, and a mother to support. And I thought, 'This distasteful, onerous group [HUAC] isn't worth spending a year in prison.' So I did something no one else had done. At the end of my testimony, a congressman asked if I had any comment or advice for them, and I spent twenty minutes criticizing what they were doing."

Following completion of *Hangman's Knot*, Roy went back on the blacklist. But the success of the western film (starring Randolph Scott) and his subsequent release from the blacklist led to a full-time job as a director/producer at Columbia. His employment there was short-lived. "My failure to get Harry Cohn to approve any of the pictures I wanted to produce led me to leave Columbia. . . . I was then offered a job by Bill Orr at Warners to produce television shows."

Roy's first assignment for Orr was to salvage *Cheyenne*, which, after just a few episodes, had drawn the wrath of its sponsor. Roy stepped in and overhauled the story lines, which he said were "aimed at children" (*Beating the Odds*, Goldenson and Wolf 1991). He also ditched Cheyenne's sidekick and reworked Clint Walker's character into a no-nonsense drifter.

Following his success with *Cheyenne*, Roy was allowed to develop his own series. *Maverick* was the story of a gambler and an antihero who generally put his own needs above those of anyone else. *Maverick* was an instant hit, but the production schedule was grueling, with each episode requiring eight working days. Since the shows were being broadcast every seven days, the point was fast approaching at which it would be impossible to meet the next air date. Roy realized that the studio needed to have two episodes in production at the same time. Since Garner could not be in two places at once, Huggins hired Jack Kelly to portray Bret Maverick's brother Bart. The two Mavericks split up the workload, and Roy's show was back on schedule.

77 Sunset Strip was Huggins's last big success at Warners, and, while it too was a groundbreaking show, it was vintage Huggins. Robert Thompson noted in *Prime Time, Prime Movers* that Roy's Los Angeles–based private-eye drama often used plot lines from *Maverick,* a trick that Huggins would also use with *The Rockford Files* nearly twenty years later. Thompson also praised the significance of Huggins's producing so many popular, film-style TV shows while at Warner Brothers. "Roy was a key creative personality in effecting this changeover in the look and feel of Network television" (Marc and Thompson, 1995).

Huggins moved over to Fox, where he first pitched *The Fugitive,* but the reception was chilly—so much so that he left after a short time and went to work for Universal. ABC eventually purchased Roy's tale of the fugitive physician, and the show was a solid hit. The series finale netted a record-breaking seventy-two share, with more than twenty-five million households tuning in to see the one-armed man get his comeuppance. *TV Guide* recognized *The Fugitive* as the best new show of the 1963–64 season, and, thirty years later, named Huggins's signature series as the best drama of the 1960s.

While *The Fugitive* was off and running, Roy became Universal's MVP, cranking out such dramas as *The Virginian* (a highly rated ninety-minute western), *Run for Your Life,* and *The Rockford Files,* the latter of which he produced with his protégé Stephen Cannell. "Roy would never accept bad film," Cannell said. "He was adamant about it. He was a real strong hand at the tiller, too . . . in terms of dealing with the studio, dealing with the network, dealing with the actors. He had a definite sense about what it was he wanted from the show, and he managed to always get it. He challenged the film to make him like it, and any little thing that was wrong would sour him. So he had an editorial process, which he called, 'Peeling the Onion.' He would run the picture, then take out all of the 's' factor, that is, the 'shit' factor. Sometimes it was important material that you needed for the story, and people would scream, 'You can't take that out, Roy. People won't understand!' And Roy would say, 'It's the 's' factor, it's out.' He would say, 'I don't care how short this film gets, I'm going to get all the 's' factor out, and then we'll carefully add to the footage, even if we have to use 'stock' until we're back on footage.' Everything that was left was going to be acceptable material to Roy." And what material it was. *The Rockford Files,* starring *Maverick* veteran James Garner, became an instant classic.

Television fans also have Roy to thank for another creation. He was the innovator of the Movie of the Week concept, which ABC used to "jump start" its television network (*Beating the Odds,* Goldenson and Wolf 1991).

Roy Huggins left series television after producing *Blue Thunder* for NBC, but then returned at the request of Cannell to help with the early-1990s cop drama *Hunter.*

Before the decade was over, though, big-screen producers Arnold and Anne Kopelson bought the film rights to *The Fugitive,* and Roy's doctor-on-the-run saga became a major motion picture. A sequel (*U.S. Marshals*) followed; then, in 2000, *Fugitive* phile John McNamara, under the aegis of the Kopelsons, brought the Huggins classic back to television. Roy was back, too, putting in long hours on story and script discussions. And so, just like Bret Maverick's crafty old poker-playing Pappy, Roy just keeps popping up and producing winning hands . . . by accident, of course.

I spoke with Roy on several occasions in 2000 while he was dividing his time between *The Fugitive,* his autobiography, and his loving wife, Adele.

Longworth: I've grown up and grown old watching all the Roy Huggins shows.

HUGGINS: (*Laughs.*) Well, you were awfully young when I did *Maverick.*

Longworth: Speaking of *Maverick,* in a book called *Warner Brothers Television* the authors credited your early Warner Brothers TV dramas with saving the ABC network.

HUGGINS: They did. No question about it. *Cheyenne,* then *Maverick,* and *77 Sunset Strip,* and then all the imitations of those three shows. Those shows were imitated very widely at Warners.

Longworth: Today we think of networks as being very powerful corporate entities, and it's hard for younger folks to imagine a time when that wasn't the case.

HUGGINS: Well, they were just learning how to do it, and ABC was actually leading the way in the field of how to do it [hour dramas]. It was Leonard Goldenson who set the tone for television in the '50s, and from that point on. Because up until the point when Leonard came along, television was radio with pictures. And it was done in New York. It was done live. It was done in half-hour segments. It was owned by sponsors. Everything about television [changed] after Leonard Goldenson made his deal with Warners.

Longworth: And of course, westerns reigned for most of the late '50s and early '60s.

HUGGINS: They were all over the place. Actually the first one-hour television series was *Cheyenne.* There was a show that preceded it from Disney, but it wasn't a series.

Longworth: That's right, because *Gunsmoke* started out as a half hour.

HUGGINS: Right, and the one from Disney was a miniseries. They never intended it to go for ten years.

Longworth: *Cheyenne* was a great show.

HUGGINS: Well, I only did it for the first year. And I don't know what kind of a show it was after that, although it got into the top ten in its first year.

Longworth: What was your involvement on *Cheyenne?* Did you create it? write it? produce it?

HUGGINS: I didn't create it. They had already done three of them when I took it over. The sponsors were saying, "We will sue you for malpractice if you don't start delivering some shows we can use."

Longworth: Which sponsors were angry?

HUGGINS: Oh, Monsanto and big companies like that. And they were sending viciously critical telegrams, and Bill Orr called me in and said, "Roy, will you take over *Cheyenne?*"

Longworth: So when you took over *Cheyenne,* did you write *and* produce?

HUGGINS: I write and produce every show I do.

Longworth: Didn't you feel a lot of pressure?

HUGGINS: It was a lot of hard work, but I felt no pressure. You know why? Because, as I said, we were all just learning what television was. So I didn't feel any pressure because nobody knew what we were doing. I didn't know what we were doing. I didn't know about stock. I had to find out. I had to go to J. L. Warner and say, "Hey, you've got a movie here with some great footage of the cavalry (*laughs*) and I need it," and he said, "Why not."

Longworth: You never know 'til you ask.

HUGGINS: That's right, and he didn't know that his stock [footage] was worth money.

Longworth: What was the work environment like at Warner Brothers Television in the early days? Was it a nurturing, highly charged, creative environment for writers?

HUGGINS: It was like a kindergarten. (*Both laugh.*) I keep repeating myself. Everyone they hired was on his own. Of course, there's a thing called the bell curve, and it applies everywhere. So the next time you go to your doctor, remember that. (*Both laugh.*) But I was on my own. I was absolutely left completely alone. In fact, Warners had a unique arrangement with ABC. ABC wasn't allowed to interfere with Warner Brothers productions, which Warners did not deserve, because they *needed* the interference. (*Both laugh.*) When ABC wasn't allowed to interfere, I was set free to do whatever I wanted to do, and I did.

Longworth: Is it harder to write a western than it is a crime drama?

HUGGINS: No.

Longworth: Any difference at all?

HUGGINS: Oh yeah, there's a big difference. The protagonist in a western is inherently more interesting because he lives in total freedom.

Longworth: Sort of like you.

HUGGINS: (*Laughs.*) You know, he rides into the town, ties up his horse, goes in, orders a drink, drinks it, never pays for it.

Longworth: That *is* you.

HUGGINS: Yeah. But have you ever seen a cowboy in a western pay for a drink?

Longworth: Not often.

HUGGINS: And nobody, of course, asks him for an ID.

Longworth: It's strange that *Maverick* did so well, because other westerns of that era were deadly serious, whereas *Maverick* had humor. Wasn't that risky?

HUGGINS: The one thing *Maverick* never was, was tongue-in-cheek. It was never campy, except when someone got away with something on the set while I wasn't looking, and I got stuck with it a couple of times. *Maverick* actually had an anti-tongue-in-cheek attitude. *Maverick* was a satire, but made by a man who was very skeptical of satire. (*Both laugh.*) So you better tell a good story, and it had better be plausible, or no one's going to watch it. And then you can be satirical.

Longworth: But what about the send-up you did of *Gunsmoke* titled "Gun Shy?"

HUGGINS: The first cut of "Gun Shy" was so bad, I almost took it off the schedule. It was just awful. It was campy, because the writer, who was a campy fellow, went down on the set and seduced the director into doing all kinds of silly things that were not in the script. I rewrote the script, and I'm seeing the dailies, and I'm losing the battle. The writer is stubbornly staying there working on the director, and we finally get this awful picture. And I say to the writer, "Look, I'm going to do a preview," which was never done in television, and it accounts for some of its differences from theatrical film. But anyway, I let him suggest some of the people to invite, and they watched the film, and they hated it. In fact a good friend of mine stood up and said, "Well Roy, I guess you got us in here to show us what a great show you did, and it stinks." And I said, "Now I can talk to you. Now I can tell you why you're here. I think it stinks too. Now I'm going to re-cut it and show it to another group," which I did. And that group liked it, but *I* didn't, because I wasn't able to get all of the camp out of it. The *New York Times,* for the first time in my life, gave me a bad review. And I agreed with them every word, 'cause I wasn't able to get the shit out of it. It was campy, and believe me, it's not a *Maverick*.

Longworth: *Maverick* enjoyed a long run on ABC ending in 1962. And though you have been responsible for so many dramas, you are best known for one that happened to appear a year later, namely *The Fugitive*. Over the years since, it had been widely reported that the series you created was based on Dr. Sam Shepherd, who, we're told, was unjustly accused of his wife's murder. Set the record straight.

HUGGINS: He was very justly accused, guilty as hell, and *The Fugitive* was not even slightly based on the Shepherd case.

Longworth: A few industry insiders know that, but clear up the misconception for everyone else.

HUGGINS: Well, I'll clear it up with facts, not with opinions. I sold *The Fugitive* to Leonard Goldenson [ABC chairman] in 1960. The Shepherd murder case took place in 1954, I think it was. I didn't hear about it, and I don't know if anyone in southern California heard about it, because it was a murder case in Ohio. I made him [Richard Kimble] a doctor because, one, people like doctors, and two, his being a doctor could create suspense on many occasions when he is forced to behave like a doctor while he's dressed like a plumber and put himself in jeopardy. So that's why he was a doctor. But that's why people said, "Ah, the Shepherd case," because Kimble was a doctor. Now a year later, F. Lee Bailey took over the Shepherd case and got a new trial for him. That was a year after I had sold it. So all you have to do is follow the dates to see that the show had nothing to do with the Shepherd case. And incidentally I don't really care. Any publicity is good as long as it isn't true. (*Both laugh.*)

Longworth: Well, then perhaps Bailey used your show to help his client because, one way or another, *The Fugitive* certainly helped to bring more attention to Shepherd's case.

HUGGINS: Yes, it did. As a matter of fact I got a very sneaky letter from Boston where F. Lee Bailey's office was, saying, "Gee I like your show. Tell me, where did you get the idea for the show? I would really like to know because I'm such a fan of your show." And it was probably F. Lee Bailey's secretary. (*Both laugh.*)

Longworth: Did you respond?

HUGGINS: Yeah. (*Laughs.*) I responded with the truth, which is what I just told you.

Longworth: Well, if your suspicions were correct, then they might have been trying to bait you for a potential legal action.

HUGGINS: They were probably hoping like hell that I would say I based it on the Shepherd case.

Longworth: What do you say, though, to someone who can't believe you didn't hear of the Shepherd case for six years leading up to the sale of *The Fugitive?*

HUGGINS: What I said was this. I don't remember reading about it in 1954. I may have, but I don't remember it. But you could check the newspapers in Los Angeles for that day, the day of the murder, and you might find it on the back page, but it wouldn't have been a headline. So therefore, I wouldn't have read it. Then when it became a much bigger story, I had already sold the show. The show had been sold a year before the Shepherd case came back into prominence. So the facts are very clear to anyone who wants to follow them, but no one has ever done that. It is still said to be based on the Sam Shepherd case, and I really do not care.

Longworth: You mentioned earlier that a television studio was smart to make sure that the producer was also a good writer. Has that always been the case?

HUGGINS: No, I don't believe it was always the case. And there were always exceptions. The guy who did *Naked City* was not a writer. He was an old-fashioned producer. So there were exceptions. As a matter of fact, the importance of the writer/producer was discovered in television during my day, from 1955 to 1960. Then, in the '60s, by that time, it was well known that if you wanted a successful TV show, and it was a drama, you had to get yourself a writer to produce it.

Longworth: Well, while we're in the '60s, tell me exactly how you decided not to produce *The Fugitive* after you created it.

HUGGINS: I was going to UCLA. I had promised myself, from the time I took my first job in movies, that I was going to go back and finish the two years that I put in already. I sold *The Fugitive* to Leonard Goldenson while I was at UCLA, and Leonard wanted me to produce it, and, not only that, but offered to put me in business. He said, "You can do it at a studio if you want, but you can do it on your own?" What was motivating me were two things. One is that I had had a year of trying to find out if this idea [*The Fugitive*] was any good, and anyone I told it to, hated it. I had thought it up in 1960. I was in charge of television at Fox at the time, and I told the head of Fox, Peter Levathes, that we would start with this show, because I had a deal that made it worthwhile to let them have the television rights to *The Fugitive.* So I told him the idea and he thought it was just dreadful. As a matter of fact, he lost confidence in me completely. So I started telling it to my closest friends, and I remember telling it to Paddy Chayefsky, and after I finished telling it to him, he said, "Now let me get this straight, Roy. You want to do a series about a man who has been found guilty of killing his wife, and he's now running from the law. And that's your idea for a television series?" And my friend Howard Browne said, "Roy, you've got a great reputation in television. Don't blow it." Those two guys are dead, but Dick Bare is still alive, and Dick said, "Roy, for God's sake, don't do it," although today he claims, "Oh, no, I liked it." (*Laughs.*)

Longworth: You've mentioned several times that you wrote it in 1960, but it took several years to get on air.

HUGGINS: Well, I put it in a drawer for a year. I just forgot about it. I wrote it off as a bad idea, even though I had thought it was a great idea when I thought of it. So I put it into a drawer and forgot it, and then Dan Melnick called me up one day and said, "Leonard Goldenson is coming out to L.A., he's got a short list of producers he wants to talk to, and you're on the list. What time can I put you down for?" And I said, "Dan, I can't meet with Leonard. I've left television. I'm in graduate school at UCLA trying to get my Ph.D." Now Dan had been very good to me while I was at Warners. And he says to me, "Are you telling me that I've got to say to Leonard Goldenson that Roy Huggins won't meet with you?" And I said, "Well, Dan, I have an idea that everybody hates. Everybody without exception thinks it is a repulsive idea. Now if it doesn't make any difference to you, I'll meet with Leonard and I'll tell him that idea." And he said, "Fine, when?" (*Both laugh.*) And when I went into that meeting, the room was filled with his vice presidents. And as soon as I told them what it was about, they started rapping their fingers on their chairs, looking at their watches, kicking their feet. The head of programming, Tom Moore, got up, said, "Bye Roy, I've got a plane to catch," left the room, and came out with a suitcase, because in those days we met in a hotel room. They didn't have that beautiful office that they now have in Century City. And he left. I was barely able to finish, when Leonard Goldenson said, "Roy that's the greatest idea for a television series I've ever heard." And he was the first person that I ever told it to who liked it. But you know that he almost took it off the schedule?

Longworth: Why?

HUGGINS: Because he had [received] complaints about it. Everybody hated it. Leonard Goldenson sat down with me at Universal when it went on the air, and had been on the air for maybe six or eight weeks, and said, "Roy, did you have any trouble with that idea before you told it to me?" (*Both laugh.*) I said, "Why do you ask that, Leonard?" He says, "I almost took it off the schedule. Tom Moore hated it, and I got letters and threats of boycotts because there were people who thought it was un-American." One of Leonard's vice presidents said to me, in the presence of Leonard, he said, "That [*The Fugitive*] is a slap in the face of American justice every week. It is un-American."

Longworth: Well Roy, don't you think that the vice presidents and some of those people threatening boycotts reacted that way because of their perception of your former involvement with the Communist Party?

HUGGINS: I believe the guy who stood up and said, "It's a slap in the face to American justice. It's un-American," was probably remembering that I had once been a Communist. Yeah. In fact, I've often thought that that might be the only time I ever, knowingly, ran into someone who was being motivated by my political past.

Longworth: But, in any event, Goldenson withstood the pressure and kept it on the schedule. What does that say about him?

HUGGINS: Well, it says a lot of great things about Leonard, but mainly it just says he knew a good thing when he saw it, because it went on the air, and no one objected to it.

Longworth: But getting back to the original question. Why did you give up the opportunity to produce *The Fugitive* every week, and let it go to Quinn Martin?

HUGGINS: Well, here's what happened. When Leonard said, "How do you want to do it?" I said I can't do it at all. And Leonard says, "What do you mean you can't do it?" Now the vice presidents were all looking at me in a completely different way. Now they were looking at me as if they had just happened on to a madman. A man is being offered air time, and he's saying, "I can't do it?" I mean, really, it was quite a meeting. (*Both laugh.*) I said, "I have been accepted in the graduate school at UCLA. When they accepted me, they rejected somebody else. I can't go to them now, Leonard, and say, 'Hey, I'm quitting. I've got a better offer.'" And I said, "Leonard, I wouldn't do it anyway because I want to finish what I'm doing at UCLA," but that doesn't mean that you can't do the series. I can find someone to produce it, make a deal with him, someone acceptable to you." I think I used the term "producer proof"—the show, as I used to say to my wife, is "producer proof." I brought up several names that I was willing to make a deal with. One of them was

Quinn Martin. They liked him because he had just done a show for ABC. So I met with Quinn Martin and made a deal with him for television rights, only. I kept everything else. I kept movie rights, book rights, dramatic rights, all that. So I made a deal with him for the television rights, but I kept a percentage of the profits and royalties.

Longworth: Did you have input into the creative process of the show?

HUGGINS: Only in the case of the pilot because I promised Leonard that I would. Leonard used the word supervise, but I don't believe I supervised the pilot. I did monitor it, and I did meet with Quinn Martin and asked him to make several rather large changes, which he made.

Longworth: Were you ever consulted after that?

HUGGINS: I chose not to be, I asked not to be, because I was rather busy doing what I was doing.

Longworth: Isn't it kind of ironic that you didn't want to be consulted then, and now, forty years later, it's been revived, and they really *do* rely on your input.

HUGGINS: The reason for that is I was concerned with the extent to which Quinn Martin was going to be free of any feeling that I was hovering over him and telling him what to do. I had already found out by that time that no producer can operate if there is someone out there who can say, "You can't do that," or "You have to change this." If that happens, you cease to be productive, and you can no longer create anything. You've got to feel that whatever you come up with is going to go on the air or you're not going to come up with anything.

Longworth: Was that the only series that you created in which you declined to have input week by week?

HUGGINS: No. There was *The Outsider.*

Longworth: That was 1968.

HUGGINS: Yeah. The pilot was the best I ever did. It won the Directors Guild Award for that year. You can rest assured that, when a director wins an award, it's because he had an awful good script, or you aren't going to win. And I hope you realize that that's a general truth, and not just an opinion of mine.

Longworth: So why didn't you stay involved with *The Outsider?*

HUGGINS: After I shot the film, we had so much trouble editing out the "s" factor. That was short for "shit" factor . . . and although I really liked our star, Darren McGavin, he's a nice guy, I just didn't want to go through that. So I not only never had anything to do with *The Outsider,* but I never even saw it.

Longworth: But you created it?

HUGGINS: Oh yeah, I owned it.

Longworth: But didn't that series concept sort of resurface later on with *The Rockford Files*, which was also about a private eye?

HUGGINS: That may have been in the back of my mind, but I came up with *The Rockford Files* because I got a call from Jim Garner telling me that he was willing to go back into television, and was even willing to work at Universal, and did I have anything.

Longworth: Yeah, because Universal treated him pretty badly.

HUGGINS: Yeah, I know. He had sworn he would never work at Universal again, even then, but, of course after *The Rockford Files*, he was even more down on them. So, anyway, in the case of *The Rockford Files*, I was much more consciously doing *Maverick* as a private eye, because I came up with the pilot story for Jim Garner at his request.

Longworth: That doesn't happen too often in the business, does it?

HUGGINS: No, but in both cases, in *Maverick* and *The Rockford Files*, I came up with the story *because* of Jim Garner. I had used him in a thing called *Conflict*, he played a con man, and I expected nothing from him. He had been miscast in everything up to that time. And I went to the dailies, and here was this character being created far beyond my wildest dreams. I had written the character, and the character was *Maverick*, but I never expected to see it on film, but there it was and I thought, "My God, I've got to do a series with this guy." So *Maverick* was a series that was written for Jim Garner. *The Rockford Files* was a series written for Jim Garner. The pilot story was written by me with Jim Garner in my head as I wrote it, and Jim was also in Steve Cannell's head when he wrote the teleplay.

Longworth: Why are you able to create characters like Rockford, Kimble, Maverick, Baretta, and others that, year after year, decade after decade, viewers always seem to relate to and enjoy?

HUGGINS: Probably it's a different reason each time. In the case of Rockford and Maverick, I think people had become very cynical. Patriotism as an emotion has taken a pretty steep drop, at least in our country. And cynicism . . . certain simple ideas, such as treating others as you would have them treat you, have given way to "What's in it for me?" The characters Jim Garner played, his whole approach to life, was "What's in it for me?" He was also inherently decent but [was] always motivated by money. Rockford was the kind of guy, who, before he took a case, had to make sure they could afford it. And if they went to lunch, and it was a beautiful girl, and they talked about the case, she paid the check. (*Both laugh.*) He liked money.

Longworth: How did you hook up with Stephen Cannell, who worked with you on *The Rockford Files?*

HUGGINS: I discovered Stephen Cannell. And by the way, the description you gave of me in being able to come up with these wonderful characters? That doesn't fit me as well as it does Cannell. Maybe the leads I came up with were interesting characters, but when Cannell would write a script for me, the incidental characters were the interesting characters. In my pilot story, the character who became Angel was just a character. He was there to serve the purposes of the story, and that was all. He was never supposed to be seen again. Well, Steve Cannell wrote a character who was so interesting. He didn't have to, he just did; it's instinct. He can't allow himself just to write a "for the purposes of the script" character. He wrote Angel. And Angel was an absolutely incredible character. An untrustworthy, evil, little shit, who, for some reason or another, Rockford liked. (*Both laugh.*)

Longworth: Speaking of Stephen, he appeared before Congress and criticized mega-mergers among television networks, and the trend toward vertically integrated control of product, saying that independent studios were being squeezed out, and that programing would suffer as a result. His solution is for government to reinstate the Financial Syndication [Fin Syn] law. Do these trends disturb you?

HUGGINS: I left television because of it. I was at Universal, and I had kept a contract in my desk for probably seven months (unsigned). It was a six-year contract guaranteeing me a profit share of everything I did. And for the first time in my life, people from the network who had never written a story or had to do anything to prove that they knew how, were telling me how to write stories. So I never signed the contract. I left television in 1985, and came back only because Steve Cannell asked me to help him on *Hunter*.

Longworth: So you were financially comfortable enough to walk away?

HUGGINS: Yeah, I would say I was *just* comfortable. I really didn't have to work again. When I did go back to work, it was for other reasons.

Longworth: It has to be flattering to you that, here in the new millennium, another young producer has embraced a show that you created.

HUGGINS: It's more than surprising. It's astonishing. (*Laughs.*) It's so unusual for any idea to have any kind of connection to the audience forty years later.

Longworth: Why is there a timeless appeal to *The Fugitive?* Why does that character and that story still interest people?

HUGGINS: I think there are two reasons. One is that the character is really the western character. He rode from town to town, stayed a while, and moved on. And he doesn't have any ID. (*Both laugh.*) So he's living like a western hero. That may have something to do with it. And the other thing, of course, is he is running constantly. The pursuit never lets up. It's the only show in history in which, if the hero just walks down the street, you have suspense.

Longworth: OK, but why do people like that?

HUGGINS: Because they like suspense. Also I think, there is somewhere deep in the souls of most people in our society, [something] that loves the idea of being an outsider and almost forced to be unable to make commitments. Although I say this with great reluctance, because I'm not a social psychologist, and I could be all wrong, but it's just a hunch that there is something there that is deeply ingrained in the character of modern man.

Longworth: What is your level of involvement with the new series? Do you get calls from John asking, "What do you think about this?" Or, have you given him any pointers?

HUGGINS: Just the opposite [of what] you implied in your question. Just the opposite. And with every script, I get every change. I get every foot of film that they shoot. I get that in the form of dailies. I meet with John, and I meet with his story editor, and we have arguments. We don't always agree. But I'm much more deeply involved than I ever expected to be. And I'm not even sure if I want to be. (*Both laugh.*)

Longworth: Are there changes made to the scripts based on those arguments?

HUGGINS: We argue about whether he [Kimble] would say [a particular thing] or not. And I would say, "That's out of character." And we would argue about that for a while. I guess I'm batting about .750. (*Both laugh.*) The final word is John's and I know that, even if no one had ever said that to me, and, as a matter of fact, no one ever has. Only one man can run a show. You can't have somebody else who can tell you, "You can't do that." If that's the case, you can't do anything; your creative juices dry up.

Longworth: In the 1990s comedies ruled the roost on TV, and now, good dramas have made a comeback. Why is that?

HUGGINS: Well, I think those things are cyclical. In other words, a good comedy will come along and it will get an audience, so it will be copied, and that comedy gets an audience, and pretty quick the only thing they want to do is comedy. I remember when no network was interested in buying a one-hour drama. They were looking for half-hour comedies. And they always believe when that happens that, "This is it, this is the future." And then they get quite a shock when, ten years later, they're looking for just the opposite. But it is cyclical. Movies were like that. Westerns used to come in for a few years, and then they would drop, and then a few years later they would come back.

Longworth: Are the really good TV dramas today better than the dramas when you started in the business, or are they not as good?

HUGGINS: I think that they're better.

Longworth: Why?

HUGGINS: The reason is this. When it started, there was an attitude toward television that prevented good writers, good directors, from [doing television]. They wouldn't do it, because they thought it was a step down. It still exists, but not as much. So television can now attract a much more talented group of writers and directors. Also they do learn. They learned from us what doesn't work. How to do things better.

Longworth: But a good story is a good story, whether it's *Cheyenne* or *Law & Order*, right?

HUGGINS: Yeah, except that *Law & Order* is better than *Cheyenne*. *Law & Order* is a very good show.

Longworth: Well, I would have thought that your ego would have forced you to side with shows like *Cheyenne* over *Law & Order*. (*Both laugh.*)

HUGGINS: Well, I wish I could have said the opposite, but I just don't feel that way. *Law & Order* is a very good show. I don't think it's any better than *Maverick* was, because *Maverick* was very original. *Maverick* was almost like the *Who Wants to Be a Millionaire* of its day. It went on the air and killed everybody.

Longworth: Here you are, having written, produced, directed television dramas in the '50s, '60s, '70s, '80s, '90s, and now in the new millennium. Six different decades. How has your work week and work *load* differed over time? Has it always been the same grind with the same tough production schedules?

HUGGINS: My case was so different from anyone else's in my day. That may no longer be true. There may be people out there now doing the same thing I did, but I would get in my car and drive 5,000 miles with tape recorders on the seat next to me, and come back with ten to twelve totally worked-out stories. Stories that, when they were transcribed from the tape, were longer than the script. That's unusual. There's a member of the Writers Guild named John Thomas James, and whenever I get the Writers Guild booklet listing membership, I always look up to see if he is still carried as a member, and he is. He even has a different agent from me, for some reason. How that happened I'll never know, but John Thomas James is me. (*Both laugh.*) They think he's another member.

Longworth: John Thomas James is you?

HUGGINS: Yeah, those are the first names of my three sons. He got more fan mail than I did. For fun, we had a parking spot for John Thomas James at Universal.

Longworth: What screen credits did John Thomas James receive?

HUGGINS: He got story credits on almost everything I did at Universal, and once in a while, John Thomas James would write the teleplay.

Longworth: (*Laughs.*) Earlier you said people looked at you like you were a mad man?

HUGGINS: Yeah.

Longworth: You are.

HUGGINS: (*Laughs.*) Well, you know what? Steve Cannell used to say to me, "Roy, you shouldn't do that. You should use your own name." Because, you know Steve had that signature of himself at the typewriter? Steve knew something that I didn't know, which is that name recognition in Hollywood is like owning a gold mine.

Longworth: So why did you do it?

HUGGINS: I was ignorant. (*Laughs.*)

Longworth: I mean, seriously, did you use those names as a joke?

HUGGINS: No, you see, my name was already on screen as executive producer, "a Roy Huggins Public Arts Production," and if I hadn't used a pseudonym, it would have been on there as author of the story.

Longworth: Boy are *you* modest.

HUGGINS: Not really, 'cause my name was there.

Longworth: You're either modest or you're stupid.

HUGGINS: I think stupid is the word. (*Both laugh.*)

Longworth: Let's talk for a moment about women and minorities in dramatic television. Up until recently, very few women have had their own drama series, and very few African Americans have had their own series. Thinking back to your days at Warners, then Universal, did producers of your generation purposely shy away from creating series for a person of color or a woman? Did you just not think about it? Were you prejudiced? Or did you think they wouldn't attract the ratings?

HUGGINS: Well, you have to separate women from blacks. Because if you had come up with a series for a black person then, they would have sent a little notice to Warners and to all the other studios in town, "Don't ever hire this man, because we won't use anything he does." They actually turned down a theme song I had on *Baretta*, sung by Sammy Davis, Jr., because it was, quote, "too black." So we just didn't use it.

Longworth: So you had to change it to "Keep Your Eye on the Sparrow?"

HUGGINS: Yeah, we had to change it, change the style of singing. And Tom Moore came to me one day when I was doing a show starring that good-looking guy, Gardner McKay.

Longworth: *Adventures in Paradise.*

HUGGINS: Yeah. And I'm not going to quote him, because this is too important to make any mistakes that could be embarrassing to Tom Moore, but I had a conversation with him, in which I got the impression that he would really be happier if I didn't use so many dark-complected people in the show. Now, after all, McKay was in the South Seas. (*Both laugh.*)

Longworth: I didn't know you had anything to do with *Adventures in Paradise.*

HUGGINS: Well, when I left Warner Brothers, for a brief moment I was in charge of television for Twentieth Century Fox, and that's when I presented *The Fugitive* to the head of that company [Peter Levathes] and that was the end of my career at Fox. (*Both laugh.*)

Longworth: But what about women in lead roles?

HUGGINS: I would have been delighted because I did make very good use of women in *Maverick* and other shows. Samantha became a tremendous character in *Maverick.*

Longworth: But no matter how great Samantha was, the show wasn't titled, *Samantha.*

HUGGINS: Oh, it sure wasn't.

Longworth: Today we have more and more women starring in their own drama series, so again, I ask, why didn't producers such as yourself create shows that starred a woman?

HUGGINS: I'll try to answer it, but I have a feeling that the true answer is that I was insensitive to the problem. And I'm sure I was typical of most white males at that time. We really didn't recognize a problem with women; after all, (*he says jokingly*) "they had their place." (*Both laugh.*) But seriously, if it had occurred to me, I probably wouldn't have done it because I would have known that the networks would have said "No." Their theory probably was that men really determine what show the family is going to watch. When they decided that it was women who decided what the family watched, then they started making shows with women.

Longworth: What made things change, though? Were the networks wrong before, or did they have the wrong research, or were women themselves changing?

HUGGINS: All of the above. Things did change. But it was also true in the late '50s and early '60s that it just never occurred to anybody.

Longworth: What about the trend toward more profanity and nudity in TV drama these days? That's something you didn't have to deal with or have at your disposal many years ago.

HUGGINS: But I wish I had. (*Both laugh.*) Listen, when you have to change a line where someone says, "danged"—"Well, I'll be danged," and someone comes to you and says you have to change the word "danged," and you say, "Why?" And they say because it sounds to some people's ears like "damned." And I said, "What do you want me to do?" And they said, "change it to 'darned.'" And I would say, "Oh for Christ's sakes, I guess I'll take it out." I once had a huge meeting with all of the people involved with Standards and Practices. And I said, "Look, the reason for this meeting is, you won't allow any of us to use the word 'bastard,' and I would like to know why, because we need a few words that sound like the way people talk. It would help if you would let us say 'bastard' on occasion."

Longworth: And what show was this?

HUGGINS: It was every show. (*Both laugh.*) I was talking about a word, "bastard," that I wanted to use in my shows.

Longworth: You needed a "bastard" in every one of your shows?

HUGGINS: Yes. And they wouldn't budge. So you're asking me how I felt? I'm telling you how I felt. I didn't like it. I opposed it. And then all of a sudden one day, I told them, "The only reason you take this rigid position is that many of your smaller affiliates are owned by blue-nosed, ignorant people of whom you are afraid. In other words what it comes down to is not a matter of taste, but a matter of money. And you're taking this rigid position because you're afraid it might cost you another affiliate. And that's a bad reason."

Longworth: But, Roy, I can't imagine Bret Maverick saying "bastard."

HUGGINS: I can. (*Both laugh.*)

Longworth: What about nudity?

HUGGINS: Again, money is the reason for nudity. As soon as the moviemakers discovered that nudity sold tickets, they gave us more nudity. But the television networks have not done it to any great extent. They do now and then when they have an excuse they can use when they get into the argument. But that doesn't bother me. I think it should be confined to shows that are on after ten o'clock.

Longworth: We've talked about some of the really tough situations that you've faced, but have you, in your mind, had any real failures in television, and if so, what did you learn from them?

HUGGINS: I had two failures. *The Outsider* was a failure because I didn't produce it. I think it would have been a success if I had produced it, because my storytelling style is so different from other producers'. But I had one failure that I *did* produce. And it goes like this. I'm in New York, and I've had a meeting at NBC. The head of programming asked me to have lunch with him at the Russian Tea Room. And he says, "Roy, we want you to produce a private-eye series that takes place in the 1930s." Over the course of a long lunch, I told him that the thing that makes a private-eye show entertaining is that the hero goes through every episode making sardonic comments on society, and who gives a shit if he's making sardonic comments about the '30s? (*Both laugh.*) They like him because he makes sardonic comments about contemporary life. And the NBC executive said, "No, no, the '30s are interesting." So I said, "Look if you want me to do a series for you, I think it will fail, but I will do it, and I will do the best job I can do, but I think it's a mistake." And I did it, and called it *City of Angels*, but that show failed, for the very reasons that I gave.

Longworth: Earlier you talked about how you played down your name recognition for screen credits. Today, Aaron Spelling, a contemporary of yours, is a household name but Huggins is not, yet both of you have contributed significantly to the history of dramatic television. Do you wish now that you had been more aggressive with getting your name out there?

HUGGINS: I suppose I have to say yes, but it's misleading because the truth is that, although I *do* think about it now and again, if I had to do all over I probably would have done it the same way. I still don't see what that is except in terms of making money, and I knew from the very beginning that I was never going to make the kind of money that I *could* make, because I never dealt with the networks the way they like to be dealt with. I never actually *went* to the networks. The networks never actually knew me. I would say a dozen heads of NBC came and went without my ever meeting them, and I never tried to. And that can be costly, because you might get an extra show on the air if you've made a buddy out of somebody, but I had never wanted to do that. I had other priorities. It wasn't snobbishness or anything like that, it was just that I was in the damn business by accident and I behaved that way. In fact, Harry Cohn over at Columbia Pictures once said to Ben [B. B.] Kahane, "You know that Huggins guy? He doesn't look like a producer, he doesn't smell like a producer, he doesn't think like a producer." And it's true, I didn't.

Longworth: Sounds like you have a pretty thick skin, but did any critic or comment ever really get to you?

HUGGINS: I have had some terrible things said, and have never responded to them at all. I've had things said that were totally erroneous, and I can prove it. (*Laughs.*) I still didn't respond. I've never, ever, ever, responded to a critic, or to anybody who, for some reason or another, decided to take a crack at me. It hasn't happened often, but it has happened, and my reaction has been to do absolutely nothing about it.

Longworth: What kind of TV dramas do you watch these days?

HUGGINS: I saw a wonderful show the other night called *The Practice*. And believe me, if I had the time to watch television, I would watch *The Practice*. Also, *Law & Order* I think is one of the best shows on television, and I watch it quite frequently.

Longworth: Why don't you have the time?

HUGGINS: Well, right now I'm putting in a lot of work on *The Fugitive*. And actually I'm writing a memoir that will never be finished. I'm up to around 1952. (*Laughs.*) So, obviously, I'm going to have to live an awfully long time to finish this book. (*Both laugh.*)

Longworth: Did you ever think, while creating *The Fugitive*, that you'd be having to put in long hours on the same series forty years later?

HUGGINS: If anyone had told me that, I would have said that they were absolutely insane.

Longworth: Yeah, but that's what people say about you.

HUGGINS: (*Laughs.*)

Longworth: Last thing. If tomorrow you were called in to a network president's office and he or she said, "Roy, we have an hour to fill, and we need an idea for a series right now," what would you say?

HUGGINS: I'd say let's do a series about twenty-six guys who are trapped in a space vehicle and they can't get out, but every week, one of them is murdered. (*Both laugh.*)

Longworth: Roy, you've just ripped off *Big Brother*.

HUGGINS: (*Laughs.*) I really have not watched any of those shows, so I shouldn't make fun of them. But yeah, I was making fun of that kind of show. I haven't seen them because I can't imagine how they could possibly interest me.

Longworth: Of all the characters that you've created for television, which one is most like Roy Huggins?

HUGGINS: I suspect none of them, or all of them. (*Laughs.*) Well, the slight cynicism that was there in *Maverick* and *The Rockford Files* is certainly a part of me, although it is not philosophical cynicism, it's behavioral cynicism. I guess it's skepticism. I am very skeptical of almost everything.

Longworth: If you should get in trouble with the law tomorrow, and had to go on the lam as a fugitive, would you take on the identity of John Thomas James?

HUGGINS: (*Laughs.*) No, but I might *write* in order to pick up money. (*Both laugh.*) Because, you know what? That is a job [writing] that you can do anywhere. And I might do that.

Longworth: You could survive anywhere.

HUGGINS: And I can still write stories. I don't do it, because I don't have to. One of the things is that I never have liked writing. It was always a terrible chore.

Longworth: I've been talking with you for almost two hours, and I thought you enjoyed writing.

HUGGINS: No. I don't like writing. As a matter of fact, I have in my computer a voice system, which allows me to skip writing and all I have to do is talk. Now I enjoy *having* written.

Longworth: But the process itself is—

HUGGINS: Is very hard on me. It's a struggle. I mean I don't write slowly, I write very fast. Steve Cannell, though, *loves* to write. He gets up at five every morning and sits in front of his typewriter for hours.

Longworth: What do you do at five in the morning?

HUGGINS: I sleep. (*Both laugh.*)

Longworth: Well, thanks for doing this.

HUGGINS: Best of luck.

Longworth: Oh, by the way, do you happen to have any old photos that were taken on the set?

HUGGINS: No, I made it a point never to go out on a set.

Longworth: You never went on a set?

HUGGINS: Only when I was directing.

Longworth: It's called professional courtesy.

HUGGINS: That's right! You go on a set, nothing is happening, and it can escalate boredom to ecstasy. (*Both laugh.*)

MARTHA WILLIAMSON | visionary

Martha Williamson. COURTESY OF MARTHA WILLIAMSON.

TELEVISION CREDITS

1986–88	*The Facts of Life* (NBC)
1988–89	Raising Miranda (CBS)
1989–90	Living Dolls (ABC)

1990–91	*The Family Man* (ABC)
1992–93	*Jack's Place* (ABC)
1994	*Under One Roof* (CBS)
1994–	*Touched by an Angel* (CBS)
1996–99	*Promised Land* (CBS)

МЖ МЖ МЖ

There is overwhelming evidence that, in Old Testament times and during the life of Jesus, women were generally regarded as second-class citizens. Leviticus (27:1–8) suggests that a woman was worth only half as much as a man. Paul, considered by some to be the poster boy for chauvinism, once advised Thessalonian males on how to buy and possess a wife, much as they would a vessel.

Making a case for the existence of influential women in Biblical times, however, Evelyn and Frank Stagg in their book, *Woman in the World of Jesus,* pointed to, "the risen Christ's commission of Mary Magdalene to inform doubting Apostles that he was not dead, as a solid Biblical basis for not only women's privilege in ministry, but her responsibility for it." Even so, it is clear that, then as now, women in leadership positions, both secular and religious, are a rare commodity. It is not surprising, then, that Hollywood crossed over into the new millennium with only a handful of female executives and showrunners in the drama genre. One of them is Martha Williamson, and her career, like that of Mary Magdalene, established a "solid basis" for women with a responsibility for ministry.

Martha is in a very small minority: she is the only female television executive to helm a show about God. But unlike some militant trendsetter content to simply make a point with a niche following, Martha's approach has captured mainstream audiences and netted huge profits for the network, as well as for her company, Moonwater Productions. She has proven that mixing religion with show biz can be a winning formula. Just as opportunities for women in television drama have finally expanded of late, the establishment of Williamson's "God genre" was a long time coming, and, perhaps, long overdue.

While Martha's ascendancy to the top of her profession is phenomenal, so is the fact that her show is still the only one of its kind on broadcast television, something that is particularly significant in light of various polls taken over the past few years. 85 percent of Americans believe in God, and 54 percent claim to be very religious (*George*, January 2001). In addition, 69 percent say they believe in angels, and 61 percent would like to see more references to God on prime-time television (*TV Guide*, March 29, 1997). Imagine if those survey respondents, instead of demanding more shows about God had, for example, said they wanted to see more stories about "twenty-something apartment dwellers." Imagine what would happen to a programming executive if he or she disregarded that polling data. Yet, at this writing, and with all the data in hand, network television offers only one prime-time drama with God at its core.

Martha, like women in the workforce in general, is still swimming upstream. The fact is that faith in God is looked down upon by many in the Hollywood community, but such skepticism does not bother Williamson. In fact, she is, well, skeptical of skepticism. In an interview with Marsha Scarborough for *Written By* magazine, Williamson said, "The inscription over the gates of Hell in Dante's 'Divine Comedy' reads, 'Abandon all hope ye that enter here.' A lot of people think that might as well be the inscription above the gateway to Hollywood. Don't believe it." It's just that kind of positive faith (along with talent) that has made Williamson one of the most successful producers in the history of television. She still holds the distinction of being the only woman to fly solo on two dramas at once (she created *Promised Land* for CBS as well), and she is also still one of only a few females who run a prime-time drama series.

Commenting on the relationship between God and television, the Reverend Robert Schuller told *TV Guide*, "Before religion is allowed to board TV, it should pass three security checks: Does it build faith; Can it inspire hope; and, Does it generate love?" Clearly, *Touched by an Angel* passes with flying colors. So does Martha Williamson.

Martha Williamson was "created" in Denver, Colorado, by loving parents who were partners both at home and at work. Together they ran a small financial-consulting firm from the 1940s to the '60s. Not surprisingly, her mother made a huge impression on Martha about her own potential. "It never crossed my mind that women couldn't succeed in business because I grew up with that role model" (*Written By*, April 2000).

Martha's mother was an activist but never admitted to being a feminist, and her instincts in that regard helped to influence Martha as she made her way into a male-dominated world. "Early on there were a couple of guys who pinched my butt, and told me to go get coffee, but I took care of them swiftly," she recalls. "Spending years in sitcom sharpens you up. If you can't handle sitting around the table with a bunch of men who are going to give you everything they've got to see what you can take, then go away. You're not going to change them. That's the business. I never really worked hard to be one of the guys. Anybody who's worked with me will say I am clearly, uniquely me. I never pressed a feminist agenda" (*Written By*).

In elementary school Martha's agenda included being a singer. It was a logical goal considering that both her parents, as well as her two sisters, all possessed extraordinary musical abilities. Growing up, Martha taught Sunday school, went to Bible camp, and joined the Teen Republicans. She also displayed an early talent for writing.

WILLIAMSON: I was writing as a kid. I was writing from the time I could literally hold a pencil, and I would write everything. I wrote little miniplays, I wrote a terrible novel that was seven pages long.

Longworth: What was the title?

WILLIAMSON: (*Laughs.*) *On Gossamer Wings.* No pun intended.

Longworth: You've always been into the wing thing, haven't you?

WILLIAMSON: Yeah, isn't that terrible? I had heard that song, (*she begins vocalizing*) "A trip to the moon on gossamer wings, just one of those things." I was fascinated with that phrase, "gossamer wings," but I didn't know what gossamer wings was. To me, it represented a sense of freedom, and I couldn't wait to grow up. Not because I wanted to get away from my parents, but because I just wanted to get out and start living life. So it was your basic seven-page novel about a girl who went to New York in search of fame and fortune. But it was just that desire to write. I also wrote terrible poetry. I wrote songs, and I wrote stories. When I got into junior high school and discovered that English class was all about writing, I was in heaven. And that was my greatest joy. I just couldn't wait to see what my next assignment would be, because I loved to write.

Martha traveled east to attend Williams College in Massachusetts, a school famous for its annual Theater Festival. Not surprisingly, though, she turned her time and talents toward singing.

WILLIAMSON: I had a very wide range, nearly three-octaves at my peak, when I was really singing. I sang in choruses, I sang in the group the "E Phlats" at Williams College. We were always in demand at Ivy League group sings because, at the time, we were the only mixed-sex group. Not mixed sex. (*Laughs.*) Oh, you know what I mean. Coed groups.

Longworth: The mixed-sex group is a whole other chapter.

WILLIAMSON: Yeah, we had boys and girls, and everything else between. (*Laughs.*) I did a lot of singing with the group, mostly as a soloist. I loved Broadway musicals. I sang along with Judy Garland, and memorized her Carnegie Hall album.

After graduation, though, it was writing, not singing that allowed Martha to make a living. She began by crafting jokes for comedians. Then, in 1980, she landed a job writing for Carol Burnett. That was followed by a stint on the NBC sitcom, *The Facts of Life.* In 1988 she wrote and produced *The Family Man* (CBS), starring Gregory Harrison, and followed that up with *Jack's Place* (ABC), starring Hal Linden and John Dye (who would later join the cast of *Touched by an Angel*). In 1994 she served as co-executive producer on a pilot drama for CBS, *Under One Roof.* The show, which Tim Brooks and Earle Marsh (*The Complete Directory to Prime Time Network and Cable TV Shows*) describe as a "multi-generational black family," starred James Earl Jones. CBS declined to continue with the innovative series, and Martha was devastated. The cancellation, however, was a blessing in disguise for Williamson, who was immediately offered another job by the network. CBS was unhappy with a new pilot about angels, and they asked Martha first to view it, then to come on board and revamp it. In the book *Touched by an Angel* (Williamson and Robin Sheets), Martha spoke of the opportunity to become an executive producer (E.P.) for the first time in her career. "I had been a P.A. [Production Assistant]," she said. "I took the producer's dog to the vet . . . the Armanis to the cleaners, and I knew the Xerox repairman by name. I had strung cable as a grip for a film company, interviewed guests for a game show, supervised scripts for a Broadway musical. I'd written jokes for comedians, wrote sitcoms, and I had taken meetings, done lunch, and been in development. I had done everything but be an E.P."

Williamson had paid her dues, and, after getting CBS to agree with her vision for the new faith-based show, she signed on to run what became known as *Touched by an Angel.* Referring to her as "The Jesus Girl," network brass had faith in Martha, but not enough to make a long-term commitment. Upon starting production on the series, cast and crew were required to have a "company" physical and to fill out an insurance form, one line of which covered projected length of employment. When co-star Della Reese noticed that the nurse had filled in the blank with "six weeks," she refused to sign until it was changed to "ten years." Clearly, Martha's faith was contagious, and while the show went on to be a big hit, the "Jesus Girl" and her cohorts initially faced rough sailing. Premiering in the fall of 1994, *Touched by an Angel* aired on

Wednesday night and was summarily pounded in the ratings by the ABC comedy *Roseanne*. With cancellation looming, CBS agreed to give Martha one last chance to prove herself, by offering up a Saturday-night placement following *Dr. Quinn, Medicine Woman* for two weeks in February and March of 1995. Thanks to the new time period and to a print campaign by a number of celebrities who had guest starred on the show in its first thirteen episodes, audiences responded. By the third season, *Touched by an Angel* was finally given its Sunday-night time slot, where it remained a CBS staple (it moved to Saturdays in September 2001).

Critics, of course, were slower to respond. During the first season, *USA Today* wrote that "CBS must be touched in the head," and *Entertainment Weekly*'s Ken Tucker criticized the show's "stilted dialogue." Tom Shales of the *Washington Post* sniped, "It's so goody-goody, and a throw back to something Michael Landon did much better in the eighties." Eventually, most of the mainstream media came around to Martha's way of thinking. Matt Roush of *TV Guide* admitted, "I've since had to eat my words."

In a surprise move, though, the grassroots organization Viewers for Quality Television challenged *Touched by an Angel*'s plot resolutions, and in 2000 refused to endorse the series. VQT's Dorothy Swanson charged that "Even religious people know that it is not as simple as if 'God loves you' everything is going to be OK." And Martha's buddy Tom Fontana, Emmy-winning producer of *St. Elsewhere* and creator of *Oz*, told *TV Guide*, "Finding God is an ongoing adventure. To happily resolve that in an hour would trivialize the struggle." Williamson, of course, defended her vision, and in that same article said, "With other series you can have people talk about both sides of any question and they end up with it up in the air. Fade to black. We can't do that. We ultimately have to come to a decision from God's point of view, which is tremendously difficult sometimes" (March 29, 1997).

Difficult, perhaps, but rewarding as well. Each week Martha is inundated with kudos and testimonials from people whose own burdens have been lightened just from watching *Touched by an Angel*. One such letter was paraphrased in a *People Magazine* article recounting the testimony of a teenager who was on the verge of committing suicide. The girl happened to see an *Angel* episode about AIDS patients trying to kill themselves. The teen wrote to series star Roma Downey, "When I saw the pain on your face at the thought of those girls dying, it suddenly occurred to me that it might matter to someone if *I* died" (February 2, 1999).

CBS president Les Moonves is surprised neither at the impact *Touched by an*

Angel has on viewers nor of Martha's extraordinary success. *"Touched by an Angel* is still probably the most underrated show on television," he says. "It works because it is truly one woman's vision all the way through. Martha believes what she is doing. She is empowered by what she is doing, and feels such a sense of duty in her show. She's someone who understands what an obligation it is when you do a show like that to be entertaining, and, at the same time, be uplifting. And, it's a very hard thing to do, because if you sort of telegraph the fact that you're going to be uplifting, then nobody's going to watch you. First and foremost you have to be in entertainment, and you can get your message there. Martha believes in that message. She believes in the power of television, and how important her mission is. And it really is a mission. I can't imagine the show being done without her." Moonves is not alone in that view.

I caught up with Martha while she was in Washington, D.C., immediately following a transcontinental flight and a day before she was to travel to Williamsburg to speak at a Congressional retreat. She was exhausted from the flight, from staying up all night with her baby daughter Isabel, and from just being Martha, which could wear down almost any mortal. We spoke over a two-day period.

Longworth: Martha, I'm sorry you don't feel well.

WILLIAMSON: Thank you, and after all this time we finally get together.

Longworth: It's a good thing you and I aren't dating. I'd think you were—

WILLIAMSON: (*Laughs.*) trying to break up with you. (*Laughs.*) You know I was talking to a friend of mine last night who I just adore and she said, "We don't talk anymore," and I said, "you and I need to talk for twenty minutes and I haven't had twenty minutes to myself forever."

Longworth: Lack of personal time is standard operating procedure, isn't it?

WILLIAMSON: It is, and it's a hard thing to keep a family and relationships and friendships going. I think the most difficult experience I ever had was writing the two-hour China episode that we did, which is perhaps in the top five of all the episodes that I am most proud of. And it was essentially a two-hour Movie of the Week, with seven acts, and it took a long time to get that episode approved because it was going to be longer and have a bigger budget. And it took a lot of research. By the time I was finally able to sit down and lock myself away to write it, I essentially had seven days to write seven acts. I was cranking out an act a day, locked up alone in a cabin outside of Salt Lake City in the hills with nothing but deer. In the middle of that, my mother had a heart attack. And I knew if I stopped and went to see her, we were not going to make the show.

Longworth: And you have hundreds of people depending on you.

WILLIAMSON: There are hundreds of people depending on me to get that script done, and there's an air date. You know, time and television wait for no man. And so I called my sisters and said, "You must let me know if her condition deteriorates, but I have to stay here until the last possible moment." My mother had surgery, and she got on the phone with me and she understood completely. She said, "You've got to do what you need to do. This is what you were made for. Do it."

Longworth: Your mom was always your role model, though, wasn't she?

WILLIAMSON: Oh yeah. As a matter of fact, I just discovered right next door to this hotel is the American Association of University Women, the headquarters for their educational fund. And my mother had been the treasurer of the AAUW for many years, right at the time when women's lib was born. She recognized very quickly that nothing can be done without money and education. And if you control the money, people listen, and they don't care if you're a man or a woman. (*Laughs.*)

Longworth: I know you grew up in Denver, but were you born there as well?

WILLIAMSON: Born and raised in Denver. I had two sisters, and they were both much older than I, about twelve or thirteen years older, so I was the baby, benefitting a great deal from having a lot of attention and being the object of "show and tell" at school. But they had lots of fun trying to teach me things when I was little. I essentially had two live-in tutors.

Longworth: Didn't you dream of becoming a professional singer?

WILLIAMSON: Just last night, somebody came up to me and told me their favorite episode of all time is "'Til We Meet Again" [episode number 210, January 1996], which is the story of when my father passed away.

Longworth: And you and your sisters are singing to him.

WILLIAMSON: Right, and that is a fairly accurate depiction of the musical background in our family. We all sang. Everyone played an instrument. But having come late to the party as the baby, after my family had existed for thirteen, fourteen years, everybody already had their harmonies worked out. Everybody already had the instruments that they played, so I was always looking for some place to fit in, in the musical life of our family. And in that show, it was only *when* my father died that I literally took the part that he would normally have sung, and my sisters and my mother and I sang to him when he passed away. But we loved music. I loved it when I was in college. I wrote musicals with my friend Marc Lichtman, who is now the composer on

Touched by an Angel, and has been the composer ever since we began. It's interesting, but as I talk to you I realize a lot of the values that my father was trying to teach me as I grew up were taught through the songs that he taught me to sing. He was tremendously nostalgic, a sentimental fellow, born in 1901. And he learned songs from his grandfather, who had sung in the Civil War. And so, I can sing old Civil War verses.

Longworth: Camp songs.

WILLIAMSON: Yes, the old Civil War camp songs. I can sing those as well as the songs that my father learned at college. So I really did not grow up listening to rock and roll. It wasn't that my parents forbade it, by any means, I just wasn't interested by the time it came around, because I so loved the music I had already been exposed to.

Longworth: You were quite the singer at Williams College, which was home to the Williamstown Theater Festival, where our friend Tom Fontana was active. By the way, Tom told me that he wanted to marry you.

WILLIAMSON: *(Laughs.)*

Longworth: Of course it's moot now because you're married, but I just can't imagine that particular pairing, you know, your influence over *Oz,* and his on *Touched by an Angel.*

WILLIAMSON: I would never consider myself the kind of writer that Tom Fontana is, and I mean that in the best sense, because he's just brilliant. But I know if someone had come to me and said, "Would you do *Oz?*" that my instincts for the show would not be that far off from what Tom does.

Longworth: That would surprise some people, wouldn't it?

WILLIAMSON: Yes, it certainly would. However, there's something that I learned very early and I'm glad I did. I worked on trying to get into the Writers Guild and make my "points." Remember how you had to make so many points before you were a full-blooded member? Anyway, I got a job working as a writer for an HBO special, *Joan Rivers Salutes Heidi Abramovitz* (*both laugh*), and I didn't even know who Heidi Abramovitz was, but it was a job. I was by far the youngest writer on the show, and I had no real experience. This was a gift that someone essentially had given to me to say, "Here, this is going to help you get some credits under your belt," and I was there to learn more than anything else, truly. There were people on that show who had incredible comedy credits, grand old men of the business. And then there were some people who were very new and hip, and wrote for *Saturday Night Live.*

Longworth: So while people might be surprised to know that you could write for *Oz*, they would also be surprised to learn that you cut your teeth on comedy.

WILLIAMSON: That's right. But I never *did* get the concept of Heidi Abramovitz. I guess she was just a, uh,(*pauses*)

Longworth: A slut.

WILLIAMSON: Is that what she was? (*Laughs.*) Well, my friend Marilyn Osborne, who is a remarkable writer, once described my writing as "sophisticated innocence." I was totally capable of writing Heidi Abramovitz jokes, but it upset me. It disturbed something in my spirit, and I didn't like myself as I did it. I ended up withdrawing from the show. I ended up getting a credit on it, but I released my points and residuals. I was happy to go because I didn't feel good about it. It wasn't a moral thing, it wasn't that I was Little Miss Goodie Goodie. I wasn't walking around holding a cross in front of me saying, "This is wrong and an offense to God." It just didn't make me feel good about myself. Now I will sit and watch *The Sopranos*, and marvel at the deep levels of metaphor that you find in that show. I find it fascinating. I could watch one episode over and over again, and find something new. It is hard to watch things on television that you admire so much without turning off the remote control and saying, "I wish I could do that." Now it's funny, and I hope before you go to print about my experience, we'll be really, really clear on the background. I've never seen anybody get it completely right, and I suspect that if anybody does, you will be the one; I've never seen anybody get the chronology of *Touched by an Angel* down right. My point being that, the show was not my idea.

Longworth: Well, you're being too modest now. Yes, John Masius created *Touched by an Angel*, but even John will say that it's your show. But since we're on the subject of *Touched by an Angel*, and we've alluded to things that might surprise people, let's see if I can surprise *you*. Here I am closing in on fifty, I'm an old married guy, try to be macho, but I've caught myself watching a couple of episodes of *Touched by an Angel*, and I'll start to tear up. Does that surprise you? And, what does that say about the demographics of your show?

WILLIAMSON: No, it doesn't surprise me. I'm sure you've done so much research that you've heard of the newspaper reporter who interviewed me. It was twenty-five minutes of a straight, tough, somewhat cynical interview. And then he said, "OK, lets go off the record. My wife and daughter watch your show, and they made me watch the show, and I started crying, and I'm really upset about that. Why?" That was amazing to me to hear a consummate professional say that. A man who only got where he was by being a "just the facts, ma'am" kind of guy. This was a reporter who did not suffer fools gladly. And it upset him. Well, I have maintained all this time that what we tapped into was an audience of people in this country who have not been given permission to feel. They've only been asked to react. Look at shows like *Playhouse 90*, and this is what people were watching in the '50s. Televisions were not available to everybody then, and your demographics were different. They also had a lot of (sophisticated) game shows back then. Who on earth today would sit and watch them ask questions about "Who gave St. Crispin's speech?" Today, they just ask, "What's the name of the fourth Beatle?" (*Both laugh.*) But the point is that the demographics changed significantly when television sets got cheaper. And it's not a judgment about intellect as much as it is, suddenly you are talking to teenagers who have televisions in their room, and families who have TV sets all over the house, and kids with disposable income, so you're going to go for MTV. You're teaching kids not to have to think for more than three and a half minutes.

Longworth: So you're equating that with your theory that we're not allowing ourselves enough time to feel anymore?

WILLIAMSON: Our emotions have been told to shrivel, and we're doing the best we can to do what television is asking us to do, and it's wrong. We say, "We're going to show you *Friends,* and you're going to laugh, and it'll all be over in thirty minutes." Look at *I Love Lucy.* I remember having a conversation with a man who said to me, "What's the matter with TV today? Why isn't TV the way it used to be with shows like *I Love Lucy?* And I said, "Well, wait a minute, *I Love Lucy* was sort of the beginning of what I think is mass television appeal. And, what were the values that were being taught there? You can't get anything you want unless you lie to your husband and manipulate him." And that was the message that little kids were growing up with. Adults would look at it and say, "That's funny amusement," but for a little kid, thirty minutes was a long period of time. You watch Lucille Ball crawling on a ledge, getting her head stuck in a pot, and then lying to her husband so she finally got what she wanted, and those were the messages that were being passed along. I think, down the line, I suffered more from watching television. I gained as much, but I suffered as much, too. I got the wrong message about relationships. I got the wrong message about general honesty. My sisters grew up listening to the radio, and they used their imaginations in a way that I did not. At any rate, there's a generation of people that began in the '50s to live as though a hidden camera was watching them. That you say things for the sake of being funny. Do you know what I'm saying?

Longworth: Yeah, and we're almost coming full circle, or perhaps we've never left the circle, with *Survivor.*

WILLIAMSON: And the real interesting phenomenon between the first and second *Survivor* is that the first one was so new and so unfamiliar, we recognized it in many ways, as an un-self–conscious experience, and it seemed strangely genuine in a medium where nothing is genuine. (*Laughs.*) And watching those people, they did not at the time realize what media celebrities they were about to become, and their behavior in the first *Survivor* series on the island is much different from the second one—where everybody knows what the stakes are now. They're all better looking. They're more glib. They have something to compare themselves to, and we have something to compare *them* to, and suddenly, it is now a performance. And I compare that to the fact that my sisters simply lived, but I was aware that life was becoming a performance. I have talked with many of my friends with whom I grew up, and they have recognized the same thing, that their life in some way was in danger of becoming derivative of a televison show. (*Laughs.*)

Longworth: But are you saying, then, that you succeeded in your chosen profession in spite of the fact that you grew up with that kind of televison?

WILLIAMSON: No, most certainly *because* of it in many ways. I personally think I have succeeded because I watched so darn much television. I love it, and I recognize the incredible power of television. And I think that the success of *Touched by an Angel* comes from the fact that people have grown up with television for so long, and I've always been highly aware of the fact that we are doing an eight o'clock show. You cannot compare *Touched by an Angel* to *The Sopranos* or *Oz*, or anything that isn't at eight o'clock, simply for the reason that, as a producer, I am very much aware of who my audience is. And I take the fact that this could be the last show that a child sees before he or she goes to bed at night very seriously. Many a time I have erred on the side of Tom Fontana rather than Michael Landon (*laughs*), personally, for the sake of telling a more dramatic story, but there are built-in parameters that you have to respect, and I respect them. And that's one of the toughest things about writing this show and one of the things people love about the show. They know that they are safe there.

Longworth: Well, you're trying to present positive role models for people, especially young people, and that's good. So it must concern you that some producers and executives in TV continue to promote some not-so-positive role models, for example, showcasing anorexic-type actresses who are role models for young girls.

WILLIAMSON: What I think about when you say positive role models is that, every week, we present someone in a situation where they have a choice to make, and we challenge them to make a choice that is not necessarily self-centered. The thing that disturbs me about role models being developed is . . . that people are making decisions out of selfishness. It's always about "You've got to do what's right for you." How many times have we heard this on a show? "You've got to listen to your heart. If it's not making you happy, then you've got to get out of this." Those are things we hear over and over again, which, I think, come directly from the '70s "Me Generation," and it's false religion of self that we have absorbed so naturally without question. And that is what I'm questioning with the show. We set up role models and they all unquestionably live with situational ethics, and that, to me, is very dangerous. The thing is, Jim, you talk about role models. I feel that, in the same vein as "me, me, me" in the '70s, it has now just become part of our culture and remains unquestioned for the most part, certainly in television. In the past it was, "I'm not going to give my child any religious training at all, and then my child can make his or her decision when they grow up." And, inevitably, they don't make any decision at all because they weren't even given something to rebel against. (*Laughs.*) And I think it's very positive to offer *Touched by an Angel* in syndication, five nights a week, so that young people today are given presentation of God as a creator of the universe who demands truth and honesty in our lives. And then you can reject that down the line, but at least there's been one stake put into the ground as a marker.

Longworth: You said earlier that you felt uncomfortable writing certain kinds of comedy; you also have begun to share some of your views on life. I'm wondering, did your time spent writing comedy, as well as your own personal experiences, help to make you a better writer of drama?

WILLIAMSON: Yes. Good question. Here's the thing that I learned about comedy. Never be afraid to rip it all apart and start all over again. There's always another joke, there's always another line. If it's not working, back up and find another road. One thing that I learned is to work very quickly, and that has worked for me and against me. I envy David Chase doing only thirteen episodes a season. I won't insult him to suggest that's a luxury (*laughs*) because I know how hard he must work, but I think I would do very different episodes of *Touched by an Angel* if I had the same amount of time to do thirteen episodes instead of twenty-six. And yet, my experience in sitcoms has totally prepared me to make those shows on time and on budget, and crank them out with the best possible quality that you can expect under the circumstances. That I learned from doing sitcoms. There's nothing like doing a four o'clock show with a live audience, and having an hour at dinner time to rewrite the second act to make it funnier before it shoots again. Another lesson I learned from comedy is what we refer to as comedy cul-de-sacs (*laughs*), you know, when you start down a road and you're trying to get to a joke, and then you hit a dead end. And no matter how hard you work to get to that joke, and no matter how hard you hoped it was going to be funny, it just isn't working, so don't try to plow through. Stop, back up, find another road to take. And I learned how to go down those roads very quickly. For example, someone suggests, "What if Monica were a house painter?" I have learned very quickly to say, "OK, if she's a house painter, then that would lead us to "x," and "x" would lead us to "y," and "y" would lead us to "z," and this will help, and that will not help. Let's back up and let's go." And we save a lot of time just by very quickly being able to extrapolate from an idea and go to the end of it, and see if it works. And, if not, give up and start down another road. Also, in comedy I learned that there was so much more I wanted to explore that I couldn't because of the time constraints and because you had to have two jokes on every page. I became frustrated with comedy, because I wanted to stop and talk about things. And it was a glorious day when I sat there on Maple Drive having lunch with my agent, Beth Uffner, and she just looked at me and said, "Maybe you're not supposed to do comedy." Suddenly someone had given me permission, and I raised both my hands over my head and said, "Hallelujah, you're right." I had personally gone down the comedy cul-de-sac and was too afraid to turn around and go back and start over. But I did. And that was the turning point for me.

Longworth: There are still only a handful of women producers and showrunners in dramatic television. The question is, why? Why in the year 2001 should I even have to be asking this question?

WILLIAMSON: Personally I feel that we are beyond it. I would not have said that even five years ago. But look at the women who are running shows now, and there are many. Not that there are ever enough, but I don't feel that it's the way it used to be. The way it used to be is the same problem you found in banking and wherever. There are boys' clubs and quotas that were met, but nobody genuinely looked at a woman as a serious executive.

Longworth: CBS CEO Les Moonves told me that he thought that we had turned the corner on being a gender-blind industry.

WILLIAMSON: I think we have, I really do believe we have turned the corner. I don't think there is anything more gender blind than an executive producer who desperately needs a good writer. And you don't care if that writer is a twelve year old who speaks a different language, but can turn out good scripts, you don't care. You *want* the product.

Longworth: Can women write for women as well as men can write for women?

WILLIAMSON: Oh, you're so mean. (*Laughs.*) Sure they can. They might write more accurately, but it doesn't necessarily mean they write better. The best writers are people who are not just observant, but empathetic. And I look at David Kelley, who does wonderful writing for women, but he also makes a point of sitting and listening to it. And there's a lot of women who don't listen to themselves.

Longworth: What do you mean?

WILLIAMSON: I believe women are naturally more verbose. It's a gross generalization, but I still feel that women are more likely to bond quickly and share their most intimate secrets with women they hardly know (*laughs*), while men are still stuck in "What about those Yankees?" But on the other hand, women can tend to fall into certain patterns of conversations with each other, and we're almost waiting for our turn to share our story, but we're not trying to listen to what others are saying. If you are a writer you have to be able to listen to each other. That's why a male writer who listens can always write better for women than a female writer who doesn't listen. So, in my opinion, listening is really the factor as opposed to just gender.

Longworth: OK, then let me try and trap you on something. If your theory is true, and empathizing is that important, then you should require all of your writers on *Touched by an Angel* to be Godfearing fundamentalists.

WILLIAMSON: We have Buddhists, atheists, we have . . .

Longworth: Right, so how can they empathize with your philosophy?

WILLIAMSON: Number one is, these are good writers who empathize with the human condition. These are people who could write just as easily and just as well for *Star Trek*. You have to be able to deal with what's going on with the human heart. The challenge of *Touched by an Angel* has always been that we have our own "prime directive" (*laughs*) and you can't mess with this "prime directive," and at the same time it creates very specific parameters that any writer will recognize as the show's Bible, no pun intended. On *Star Trek*, for example, you're not allowed to change the evolution of a life form, and if you do, it is going to create conflict. But you don't change the fundamental rules of the series.

Longworth: It's interesting that you used the *Star Trek* analogy. As you know, John Masius sent me a tape of the original pilot for *Touched by an Angel*.

When you took over the series, you came in and really changed the concept of what John had envisioned an angel should be and do. Why tamper with it and change *that* "prime directive?"

WILLIAMSON: Oh, I remember exactly what it was. The fundamental change occurred the morning that I went in to discuss the show with the network and say whether or not I would accept it. I had done *Under One Roof* with Thomas Carter [*The White Shadow*]. I had fallen in love with *Under One Roof*. It was a very deep, powerful family drama. Race relations has such a fundamental place in my heart and I wanted that show to work so desperately. And when they did not pick it up, I was so angry. It was a Wednesday morning, and I got a call from my agent saying, "The network still wants you. They've got another show and they're sending over a tape," and that was the Masius pilot. I didn't like it, and I acknowledge that I was already angry at CBS (*laughs*), so certainly that colored some of what I felt. They sent me something called *Angels Attic* and I couldn't understand why they picked up that show and wouldn't pick up *Under One Roof*. The first scene on the pilot is of some dippy girl popping out of the ocean, sort of a cross between *I Dream of Jeannie* and *Splash*, and the first thing I heard was a drug joke. Now I don't know what version of the show you saw, but the version I saw, these guys on the beach were making bong jokes.

Longworth: Yeah, the guys who found Monica after she landed in the ocean.

WILLIAMSON: Then I watched the show and I wasn't particularly driven by it. I didn't like to see all the special effects. It felt like somebody's idea of what angels were without any connection to who God was. I had spent fourteen years in show business by that time, and never once had a desire to impose my Christian ethic on a show. I certainly had drawn from my Christian experience when I wrote certain shows, but I never tried to go out there and proselytize and use network television to do it. But, if somebody is going to come to me and *ask* me to do a show that involves an element of my faith, I cannot betray that. Let's say somebody had asked me to do a show about the old West. My first instinct would be to move it to Colorado, let's go to Central City during the silver-mining days, because I *know* that. *That* I understand. I know how to write that. But you come to me to write a show about an angel and you show me somebody who is a recycled dead person, which I don't believe exists, well—there's nowhere in the Bible that suggests that. Monica raises a dog from the dead, which is in direct opposition to my belief that human beings who are either dead or living do not have the power of life over death. God has the power of life over death. There was flying and wings, things that perpetuated myths about angels that, in my mind, tended to trivialize the whole realm from which angels come. I am not an angel person. I don't collect angel tchotchkes. I never gave angels much thought. But they are part and parcel of the Christian faith. And, by the way, there are angels in the Old Testament, as well. But none of them ever looked like this. So if you perpetuate the fairy tales about angels, then that's what people believe.

Longworth: But if Satan was originally an angel himself, why can't you portray angels as having diverse aspects about their existence?

WILLIAMSON: Well, it goes back to the *Star Trek* thing, and to the eight o'clock time slot. I was very clear that this had to be a simplified show. You cannot get into the deep levels of self examination that you could on *Picket Fences*, or *NYPD Blue*, or *Ally McBeal*, for heaven's sake. It's for one reason. It's an anthology, and you are essentially writing a pilot every week, which people tend to underestimate a lot. It is incredibly difficult to create a brand new set of characters every week. I mean, the angels are there to *support* these characters. Look at Angela Lansbury. She was essentially the star of the show, and whoever the guest star was, they walked in, got killed, and got carried out, but basically you did not have to do a lot of character development. *ER*, the same thing. You have the same people every week, and new people get rolled in and they walk out. (*Laughs.*) But basically you are dealing with familiar characters, and each week you can peel another layer off of these characters. *We* can't do that. And so, I knew that we had to make very specific rules, just like *Star Trek*. This is what I said when I walked into CBS. "The pilot that I have seen has given me no rules. I don't know the realm from which these angels come. I don't know what their parameters are. I don't know what their message is. I don't know what Monica is there for. I don't know if she's supposed to be healing someone every week, or meddling in peoples lives, or if she's undercover." There were no rules, and people in television need to know the rules, particularly at eight o'clock. What's interesting about shows like *Ally McBeal* is that, once you start directing toward a more sophisticated audience, then breaking the rules is a very hip thing. *Seinfeld* was the anti–*I Love Lucy*. It broke all the rules of sitcom, and that's what made it so wonderful and so hip. But you had your characters that you were willing to go on the ride with. We have angels who cannot go on the ride. Your question is, well, why *don't* they go on the ride? Why can't they look into their hearts and struggle with their faith? Because it's an anthology and because it's at eight o'clock. Because we're not there every week to watch angels struggle with their faith; we're there to meet new people every week. And again, I was very, very clear that this had to be a show for the whole family. To be honest, I love this show with heart and soul. It has been my baby. I have protected it, I've stayed up all night with it (*laughs*), I have fought for it. With the exception of getting married and adopting my child, it is the most important thing I've ever done in my life. And yet, I am very clear that to some degree I've always known that I was trapped in an eight o'clock show, writing eight o'clock material.

Longworth: And it is very personal for you too, for example, having gone through an abortion years ago, and ending up writing an episode inspired by that. You also wrote an episode about the family singing together at their dying father's bedside, which was autobiographical. My point is that on most shows, the producer will tell you that coming up with stories is a team effort, but with *Touched by an Angel* it is oftentimes about you sharing a story that is cathartic for you.

WILLIAMSON: Yes. And I did a lot of therapy. I think the Writers Guild *requires* that you go into therapy. (*Both laugh.*) But I stopped therapy and stopped writing in my journal when I started working on *Touched by an Angel*, one because I was just so darn tired, there was no room for anything else in my life except to live and breathe that show. But secondly, you're right, it was very cathartic. I would say that in the last few years I've had to spread around the responsibility because you can't keep that pace up all by yourself forever. With David Kelley, for example, it's my understanding that he doesn't get involved in the day-to-day producing as much as he just sort of sits there and cranks out the script. And, because of the nature of this show, because every week you're in a different world, different places, the anthology format creates the brand new potential for disaster every week. (*Laughs.*) We'll do a comedy one week. We do a very, very heavy drama the next week. We'll do a very sentimental show the following week, then we'll do a big extravaganza, with high production. Every single week it's something different. So I've had to be there, and present, and on the set.

Longworth: With sitcoms, there was an old rule of thumb, that you knew the writers were getting burned out when they sent the cast to England for an episode.

WILLIAMSON: (*Laughs*) or Hawaii.

Longworth: Similarly, I noticed a change in your show not long ago where you shifted from the interpersonal stories to doing topical, political issues, going to the Sudan, etc. Weren't you afraid that your audience might not like that direction?

WILLIAMSON: Interestingly enough that was the opposite of burn-out. The early stories were very, very personal stories and there was always an element of some experience I had had, and there still has to be something that I can personally relate to before that script is completed. Everybody pretty much takes it for granted that, whoever writes the first draft or the second draft, I will always end up writing the revelation scene, and taking a complete pass at the whole script. Our process now is very different from what it used to be. We have a table that works almost more like a comedy table than a drama table. I have a friend who went to work for *Providence* for a while, and I was told that they all sit down, break all of their stories, and find the arc for the whole season. They assign the scripts and everybody goes away for a month and writes their scripts. And then they come back and turn them in and get notes, and they come back and turn in their second draft, and basically each writer takes their script and refines it and refines it, based on the notes from the executive producer, the showrunner. Ours is different. One, we didn't really have a big writing staff at the beginning. Secondly, CBS was really nervous and unclear about what the show was supposed to be, and the truth was I had essentially three weeks to figure it out myself. I knew it was not going to be anything like the Masius pilot except that we were going to keep Roma and Della.

Longworth: Speaking of Roma, let me digress for a moment. Is Monica supposed to be your alter ego? I mean, there is a resemblance between the two of you.

WILLIAMSON: Isn't that funny? I had nothing to do with casting Roma. As you know, Roma and Della had been cast in the original pilot. I'm the extra-large version of Roma. (*Laughs.*) She's a tiny little thing. We're both Irish. Her people are from the North, and my people are from the North and the South. As the story goes, my grandfather was Roman Catholic, and my grandmother was Protestant, and so they had to get married secretly.

Longworth: Same with my wife and me. She was Baptist and I was Episcopal, so we had to marry secretly, as well. It's as flammable as the Irish conflict.

WILLIAMSON: (*Laughs.*) Thank you, that's quite an honor to be compared to your situation. (*Both laugh.*)

Longworth: But let's get back to your accepting CBS's offer to take over the show, which, by the way, almost didn't make it.

WILLIAMSON: It almost didn't make it. But I also knew that, despite CBS wanting it to be about recycled dead people and they wanted more special effects and more "angel stuff," I just knew that this show was definitely not going to succeed if I spent more time trying to please *them* than I did trying to please myself.

Longworth: Pretty risky. They could have shown you the door.

WILLIAMSON: It was very risky. I remember once in the second season I showed the network a script and everyone read it, but not a single person understood it. They said, "What is this?" And I sent it to my agent, who has now finally retired, and even Beth said "I don't get this." That was a very important moment for me. I said, "Either you folks trust me with this show or you don't, but I'm telling you, it's going to be special." And it was. And I later got the phone call back from the network, who said, "You were right," and that was a big turning point because they left me alone after that. But let's go back for a moment to your question about is it the writers, is it me? Was there burn-out, and so forth. For me, those first couple of years were essentially about survival and truly putting my stamp on it. Not because I wanted to put my stamp on it, but because I *had* to put *a* stamp on it. And I only knew one person to go to for that. (*Laughs.*) If you don't have a clear vision of a show, it does not succeed. You can go high brow or you can go low brow. David Kelley has a very clear vision. Tom Fontana has a very clear vision. Chuck Norris has a very clear vision. You can waste time day after day after day trying to incorporate two or three or four visions, and all you're going to get is a mess. And one of the challenges for women is, "If a woman was doing what Dick Wolf was doing [several spin-offs from the same series] with the same vision and the same commitment and the same demand for a particular message for *Law & Order,* then people would call the woman producer 'Janet Reno' or something." And that's tough. For me, I had a unique challenge in that you have to be tough and you have to be committed, and you have to be uncompromising in terms of the quality and the message of the show. And, at the same time, this tough, uncompromising person is talking about love and forgiveness. (*Laughs.*) So you automatically set yourself up for criticism, because they'll say, "Well, who is she?" But I knew what we had to do, and they were either going to like it or they weren't going to like it. At the end of the day, I mean at the very end of your day, at the end of your career in Hollywood, when you're sixty-five years old sitting in Jerry's Famous Deli with your old buddies remembering the old days, that's about all you've got left, truly, is that you did it your way, whether they liked it or they didn't. But there are so many compromises that get made in television that if you compromise your integrity, too, then you might as well just get out of the business.

Longworth: Well, I won't tell Don Bellisario that at age sixty-five you're supposed to retire and sit in the deli.

WILLIAMSON: (*Laughs.*) Let's say seventy-five. But there are so many people that made so many compromises just to keep working, and God bless 'em, cause we do what we have to do to keep working, but if you do it too much and too often for too long, you're not going to have anything to show for it. And that's what I'm really proud of with *Touched*, is that I wanted to play in the bigger leagues, the nine o'clock and ten o'clock leagues, but I was given something that frankly I *did* know how to do, and I did it.

Longworth: And with these policy issues that Senator Brownback and others have worked with you on, you're really sort of doing nine and ten o'clock stories, but you're doing them at eight.

WILLIAMSON: Thank you, and that was my next point, which is I'm very sensitive to what is burn-out and what that means. There's no question that I have come close to that at times, and this is when my faith has come through. I really do pray about the scripts that I write. I really do rely on God more than myself. When I start relying on myself to come up with these ideas, and crank them out, that's when things feel flat, that's when I feel uninspired. That's when I start to get worn out. And what has been wonderful for me is to try to reinvent the show when all the typical television tools to reinvent itself don't apply. You can't get anybody pregnant on this show. (*Laughs.*) You can't marry them off. But when we started recognizing that this was a show people are watching to be encouraged and inspired on a Sunday night before they have to get up and crank it out for another week out in the "jungle," then maybe we also have created a space where we can challenge these folks, too.

Longworth: Les Moonves said you are on a mission with *Touched by an Angel.*

WILLIAMSON: (*Laughs.*)

Longworth: Do you agree, and what is that mission? What's the goal?

WILLIAMSON: I didn't start on a mission. I did not walk into CBS with a flag saying, "Here's my mission." As I got involved with *Touched by an Angel*, I realized we had something very special. We had a show that dealt with something that 85 percent of the country holds near and dear, and that is their religion, their faith. And this could never be a religious show. I don't even consider myself to be religious. This show presented me with certain parameters, and I broadened them in some places and narrowed them in others. As a result I discovered that I certainly had a mission. I had the challenge to make this show a success. That's what they hired me for. CBS doesn't want a religious show, they don't want a mission, they just want a hit. And so, that was number one. I thought, "How do you make a hit out of something like this?" And, to remove the fantastic element from it right away seemed the obvious thing to do, because up until then, with all due respect to John Masius and the first pilot, you could have switched out the angel and made her a genie. You could have made her a witch. You could have made her an alien, and the show would have been the same because people would have seen it as a fantasy. I knew that my goal had been accomplished when, after the second season, television critics stopped referring to *Touched by an Angel* as a fantasy and began calling it a drama. Early on they called it a fantasy, and this is one of the things that always makes me crazy, is when people say, "The critics hated the pilot," or "It originally got terrible reviews," because most of those critics saw the pilot and never saw the first episode. And so, we were coming from behind the starting line, because everybody was reading a review of a show that didn't exist. So I can take the element of fantasy out and recognize to the audience that I wanted them to watch a show where angels and God are *not* a fantasy. These are very, very sacred things, and you don't mess around with that. I think *Highway to Heaven* succeeded for two reasons. Number one, Michael Landon. He could have come as the magic plumber and he would have succeeded in that show. But secondly, he was very, very wise never to insult the source of the angel's power. And that was God.

Longworth: Was *Highway to Heaven* your model for how to create rules in a show?

WILLIAMSON: No, I didn't really have a model. To be honest, watching that pilot, all I did was the opposite. It was very easy. You looked at the pilot and went, "Michael J. Pollard is creating death as a terrible thing." Well, only a few years earlier, I had seen my father pass away, and death was not an ugly thing. Yes, people can actually die in terrible ways, but the moment of death is not bad at all. And once again, I felt that creating a character for children to see death as a terrible thing, was, in itself, a terrible thing. I could not justify perpetuating that at all, and that's why I made a point in the first episode of having Charlie Rocket, who played the Angel of Death at that time, run into Monica and make a point of saying, "I just took Mr. Morgan home, and it was beautiful." That was very important. Secondly, Monica having the power over life and death. No! Just do the opposite. God has the power, God doesn't make mistakes. There was a line in the Masius pilot—

Longworth: "God doesn't give you any more than you can handle."

WILLIAMSON: And Monica says, "That's a lot of crap." Well, my jaw dropped open. And it seemed to me that it was just an attempt to be hip without any recognition of the only audience that's going to watch a show like this, a family audience that most likely is going to be offended by that.

Longworth: But remember where John was coming from at that time with his own personal situation. And it made sense that an angel would question another angel who says "God doesn't give you any more than you can handle." But because of your life experiences, you're coming at it from a different perspective than did John, and that didn't make either approach bad.

WILLIAMSON: Right, but if there was a mission for me at all, it began to form at that moment, because I began to recognize that the highest and best use of television is to inspire people to examine themselves. At the same time, why not use television to encourage people? I don't personally believe that we're encouraging them with false information. I am a living, breathing testimony to the grace of God, and people will roll their eyes and say, "Oh boy!" but anybody who is searching for truth, making a genuine search for truth, cannot discount Christianity in their search.

Longworth: Well, you seem to be pretty knowledgeable about these matters, and that reminds me of an episode with Kirk Douglas, where Tess [Della] was producing a variety show, and she tells Kirk, "I know all sorts of things. It comes with being a good executive producer," and I started to laugh.

WILLIAMSON: (*Laughs.*)

Longworth: Was Della describing *you?*

WILLIAMSON: It's so funny because that was not my line. It was Joseph Telushkin (a rabbi) and Alan Estrin's line, but I found it very amusing. They were freelance writers for that episode. But this is a show where you really need to recognize that it's just like anything else that makes a good series. You know what the rules are, and you're comfortable with them, and that's why you invite the show into your house every week, because it's something familiar and it's not going to demand that you're constantly keeping up. And that's sort of a default position, and you certainly don't want to encourage people to stop thinking, by any means. You look at the shows we do, and we're trying to encourage people to think all the time, but to think *and* give a place for their hearts as well. It's unfortunate you hear the word "angel," and suddenly everyone devalues the show because they will either call it a fantasy or simply consider it sentimental tripe. If you look at our show and look at all of the stories that we have done, we have never compromised the message just to tell the story. I mentioned the dramatic cul-de-sacs earlier, and we've never adjusted the message just to fit the story. We always go back and adjust the story to fit the message.

Longworth: You once commented to *TV Guide* writer Daniel Howard Cerone (March 29, 1997) that "You never know when you might be entertaining an angel."

WILLIAMSON: (*Laughs.*)

Longworth: So how do I know that I haven't been entertaining an angel during these interview sessions?

WILLIAMSON: That's so funny. (*Laughs.*)

Longworth: I mean, how do I know?

WILLIAMSON: (*Laughs.*) Go back and read the *George* magazine article. (*Laughs.*)

Longworth: But so what if you've made a journey. You can still be an angel.

WILLIAMSON: But see, I believe that angels are created beings by God, and that they really do go back and forth, and bring healing and comfort and deliver messages. And I don't believe that they have a human experience. If there's one thing that I've bent the "rules" on from the Bible, it's that we have sent Monica as an angel to explore what it's like to be a human being and experience more human emotions.

Longworth: But you do a lot of good works here on earth, and you're human, so even though my question was humorous, the point is still, can't humans do angelic work on earth?

WILLIAMSON: I hope so. (*Laughs.*) When I look back and realize the small circumstances that, had they been slightly different, I would not be working on *Touched by an Angel* today, and how different my life would be. Because I came to *Touched by an Angel* with a certain degree of faith. I didn't realize how much I needed it until I started doing this show and truly relying on God. Relying on sitting at that computer, putting my hands on the keys and saying, "OK, it's not my will, but yours." I'm not saying that I channeled anybody. I'm not saying that God magically pressed all of the keys (*laughs*), but God gave me peace and clarity, and that has been responsible for one hundred and fifty–plus shows. Not because I was out there trying to get my vision so that I could go out and get another show, and push my career on and on. It became very clear to me very early on that, if I never did anything else, this was what I was supposed to be doing.

Longworth: Yet the thing you speak of even more fondly than the show is your family, your husband, Jon, and daughter, Isabel. Women have struggled to have a place in drama, both on screen and behind the scenes, and here, you've sort of made your workplace your *family* place too.

WILLIAMSON: I am not exaggerating. I wish I could express how much of a family we have on that show. We have shared everything. Roma's divorce. Roma's marriage. Roma's baby, not in that order. (*Laughs.*) We have wept, we have laughed. There have been deaths on our show. I met my husband, Jon, on our show. Sitting in the writers' room one day I said, "Folks, I think I'm going to come out of the closet and talk about my abortion experience." I remember calling up Les [Moonves] and saying, "This lady from *George* magazine asked me these questions, and it's not something I *want* to do, but I think I'm supposed to talk about this. Because if I don't, it is antithetical to the message that we give on the show. How can I talk about honesty and family secrets and the damage that they do, and the value of life, and then keep these things to myself? If it could help somebody then I think I should do it. But I want to know if you're comfortable with my doing this." And Les said, "Martha we love you" and (*pause*), It chokes me up. (*Her voice breaks with emotion.*) He said "We love you so much, and we'll stand by anything you do."

Longworth: Les is a great guy.

WILLIAMSON: Yeah, and I went, "OK, I'm going for it." And I sat down with everybody in the office, and I said, "I'm going to tell you a story here, and I want you guys to know I don't know if that means people will start to point to me and say, "There's the angel lady, and she's not such an angel anymore," or they'll say, "Maybe there *is* something to her faith because it brought her to a moment where she could do this."

Longworth: And maybe they'll say, she wasn't ready to be a mom then, but now she has a beautiful baby daughter.

WILLIAMSON: Isn't that true. Of all the times for that [the interview with *George* magazine] to have happened, Jim, it all came about the month before we went to China, and I believe it was God's gift to me. Just like every gift that God gives us, we have to have the courage to accept it. And this was a gift he was offering me at the perfect time, saying to me, "You get this out now, so when Isabel comes, you'll feel free." And that was a wonderful thing.

Longworth: Interesting how your life has crossed into your program, which is not usually the case with most showrunners. The family at work is fused with your family at home, and both are joined in a mission that is largely your personal vision.

WILLIAMSON: I think so. One thing many people have said to me is,

"Martha you just spill your guts out there for fifteen, twenty million people every week. Why?" And I said, "First of all, I do my best writing when I'm being honest. And, secondly, I just feel very strongly that this is the place and time to set examples of self examination." If people can watch *Touched by an Angel* and hear genuine sincerity, either it'll make them uncomfortable, which is good, or it will encourage them and comfort them, which is also good. One time there was a man attending a panel discussion with me, and he stood up and attempted to humiliate me by saying that all my earnestness was very disturbing because there are no answers in the world, and life is what we make it, and there really is no God, and—

Longworth: That was me, by the way.

WILLIAMSON: (*Laughs.*) That was you? Well, you had a nice head of hair, but that was about it. (*Laughs.*) I just sat there and thought, "This is a man who has seen the show, and is very upset by the fact that it moved him." You could just tell that what had happened was he had seen a show that pressed so many buttons in him. Darned if he was going to let it get to him. But that's good because, for example, one day when my husband had his heart attack and was lying in a hospital being given the last rites, he knew that none of his credit cards were going to save his life. Neither his agent nor his manager were going to save his life. His union couldn't save his life.

Longworth: I don't know about that one.

WILLIAMSON: (*Laughs.*)

Longworth: I think the union can still get to you after death, can't they?

WILLIAMSON: (*Laughs.*) . . . and all he knew was to call out to God, and he had to fight to survive a terrible attack and was in a tiny Canadian hospital with fourteen beds, and no surgeon who had a clue as to how to save his life, and he fought to survive. But once he did that, he was no longer fighting alone. If somebody has seen *Touched by an Angel* at some point in their life, and let's say they *do* consider it a fantasy, the day they need God, they will reach out to Him, and they're not going to care if it's a fantasy or not. There are no atheists in foxholes. And I love the idea that there are little children watching the show in syndication even now, and ten years from now, who are going to, maybe one day, say, "Maybe that show was right. Maybe it had something." That's a legacy for all the great television shows that have ever been. There is not a child who will reach out in times of trouble and grab for a lesson from *Seinfeld*, but they might grab for a lesson from *Touched by an Angel*.

Longworth: Thanks for spending time with me.

WILLIAMSON: I'm so sorry it took over a year for us to get together.

Longworth: As you know, in my thirty years in the business, I've interviewed everybody from Bob Hope to Elizabeth Taylor. I even did an entire half-hour TV special with Red Skelton. When people ask me if there was ever anyone I wish I had been able to interview, they think I'm going to say Sinatra. But I say to them, "You know, if I could have just gotten that damned Martha Williamson to return my phone calls."

WILLIAMSON: (*Laughs.*)

Longworth: So you're off to Williamsburg to speak at a Congressional retreat. Are you going to make policy there?

WILLIAMSON: That was the original plan. (*Laughs.*) No, my plan is to simply share the challenges that I've had as a person of faith in Hollywood, and compare that to how these guys have such a challenge to reach across the aisle. But I don't know if they know how to do that. One senator confided in me briefly last week. He said, "You know Martha, we don't know how to connect with each other on a personal level. We've got a lot of old-guard people who are very uncomfortable talking about anything but budgets. Yet if we don't find a way to lovingly approach the work that has to be done on both sides of the aisles over the next four years, it's going to be very ugly." And I asked him, "Do you have any clue why they want me to be speaking to them?" He said, "It's because you're spiritual without being religious, and you have a story to tell." You know, the bottom line of so many of these things is really fear, and if we can recognize the fear that we see in each other, then we have two choices. We can manipulate that and capitalize on it, or you can address it and empathize with it and compare your fear to their fear. I know that people carry around such secrets. That was my experience with the *George* magazine article. I finally said, "You know, if I talk about [my abortion] I may never be able to run for office, not that I ever would want to, but I can pretty much guarantee if I talk about it, that they—

Longworth: They would hammer you on it.

WILLIAMSON: They would hammer me someday, and it would all come out. And I thought, I have a deeper hope than that, and I have peace with God, so what if they hammer me? (*Laughs.*) I got hammered enough. I remember when we brought out *Promised Land,* somebody stood up in the press tour and accused me of being a white supremacist (*both laugh*) because the kids on the show were being homeschooled. And I said, "They're homeschooled because it's a series about people who live in a trailer and are always on the road! They don't live in a neighborhood." (*Both laugh.*)

Longworth: Well, I've had a great time talking with you, even if you *are* a white supremicist.

WILLIAMSON: (*Laughs.*) You've been so wonderful and so kind.

Longworth: I had to be. I couldn't be sure that I wasn't entertaining an angel. (*Both laugh.*)

4

ANTHONY ZUIKER | Master of Forensics

Anthony Zuiker. PHOTO BY TONY ESPARZA.
COURTESY OF CBS PHOTO ARCHIVE.

TELEVISION CREDITS

2000– | *CSI: Crime Scene Investigation* (CBS)

MW MW MW

One day when giving directions over the telephone to his pal Joe Garagiola, Hall of Famer Yogi Berra said, "When you come to a fork in the road, take it."

Still only a television rookie, young Anthony Zuiker has come to many a fork in the road, and he *always* takes it. To Zuiker, Berra's malapropism would make perfect sense, for there's nothing Anthony won't try and there's never any hesitation about trying something in which he believes. Zuiker, by his own admission, is a risk taker, a high-stakes gambler in life, which is consistent with his Las Vegas upbringing and evident in his creation of *CSI.* "Ever since we were kids, fourteen and fifteen years old, we would hang out in the sports books. We would bet sports, little two dollar parlays, at places like the Castaways Hotel, which is now the Mirage, 'cause that's what Vegas kids *did* in high school. If you watch any of the *CSI* episodes, you'll see references to sports betting because that's part of our culture, part of our heritage. New York City kids do their thing. California kids do their thing. Nebraska kids shuck corn, but we bet sports. And I guess it got me into a sort of gambling mentality of taking risks. I've always been a guy who'll gamble on life. Sometimes it pays off, and sometimes it doesn't."

Mostly it *does* pay off, though, and that in itself is remarkable. But there are many remarkable things about Anthony Zuiker's brief career, most notably that his first foray into network television is a huge success. Anthony's creation, *CSI: Crime Scene Investigation,* is a phenomenon that even chief investigator Gil Grissom couldn't explain. Returning to Yogi Berra's sport for an analogy, Zuiker's success is like that of a college freshman accidentally wandering into a major league baseball game and pitching a no-hitter in his first appearance. It just doesn't happen. It can't happen. But it did happen for Anthony Zuiker, and he took the fork that got him there.

Anthony Zuiker was born on August 17, 1968, in Blue Island, Illinois, near Chicago. His mother and father divorced when Anthony was just six months old. His mother, Diana, then moved to Las Vegas, where she became a cigarette girl at the Riviera Hotel under the code name "Linda Winston" during the twilight of the mob '70s. She remarried, and her second husband, David Orfin, became Anthony's stepfather. "My parents were really great," Anthony says. "They both worked Vegas hours, which was pretty much one P.M. to eleven P.M. So I would come home from school, and [be there] from five to eleven P.M., which was a lot of time alone and was actually the beginning of my being a creator. I was an avid sports lover, and I would sit in my room for hours inventing sports board games using dice. It wasn't like we were this close-knit family that did picnics and stuff together. My stepfather wasn't that way. He was a reserved man who worked very hard. My mother would guide me, but for the most part she let me do my thing. I'd bring her a bunch of ridiculous ideas, and she would say, 'That's great honey, that's great,' and I would be happy, and go away. But because of the abnormal hours of the hotel industry, she couldn't be overly involved in my life the way I would like to be involved in my child's life when he gets to be that age. But what she couldn't provide in terms of time, she continued to compensate with support and love, and still does to this day."

Creating stories and games as a child gave Anthony the imagination to come up with *CSI*, a TV series about crime scene investigators, which became the hottest new drama of the 2000–01 season, and, ultimately, launched his career. But it was a particular fork in the road that led Zuiker from one kind of forensics to another. "Here's the big irony," he recalls. "When I was in tenth grade at Chaparral High School, I took the elective 'Forensics' because I thought it was like *Quincy*. I thought the subject matter dealt with dead bodies. I quickly found out that forensics was not medicine, but actually speech. I arrive to the first day of class, and my instructor informs me that I'm going to have to recite poetry and prose and do dramatic interpretation. I was terrified, but I stuck it out. I was the worst speaker in the world, but forensics helped me become a better speaker, and, the funny thing is, fast forward twenty years, and now I'm doing a forensics show." (*Laughs.*)

Early on, though, it was *speech* forensics, not criminal forensics, that made Zuiker a hot property, and he was recruited by and attended several colleges that sought out his talents to boost their chances in competitions. "I went to five universities," Anthony says. "I had competed in forensics at Chaparral High School. I won two state championships and went to nationals my junior year in the dramatic interpretation category (with *The Elephant Man*). My freshman year of college I attended the University of Laverne, in Laverne, California, on a full forensics scholarship. Then I was recruited by and received a scholarship to Mount San Antonio College in Walnut, California, and another to Cal Poly Pomona [California State Polytechnic University, Pomona]. From there I was recruited to go to Arizona State University. I went there for a year and took third place in the nation in prose interpretation. I also got to the speech semifinals with my *German Cockroach* expository. Competition on the collegiate level was brutal. You're on a plane every other day. You are constantly missing class. Holding down a part-time job was never an option. Money was scarce, so I found myself literally starving in Arizona. After competing in nationals, I then went to UNLV for another year and a half, and received two degrees, one in communication and the other in philosophy. I graduated with distinction and thought it was then time to start my life."

Before his forensics irony could manifest itself into a hit TV show, however, Zuiker first had to survive his "wilderness" years, which began with a venture into the world of stocks and bonds. "I went to work for a friend of mine as a wire operator at Dean Witter," he recalls. "A wire operator sits by the teletype and enters stock and bond tickets to and from the New York Stock Exchange. [That] was before brokers had online access computers. So I did that for a couple of years, and then went to Merrill Lynch as a stockbroker for about a year. I loved the 'gambling' aspect of the stock exchange. It was really exciting and fast paced. The problem was that I didn't really believe in selling intangibles. My heart just wasn't in it. I found myself at age twenty-four changing direction and getting back to what excited me: creating. I was even designing billboards for sex shops. (*Laughs.*) I walked into this sex shop and said, 'OK, I'll make you a deal. You either give me five hundred dollars cash, or five hundred dollars credit, but I've got a billboard idea that can't lose.' My mock-up portrayed three blow-up dolls all lined up in a row, and a caption that read: 'Picking up airheads just got easier' (*laughs*).' The owner belted out a huge laugh, opened us his cash register, and paid the five hundred dollars. It was creating. It was writing. And I got paid. In addition to creating billboards, I started writing business letters for hotel executives at two hundred dollars a pop. I did that for six to eight months and decided that I needed something steadier. Now I had always wanted to work for Steve Wynn, the modern-day pioneer of Las Vegas. Mr. Wynn, who previously owned the Mirage Hotel, is a visionary, and I decided that I would take any job I could get and work my way up in that hotel, because Mr. Wynn's the kind of visionary who can recognize people with talent. So I'm thinking to myself, 'This is my last hurrah. Either I'll make it in this company, or I'm screwed, because, frankly, I'm out of options.' So I bit the bullet and took a job as a tram operator at the Mirage. It would prove to be the single best job of my life. Where else can you meet four hundred people from around the world, every four minutes? I remember my first week, this Japanese couple walks up to me, and I ask them, 'Where are you from?' And they tell me in Japanese. So I then ask them, 'How do you say, "My name is Anthony," in Japanese?' And they tell me. Next thing I know, I've written this thing called the *International*

Phonetic Language Booklet. It's got phrases like, 'Welcome to the Mirage,' 'How are you?' and other phrases in twenty different languages. Then Steve Wynn's mother, Zelma, was on the tram one night, and overheard me speaking Korean to some guests, so she pulls me aside and says, 'How did you know how to speak their language?' I pulled out my literary creation and said, 'I made up this booklet for the tram because I want to communicate better with guests, and move up in your son's company.' (*Laughs.*) Word spread throughout the hotel like wildfire, and next thing I know, I'm writing booklets for security, for the front desk, the bellman, etc. The bellmen start making money hand over fist because suddenly they know how to speak Japanese. (*Laughs.*) The whole place was up in arms. As a result, I got promoted from tram operator to bellman, and that's where the real problem started, because all the bellmen were jealous, asking each other, 'Who's this tram guy carrying bags?' I got cornered in the elevator by two bellmen who threatened me, saying, 'You're making a lot of trouble around here.' And I said, 'Why? Because you're making nothing but cash?' They had no reply. (*Laughs.*) So after about six months of that, I said to myself, 'This is a dead-end tip job, it's time to make a move.'"

Zuiker's writing skills had put him on the road to becoming a hotel executive, but it was actually an earlier work, not the language booklets, that presented him with his first big break in show business. "I got a call from a childhood buddy's Hollywood agent who says, 'You wrote something in your high school forensics competition that had to do with a horse race, and your friend has been auditioning with it, and getting jobs from it. I was wondering, do you have the entire screenplay, or can you write a screenplay?' Luckily, this phone call came at a transitional period in my life. My boss, the supervisor in advertising, hated me. Making my decision to roll the dice and write a screenplay was a no-brainer. I then walked three miles from the Mirage to Maryland Parkway. I went into a bookstore and bought three books by Syd Field on how to write screenplays. I wrote *The Runner,* my first screenplay, in six weeks. After all that work, the agent read it, and wasn't interested, so all I had was one hundred seventeen pages of paper held together with two brads, and a boss who hates me. Now what? Then I got a phone call from a friend of a friend who knows a friend, who knows a director of several low-budget movies. I fly out with my screenplay to meet the director and ask him to take a look at it. He gives me the 'Kid, you're wasting your time' speech, and I get back on the airplane dejected. Once again, I was at a dead end and out of options until the phone rang the next day. After that, my life would never be the same again. The director *did* read my script, and he told me it was brilliant. He says, 'I'm going to offer you thirty-five thousand dollars.' And I'm like, 'Where do I sign?' I went back to the Mirage and told my boss, 'I just sold my screenplay, and I'm outta here in twenty-four hours.'"

Longworth: In which language did you say that?

ZUIKER: A lot of languages. So I tell my wife-to-be, Jennifer, that I'm going to Hollywood, and she says, "Well, you're sure not leaving me here!" So she quits her job, and we go to Hollywood not knowing a soul. We lived in the Hollywood Towers, and I go into production with Ron Moler, who owns Aspect Ration, a trailer house. *The Runner* was to be his directorial debut. Meanwhile, the script gets passed around town and creates a buzz. Suddenly I go from not knowing anyone to being represented by Industry Entertainment; CAA; and Barnes, Morris, Klein & Yorn. So even though Ron was in preproduction, it didn't look like the money would come together. Then, a big studio offered a lot of money to buy the project. Unfortunately, they wouldn't make the film with Ron directing, and Ron wouldn't step down. So instead of making a big-budget movie, we made *The Runner* as an independent, low-budget movie. And even with the cast of Joe Mantegna, Courtney Cox, and John Goodman, it still went straight to Blockbuster Video's "Guaranteed or It's Free" section.

Zuiker's first studio job "netted" nothing but frustration. "I did a rewrite of a screenplay called, *The Harlem Globetrotters*, which is probably the best piece of work I've ever done, and my biggest disappointment that it didn't get made," he recalls.

Although the *Globetrotters* project was shelved, it did catch the eye of Bruckheimer Television, which wooed Zuiker to develop *CSI*, the story of crime scene investigators and how they solve unusual crimes in and around Las Vegas. But even with Bruckheimer's clout as a major filmmaker, *CSI* would be rejected by two networks before eventually finding a home at CBS. Bruckheimer recalls the pitch. "We were at ABC, Fox, and CBS. And CBS bought it right there in the room. It was all done over a two-day period. To me it was a slam-dunk to do it. I don't get it, but they [networks] have their own criteria for what they think is going to work on television. I can't jump into their minds. Certain networks look for things that are already on TV, to try and duplicate it. But I always look for things that you *don't* see on TV. That's how we approach our features and how we approach everything else."

Les Moonves, CEO of CBS, also admits that *CSI* was not a slam-dunk. In fact, according to *Entertainment Weekly, CSI* was "the last script purchased by

'The Eye' for the 2000–2001 season. It was the last pilot shot, and the last show added to the schedule" (March 30, 2001). Still, the show made it to air, producing unexpected results. On October 6, 2000, *CSI* premiered to an audience of 17.3 million (source: Nielsen Media Research), making it the highest-rated new drama of the season and surpassing *The West Wing*'s premiere the previous fall by more than one-half million viewers (*Entertainment Weekly*, November 10, 2000). In fact, the series was so successful that its distributor began taking bids for long-term syndication deals before *CSI* had completed its first season.

There was initial criticism from those in the police community, and, according to Chad Graham (*The Hollywood Reporter*, January 23, 2001) "even some forensic specialists weighed in." John Houde, a veteran of twenty years as a forensic scientist, said *CSI* was "make-believe entertainment." Houde charged that "the show has as much to do with criminalistics as *Baywatch* has to do with being a lifeguard." But Houde was also in the minority, because audiences and critics alike praised Zuiker's innovative drama. *TV Guide* said of the new crime series, "little did TV bosses know that the biggest new stars of 2000 would be maggots, decomposing pigs, and torn fingernail fragments" (December 16, 2000). Matt Roush revisited the show in January of 2001, saying, "*CSI* has improved steadily . . . the crimes are mystifying and the criminalists are fun to watch in their competitive zeal." *Entertainment Weekly*'s Mike Flaherty penned a cover story in which he lauded the innovative series as, "Proactive, but not salacious, violence-based, but not violent, visually stunning and disturbingly graphic, *CSI* is the perfect show for the new younger demo-hungry, but still geezer-centric CBS. It's *Welcome Home*, and *Holy Crap* rolled into one hip, Nielsen-dominating package" (March 30, 2001). *CSI* was also listed in *Entertainment Weekly*'s "Best & Worst" issue, with the magazine calling it, "an old fashioned mystery series, with a canny combination of high tech gadgetry, and a hard boiled tone that's been missing from TV since the marvelous 1980's flop *Crime Story* . . . the fact that this new show is actually popular makes its artistic gloss all the more bright."

Anthony Zuiker's future is bright, as well. In addition to co-producing *CSI*, he is at work on a film script with director Tony Scott (*Top Gun*) and Fox 2000 about the Hell's Angels. He also enjoys spending time with his soulmate, Jennifer, and their son, Dawson.

I spoke with Anthony on many occasions, both by telephone and at his office in Santa Clarita. Our first conversation took place just after he had read a copy of *TV Creators*, volume one. "Awesome," he said of the book about other producers, "I'm all over this!" In fact, Zuiker seemed genuinely surprised at his being included in this second volume, proving that even a confident risk taker sometimes just doesn't know his own strength. Says Jerry Bruckheimer, "You always look for a writer with a unique voice. That's what writing is about, and that's what television and features is about, is somebody who understands theme, character, plot, and story. For Anthony, that comes very easy."

CSI is a huge hit, and Zuiker's innovations in the series have changed the way that we look at crime dramas. In a sense, he brought us all to a new way of enjoying television, to a new "fork in the road," as it were, and we took it without hesitation.

Longworth: Does anybody ever call you "Tony"?

ZUIKER: Not if they expect to live. (*Laughs.*) My mother does. She says, "You're 'Tony' to me, you're not Anthony, and I don't care what kind of business you're in, it's 'Tony.'" (*Both laugh.*) So I say, "OK, Mom, you're the boss." She's cool.

Longworth: I know that you created a lot of board games when you were younger. Did you ever try to sell one of them to Milton Bradley or some other big company?

ZUIKER: Yes. Since the age of fourteen I have invented three hundred and seventy-five different sports board games. I had a small trademark company called *Make the Pros.* It became a huge hit with all my Vegas friends, and I called Mattel and talked to a representative there, like nine times. I drove down to their annual shareholder meeting and had coffee with him, and he said he'd see what he could do. He never called me again, and that was the end of it.

Longworth: Everything you create seems to have something to do with the roll of the dice.

ZUIKER: Absolutely.

Longworth: Tell me what TV shows you enjoyed growing up.

ZUIKER: I loved *Three's Company, CHiPs,* and *The Honeymooners.*

Longworth: That was a set up question because I thought you were going to say that you really liked *Quincy.*

ZUIKER: I did, but it wasn't one of my favorite shows.

Longworth: So then, you didn't want to be a medical examiner or a CSI?

ZUIKER: No.

Longworth: Among your earlier jobs was that of letter writer. Since this is a book about writers, tell me about that experience.

ZUIKER: I love to write copy. I love to write letters. It was a challenge to see if I could write a letter that would be persuasive enough to get exactly what I was asking for.

Longworth: Well, no offense, but if I'm the CEO of a hotel, and a twenty-three-year-old guy walks in and says, "I can write really good letters," why would I even give you the time of day?

ZUIKER: Because you'd be surprised how many people cannot write letters. And if they threw me out of their office, what do I care? Because, guess what? I wrote five different letters for five different hotels, and I wasn't thrown out. I wrote letters for one hundred to two hundred dollars apiece, which was like a million dollars to me back then. You see, a lot of times, secretaries don't know how to communicate what their bosses want to say. So I'd say to the presidents of these hotels, "If you ever need me to come in and write a letter in twenty-four hours, I can do it." And I'd give them a couple of sample letters, and shake their hand, and I'd leave. I even wrote a love letter for a barber so he could get his girlfriend back. And it worked. (*Both laugh.*)

Longworth: You once had to put your "speech" forensics skills to work by pitching a big film star. Tell me about it.

ZUIKER: I was called in to meet with Leonardo DiCaprio and pitch him an article he liked called *Hood Fellows.* The way writers get jobs on a project like this is to come up with a complete take on the movie, and then pitch it. The hard part was this was one of my first pitches, and I'm pitching one of the biggest stars in America. It was between me, Scott Frank [*Out of Sight,*] and another writer. Scott had been up for an Oscar the year before, so there we were, the tram guy up against an A-list writer. (*Both laugh.*) So I'm nervous and jacked up at the same time. I put on my big mafia sunglasses, and went for it. I say to Leonardo, "Let me tell you a story." And I'm cussing and acting, doing the dialogue, switching characters just like in speech competition. (*Laughs.*) This guy [DiCaprio] is rolling, crying, laughing his ass off. And when I was done, he gave me a big hug and said, "You know what? You got the job."

Longworth: How did you hook up with Jerry Bruckheimer?

ZUIKER: Jonathan Littman, who runs Bruckheimer Television, sees a copy of *The Harlem Globetrotters* script. He called and said, "I read *The Globetrotters* and I cried my eyes out. Could you come in and talk about television?" So I said, "Sure." Now about a month before that, my wife is watching this [cable] TV show on forensics. I thought to myself, "This is so interesting. This is an uncharted world." So I go in to meet with Littman, and he says, "What do you want to do for TV?" and I said, "I gotta be totally honest. I've got to do something about forensics. It's totally insane. Nobody's ever done it. I've watched these *FBI Files* shows. I can't stop watching them. I tell you, there's a series there." He says, "Fine. Let's call the head of criminalistics in Vegas and see if you can ride along and learn anything, and see if there really is a series here." There's only one problem: the pitching season ends in August, which meant after six weeks of research, I wouldn't be able to go into the networks until late October. I knew the research was crucial, so I took the risk. I met with a lieutenant and requested the bloodiest, goriest, hairiest shift. Fuck day shift. I want these guys eating lobster bisque at four in the morning. I want to show Vegas, thirty million people every thirty days, where anything can happen; it's a transient town. Give me the blood and guts. My wish was granted, and the next thing I know, I'm on the graveyard shift with these guys, driving in CSI Tahoes. They've got guns, they're on "walkies." They're all smooth-looking kids. They're all intelligent. And when you walk into these crime scenes, the crime has already occurred. The next thing you know they're processing evidence and telling me what happened verbatim. And I'm like, "Whoa! How do you *know* this shit?" They say, "Well, there's blood spatter here, hair follicle here, blah blah blah blah blah." Things took an especially interesting turn one night while I was on the job taking notes, and we get a sexual assalt call. Apparently, one girl had picked up another girl at a bar. They go back to a hotel, walk into the room, and there's three guys waiting for the girl who got picked up. They block the door and rape her. Fortunately, the police immediately catch the three guys. The victim is in protective custody, but they can't find the chick who lured her there. So here I am rolling up to the crime scene, and a CSI says, "Hit your knees and look for semen. Comb the carpet." (*Laughs.*) So here I am, a screenwriter looking for semen. I'm on my knees crawling around. I lift the bed skirt, and out of nowhere, a hand comes out and scratches my face. I'm screaming, "There's someone under the bed!" They lift the bed up, handcuff her, and that's where I got the idea to have Holly shot at the end of the pilot. (*Both laugh.*) So after all my research, I'm finally ready for my big pitch at ABC. I'm all fired up, I give them my pitch, and they pass.

Longworth: And you said, "But I was on my knees looking for semen!"

ZUIKER: (*Laughs.*) Yeah. "But I was looking for semen, man! That's got to count for something!" But they passed. I fly out a week later, and moments before I walk into CBS, Jonathan Littman says, "We've got some bad news again, Anthony. NBC and Fox don't want to see you, it's too late. CBS is our only chance." Well, I need a whole *room* full of people when I pitch. But when I walked into the room, it's just Nina Tassler [CBS], Jonathan, and me. Since it is really difficult for me to pitch to only one executive, and I was sure we didn't have a chance, (the other networks had passed), I simply closed my eyes and pitched very slowly. Miraculously, when I was finished, Nina says, "Great, I want to buy this. Start right away." I couldn't believe it. I was in shock.

Longworth: But for that brief period before CBS signed on, what was it like having three networks pass on your show?

ZUIKER: I gotta tell you, it was like, "What am I going to do?" All those weeks I was pissed because I knew I had something good here, and I knew there was a chance nobody would buy it because I was too late.

Longworth: If the real-life CSIs taught you how to write about dead people, who and what taught you how to write drama?

ZUIKER: The books taught me the format.

Longworth: But I've read those books. If you don't have talent, those books can't help you.

ZUIKER: No, you're right. Where does the talent come from? I don't know. I hopefully have the unique ability to listen to my characters talk, and then I translate what they say, and I can understand the situations that they're in. And, working with Ann Donohue and Carol Mendelsohn, who are far better writers than me, keeps me honing my craft. My contribution is I feel that I have a gift for dialogue. I don't know where it comes from, but, hopefully it keeps coming. But in the beginning I was more worried about format because those books tell you that if you don't have the proper format, or, "If you use three brads instead of two, it shows you're an amateur." Or if you use colorful cover pages "You won't get your foot in the door." I was more worried about looking like an amateur than what was on the page because I *knew* I could write it.

Longworth: The expenditures on the pilot for *The Fugitive* are legendary now. They spent about six million. What was the story on *CSI?* Did you have carte blanche on your pilot?

ZUIKER: No, I mean we were such huge underdogs. *Survivor* broke the mold for us. CBS started going for a younger demographic, and they wanted something edgy and cool. And *Run Lola, Run* had just opened theatrically. We loved the way they told three different stories, we loved its style. We were determined to write an edgy show that did re-creations and re-enactments. And we went for it. But these things don't get green-lit unless you have the right people pumping it up. I was told by Nina, "You should meet Billy Petersen because he's been trying to do pilots with us for seven years. He might be perfect for this." So he and I met at the Beverly Wilshire and had coffee. I pitched him, and we sat there for four hours. We were so loud, we almost got arrested. And we became brothers ever since then. He came on board, and he helped develop his character and helped develop the pilot. And so I had Billy Petersen attached, which helped because Les Moonves loves Billy Petersen.

Longworth: But I notice that Petersen had a producer credit from the get-go. What is his role in that respect?

ZUIKER: He's involved with the scripts. He's involved in the tone of the show. He's very hands-on, and he's a brilliant guy.

Longworth: OK, so to use a sports analogy, William Petersen is your franchise player, but how important is it for you to put the right team together, meaning other actors, writers, etc.?

ZUIKER: Billy is our star, as is Marg Helgenberger. I am in a backseat position, a learning mode on this show. I am not the typical creator that calls the shots. Carol Mendelson is the showrunner, she's our boss. Ann Donohue is also an executive producer and our most senior writer. I'm a co-executive producer because I created the series, and I was able to convince Billy Petersen to get involved. And now I'm working alongside the two executive producers and helping the show maintain its hit status.

Longworth: What is your level of input each week?

ZUIKER: I have input on everything. Stories, rewrites, casting, editing, and post. I'm consulted with decisions, but ultimately I don't have the final decision; I haven't earned that right yet. And hopefully in a couple of years I'll have a show of my own and I'll be able to do that. I'm more than happy to be in a learning position right now. What people don't understand is that when you write the first television script of your life and it becomes the highest-rated drama in the country and up for Golden Globes, it doesn't mean that you're calling all the shots. You have to find your position and work as a team, because it's such a team effort from top to bottom. I know David Kelley and Chris Carter and those guys write their own episodes and call the shots, but those guys have earned the right to do that. They've been in the business ten, fifteen, twenty years. I've been in the business a year.

Longworth: It's refreshing that you have that attitude, but, at the same time, if I asked you to go to the moon tomorrow to develop a series, you'd probably say, "OK, I'll leave in an hour." I mean, it seems to me that you have a history of and an ability for doing pretty much whatever you set your mind to.

ZUIKER: Yeah, I'm not a dumb guy. But I'm not an egomaniac who comes in with his first show and tries to take over and fight over how the vision has to be his way or no way. That's not the way TV works. The show is successful for a reason, because we all respect each other's vision. We realize that it's not all just my vision, that there's a collective vision for the show. We all pitch in.

Longworth: I know you've been asked this question repeatedly, but were you surprised at how well *CSI* did right out of the chute? What makes the show so engaging to audiences?

ZUIKER: I gotta be honest. I am not surprised, but I'm encouraged that, once you try and break the mold and write something different, America's not going to chastize you for it. And I think what makes it so engaging is the fact that it's an uncharted world. I'm thirty-two years old, and I thought that cops did fingerprints. I had no idea that CSIs are the ones who analyze blood. When you can show America a whole new crime-solving world that they've never seen before, combined with a good cast and good story lines, hopefully, you're going to have a hit show on your hands. And I think that's what we've done. The level of writing of the women who work here, and what they've done with episodes about bombs and about arson, I mean, the level of intricacy in the writing is second to none. It's really brilliant.

Longworth: And how many writers do you have?

ZUIKER: We have six writers.

Longworth: And how many are women?

ZUIKER: Three women. We have Carol, Ann, and Liz Devine.

Longworth: I don't mean to sound sexist, but most girls I knew growing up didn't like dissecting frogs, much less cutting open dead bodies. Most women don't even like to bait a hook. Yet the demographics on *CSI* show that women love it. Why is that?

ZUIKER: I think because we handle gore in a responsible, forensic way. We don't show gore for the sake of showing gore. We learned in the pilot that we had to tone down the gore in the opening scene or else the audience would change channels, because they might have thought the whole show would be this gory.

Longworth: There are people who say, for example, *Law & Order* is a "man's show." It's an adult show. And yet, *CSI* pulls in all demographics with equal loyalty.

ZUIKER: Well, I think crime solving doesn't have to be geared specifically to men or women. I think re-creations and re-enactments are interesting to both sexes. And I think kick-ass visuals, actually showing the micro, instead of the macro, is fascinating. It's not every day you're able to see what a hair follicle looks like at the four hundredth power. And when you can bring that to America, that's interesting. It's interesting to a six-year-old girl or boy as well as to an eighty-year-old man or woman.

Longworth: Also, a lot of us are closet gamblers, so does the Vegas locale play into the appeal of the show?

ZUIKER: Well, luckily I'm from Vegas, and I know Vegas. And the smart thing to do in television is to choose a venue where the audience has some sort of association. I believe almost everybody has been to Las Vegas. What I attempted to do in the pilot and setup for the series is to show America that Las Vegas has elements that are just like anyplace else; that it's not only about the strip and gambling, but there's a whole other world as well. And that's the key to our success. Because if you just do a show where somebody ends up dead in a hotel room, and somebody jumps off a building because they were gambling too much, and it's all Vegas, Vegas, Vegas, it'll just get old. I also want to show you the things you've never seen on TV or in Vegas, like the two blackjack tables in a gas station that are a mile outside of town where you can buy corn nuts and play twenty-one. (*Both laugh.*) That's a place you never see.

Longworth: But could *CSI* have worked in any city? What if Tassler had said, "I love the idea, but can you make it Cleveland?" Would it have become the hit show that it has?

ZUIKER: I don't think so. I mean, let's pick three other cities that are popular: New York, Los Angeles, Chicago. It's hard to work the graveyard aspect in those cities because they shut down at a certain time. But Vegas is twenty-four hours. It attracts a lot of people, just like New York and Los Angeles, but I think the venue is much more exciting. You know, the pulse of the town goes with the pulse of the tone of this show.

Longworth: One of your producers, Sam Strangis, was quoted in *TV Guide* as saying that *CSI* is shot like a feature film. How so? And why?

ZUIKER: Well, Jerry Bruckheimer has a philosophy that he wants to shoot "minimovies" for television, and when we hired Danny Cannon to direct the pilot, Danny and Jerry were really in cahoots in terms of how the tone should look, the coloring. Jerry has a philosophy that people watch television by pressing the channel button over and over and over again, and he wants to go to *CSI* and go, "Whoa! What show is that?" I think a lot of television shows are shot in a very conventional television-type way, and we've done things in terms of color, lighting, in terms of cast shadowing, and grains of texture to really make it look like a feature, and give people something extra in their living room.

Longworth: You once said in an interview that with *CSI* you were sending a message to criminals.

ZUIKER: Absolutely.

Longworth: Well, are you attempting to do what Adam Walsh has done with *America's Most Wanted?* How much of a role can your show play in terms of helping society?

ZUIKER: I think we send a message to America, and I think we send a message to criminals, that there are people out there who can solve almost any crime using incredibly sophisticated methods. Hopefully, our show could make a criminal [think] twice.

Longworth: And *CSI* may be significant for another reason. Following the O.J. Simpson trial, people began to have a negative view of CSIs and medical examiners. Are you getting feedback from those professionals thanking you for portraying them in a positive way?

ZUIKER: Yeah, I've got a very strong relationship with the lab director at the [Las Vegas] Metropolitan Police Department and strong relationships with Daniel Holstein and Yolanda McLary, which the series is loosely based on . . . and in terms of CSIs, they're over the moon. I've been invited to conferences all over the country to speak. The CSIs have gone out of their way to thank us for putting them on the map. I think the detectives in Las Vegas are a little bent out of shape because they feel that we're taking away their thunder. And my attitude is, "tough." (*Both laugh.*) They've had detective shows for forty years; let's give these nerdy forensic scientists their due.

Longworth: Dr. Marcella Fierro, the Virginia chief medical examiner who is believed to have inspired Patricia Cornwell's Kay Scarpetta character, once told me that her only problem with *Quincy* was that it was unrealistic for him to have free rein outside of his jurisdiction. On your show, though, you really strive for realism.

ZUIKER: We have the best insurance policy a show can have: Liz Devine, a former veteran CSI from the Los Angeles County Sheriff's Office. She was recruited by the show to insure its authenticity. She was so impressed by the tone and the realism of the show, she opted to make a career change by leaving her criminalistics career to work full-time on *CSI*. In fact, episode fifteen, titled, "Too Tough to Die," was written by Liz and loosely based on her experience on a case when she was in the field.

Longworth: It seems to me that the series is getting better as it goes on, and perhaps that's as it should be. Or maybe it just took me time to get invested in it. Is that to be expected—where a show takes a certain amount of time to hit stride with an audience?

ZUIKER: As the audience is adapting to watch the show, we're adapting as writers. The show keeps growing every day and every week, and when you compare the latest episode to the pilot, the latest one is just so much more mature and lucid. But that's the evolving process. Every week we want to constantly challenge ourselves and push the envelope, and keep ourselves interested. Hopefully, we'll write a hundred episodes of something that we're really proud of.

Longworth: Dick Wolf and John Wells talked with me about character-driven dramas versus story-driven dramas. In fact, John thought that *Law & Order* would be on longer than *ER* because *ER* is character driven, whereas *Law & Order*, being story driven, will never run out of ideas. Where does *CSI* fall in that spectrum?

ZUIKER: I think we're more story driven than character driven at this point. We know right now that people really love the process, when we let the visual take over to see how you "string a room" or watch how the process of DNA works. I think the nature of the show works because it involves deconstructing a crime in a way that audiences have never seen before. There are still hundreds of stories to tell, so hopefully our audience's appetite for story-driven episodes versus character-driven ones will sustain. We keep developing our great characters to enhance the story—but we are probably about 60 percent story-driven and 40 percent character-driven.

Longworth: One of my favorite shows is the original *Perry Mason*. But it seems that we've evolved to a point where the old-fashioned mystery, including *Murder, She Wrote* or *Diagnosis Murder*, is not the "in" thing in Hollywood anymore. Can *CSI* change that trend back to where the old-fashioned mystery *is* a respectable drama?

ZUIKER: When I pitched *CSI* to CBS, I hoped we could give the audience crime-solving fun for an hour, along with flawed yet compelling characters. If the evolution of the show brings us back to the old-fashioned way of mystery, great, but that's not something that we're striving for. We're just trying to write kick-ass shows that are different and cool, and stay ahead of everybody else.

Longworth: What kinds of things do you and your wife Jennifer like to do?

ZUIKER: We like to go to nice restaurants, watch movies, and spend time with our son, Dawson.

Longworth: What about TV shows? What do you like to watch, other than *CSI?*

ZUIKER: We watch *The Sopranos* religiously. I actually just started watching it, and I think it's an unbelievably brilliant show. I think David Chase is a god. We also love *Behind the Music* and *E! True Hollywood Story.*

Longworth: When we spoke a couple of weeks ago, you said that what was really weird for you was dealing with the "transition between your old life and your new life." What exactly did you mean by that, and what have you learned as a result?

ZUIKER: The biggest difficulty is that the show is incredibly demanding and is a huge time commitment. Since *CSI,* I don't get to spend as much time as I'd like to with my family and friends. Also, I had to learn to deal with the fact that three and one-half years ago I was making eight dollars an hour, and now, well, I'm thankful for the money that I make, but it's hard, too. It's a lot of extra work, and people cannot believe that you can get depressed from that success. You're like, "Why is this happening to me?"

Longworth: Were you less depressed when you weren't dealing with success, such as when the *Globetrotters* script wasn't picked up?

ZUIKER: I love the work I've done on *CSI,* there's no question. But I wrote every word of *The Harlem Globetrotters* from my heart—I put everything I could into it. And I think that's an important movie for America and for African Americans. It's about a group of people who didn't get their due. And I would love to be able to bring that to the world. Unfortunately, the studio had a different vision of the movie than I did. If I could trade in the success of *CSI* for one more shot at that film, I'm not sure I wouldn't do that. I really think that was one of my best scripts.

Longworth: Do you want to do any more TV series? You said you and Jennifer have a five- to ten-year plan.

ZUIKER: I already have two or three ideas for other TV shows. I'm just jotting notes down right now.

Longworth: I bet that one of them is titled, *Property Room Clerk?*

ZUIKER: *(Laughs.)* I don't know.

Longworth: After all, you could take any idea and make it work.

ZUIKER: That's funny because that's what some big producer said. He said to remember that you can take nothing and make it something, and that's important.

Longworth: Still, you're putting in a lot of hours these days, and I can't help but think of how Grissom can look at a corpse and tell a lot about the deceased. If we found you dead, slumped over your desk tomorrow, what would your corpse reveal about you to the CSI?

ZUIKER: He'd probably say, "This guy's got a big smile on his face. And he's got all kinds of balls, and he went for it."

Longworth: And the CSI can tell all that from the smile on your dead face?

ZUIKER: Absolutely. It's funny . . . my wife gave me the best compliment. She said, "You're so much more confident than when I first met you, and it's really a turn-on." (*Both laugh.*)

Longworth: Do you have a copy of the little multilanguage booklet you wrote for the hotel?

ZUIKER: I might have one stashed away somewhere, but it's classic.

Longworth: Sure, because that booklet is your life story.

ZUIKER: Absolutely. And here's the motto, are you ready?

Longworth: Go ahead.

ZUIKER: The International Phonetic Language Booklet motto is, "Because there's no better way to respect a customer than to speak their language." (*Both laugh.*)

Longworth: Well, you're certainly speaking *everybody's* language now with *CSI*, don't you think?

ZUIKER: I think so. I hear people talk about it in restaurants and it's so cool.

Longworth: And you no longer have to be on your knees hunting for semen samples.

ZUIKER: I hope not. My goal is to be in business a very long time. The greatest thing about being a writer is thinking of a new scene, inventing a new character, or hearing a new song. Those private moments are the things that keep me going, and I wouldn't trade being a writer for the world.

5

GLENN GORDON CARON | Intrepid Explorer

Glenn Gordon Caron. COURTESY OF GLENN GORDON CARON.

TELEVISION CREDITS

1980–81	*Breaking Away* (ABC)
1982	*Remington Steele* (NBC)

1983–84	*Murder, She Wrote* (CBS)
1985–88	*Moonlighting* (ABC)
1999–2000	*Now and Again* (CBS)
2001	*When I Grow Up* (Fox)

MM MM MM

christopher Columbus traveled in a new and different direction from everyone else and did so at considerable risk. Cortez journeyed far to discover Mexico long before NAFTA made it profitable. Magellan did the unthinkable by proving the world was round when he became the first person to circumnavigate the globe. And Charles Lindbergh helped to make that globe just a little more personal.

History is replete with explorers. Men and women who thought outside of the box. Pioneers whose vision opened up new paths for us to follow and enjoy. One famous explorer said of his exploits, "I always think disaster is an inch away." That explorer is Glenn Gordon Caron, and, on many occasions, he has ventured into uncharted territory so that television could be a better place for us to settle in.

The funny thing, though, is that Caron does not look like an explorer. In fact, he does not even look like a television producer. Bruce Fretts said it best when he observed that Glenn "resembles a rumpled, suburban dentist more than a Hollywood producer" (*Entertainment Weekly*, November 26, 1999). Of course, looks can be deceiving. Depending upon what tabloid accounts you believe, Glenn is an egomaniac. He is tough on actors, has a bad temper, and is downright dictatorial. But even if those assessments are true, the fact is that the captain of any ship occasionally has to display such qualities, otherwise the crew cannot reach its destination. In any case, it is Fretts's description that most accurately hits the mark. Glenn is self-doubting, not self-absorbed. His humor is self-deprecating and intellectual, but never meanspirited. Given the choice, he prefers listening to others over talking about himself. Even when he is preoccupied with pressing matters, he is sensitive to the needs of those around him. In short, the totality of the man and the complexities of his nature allow him to create, innovate, explore, and lead.

Early on, Caron discovered that a detective drama disguised as a romantic comedy could succeed. In a master stroke that only Bob Vila could appreciate, he also discovered that you could break through the fourth wall without tearing down its foundation. He discovered how to incorporate three different genres into one series by injecting science fiction and comedy into a drama. And, in a more recent outing, he set sail for yet another destination, hoping to discover how to create a "dramedy" about the complexities of infidelity.

In nearly every television series in which he has been involved either as writer or creator, Glenn presents a common theme, namely that "we only want what we cannot have." Moreover, it is a theme that in some ways has followed his own career path, because at every juncture, and no matter how successful the project, Caron keeps exploring.

Although born in Brooklyn, New York, in 1954, Glenn grew up in Oceanside, an appropriate setting for one of television's most skilled navigators. His parents were of modest means, and his father sold sweaters to support Caron, his mother, and his older sister. There was no history of show business in his family, except in a somewhat protracted way that only Glenn could appreciate. "My sister's name is Leslie Caron, and my wife's name is Mary Martin," he explains. "It's a musical comedy family. What can I tell you?"

Not surprisingly, Glenn loved the comedy of *I Love Lucy* and spent a lot of time watching offbeat shows like *The Monkees* and *The Wild, Wild West.* In later years Cybill Shepherd would claim that she introduced Glenn to the art of writing comic banter by suggesting he watch old Howard Hawks films. But in truth, Caron had been exposed early in his childhood to such byplay. "I watched *I Spy* a couple of years after its first run, and I was quite taken with that," Caron says. "I thought that was really neat. I remember the banter between those two guys [Bill Cosby and Robert Culp]. I also remember seeing *Butch Cassidy and the Sundance Kid,* and thinking, 'God, it's great when people talk that way.' I think there may be some of that when you look at Maddie and David [in *Moonlighting*] and even Theo and Michael [in *Now and Again*] . . . there is a kind of music to that banter that is very specific." On that note, Glenn began to dream of one day making films with such "musical" dialogue. Toward that goal he applied to Boston University's School of Communications. "I thought, communication? That's sort of like filmmaking. And my dad sent them a check and it bounced. So I had to find another school in a hurry."

Caron was accepted at Geneseo, a college in the State University of New York system, where the tuition was only four hundred and forty dollars per semester. He then snagged a scholarship to Hofstra University. "There was a film teacher there named Walter James Miller, and he ran a film-writing course. He was the first person to actually say to me, 'Hey, you're pretty good. You have a talent for this.'"

Miller was right, but it would be a while before Caron would have a forum in which to display that talent. "I got out of college and had absolutely nothing, so I promptly went to work for a gas station," Caron recalls. "I worked the graveyard shift, which began at midnight. My wife was a couple of years behind me in school, and she still has a letter that I wrote to her during that period. I changed jobs, and in my letter I told her that I had finally broken into 'show business.' I announced that I had gotten a job as the assistant manager of a movie theater. (*Laughs.*) In the meantime, I was beginning to write scripts. I had no idea what to do with them, or how to get them to anybody, but I was writing film scripts."

The writing paid off. Just two years out of college, one of his scripts landed Caron an opportunity to write a pilot for NBC. That led to a short stint on *Taxi* and several more writing assignments, including the TV version of *Breaking Away*. Although *Breaking Away* lasted only six episodes, ABC was impressed enough with Caron's scripts to let him try his hand at creating. His first two attempts, *Concrete Beat*, about a newspaper columnist, and *Long Time Gone*, about a private eye and his son, both appeared as a Movie of the Week, but neither were launched into a series. Then Caron was given one last shot by ABC. With pressure mounting to develop a two-hour TV movie that could then make it onto the network's weekly schedule, Glenn-the-explorer set sail and discovered the world of Maddie Hayes and David Addison. His creation was *Moonlighting*, which starred Cybill Shepherd as a former model who owns a private-investigative agency, and the then-unknown Bruce Willis, who portrayed the head dick. The show premiered as a spring replacement in 1985 and was promoted as a comedy. It was also one of the first prime-time series to be co-owned by ABC during the fin-syn (financial syndication) era, and it was one of the most expensive shows to produce, costing a whopping 1.2 million dollars per week. But *Moonlighting* was on a fast track to cancellation until audiences made a discovery of their own during summer reruns: the show was great fun.

Despite its signature comic banter between the two stars, *Moonlighting* in its second season was reclassified by the Television Academy as a drama, resulting in sixteen Emmy nominations that year. But while on-screen chemistry abounded, there was mounting bad blood behind the scenes. In her book *Cybill Disobedience*, Shepherd indicates that she was the third wheel in a two-wheeled boys' club that was run by Caron and Willis. She also claims that

Glenn resented her for getting pregnant during production, which led to rumors that Caron was a sexist. *Moonlighting* co-star Allyce Beasley, however, defended her boss, saying, "I didn't feel Glenn is sexist. I don't think he was unfair" (*TV Guide*, January 14, 1989). Nevertheless, reports of heated arguments between star and producer escalated. Shepherd's assistant told *TV Guide*'s Louise Farr that one confrontation in particular was "like a volcanic eruption" and that Caron's treatment of Cybill at that meeting was "horrible, real demeaning." The feud became so well-publicized that Caron even wrote an episode in which Hollywood reporter Rona Barrett goes behind the scenes at the Blue Moon Detective Agency to investigate rumors of conflict between Maddie and David.

After four seasons, and with ABC not wanting to lose its star, Glenn chose to walk away from the fights and from the series that he had created and co-owned with the network. The show lasted only one more year. During Caron's tenure with the series, *Moonlighting* ranked as high as ninth in the ratings and developed a loyal audience. Robert Thompson (Syracuse University) writes in *Television's Second Golden Age* that critics were just as enthralled as viewers. *The Chicago Tribune*'s Steve Daley called it "The best written show on television.'" Other observers tagged the series as "risky," "Russian roulette TV," "an anomaly," and "something truly different in the medium." Thompson himself noted that *Moonlighting* took a traditional genre (the detective show) and transformed it, much as *Hill Street Blues* and *St. Elsewhere* had done for the cop show and the hospital show, respectively. According to Thompson, "Quality TV breaks rules."

After nearly a decade's absence from the small screen, Caron returned to break some more rules with his series *Now and Again* for CBS. This time, Glenn-the-explorer decided to interject science fiction into an offbeat drama with comic overtones. The premise is that, after a middle-aged husband and father is hit by a subway train, a covert government agency transplants his mind and spirit into the body of a young bionic man (Eric Close). This "new" man is reluctant about being used to fight terrorism and frustrated by his feelings for his "widow" (Margaret Colin), who no longer recognizes him as her husband. Caron told *Entertainment Weekly*'s Shauna Malone, "This show isn't exactly classified . . . it metamorphosizes every week" (September 10, 1999). He also told *TV Guide*, "I don't want the audience bored. So just when you think the story is going to zig, a lot of times it zags" (December 25, 1999). But audiences might have been confused by all that zagging. They might have been confused by the innovative premise or put off by a genre cocktail. Perhaps they were even confused by the title and by the male lead. After all, Ed Zwick and Marshall Herskovitz's *Once and Again* boasted a similar moniker, and its star Billy Campbell could pass for Eric Close's older brother. Some media analysts predicted Caron's show would be a hit with women, who could live vicariously through Margaret Colin's unexplained attraction to her younger male co-star. Given time, the series might have been a cross-gender cult classic. Matt Roush of *TV Guide* wrote of *Now and Again*, "The characters are developing wonderfully, and the show's heart is in the right place."

But good intentions do not count for much in television anymore. Gone are the days when a slow starter would be left alone in a good time slot to find its rhythm and its audience. CBS president Les Moonves, who had promised Caron a free hand with *Now and Again*, pulled the plug after only one season. "Glenn is one of the most innovative minds in the business," Moonves said. "It was probably one of the most difficult decisions we made at the end of last season because *Now and Again* was such an interesting show. It was faced with two problems. First, it was an extremely expensive show to produce, and, second, though its audience was very loyal, it didn't seem to be growing. And, unfortunately, we have to make those calls about which shows are looking brighter for the future. But talk about innovation. From *Moonlighting* to *Now and Again*, Glenn thinks like no one else. I think part of the problem was that, because Glenn is such an original, it was hard for him to get help from other people. Therefore, he almost had to write, produce, and direct everything himself, which is a terrible strain on someone and proved to be very difficult. But God knows what a great mind, though. Glenn is a great guy."

Following the demise of *Now and Again*, Caron began working on *When I Grow Up*, an offbeat "dramedy" headed for Fox. As with his previous discoveries, this project explores new territory via a mixture of genres. Caron told *The Hollywood Reporter*, "It's a romance and combines a lot of different genres—it's a comedy, it's a drama, and there's music" (January 17, 2001). Unfortunately, however, when the 2001 industry strikes were averted, Fox became less concerned with stockpiling programs and Glenn's new series was never aired, though seven episodes were produced.

Most pioneers and explorers are misunderstood, so it is not unusual that we cannot always appreciate a Caron series from the outset. But in retrospect, the treasures of his voyages have yielded a wealth of material from which viewers have continued to benefit.

In an episode of *Moonlighting*, Maddie flies into a tirade after having been fired by a client. As the ranting continues, David turns to a shocked observer and says, "She gets like this. Too much television." Perhaps, but as long as Glenn Gordon Caron is writing it, we can never get too much television.

I spoke with Glenn on many occasions, first during production of *Now and Again,* then again several times following the show's cancellation.

Longworth: What kind of television shows influenced you when you were growing up?

CARON: I was quite taken with *I Spy.* I thought that was really neat. The only reason I mention that is because I remember the banter between the two guys.

Longworth: Did that inspire you to want to write?

CARON: It was the furthest thing from my mind; I really wanted to be a film director. I don't think I understood that films were written or that television shows were written.

Longworth: They just happened.

CARON: Yeah. Actors acted them, directors sort of conducted them, but I wasn't aware that somebody actually wrote them.

Longworth: You thought the actors just showed up and talked?

CARON: Well, I wasn't a stupid kid, but yeah, it never occurred to me that someone sat down and wrote these things. I don't think I really became aware of writing until in my teens, having decided that I wanted to be a film-maker, a director, I realized I couldn't afford to go to film school. At that time, there were really only three in this country, and they were all pretty much inaccessible. I thought, "Well, there goes that. I'm just not going to be able to be any kind of a filmmaker." And someone said to me, "Why don't you *write* a film? That only costs about three bucks." I thought, you know, maybe that makes some sense. I wonder what those look like, film scripts? At the time the only film script that I could buy that was available in the stores was *Butch Cassidy and the Sundance Kid,* which had been published in paperback form and was written by William Goldman. And I literally took it home and studied it, and then taught myself to type, and began to write what I thought were movie scripts, based on this one very narrow example of what a movie script was. That was the first time that it ever occurred to me that writing was an option.

Longworth: So there was absolutely no show-business background in your family, or anyone who was a writer?

CARON: No. And the whole idea of suggesting you do that for a living was anathema to my mom.

Longworth: Why?

CARON: Well, I was the first one in my family to go through four years of college, and then to do that and go into something as flighty as show business is ridiculous! (*Both laugh.*) So it wasn't something you talked about.

Longworth: What led you to Geneseo?

CARON: To be perfectly honest with you—

Longworth: And don't tell me you wanted to get laid.

CARON: Well, Geneseo was very, very inexpensive. And, additionally, it was 70 percent female. (*Laughs.*)

Longworth: Were you a ladies' man in college?

CARON: Oh, gosh, I don't know about that. I certainly liked women. (*Both laugh.*) Having said that, I've been married twenty-one years. I've always liked being around women. But the main thing was they were very anxious to get some males in there to balance the scales.

Longworth: Let's veer off for a moment. Since you just told me that you love women, I want to make you angry for a moment.

CARON: OK.

Longworth: Some women in the industry dislike anyone who portrays females as victims or as totally dependent on men. *Remington Steele* stars a woman who can't let anyone know she owns her own agency. *Moonlighting* stars a woman who needs a man to front for her agency. And *Now and Again* stars a woman who is still struggling with being on her own because she's used to having a man take care of her. Is there a chauvinist thread that runs through shows on which you work?

CARON: Well, I'm probably not the one to ask. I certainly don't think my work is chauvinistic at all. What I'm attracted to are interesting stories about men and women. I was always aghast at Cybill's take on the show, which was that she was a victim. The truth was that David Addison knew no more about detective work than Maddie Hayes did, and didn't pretend to. And if you take a step back and say, "OK, who's the smart one and who's the mentally challenged one in this relationship?" Really, the smarter one was Maddie Hayes. So I was always sort of puzzled by that. It always seemed to me you really had to work like hell to make that charge about *Moonlighting*. In the case of *Now and Again*, the woman hasn't spent a lot of time working for a living of late. Her energy has gone into the household. It's probably not a very popular idea, but the fact remains that there's a considerable part of the population who lives their life that way. I don't think they are any more or less worthy of having stories told about them than anyone else. She then loses her husband. Now, I don't care if you're a man or a woman, the loss of a loved one is going to be, for a period of time, devastating. So I don't think it's a gender-specific tale.

Longworth: So you're not concerned about women being defined by the men they're with. You're saying it's not gender specific in terms of who relies on who?

CARON: One of the things about television is that you probably jam whatever political doctrine you have and make it fit that particular story. I look at *Now and Again* and say it's a story of a woman who suddenly discovers a younger man being attracted to her. And for the life of her, she can't understand why. I look at that and say, OK, I'm taking the normal sexual stereotype and turning it inside out. Normally it's the younger woman who is the object of desire. It's the man who is older. So it's not a chauvinistic tract; I see it as a very enlightened tract. I like to think of myself as a very enlightened person. Again, I *love* that there are men and women. (*Laughs.*) I'm serious. I may in fact *be* a chauvinist and not know it, but I'm not aware of it.

Longworth: What was your first big break in show business?

CARON: I'm in college and in 1975–76 it was the height of the recession. I had switched from communications to drama. After working at the gas station and the movie theater, I finally got a job in advertising that I did for about two and a half years. In the meantime, I had been writing film scripts. So someone that I had gone to school with went to work as the secretary at a very small production company in New York City and gave one of my scripts to a gentleman who worked there. That gentleman, Stu Sheslow, went on to work for Fred Silverman when Fred moved from ABC to NBC. (Stu brought Tony Danza to California to audition for *Taxi*.) He called me one day and said, "Fred Silverman has an idea for a pilot." And he told me the idea. I said, "That's the stupidist idea I've ever heard." And he said, "Well, we have a meeting about it on Friday at Universal." I said, "Universal on Park Avenue?" See, my whole frame of reference was Long Island, New York City, and upstate New York. That was everything I knew. He said, "No, Universal in California." And I say, "My God, how do you get there?" (*Both laugh.*) He said, "You *fly* here!" And I said, "Wow, who would pay for that?" He said, "Well, not us. Nobody knows who you are." So I really kind of forgot about it. I thought it was such an absurd idea that it sort of left my mind until I got home that night. I was living with my wife; we weren't married yet, but we were living together in Chelsea. And she said, "What happened at work today?" I said, "Stu called, he wants me to come to California." She said, "Well, why don't you do it?" And I said, "Well, how on earth will we ever pay for it?" She said, "We'll put it on a credit card, and we'll figure it out later." And I said, "Well, what about work?" I had this job, and I was making one hundred and forty dollars a week. And she said, "Just call in sick." And I said, "Well, that's a lie." You have no idea how naïve I was. So in the deep recesses of my badder self, I found a way to call in sick. So I went to Kennedy Airport and I got on this "building with wings." I'd never been on a big jet before. I couldn't believe this thing was in the air. I couldn't believe we were going to California. As a die-hard New Yorker, of course, I got off the plane, went to the curb, got in a taxi, and said, "Take me to NBC." (*Both laugh.*) And fifty-six dollars later, they took me to NBC. I had sixty in my pocket. Of course I was convinced that when we got to NBC the guard would say, "That's ridiculous, there's no meeting here." But indeed I got there and there *was* a meeting! And it was me, Stu Sheslow, a young executive named Brandon Tartikoff, another young executive named Dick Ebersol, Warren Littlefield, and a gentleman from Universal Television whose project this was going to be. The guy from Universal looked at me and said, "Where are you from?" And I said, "I'm from New York." And he said, "What have you done?" And I said, "Well, I haven't done anything." (*Both laugh.*) And basically the meeting was over. The whole thing lasted about thirty-five seconds. He said, "Gee, if you lived out here in California, maybe we'd let you go home and write a little story, and if we liked the story, maybe we'd let you write the script, but you live in New York!" Everybody got up and started to leave. And as they left, this horrible idea that I thought was so ridiculous started to percolate in my head. I said, "Listen if you let me do it, here's what I'd do." And then I didn't stop talking for an hour and a half. And when I was done they said, "You have a deal."

Longworth: How did you pull that off?

CARON: I think I had a tremendous amount of enthusiasm, and I think it was clear that there was a story. What they had wanted to do was, a story had come out the year before, *Heaven Can Wait,* and Fred Silverman wanted to do a show in which three people die and go to heaven. God tells them he can't really assess whether they've been good enough to come in to heaven, and says, "I'm going to send you back down to earth, probably around eight o'clock on Tuesdays." (*Laughs.*) "And you'll do three good deeds in an hour." I thought this was just a horrible idea, but somehow I got in that room, and, boy, did I get passionate about this idea. And I had a deal to write this pilot. So I went back to New York and resigned from my job in advertising. There is no bigger thrill than going into the boss's office and saying, "I'm sorry, I have to quit, I'm going to Hollywood." (*Both laugh.*) I rented a little office where Warren Littlefield still worked in this little production company in New York, and started to bang out this script, which I finished and gave to Universal. They liked it quite a bit. They gave it to a producer, who completely rewrote it, and they made it into a pilot. But that was really the beginning.

Longworth: What was the original title?

CARON: It was called *The God Squad*—that wasn't my title.

Longworth: And whatever happened to it?

CARON: Well, as I say it was rewritten and made into a pilot, and I remember calling NBC and saying, may I see it?" And they said, "Well, why would you want to see it?" (*Both laugh.*) And I said, "Well, I thought it would be educational. I thought I could learn something from it." They were completely nonplussed that somebody would want to see one of these things. But I went up to some guy's office and he showed me the tape, and I was very grateful. But it's very, very unusual for your first writing job to be writing a pilot. Normally people spend years writing episodes, and then get an opportunity to write a pilot. Because I started by writing a pilot, suddenly all these agents were calling me, saying, "I'd like to represent you." Ultimately I signed with an agent who was at ICM. And they said, "What television shows would you like to work on?" I said, "I'm not interested in television. I want to make movies." And they said, "That's great, but what television shows would you like to work on?" And I said, "I don't *watch* television." They said, "Go home, watch television."

Longworth: This is unbelievable. (*Laughs.*)

CARON: (*Continues.*) They say, "Call us up and tell us what shows you'd like to work on." So I went home and I watched televison, and that night *Taxi* premiered. It was a terrific piece of writing. So I thought, "Wow, television's gotten good." I called ICM and said, "I'd like to write for *Taxi*." And they said, "OK, we'll call you back tomorrow." Next day, they called back and said, "OK, you've got five *Taxi*s." This is unbelievable. This is like the Horn and Hardhart. You go in and say, "I'd like some pie," and they give you pie. This is so easy! (*Both laugh.*) They said, "The only thing is you have to move to California." And I said, "Oh, I hadn't planned on that." So, my wife and I got married, drove to California so I could write these five *Taxi* episodes. I showed up, and it was now the beginning of the second season, and Glen and Les Charles are running *Taxi*, and I had no idea what the process was. I'd go to these meetings and they'd say, "OK, we were thinking Louie would do this, blah blah blah," and I would go, "Oh no, Louie wouldn't do that." And they just looked at me like, "How on earth would you know what Louie would or wouldn't do? And by the way, should we remind you *we're* the guys who thought up Louie?" (*Both laugh.*) I had no idea what I was doing or saying, but I genuinely felt these things and said them, and didn't think them through. So my five *Taxi*s sort of became one *Taxi*. (*Both laugh.*) But I was in California, and I was a writer. Soon, Charles Joffe called me. He produced Woody Allen's movies, and had heard about me from Jim Brooks, who, upon hearing that it wasn't working out well [at *Taxi*] thought, "Let me tell a friend of mine about this guy who I think is talented. He just maybe needs to learn how to work on a television staff." (*Both laugh.*) Anyway, Charles Joffe was taking his first foray into television, and he called me and said, "We're doing a show that was created by this genius. Would you like to met him?" And I said, "I'd love to meet a genius." So I went over and met this guy named Steven Gordon, and he really *was* a genius. He was an extraordinary writer. And he was creating this show called, *Good Time Harry,* which was a vehicle for Ted Bessell. He asked me if I'd like to be part of the staff. The staff was myself, Steve, and a guy named Mickey Rose, who was Woody Allen's co-writer on many of the early movies. And it was sort of a half-hour version of *Sweet Smell of Success.* But it was very, very, very funny. We did six episodes. They put it on at 10:30 Saturday night. Again, this was for Fred Silverman, who was then at NBC. Steve was so upset that people hadn't embraced his show that he said, "I'll show you." So he went off and directed this movie called *Arthur,* which was a huge hit, and then he promptly passed away from a heart attack. He was one of the funniest people I've ever known.

Longworth: How old was he at the time, and how old were you?

CARON: He was about forty-six, and I was twenty-six. So it had an enormous impact on me. But the other thing that had a big impact on me was that I realized that I was spending a lot of time working very hard at something I really didn't want to do. I really didn't have a passionate interest in three-camera comedy. I wanted to be a filmmaker. And I kept putting that word out to anybody who would listen, that I wanted to do something closer to film rather than this sort of bastard medium, which combines theater and three cameras, and all that. And I'm not sure how the connection was made, but Sam Cohen, [who] was sort of the Mike Ovitz of his day, the most powerful agent at that time, called me on the phone and said Steve Tesich, who had just won the Academy Award for *Breaking Away,* was going to do a television version of [that film], and very much wanted me to be involved. I don't know what made them think of me, because there was certainly nothing in my background that suggested that I could have done it. I ended up doing the show *Breaking Away*, and it was a curious moment because I was suddenly being considered for a lot of interesting shows. These two guys that I never heard of named Steve Bochco and Mike Kozoll asked me to come in and watch a pilot that they had just done called *Hill Street Station*. At the end of the pilot I said, "Gee, I'm not really interested." And they said, "Why not?" And I told them, "I don't think *Hill Street* will last. (*Both laugh.*) I also told them they killed the wrong guy at the end. In the original pilot they killed Charlie Haid. They listened to me on the second thing, but, thankfully, not on the first. I went off and did *Breaking Away*, and it was a great experience for me. We only did six shows, and it was really what my idea of filmmaking was.

Longworth: Now, during this period of time you wrote for *Remington Steele*, right?

CARON: I did it because I very much wanted to work with Bob Butler, who is one of the people who created *Remington Steele*. Bob is a seminal figure in television. He's directed most of the important pilots that have been done in television over the last thirty-five years. He did the pilots for *Hill Street Blues* and *Moonlighting*. He did the pilot for *Batman*. He did the original pilot for *Star Trek*. I mean, Bob *is* the history of television, and I really wanted to work with him. Anyway, he had done the pilot for *Remington Steele* and was going to continue to be involved with the show. The genre bored the living daylights out of me, but I needed a job, so I went to work on *Steele*. I wrote nine episodes and had a lot of involvement with them, which I look back on with some affection because I was also friends with Pierce Brosnan, who I'm still quite fond of. But I couldn't wait to get out of the genre. I truly hated the detective genre.

Longworth: So how did all this take you to *Moonlighting*?

CARON: Well, remember I had done these six shows on *Breaking Away*, which were on ABC, and the guys at ABC were really impressed with them. And they said, "We'd like to go into business with you. We'd like to create a company to go in the series business." And they made a deal with me. They said, "We'd like you to do three, two-hour movies of the week, with the intention of one of these movies becoming a series. These would actually be called backdoor pilots." At the same time, Kozoll and Bochco called me again. (*Laughs.*) *Hill Street Blues* had lasted a whole year, and they said, "Come on and do this with us." And I really was torn. I didn't know whether to go do that with Steven, or form this company of my own. I ended up going in business with ABC, and I did two, two-hour pilots. The first was *Concrete Beat*, about a journalist, and the other was called *Long Time Gone*. Neither became series. Each one cost about two million dollars to make. And I remember having spent four million dollars of ABC's money, and they said, "OK, that's it. This time you're going to do what *we* tell you to do." And I said, "What do you mean?" And they said, "Let's do a boy-girl detective show." And I said, "What do you mean?" And they said, "Oh, you know, like *Hart to Hart, Remington Steele*." And I said, "Oh, you've got the wrong guy. Wow, do I hate that stuff." And they said, "We don't care, that's what we're doing . . . and we're going to get you one of those girls like Cheryl Ladd." (*Both laugh.*) "You'll find a guy and it'll be great. And you can do whatever you want with it." That's what they said as they sort of walked out of the room, "You can do what you want with it," and that's all I heard. And I sort of clung to that, and *Moonlighting* was very much my reaction to, "OK, you've said 'You can do whatever you want to it.'" It was my way of staying awake.

Longworth: Did you even care if the series made it or not at that point?

CARON: Sure, you create something, and you get unbelievably invested in it. Of course you want it to make it. But we did a pilot and six episodes. And I remember around the fourth episode, a really nice man at ABC named Gus Lucas, who was the vice president there, was sort of a fan and was very supportive, called and said, "Listen, Glenn, the show is like number sixty-seven or something, and I just want you to know I really like it, but I don't think it's ever going to go any higher." And I said, "Yeah, I really like it, but I don't think it's going any higher either." It was really only during the summer when the shows were in re-run that it really began to pick up speed. When it first came on the air, I think it probably puzzled people. They didn't quite know what to make of it, or how they felt about it. When we were filming the pilot, I vividly remember the first scene where we introduced Bruce and Cybill comes to the Blue Moon Detective Agency to close it down. Bruce is in his office playing basketball. He's put a wastebasket up above the door, and as his secretary Ms. DePesto comes in to announce Cybill, she opens the door, and the wastebasket falls down and lands on top of Ms. DePesto, actually covers her head. And everyone continues to play as if nothing happened. Bruce walks over to the door and says, "Gee, Ms. DePesto, you look a little pale today." She starts to introduce Maddie to David, but of course you can't hear what she's saying 'cause there's a wastebasket over her head. We put the scene on its feet and I still remember Bob Butler and Jay Daniel turned to me and said, "You don't really want to do this, do you?" (*Both laugh.*) And I said, "Yeah, of course, it's funny." And they said, "Yeah, but what about the suspension of disbelief?" See, back then, on the whole, people took these detective shows fairly seriously, which I, again, always thought was absurd. Based on some bizarre notion that (a) these people really existed, and that (b) they were actually in some kind of jeopardy.

Longworth: Well, Joe Mannix was shot every week, but never seriously wounded.

CARON: Of course! Because he had to show up next week. (*Laughs.*)

Longworth: He had a good work ethic.

CARON: That had no truck with me. But that was constantly a concern. I remember once, it was like the fourth or fifth episode, I was really sort of vexed by the fact that they had to get into a locked or guarded place. And I just didn't care, 'cause you *knew* they were going to get in there, or else you wouldn't have a scene.

Longworth: Well, you talked about suspension of disbelief in a drama, and that leads me to categorization. At first, the Academy didn't know how to classify *Moonlighting*. Do you consciously seek to color outside the lines and produce these kinds of programs that people just can't quite get a handle on?

CARON: Yeah, I don't know what the answer to that is, other than that's what I sort of do. I think our lives are complicated. There are some days when our lives are a drama, and there are other days when our lives are a comedy. There are even days when our lives are a musical, you know? So the most interesting storytelling has to accomplish some element of that stuff. I just don't like to feel limited.

Longworth: And you were one of the first to really play around with breaking the fourth wall in a detective drama, which you also did with *Now and Again*.

CARON: Yeah, but I was a little uncomfortable with that, because frankly, Burns and Allen, and Hope and Crosby were breaking the fourth wall back in the '30s and '40s, so it didn't strike me as being a revolutionary concept. I think the thing that's hard is to do it and be truly funny. Essentially since *Moonlighting*, it's become fairly ubiquitous on television now, and my disappointment is that most of the time it's not terribly effective. It isn't done with any real sense of purpose or humor and that tends to dull the effect, and that's sort of a shame. You almost feel like somebody ought to put a quota on this stuff so we don't abuse it. But I certainly was not the first; I don't feel like I was any kind of originator in that area.

Longworth: But in terms of a drama—

CARON: But like I say, I didn't know I was doing a drama. (*Laughs.*) I was trying to stay awake. My feeling was, "Oh boy, I can use this and do these things I've always wanted to do." Bruce used to comically call it film college. He'd say, "What are we doing this week?" And I'd say, "Oh, let's do a boxing show, or let's do a musical, or let's do Shakespeare." I mean, I would try any way I could to keep everybody interested. "Hey, Orson Welles is going to do a show this week! Eva Marie Saint is going to do a show this week! Stanley Donen is going to come direct an eight-minute dance number!" You know? To me, I really do work on this egomaniacal thesis of "if *I'm* interested, then chances are, *you'll* be interested."

Longworth: You've said on many occasions that your main objective was not to let viewers get bored. Are *you* easily bored?

CARON: No, but I think a lot of television is pretty doggone boring. So much of series television has become a creative template, which then replicates the template. But invariably, if you look at a history of the shows that are most enduring, most interesting, the template was very malleable and constantly changed. I mean, you look at *Seinfeld* in year one and *Seinfeld* in year seven, and they never stopped exploring. Part of our job is to entertain, and I don't know how you entertain without startling. You can't come out and tell the same story every week, and you can't tell them the same way, I don't think.

Longworth: Bob Thompson said *Moonlighting* "exceeded the industrial limitations of network television."

CARON: Oh, I've read that.

Longworth: Bob considers you to be a genius and a perfectionist, and—

CARON: Well, I had him completely fooled didn't I? (*Laughter.*)

Longworth: I'll call him and set him straight. But compliments aside, I was particularly taken with his phrasing, that you "exceeded the industrial limitations of network television," obviously referring to the fact that one week you're doing a boxing story and in the next, a rip-off of Shakespeare. Did your approach cause problems in terms of—

CARON: (*Interrupts with loud laughter.*) Yes! Tremendous problems!

Longworth: OK, then let's talk about the problems. One camp says it was because of Cybill Shepherd, the other says it was you going over time and over budget. Can we get the definitive answer out on the table? What drove you out of *Moonlighting*?

CARON: It was not an economic decision. It wasn't about that. Although I absolutely had an economic hypothesis about network television at that moment, and it's constantly evolving. The truth was, what I presented to the network they couldn't argue with. And it was very simply that there was sort of a threshold number that everybody made hour television shows for. And I said, "What if we spent more, and made better shows? Perhaps (a) more people would watch them, and (b) you could show them more often." And everybody sort of looked at me. I said, "Well, wait a second. If I could make you a show that is genuinely funny, and funny enough to make people say, 'I want to see that again the next time they show it,' and you could consistently get a thirty or thirty-five share with it, then maybe that 'in-stone' number of what an hour television series is supposed to cost could be made more flexible." And that was part of my theory.

Longworth: And their reaction?

CARON: Nobody would admit to it, because if they admitted to it, it would have changed the rules for everybody. But privately they bought it. They would publicly say, "Well, he's being irresponsible, he's doing musicals and he's doing period pieces, he's doing this and he's doing that," but nobody ever shut me down. And they always aired the show. (*Laughs.*) So people were talking out of both sides of their mouths. I used to joke that they would come in and yell and scream and threaten, and then as they would get to the door, they'd turn and go, "But don't change anything." (*Laughs.*)

Longworth: So when did *that* change?

CARON: Well, that never did change. What happened was, the show was very tough on both of the actors. They were in virtually every frame. Very, very demanding. And I don't think Cybill ever really gave any thought to that before she signed on, and it took its greatest toll on her very quickly. She would say things to me like, "Why does this have to be so hard? Why does it *have* to be so good? Why do we have to do this? Why can't we just do that? like other shows?" She wasn't really interested in putting in that kind of effort, and, indeed, a lot of the shows were shot over the backs of doubles and stand-ins, and then we'd go back in later and get her close-ups, because she stopped showing up. She would get sick. She would be unhappy.

Longworth: In Susan Faludi's book *Backlash,* she says that you and Bruce launched a campaign to curb Cybill's aggressive personality. Now, did you two guys really sit down in the lunchroom one day and say, "Hey, let's launch a campaign to curb Cybill's aggressive personality?" Where does that come from?

CARON: I think that came from Cybill's imagination. And I didn't think she had a particularly aggressive personality. I just think she didn't have a particularly strong work ethic, to be perfectly honest. I don't recall us ever clashing, but I now read the reconstructed history, which seems to indicate that we clashed over philosophical issues, and all these other lofty things, like what was funny and what wasn't funny. I remember virtually no conversations about content. The conversations I remember were at five or six o'clock in the morning, and the first call I'd get would be from Cybill's assistant asking, "When can Cybill leave? How long must she stay today?"

Longworth: So what was the chicken and the egg here?

CARON: There was no chicken and no egg. There *was* a period during which records were kept by the company that insured the show, monitoring the time between when Cybill was called to the set and when she would actually arrive. And when the Writers Guild strike hit (in '87 or '88), and no one was making television shows, we all sat down and presented the data to Cybill and her attorneys and said, "Look, here's what it costs us." And needless to say, that was a pretty volatile meeting.

Longworth: Did that have a direct effect on the number and quality of shows *Moonlighting* delivered? Were shows delivered late?

CARON: We were never good about delivering and I never did twenty-two in a year, and that was from the beginning. Late? Some of that was my fault. Some of that, as I say, was if you can't get the star to show up, you can't shoot the show. That's why I had claymation Cybills. I mean, any way I could get the show done, I would challenge her. We would be on a location that we paid a lot of money for, and she would say, "I'm going home." And I would say, "You can't go home. We have to finish the location." And she'd say, "I'm going home," and I'd say, "No, you're not, we're finishing the location." And she'd go, "OK," and instead of going home at 5:30 at night, she'd go home at 8:30 at night, which is pretty difficult for series television. A lot of people go home at 2:30 in the morning. But then the next day, she'd call in sick.

Longworth: What was the straw that broke the camel's back in terms of your leaving?

CARON: The straw that broke the camel's back was the meeting that I was alluding to, at which time ABC told us to present Cybill with an ultimatum, and say, "Look, we're going to pick up the show for next year, but we'll only pick you up on an episode-by-episode basis, so that if you don't behave, we have the right not to continue with you." And she basically said, "Oh really? Well, we'll see if you really do that." And she began to play a game of chicken with the network. Ultimately the network picked Cybill up for twenty-two episodes. The problem with that was that I had been the guy who was sent in to deliver the ultimatum for the network, and it was very hard when they picked her up to say to me, "Now you continue to run the show, and she'll listen to you." (*Laughs.*) She didn't *have* to listen to me. So that was my undoing. I said, "Wait a minute, you've put me in a terrible position here." They said, "Well, you can still write." I said, "Well, I love writing, but I prefer to do it for people that are happy to do the work. I can't continue if I can't run the show." And they basically said she looks better in pumps than I do. (*Laughs.*) And I was gone.

Longworth: So you went into a deal with ABC because they had essentially given you free rein, but then the free rein ceased.

CARON: It would be tough for me to complain about what happened with *Moonlighting.* Sure, the ending was awful, but no one could have foreseen that. I mean, frankly, again, I think Cybill went into it not understanding how hard it was going to be. I had never done it before, so I couldn't even begin to articulate to her how hard it was going to be. ABC, I don't think in their wildest dreams, anticipated the size or the magnitude or the popularity of the show. No network had *made* a show itself before. *Moonlighting* was unusual in that it wasn't made by a studio. It was me and ABC. ABC was the bank. And they couldn't have anticipated that. And none of us anticipated what happened with Bruce. There was no way to see it ahead of time, so we were all sort of making it up as we went along, and we didn't have the support systems that—say, had we made the show for a studio—would have been in place.

Longworth: What's the better system for nurturing the creative process? Working for a studio, or for a network?

CARON: Oh, I don't know. When I was at MTM, Grant Tinker was already gone and I worked on *Remington Steele,* which they had the least invested in, in terms of the culture of MTM. I had been offered *Hill Street* and I turned it down, and at one point I was approached about *St. Elsewhere,* and I turned it down. All I needed was a job. So I ended up on *Remington Steele.* MTM was a great place to work, but sure, you always prefer to be your own boss, at least I do, and that was the experience I had on *Moonlighting.* Of course for me, Grant Tinker was something of a God. I mean, put the work experience aside for a moment, and I grew up watching those shows—*The Mary Tyler Moore Show* was the first or arguably second intelligent sitcom that had been on television, perhaps after *The Dick Van Dyke Show.* I adored that ethos, and very much wanted to work at MTM, and revered what I perceived to be that whole culture. I will tell you that, while I was doing *Moonlighting,* I was working one Sunday and the phone rang and it was a reporter, I think from the *New York Post,* and he said, "Grant Tinker just did a press conference and he was highly critical of you." He wanted me to respond, and I said, "Oh well, gosh, I didn't hear what he said, I wouldn't know how *to* respond, and, more importantly, I don't know in what context he would have said it, so I really have to reserve judgment." While I'm saying this, my heart is sinking, 'cause this is one of my heroes. So the next day I put in a call to Grant—he was at NBC at the time. I was so hoping to get a call back where he would say, "Well that's nonsense, I never would have said those things." But instead one day my phone rang and it was Grant Tinker. And I said "Hi, Mr. Tinker we don't really know each other," and he said, "No, I know who you are." And I said, "This reporter called me and said you said these things, and I was certain he had taken them out of context." And there was this long silence (*laughs*) and he said, "Perhaps I regret saying those things, but I meant them." I was devastated, and what he was commenting on was a threat that he felt (and I know Steve Cannell felt, the other large independent producer at the time), that this alliance that I had made with ABC wherein the network essentially funded and owned the show was an unholy alliance, and one that threatened these companies that *they* had built, and that I was some sort of anti-Christ. (*Both laugh.*) Not only had I made that deal and gone into business with ABC, but I had actually created a hit show. And it was this *mammoth* hit.

Longworth: So you're the guy to blame for today's vertical integration and mega-mergers?

CARON: I don't think so. (*Laughs.*) But I am one of the first people to have experience with what that was like. And that's the other part of *Moonlighting* that nobody talks about, but that makes it rather conspicuous. That's the reason *Moonlighting* was never in syndication all these years; it was owned by a network and not by a studio.

Longworth: And it's only in the past decade that the ruling has been lifted to allow Networks to get back into the business of "fin syn."

CARON: Yes, because it's only now that the Justice Department has said you can be in both businesses. You can be a network, you can be a syndicator. Back then it was verboten.

Longworth: Coming away from *Moonlighting*, where you had problems with an actress who was 50 percent of the show, did that cause you to change the way you developed or cast future programs?

CARON: No. You can't do this for a living unless you're a cockeyed romantic. The whole sort of kismet that happens between an actor and a role is something that you hope to capture, and then you get the heck out of the way and let it happen. Having said that, the thing I *did* learn from *Moonlight-*

ing, though, [which] I did consciously incorporate in the structuring of *Now and Again*, is that I knew the idea of building an entire series around one person and then expecting that person to be in every scene was a destructive idea. There are two kinds of mysteries, an "open" mystery and a "closed" mystery. I always thought the more artful and interesting form of storytelling was the "closed" mystery where you're basically with the character. You learn what he learns, never cut away from him and see the bad guy twirling his mustache, and going, "That's him, that's why this is happening." *Moonlighting* was a "closed" mystery. The vast majority of television mystery shows use the "open" format.

Longworth: And why is that?

CARON: Well, *now* I know. (*Laughs.*) I had spent three and one-half years doing *Moonlighting*, a "closed" mystery, where the star was in every frame of the picture. In an "open" mystery, the first act can be about the bad guy. Then, you can cut to the secretary waiting for the detectives to come in. Then you cut to his sidekick out on the road, and it's much more production friendly.

Longworth: So, in a sense, you're saying that most producers do "open" mysteries because of constraints on time?

CARON: Well, what I'm saying is, intellectually, I'm much more challenged by the "closed" mystery. I prefer that. I think it's more artful. It's also harder to do. It's harder to write. It's harder to produce. It's very tough on the actors. So when I set about doing *Now and Again*, it wasn't an "open" or a "closed" mystery. But I purposely said, "I want to develop an ensemble as opposed to a star vehicle or a duet, because in my last experience in trying to do something where the same people are in every frame, it took a real toll. You know, even Bruce, who has an extraordinary work ethic, at certain points would come in and say, "My God, I'm exhausted." (*Laughs.*) I mean, it's brutal to try and make those air dates. So, to that extent, the *Moonlighting* experience had formed how I designed *Now and Again*. But again, I have a lot of compassion and empathy for Cybill, I mean, even at this point. My sense at the time was that she was not a terribly happy person, and I felt badly about that because I felt like, hey, we were doing great work, she was doing great work. There was every reason to be happy.

Longworth: If a show is your vision, your creation, and you're there every day, making corrections, and you're the best person to write it anyway, why do you even *need* to hire a writing staff?

CARON: It's a very good question. It's one that I often ask myself. I'm really of two minds about it. I mean, I rewrite everything that goes on in my show, OK? But the staff comes up with a lot of really original, wonderful ideas that I would never come up with on my own. They give me things to respond to. They respond to me. Sometimes they write things that are brilliant in and unto themselves, without any help from me whatsoever. I mean, it's a complicated process, and it isn't all *The Glenn Show.* Sometimes it's hard to quantify because it *seems* like, in terms of the writing, that it *is The Glenn Show,* and I feel sort of badly about that.

Longworth: In a typical week of production on a TV drama, how much time would you spend writing?

CARON: I would get up around 4:30 in the morning, hopefully be behind the typewriter by about 5:45. On a really good day, try and be done writing by eleven A.M. From eleven o'clock in the morning on, you're either editing the show that's about to go on the air, and by editing I mean all those sorts of post-production processes, editing, scoring. Thankfully I no longer do things like color correction. I've found people who are really good at that, who know what the show's supposed to look like. Except for the pilot, I don't even dub the shows. Other people do that, then I look at the dub and make changes. But the rest of your day is about that, plus being on the stage itself, and helping the director who's going to do the next show prepare, and that kind of stuff.

Longworth: What was your inspiration for *Now and Again?*

CARON: I'm a big believer in that, when your children are young, you lead them to culture. You say, "Oh, here's a book I love, can I read it to you? Here's a song I love, can I sing it to you? Here's a movie I really like, let's watch it together." And then your kids get to an age where they start leading *you* to culture. My middle child, who at the time we are talking about was around twelve, started to ask me to take her to the *Scream* movies. She started watching these shows on television like *Dawson's Creek,* and listening to music that was very specifically aimed at people her age, and she would start sharing this stuff with me. It occurred to me that once you became twenty-four, you passed into this netherworld of adulthood where you never experienced romance or ardor or passion again, based on the shows and the songs she had been seeing. That's the way the world works. (*Laughs.*) And I thought, "Wow, what a shame. Because when I was a kid, we used to go to the movies to *learn* how to be an adult, and that was no longer the case." And I started thinking, I wonder if you could do something where viewers would actually see middle-aged people having all these feelings. And then I thought, "What if I have a middle-aged person with someone younger?" And that sounded like the traditional model of the older guy and the younger girl, so I thought, "What if you turn that around, and it's the woman who's older and the man who's younger?" And somewhere in there, I thought about *Damn Yankees*, where this guy that's like fifty years old, and all he wants in life is to be a Washington Senator so he could beat the Yankees. The Devil grants his wish, and he turns into a strapping young man, only to discover that what he *really* wants is to be home with his wife. It all sort of came together in that jumble.

Longworth: So we go back to this theme of yours that, "We only want what we can't have." In fact, I recall one of the *Now and Again* episodes where Dennis tells Eric, "To keep you healthy, we must deprive you of the things that make life worth living." Even given the "Damn Yankees" scenario and everything you've told me, isn't that a bit fatalistic for a TV drama? Can't that frustrate audiences if you're not careful?

CARON: I don't know. (*Laughs.*) What I do is try and really only honestly please myself. My assumption is, if I'm really tickled, maybe they'll be tickled. But at least *somebody* will be tickled."

Longworth: If someone picked out an episode of *Moonlighting* and watched it, then watched an episode of *Now and Again,* but something went wrong on their VCR and they didn't see any credits, how would they know that Glenn Gordon Caron did those shows?

CARON: Well, I'd like to think that the dialogue was kind of erudite, and the story well told. And I think both shows are very much filled with heart and filled with ache. And I do think that's something that's unique.

Longworth: In an episode of *Now and Again,* Dennis [Haysbert], this imposing figure, who has ordered "hits" on people, all of a sudden breaks out into song, with a rendition of "Mister Rogers' Neighborhood," and I'm on the floor laughing. Let's talk about humor in drama, and humor versus jokes. What's the difference and how are you able to make them work?

CARON: To me, a joke is a very, sort of obvious and schematic, construction, whose sole purpose is to make people laugh. And it sort of exists completely separate and apart from the business of character. Humor is sort of a pure overlay of a kind of humanity and a general sort of a collision of optimism and pessimism in drama.

Longworth: And yet, in the example I cited, Dennis's humor might have seemed out of place for a drama.

CARON: But I don't think so, because as harsh as he can be, he's still capable of that kind of morbid humor.

Longworth: In *Moonlighting,* though, there *were* a lot of jokes, more deliberate humor.

CARON: I think that's true. *Moonlighting* took place in a very specific sort of TV universe. At the time, the three networks were sort of awash in detectives. They were ubiquitous, they were everywhere, which I always found hysterically funny. I used to joke that [in Los Angeles] I never passed a detective agency on the way home from work (*laughs*); to look at television, you would assume they're everywhere. (*Laughs.*)

Longworth: You never had a detective follow you?

CARON: Never. (*Laughs.*) Not ever!

Longworth: If you had been followed by a TV detective, which one would you have wanted to follow you?

CARON: Oh, no doubt, one of the ones I created. (*Both laugh.*) They're the most fun. What did you think I would have said? (*Laughs.*)

Longworth: Earlier you told me about your work schedule. Is writing a chore for you, is it just a job? Or is it still fun?

CARON: It's a little bit of both. I love doing it, and I love that I *can* do it. It's an extraordinary gift. And by the way, I really do believe it's a gift, something's that's given to you.

Longworth: You don't think it can be learned?

CARON: I don't know, I can only speak for myself. I know that I'm very lucky that somebody somewhere along the line touched me, and it really is a gift. Having said that, like anything that you *have* to do, there are days in which it is a chore, and a real grind. I mean, I have very specific memories of being in college and turning in term papers, and thinking, "Well, I'll never have to do this again." And then suddenly, every day you have a term paper due. And I'm thinking, "How did I get myself into *this?*" Directing is a very different thing. Directing is social, where you're working with a hundred people. But writing is solitary. Well, you know, because you're a writer. And in that sense, it can be very daunting at times.

Longworth: So do you want to direct more films, or develop more TV shows and do a film each year?

CARON: I'd like to do both. I've made four films. I'd love to do more television and more film. The world is different now. When I was doing *Moonlighting*, people did one or the other. It was very rare to go back and forth. Nowadays, people do both. So I'd like to take advantage of that change in the culture and be able to do both. A series is a wonderful thing and very different from making films, but I still love making films.

(Interview resumes several months later)

Longworth: *Now and Again* was not renewed by CBS. Any thought on the current trend toward networks not allowing shows time enough to find their audience?

CARON: Personally, I can tell you I was completely shocked. The possibility had always been there that we wouldn't be renewed, but I intellectually had never dealt with it, so I was truly stunned that we weren't on the schedule. It's funny, but I never thought of *Now and Again* as a niche show. I thought of it as a show, I think it's fair to call us a niche show if we were put on a heavily trafficked night and well promoted and we only attracted a niche audience. In truth, we were put on the least-trafficked night on CBS's schedule. We were given no lead in, very little promotion, and we continued to attract a core audience that fluctuated between eight and one-half, and eleven million people. So to me it was never a niche; it was clearly a show that if we were given a better opportunity, a better piece of real estate, would have done better. There's a lot of history to back that up. In truth it was the same time slot that *JAG* had been in, and done virtually the same numbers that we did. It was the same time slot as *Everybody Loves Raymond*, which, now, *JAG* and *Raymond* are the two flagship shows of the network. We won the Saturn Awards, and there was hope that we might get nominated for some Emmys. I think there's a lot of evidence that suggest the decision [to cancel] may have been made hastily.

Longworth: Do you think it had anything to do with the trend toward reality/game shows?

CARON: Yes, to the extent that, if you look at the way the company has recently reorganized itself. It's now run by Mel Karmazian, who comes out of radio, and I think has a very bottom-line mentality, which is not necessarily a bad thing. But I think there needs to be an understanding that dramatic television shows accrue value the way real estate does. *Survivor* is a terrifically successful show, but represents a different kind of investment; it's not a long-term investment. It doesn't have a tremendous amount of value down the road. The people who are in those corporate jobs are feeling more vulnerable because they need to generate a profit much, much faster. These people are much hungrier to see that their investments are earning a return. So I think there's a much quicker trigger finger. And the fastest way to do that is to put the least-expensive programming on and charge as much money as you can for it. That's just common sense. Historically, both narrative motion pictures and television shows actually *gain* value over time, but that's a hard concept to teach people. It's something you have to learn. People scoffed at Ted Turner for buying the MGM library, but nobody's laughing anymore. Suddenly there's a place for that library. You can sell them to cable, sell them on DVDs and cassettes and to satellite companies. And you can sell them over and over again. And they've already *been* manufactured, they've already been paid for. And that's something you learn. I think the culture at CBS in this moment is, "How do we squeeze this lemon harder, and get more juice out of it?" And one of the ways you get juice out of it, is long-term as well as short-term. So when you ask, why did *Now and Again* get canceled? I believe it has as much to do with that as anything else.

Longworth: So when you hear that your show has been canceled, do you immediately say, "OK, I've got five other ideas that I want to go work on."

CARON: (*Laughs.*) No. I immediately become morbidly depressed for about two weeks. And then slowly you say, "OK, I've got to pick myself up and dust myself off, and figure out if—I have to assume there is no future here—and figure out what I'm going to do next." I can only tell you that I was in a coma. The show got canceled and my wife and I went to Bermuda for our first vacation without the kids in fifteen years, and I was asleep for four days, and part of that was depression. The thought that these characters weren't going to live out their destiny, that I wasn't going to be able to finish what I started with these actors, that we weren't going to finish some of these stories, that this family we put together, this wonderful crew was going to be separated. I was devastated.

Longworth: Final question. Since the theme of your shows is usually about people wanting something or someone they can't have, what is it that *you* want, that you can't have?

CARON: Oh, I probably want that thing that we *all* want, and certainly most people in the arts want, which is immortality (*both laugh*), which is really what *Now and Again* is really about. It's really about resurrection, right? You're a writer, so you know that on some level it's all about leaving something behind. "Hey, I was here. I participated." So the thing we always want that we can't have is, "Can I do this forever? Can I live forever? Can I participate forever?"

Longworth: If you could be like the character you created in *Now and Again* and you could occupy someone else's body, whose body would you inhabit?

CARON: (*Laughs.*) That's a genuinely nutty question, Jim. I have absolutely no thought on that whatsoever. (*Laughs.*) You know what I'd really like to occupy, I'd like to occupy the mind of one of my children. If only to get some insight.

Longworth: To see things the way they see things?

CARON: Yeah, but I realize that's not really about occupying their body, but occupying their mind. (*Laughs.*) Gosh, I don't know, that sounds like a Barbara Walters question.

Longworth: Oh come on, at least I didn't ask you what kind of tree you'd want to be, like she did with Jimmy Carter.

CARON: Now *that* I have an answer for.

Longworth: Well, thanks for taking time to do this, and if you do happen to change bodies with anyone, be sure to give me a call.

CARON: Yeah, because that would be an extra chapter for the book, right?

Longworth: Right. Well, thanks Glenn. While I'm writing this chapter, I'll send you a copy of *TV Creators* volume one so you can see how volume two will be formatted.

CARON: Tell me when it's for sale, and I'll buy a copy. I'm a rich guy, let me buy one.

Longworth: Absolutely not, it will skew the book sales because my mom and my brother-in-law are the only people actually buying it.

CARON: So let me understand this. I get the first volume for free, but you're going to make me buy the one I'm in?

Longworth: Yes.

CARON: You're very strange, Jim. (*Both laugh.*)

6

DON BELLISARIO | Leatherneck optimist

Don Bellisario. COURTESY OF DON BELLISARIO.

TELEVISION CREDITS

1976–78	*Baa Baa Black Sheep* (NBC)
1979–80	*Battlestar Gallactica* (ABC)
1980–88	*Magnum P.I.* (CBS)

128

1982–83	*Tales of the Gold Monkey* (ABC)
1984–86	*Airwolf* (CBS)
1989–93	*Quantum Leap* (NBC)
1992	*Tequila and Bonetti* (NBC)
1995–96	*JAG* (NBC)
1997–	*JAG* (CBS)
2001–	*First Monday* (CBS)

MW   MW   MW

commenting on his musical ability, composer Hector Berloiz said, "The luck of talent is not enough; one must also have a talent for luck" (William A. Gordon, *The Quotable Writer*). Add to that *Time* magazine essayist Lance Morrow's theory that, "Genius may be defined as the ability to control luck," and you have a pretty good profile of Donald Bellisario. Although Don's display of talent has been consistent over the years, he is also a study in contrasts. As a former Marine, Bellisario has been exposed to plenty of coarse language, yet he abhors its use in film or television. He was an avid supporter of John McCain's 2000 presidential bid, but opposed the senator's crusade for government interference in television content. And, although a master storyteller, Don maintains that he never begins a script by writing a story.

Bellisario is the product of a bygone era when family values comprised the collective matrix that defined, then held together our nation, both in good times and in bad. He has also been masterful in adapting to and anticipating societal trends and tastes across several generations of TV viewers.

"My philosophy is always to entertain," Bellisario says. "I've been in Hollywood twenty-some years, but still have the same values and judgements as when I was a kid" (*New York Times News Service*, January 8, 2000).

CBS president Les Moonves describes Bellisario's ability to survive and succeed. "How many people do you know who have created three big hits on television? Not too many. And when you look at those shows, they're all three very, very different in tone, in style, and amazingly successful. Don is a natural leader. He is unbelievably charismatic. He surrounds himself with top-notch people. And Don is one of those guys who walks into a room and attracts attention. He really is a leader in every sense of the word. Plus, the buck stops with Don. He and I are the only ones who talk about his show. You know the number of notes I've given him in five years? Zero! Not one note about music, about editing, about anything. I just trust his taste and his ability so much that, instinctively, if he thinks it's going to work, [then] it's going to work."

Therein lies the true essence of Don Bellisario, a man who has been able to control his luck and harness his talent because of an eternal optimism about life in general and his career instincts in particular.

Donald Bellisario was born in 1935 to an Italian father and a Serbian mother. He and his brother grew up in Cokeburg, Pennsylvania, a small mining town southwest of Pittsburgh known for supplying raw material to the large steel mills. Don's family was one of the few in the area not employed in the mining industry. "My Dad was a famous athlete in the area," he recalls. "He graduated from Pitt in 1933, and he opened up this bar. He was a great man, big on community service. He would loan people money, put on fireworks shows for the town. Cokeburg was completely made up of Europeans, mainly right off the boat. And so, my generation was usually the first-generation Americans born here. There were Serbians, Italians, Croations, Russians, Poles. It was very stratified at the time. The town was owned by the Ellsworth family of Ellsworth Mining. The foremen were Germans, and the rest, the laborers, were all these different Europeans. Everybody else [but my father] was working at the mine, and that put me on the outside in some ways. It made me a bit of a loner. I had a lot of friends, but I loved to stay to myself. Now, I would never do this to *my* child, but my parents made me wear either shorts or knickers until I was in fourth grade. Everybody else in the school was wearing overalls. Some of those kids were coming to school barefoot."

Aside from the cultural diversity of his little community, Don's life was also shaped by the clash of world cultures. "You gotta understand I was a young boy during World War II," he says. "It started when I was five years old and ended when I was ten. And it was probably the most influential five years of my life. Unless you have lived through that, especially at my age, you have no idea. I watched everybody go to war. My dad's bar became the communications center for the town. I still have over five hundred postcards that were sent from all over the world during the war. I also saved all of the photographs of those who served. We lost four or five men, and that's a lot for a small town of twelve hundred people. I still remember the funerals and the bodies coming back. I remember the rationing, reading the papers, listening to the war news on the radio. I remember one Sunday we were getting ready to go to the movie, it was the only day my dad had off, and I remember my dad coming upstairs and saying, 'The Japs have bombed Pearl Harbor.' My father had this look of horror on his face and it scared the hell out of me, 'cause I thought it meant somebody was going to bomb *us*. And my dad said, 'What are we going to do?' And my mother said, 'We're going to go to the movies like we always do.' And I thought, 'Well, it can't be that bad if we're going to the movies.'"

His mother's optimism clearly had a profound influence on young Donald, who, despite being an "outsider," held the respect of his childhood friends, who even today remember his special talent. "When I see my friends now from back then, they say, 'You were always telling stories. We'd sit around and listen to your stories,'" Don recalls. "One old friend (a retired judge who was in the Marine Corps with me) said, 'It was always clear to us that you were somebody different and special. That you were going to be very successful.'"

But it was exposure to the stories of others that eventually led Don to writing his own. "I was a voracious reader as a kid. One of the first books I ever remember reading was Hemingway's *For Whom the Bell Tolls*. I also read *The Hardy Boys*." (*Laughs*.) "My Aunt Nell would always give me books for birthdays or Christmas, books by Richard Halabert. He wrote these incredible adventure stories about traveling to exotic parts of the world. At night, my mother would come into my room and say, 'Enough,' and shut out the lights, but I'd hide a flashlight under the cover so I could keep reading. The first time I remember writing was the letters home when I was in the Marines. My parents would write me back and say how interesting my letters were. I got out of the Marines, was married, had two kids, and was working my way through college toward a degree in engineering. Then I got interested in journalism. I was at a career day at Penn State, and there's a fellow sitting at the end of a table with a cigarette dangling from his lips, and his fedora pushed back on his head. I swear to God he had 'PRESS' stuck in the band of his hat." (*Laughs*.) "He was a reporter from some paper. And I thought, 'I can do that.' And that was the start of it. When I graduated (with a journalism degree), I had another child being born, so I took a job with a local paper. It's a wonderful thing to work on a newspaper because you get that gratification of putting the paper to bed and see it come out new every day. It was all done by four o'clock each day, and I'd go home, and that's when I started writing short stories. I would spend my nights sitting at this old Royal typewriter, and these stories started coming to me."

And the stories kept coming, first for the *Centre Daily Times*, then later as a copywriter for a small advertising agency in Lancaster. But Don was destined for television, and the ad business was to be his entre. "I was getting paid five hundred dollars per month, and they said they would give me a fifty dollar raise for every year I stayed with them," Don says. "I remember my mother saying to me, 'I think you ought to think about this.' (*Laughs.*) But I went with the *Foltz Wessinger Agency* and they paid me fourteen thousand dollars a year. That was 1965, and I had four kids by then. Within one year I was made creative director, and they were saying that twenty thousand dollars a year wasn't out of sight in a few years. And I thought, 'God, if I can make twenty thousand dollars a year for the rest of my life, I'm *there.*' Back then they were still doing TV commercials on slides, and I wanted to produce film spots. So they said, 'OK, if you can produce them for the same amount of money as before.' So I went over to WGAL TV and they gave me a 16mm hand-wind camera. I wrote this commercial, shot it, and edited it. It ended up winning an award, and that was when I first started making television. In 1968 I moved to Dallas to work for the *Bloom Agency* and stayed there about eight years. Then I was turning forty and I said, 'This is not what I want to do for the rest of my life.' While working on a commercial, one of the guys on the crew still had a script of a film he had just worked on [*They Shoot Horses, Don't They?*] I asked if I could borrow it, and that became my matrix for writing a script. So now I'm making seventy-five thousand dollars a year in advertising, but I decided to get out and move to California. My wife wouldn't go—she didn't want to expose the kids to the drug culture. We ended up getting a divorce. I went to work for *Paisley Productions* here in Los Angeles making half of what I was making in Dallas. The production slowed for a while, and so I sat up in the Hollywood hills and turned out two screenplays. Then one day at work this casting director sees one of my scripts on the desk and says she wants to take it home to read. Two days later she says her husband, who is a film director, wanted to introduce me to his agent."

Buoyed by the compliments on his script, *Five O'Clock Whistle,* a story about the coal mines set in the 1930s, Bellisario knew he had to pursue screenwriting. But alimony and child-support payments had nearly wiped him out financially. Still, that unflappable spirit of optimism prevailed, and Don set out once again to control his own luck. "I found a little house in North Hollywood for sixty-five thousand dollars. I thought, 'If I could just swing buying this house, something good has got to happen.' So I asked Tony Bushing, my boss at Paisley, if I could borrow thirty thousand dollars, and he loaned me the money. Then the realtor said, 'I have faith in you,' and she got the seller to give me a second mortgage. (*Laughs.*) Then *she* gave me the third, from her commission money! I had it all figured out. I had enough money to last six weeks . . . and there was no way I was going to lose this house. I thought, 'I've got to have something positive happen.'"

To the surprise of everyone but Don, something positive *did* happen. With the help of his new agent, he wormed his way onto the writing staff of Stephen Cannell's *Baa Baa Black Sheep* and became a producer shortly thereafter. Soon his outstanding work on *Black Sheep* was the buzz around Universal, and when the war drama was on hiatus, he picked up writing assignments on *Switch, Delvecchio,* and *Kojak.* That led to a turn as supervising producer on *Battlestar Gallactica* and a very short stay as executive producer on *Quincy.* "Jack [Klugman] starts telling me how to write on the first day I met him," Don recalls. "And I say, 'Look, Jack, if you're going to be the executive producer, and you have every right to be, then you don't need me.' And I'm thinking, 'I'm outta here.' So I went to the people at Universal and said, 'I'm in development.'" (*Laughs.*)

Bellisario's split with Klugman might have broken the spirit of a lesser man, but this was, after all, "lucky Don," the same man who had once charmed a real estate agent out of her commission. So, naturally, he turned the loss of employment into a life-changing opportunity by taking over a Glen Larson project starring Tom Selleck. The show was *Magnum P.I.* Supervising Producer Joel Rogosin told Tom Stempel, "The original pilot script by Glen Larson was a conventional detective show until Don infused it with the Magnum personality. It was all sort of tongue-in-cheek. It was a very difficult style to write in. Nobody but Don Bellisario could ever really write it very well. There were a couple of people who came marginally close, but not like him" (*Storytellers to the Nation*).

Magnum P.I. premiered in December of 1980 and ran for eight seasons on CBS, usually ending up in the top twenty-five and ranking as high as fourth in 1983. *Magnum* not only changed America's views about Vietnam veterans, but also established Bellisario as a hit-maker. Don tinkered with *Tales of the Gold Monkey* in 1982, but the Indiana Jones–type drama lasted only a single season. Then, during the fourth year of *Magnum* and following the success of the feature film *Blue Thunder,* Don created *Airwolf,* about a high-tech helicopter. The action series ran for three seasons on CBS.

By 1988 Bill Cosby had ushered in a new era of comedy, and the popular Cos himself helped to usher out *Magnum.* But Bellisario made sure that his *P.I.* went out on top. The series finale was watched by nearly half of the national television audience and garnered a thirty-two rating. Critics and fans alike were sorry to see *Magnum* go. Said Steve Sonsky of *The Miami Herald*, "*Magnum* has long been one of the most underrated series on television—exceedingly well-written, well-acted, clever, witty, and self-deprecating." *The San Diego Tribune*'s Grey Joseph wrote, "*Magnum P.I.* never lost its sense of humor, which makes it sad to say goodbye."

When all the goodbyes were said, Bellisario took another stab at a fantasy/action series by writing the pilot for *The Ultimate Adventure Company*, but such hour dramas were becoming too costly to make. In its place, Universal instead put Don's new, offbeat sci-fi show on the schedule. *Quantum Leap*, which ran from 1989 to 1993 on NBC, featured a time traveler who assumed the identities of different people, helping them to correct a mistake or other incident from history. Writing for *Viewers for Quality Television* in 1990, Cynthia Shannon said of *Quantum Leap*, "It is not limited by genre, time period, or tone. It has explored many elements of the human condition, from main streaming of mentally handicapped persons to women's liberation and sexual harassment, to the plight of the Native Americans, to the heart-wrenching plight of the wife of an MIA. But it doesn't always limit itself to social issues. It also spotlights personal dilemmas and relationships. The show does all this while still entertaining the audience with humor and poignancy" (Dorothy Collins Swanson, *The Story of Viewers for Quality Television*).

Quantum Leap remained popular throughout its run, but despite a lobbying effort from *VQT* to save the series and a ranking of eighteenth among all shows, NBC pulled the plug during the 1993 season.

With two bonafide hits to his credit (three if you count *Airwolf*, which is still in syndication), Bellisario could have retired to reminisce about his extraordinary talent, incredible luck, and eternal optimism. Instead, the sixty-year-old jarhead suited up for another tour of duty, this time returning to his military roots with *JAG*. "I realized, *Oh* my God, I'm not going to have a show on the air this year for the first time since 1980. So I went to my guest office and I thought, 'What the hell, I'm going to write what I want to write.' So I started to write about what was going on over in Bosnia with the no-fly zones. Women were also just being introduced into combat [at the time], so I wrote about a female pilot who is murdered and tossed off the ship. Then I had to figure out who was going to investigate this, and that's when I came up with *JAG*. JAG officers investigate, defend, prosecute, they cross the lines. So I'm thinking, 'Whoa! This is a franchise for television.'"

And so it was, but not at first. *JAG* started out on NBC in 1995 but was dropped after one season. Former NBC chief Don Ohlmeyer explained, "*JAG* was a terrific show, and Don did a terrific job with it. At the time *JAG* was on NBC, from a demographic standpoint, it just didn't fit with us. Critics like to [believe] there's something malevolent about demographic profiles of networks. There's nothing malevolent about it at all. *Caroline in the City* was a show that we [NBC] picked up and ran for five years, that CBS didn't think would work for them. They owned the show and we picked it up. There are some shows that could work anywhere, but there are other shows that have a chance of being successful on only one network and maybe not another. *Murder, She Wrote* would have never worked on Fox. That doesn't mean there's something wrong with Fox or with *Murder, She Wrote*. It just means that's the way the business is. The other point is, at the time we had *JAG*, we didn't necessarily have the patience that Les [Moonves] showed. It was not a reflection on Don's work. It was not a reflection on the quality of the show. It was not a reflection of anything other than demographically it didn't match up well with us [NBC]. It matched up better with CBS. And, secondly we didn't really have the patience to sit for two and a half years with the show."

Following cancellation by NBC, "Lucky" Don Bellisario then made a deal with CBS, where the series has risen steadily in the ratings ever since. CBS's Les Moonves recalls, "I thought, how stupid of NBC to drop *JAG*." (*Laughs*.) "First, if you saw the pattern on that show, you saw that it was growing. It was slowly growing, but it was not losing its audience. In addition, you saw the quality of the show, and I knew the quality of this guy, that given more chances this show was going to work. The show is going to be a hit. Now, we're always wrong more than we're right, but part of what you've got to bet on is who the guy is. Who is the showrunner? Who's the guy who's driving the train? And, as I've said, Don's been a true leader, and a true professional in every sense of the word."

Just as with *Quantum Leap*, Bellisario used *JAG* as a forum to address serious, relevant social issues. Bellisario told David Kronke, "A lot of people in this town view *JAG* as just a military show, a shoot-em-up. It's not. It's as well-written, directed, and performed as any show I've ever made, including *Quantum Leap*, which was a critical darling. We've tackled issues such as gays in the military, segregation issues, animal rights, all the issues that are popular among the liberals in Hollywood, and because it's a military show, they write it off" (*New York Times News Service*, January 8, 2000).

Somewhat prophetically, *TV Guide*'s Matt Roush noted, "This shipshape, mainstream paean to patriotism is likely to stay afloat no matter the competition" (September 5, 1998). Roush was proven right. Despite ABC's best effort to derail the competition with its mega-hit game show, *Who Wants to Be a Millionaire?*, *JAG* actually improved its performance among the key eighteen- to forty-nine-year-old audience. Media analyst Bill Croasdale told *Entertainment Weekly*'s Lynette Rice, "They're tuning into *Millionaire* and are then saying, 'Let's see what's on other channels,' and getting wrapped up in *JAG*'s storyline."

Once again Don Bellisario had gotten lucky with his talent. Instead of folding against the new millennium's biggest phenomena, he found a way to benefit by scoring with advertiser-friendly demographics. He hopes to keep those viewers on board for his new drama, *First Monday*, about the inner workings of the U.S. Supreme Court and the lives of its clerks and judges.

Don Bellisario is truly a gifted storyteller, whether for the small screen or during a private conversation. I was fascinated by his tale spinning and found his optimism to be contagious. We spoke at length in late spring of 2000.

Longworth: Thanks for doing this interview. I'm working on volume two now.

BELLISARIO: Why wasn't I in volume one? (*Both laugh.*)

Longworth: I wanted to tell you that my dad's favorite TV show was *Baa Baa Black Sheep.*

BELLISARIO: I was watching *The History Channel* and I caught *Baa Baa Black Sheep* with Bob Conrad and all my friends. And I called up W. K. Stratton and I said, "Now I know we're really getting old if we're on The History Channel." (*Both laugh.*)

Longworth: It seems like that show should be out on tape, or something should have been done to follow up.

BELLISARIO: I've always thought that those shows should have gone on. I mean, here we are, twenty years this fall since *Magnum* went on the air, and we have still not done a *Magnum* reunion show, which would be a *huge* hit.

Longworth: Then why haven't you done it?

BELLISARIO: Sometimes it has to do with the studio, or the star. Tom wasn't ready to do it, or wasn't willing to do it.

Longworth: But if he said to you tomorrow he was ready, would you do it?

BELLISARIO: I think now he would do it. There was a time he didn't want to do it because he had his feature career he was trying to get on track, and if he had gone back and done a *Magnum* reunion movie he figured people wouldn't think of him as a serious actor.

Longworth: How would you do a reunion without it being too sentimental?

BELLISARIO: I would contemporize it. It would take place today. I don't know until I write it. I never know what I'm going to do until I write it. (*Both laugh.*) Hell, sometimes I don't even know how the things are going to end until I'm five pages away from the ending; that's the way I work. I don't do stories. I have rarely in my career ever done a story. I was forced recently to write a story because I was shooting *JAG* down in Australia, and I had to get permission from the RAN, the Royal Australian Navy. We were going to use some of their facilities. And they said, "Well we have to see what you're doing." And I said, "I'll write you the story and send it out." So I hastily wrote a story and sent it down there about two months before I even did the script. But (*laughs*) that is the first time I've done a story since the first one I did to get into this business. And I haven't done one in between. (*Both laugh.*)

Longworth: So are you as surprised as anybody how your scripts turn out?

BELLISARIO: Yeah, always. Which makes it very interesting for me. Sometimes I'll sit down and I'll have no idea what I'm going to write or what I'm going to do. And I'm talking about creating a series. I don't have a clue as to what I'm going to do. And so I just start writing something. I could tell you how that happens on various shows that I have done. Sometimes I know how I want it to end, but I don't know how it starts or gets there. Usually I just start writing and I discover as I go along how the characters act, and then *they* do the story, I don't do the story. The characters do the story.

Longworth: A lot of people think *JAG* is just about the military. Comment on that prejudice.

BELLISARIO: Yeah, you're right about that. *JAG* is thought of, usually by people who have never seen it, as a jingoistic, military, action-adventure show. And nothing's really further from the truth. In *JAG* we have dealt with sexual harassment, we've dealt with bigotry, we've dealt with gays in the military. We have tackled issues that are not just the military, but are also issues in society as a whole. And the one thing I try to do with *JAG* that, I think, makes it different, I try to show the heroes as honorable men and women of integrity who are really trying to face the critical issues of the military today *with* honesty and integrity, and looking for the truth. I really like that, 'cause that's a very positive approach. Also, you know, when you're doing a show about the military you have Navy cooperation; well, *now* we do. We didn't when we first started the show, because they were terrified of it.

Longworth: Why?

BELLISARIO: For a couple of reasons. One, when I first wrote the pilot about six years ago, it was right after *Tailhook* so they were afraid of any kind of publicity. They were hunkered down in port. (*Laughs.*) They didn't want to go out. They didn't want to be in the press, they didn't want any kind of publicity. And, I was going to do a story about JAG lawyers. Well, *JAG* deals with all the trials and problems in the military. And all they could see was that this was going to be a show that was going to hang all the dirty laundry out.

Longworth: When did it turn the corner?

BELLISARIO: It turned the corner after I had done the show about two years. They realized that the show was really about positive people in the military and the military taking care of problems that arose—problems that arise in any large complex or organization.

Longworth: Except for the change in networks and the change in female leads, what would I have noticed as a viewer that was different between the shows you did without full cooperation and those with it?

BELLISARIO: Having cooperation means a cost savings for us. It enables us to go into their film bank and to get new footage that we had no access to before. All the footage that we had access to in the beginning I was taking out of feature films. And I was taking it from film libraries that the Navy had no control over. Now I have access to the Navy's library. I also have access to the Navy's facilities, and this is on a show-by-show basis. I'm doing a show right now that they're not too pleased with, so they're not letting me use their facilities on this show. But that's fine by me.

Longworth: Are you kidding me?

BELLISARIO: No.

Longworth: So you don't get a seasonal carte blanche.

BELLISARIO: I do not get a seasonal carte blanche, but by the same token, I don't have the Navy telling me, "Well, if you make that show, you're never going to get any help from us again." So, it's fine with me. Now and then we make a show that is too tender for them or that they feel is not in the interest of the Navy. That's OK, we'll make it elsewhere.

Longworth: What concerns them? Give me an example of one that concerns them.

BELLISARIO: The one that concerns them was a coven of witches on an Army base in Texas, and they were military people, and it raised quite a row, especially by the Christian right.

Longworth: Hey, I'm in Virginia. I know about the religious right.

BELLISARIO: (*Laughs.*) OK. Well the Army base was allowing them to worship the devil. And I decided, that's an interesting arena, let's go into that.

(*Laughs.*) So one of the writers came up with a story idea that a coven was meeting off base, and a female petty officer at the construction battalion accused the head warlock of raping her by putting her under a spell. So we have our female lead, Catherine Bell [MacKenzie], go undercover in the construction battalion as an NCO and she joins this coven to see what's going on. And she learns that they don't worship the devil, they worship gods and goddesses and they have bonfires. And one of the things they do is they dance around the fire naked, and we have Catherine Bell doing this with them, but we never show it. So we sent the Navy a script and they said they felt really uncomfortable with a Marine Corps lieutenant colonel going undercover and ending up dancing naked around the fire. We were going to use Fort Hueneme—they have a construction battalion there—but we ended up going to Fort McArthur instead, which is the old abandoned fort that everybody uses here in Los Angeles, and we just shot it there instead.

Longworth: They probably also didn't appreciate your new slogan, "We're looking for a Few Good Witches."

BELLISARIO: (*Laughs.*)

Longworth: But seriously, if you're waiting to get script approval from the military, doesn't that jeopardize your shooting schedule?

BELLISARIO: Well, no. We had a few days to make the adjustments, but we're pretty flexible. This happens rarely. In fact, this is the first time this year that they have done it. In the previous year, it happened once or twice.

Longworth: Let's talk about your mission with *JAG*, using, for example, the episode that was based on the U.S. military chopper that rammed into the ski gondola in Aviano, Italy, which resulted in civilian casualties.

BELLISARIO: In our version it was a private aircraft that caused the accident.

Longworth: But in real life the military pilot was guilty, and in your version it was the fault of a private aircraft. Do you go out of your way to be pro-military, and in this case, do a make-up call to combat the negative publicity the military received in the real accident?

BELLISARIO: I wouldn't say I go out of my way to do things like that, but I am not negative on the military person. This whole town is full of producers who do that. (*Laughs.*) I mean, everybody in this town that produces television or anything else is very negative to the military. The military is a pejorative term in what is a very liberal community. And to give you an example of what a pejorative term it is, when I first wrote *JAG*, the network said, "No, nobody likes the military." But there was enough action in it to get their appetite whetted, and we got into the court trials and that's what made it work. I don't go out of my way to make it a positive. I happen to think that what went on in Aviano is a case of where the military wasn't hotdogging it. You can't train at fifteen hundred feet for what is one hundred feet in real life.

Longworth: And you speak from experience because you're a flyer.

BELLISARIO: That's right, and when you need your military, they have to be prepared. But you say, did we sugarcoat it? We did a story once where the Navy first put females in the cockpit of F-14's and we had the pilot go down, when she should have never been *in* that cockpit. Well, we did two stories about that. One where we showed a female aviator who was just as good as a man, and *should* have been in the cockpit, and was being kept out because she was a female. Then we did another story where a female was using the fact that she was a female to charge sexual harassment as the reason she wasn't allowed to fly. So I try to show as much as possible all sides of an issue. If I can do it within one show, I'll do it. If I can't do it within one show and make it dramatically interesting and not too confusing, then I'll say, as I did in that case, we're going to do a show in which a female in the military *is* being sexually harassed, and we're going to do another show where a female officer is going to claim sexual harassment when the problem is really incompetence.

Longworth: You mentioned Hollywood's bias against the military. If you think about it, out of about six thousand TV shows that have been on in prime-time, only a couple of dozen have had military themes. With the popularity of *JAG* is there a chance that trend might reverse itself?

BELLISARIO: Well, I was glad to see Spielberg and Tom Hanks are joining us now with shows about the military. (*Editor's Note:* Following success with *Saving Private Ryan*, Spielberg's *Semper Fi* series was slated for NBC in the fall 2000 season but was delayed until March 2001, then was shelved. Meanwhile, Hanks also produced a miniseries about the 101st Airborne for HBO.) I feel we paved the way on that. I've always had a pro-military leaning, but I've tried to be balanced. If you go back to *Magnum* twenty years ago, when I created *Magnum* it was only five years after the end of the Vietnam War. This country was still punishing the warriors for the war. And that was wrong. You don't punish the warriors for what the government sends them to do. So at that time, in all dramatic series, you could not find a Vietnam vet being portrayed who wasn't sticking a needle in his arm or pulling a .45 out and shooting a bunch of people, or shooting himself, or being a sniper on a roof, or being a drug addict. You could not find a single, positive role model of a Vietnam veteran in television. When I created *Magnum*, CBS said to me, "Why do you have to do all this stuff about them being in Vietnam? Everybody hates that war. Everybody hates veterans." And I told CBS, "Don't worry, I can always cut it out if you don't like it." (*Laughs.*)

Longworth: Do you lie very often?

BELLISARIO: Sometimes when I have to. (*Laughs.*) I had a lot of Vietnam flashbacks in the pilot of *Magnum*, and I said, "I can always cut out the flashbacks." Of course, I knew the show wouldn't work if I cut them out. The pilot worked so great that they left it in. Well, a phenomena started to happen that I found very gratifying. Suddenly I was getting letters and calls from Vietnam vets from all over the country saying, "Thank God, somebody is finally showing us as normal people. We have gone through the Vietnam experience, we have come out of it forever changed, some of us for the worse, some for the better, but we are all trying to put our lives back together and go on with a normal life." And seeing these three guys on *Magnum* leading a normal life— well, as normal a life as a TV hero detective can lead (*laughs*)—it just became a landslide of people.

Longworth: So you helped the TV industry turn one corner with *Magnum*. Do you think you might be doing the same with *JAG*?

BELLISARIO: I think so.

Longworth: When were you in service?

BELLISARIO: I was in the Marines. I served between the wars from 1955 to 1959.

Longworth: Post Korea.

BELLISARIO: Technically I'm a Korean veteran. I was in the Reserves until 1963. I almost went back in to go to Vietnam. A close friend of mine came back after his second tour in '65 and said to me, "Stay the hell out of there [Vietnam]. It's getting mean, nasty, and dirty, and it's going to be a terrible thing."

Longworth: And you fly choppers?

BELLISARIO: I used to; I don't anymore.

Longworth: Did your military experience help you be a better disciplined writer/producer?

BELLISARIO: I think that discipline came out of what I did *after* the Marine Corps. I was in the newspaper business for a while, and then I got into the advertising side of it from 1961 to 1975. My television copywriting taught me brevity in writing and it also taught me how to do something in twenty-eight seconds, how to communicate a message and make it interesting. And that is still reflected in my writing. I enter a scene when it's well under way and exit at the peak. I delete superfluous words and I get right to the gist of the scene. People who have read my teleplays or screenplays consistently tell me the same thing. They pick it up, and they say they never put it down. They're amazed when they get to the end of sixty-two to sixty-five pages that it's over. People say, "It says Act Four, where in the hell was Act Three?" (*Both laugh.*)

Longworth: That's a great compliment.

BELLISARIO: But that came out of the disciplines I learned in advertising. The Marine Corps—once you're a Marine, you're always a Marine, that's why there are no ex-Marines, only former ones. And the disciplines you learn in the Marine Corps are things about yourself as a human being, just surviving in the world. That's invaluable.

Longworth: You were using black powder weapons then, right?

BELLISARIO: (*Laughs.*) Not quite. I was in a unit of thirty to thirty-five men, and the Marine Corps plan at that time (1957–58) was that Marines were always the first ones in. The Pacific war was still fresh in their minds. They developed a system to take enemy islands. Tactical nuclear weapons would be dropped and detonated at two to five thousand feet, to wipe out the enemy without damaging their runways. Shortly after that, we would be parachuted in to set up communications and land marine aircraft on the captured runways. We would practice this on Pacific islands. Of course, we didn't drop any tactical weapons. (*Laughs.*)

Longworth: Is that why going into a meeting with network executives doesn't seem scary to you?

BELLISARIO: (*Laughs.*) Right.

Longworth: Your son Dave works with you, doesn't he?

BELLISARIO: I have seven children, and two of them work with me. David and my daughter Julie Watson, who is running postproduction. David works on stock footage and CGI work. David is great. You ask him, "I need Navy SEALS going out of a C-130 at night over water," and he'll go, "Oh yeah, there was a film about ten years ago . . . I'll have it for you in a few minutes." (*Both laugh.*)

Longworth: Well, hold on a minute. Let's talk about nepotism. I once spoke with Grant Tinker about that topic, and he loathed nepotism, but then he ended up having Mark and John work for him at MTM studios. Apparently you never made a stand against nepotism.

BELLISARIO: No, because my son and daughter who work for me are underpaid and overworked, and always have been, because they are my children. My daughter is known throughout the industry as one of the best post-production producers available in television. She's been approached to go to other places and won't. They were raised in the business, they saw it their whole life. I didn't say to them, "Come work with me." They came to me and said, "Could we come to work with you?" (*Laughs.*) My unit is very hard working, and they [my kids] are as hard working or harder working as anybody in the unit. In fact, when my daughter was pregnant with her second child, I had to order her to stop working the long hours.

Longworth: As a big-time producer and a big supporter of the military, how do you feel about the issue of government interference in television and film?

BELLISARIO: Well, I don't like government control over much of anything. I'm a minimalist when it comes to government interference. I'm certainly not a Democrat. I've been a Republican most of my life. And back during the Nixon era I became an Independent. Recently I was a McCain supporter. (*Laughs.*) That would go without saying. (*Both laugh.*) It's difficult. I get turned off by so much of what I see in film. I don't restrict my children as to what they can see probably nearly as much as the average American would.

Longworth: You're talking about television as well.

BELLISARIO: I'm talking about television as well. I have a child who's only nine years old and a child who is fifteen years old. I'm pretty open with what they see. I will restrict them if I think it's going to cause them some emotional turmoil, but I don't restrict them on things such as nudity. That's silly. It used to be worse in television. I mean, I remember when I was making *Magnum* and they would count the "hells" and "damns." If you had two "hells" on a page, you couldn't do it. You were allowed so many "hells" and "damns" per episode per hour. I remember when they used to have a point system for violence. I was on ABC at that time, but there was a point system at NBC, too, maybe every network, where they would count the points, say if you got to three points in an hour of television, then you had to take something out. So, say you throw a punch at somebody, it's a half a point. If you shoot someone, it's a point. If you commit adultery, it's a half a point.

Longworth: Well, then, I guess Clinton was out of points early on, wasn't he?

BELLISARIO: (*Laughs.*) Don't get me started. It was really pretty silly, and I used to just barrel right through it and ignore most of it as much as I could. I'd tell them to go ahead and bleep it or do whatever they wanted. But I never went overboard with that. I was watching a show one night, and I won't mention the show, but I hear the language that's going on, and it's like, "OK, we can use these words now and get away with it, so we're just going to keep saying them over and over and over." That's disgusting. I hear music which I find repulsive to me, but I'm certainly not going to restrict it. And there are movies I won't even go see.

Longworth: Yeah, well, if you believe the movies, everyone in the military is always using bad language, but in *JAG*, it doesn't seem to be an issue.

BELLISARIO: Well, we have it. The admiral will say "damn." (*Laughs.*) And we've called somebody a "bastard" and things like that, but it's never been about foul language. So we don't overdo it. The other night we picked up the Red Cross Spirit Award for the year 2000 for positive portrayal of people in the military. We also accepted the American Cinema Foundation Award for the same thing. There are people out there, and they're not just the extreme right or religious right or Christian coalition, that recognize what I'm trying to do in creating positive role models. Of course, with the American Cinema Foundation, one of the movies nominated was *South Park.* (*Laughs.*) So we're not talking about a right-wing organization. (*Both laugh.*)

Longworth: Take me back to when you first came out to Hollywood. How did you land a job on *Baa Baa Black Sheep*?

BELLISARIO: I go in to see my agent and I ask, "How long before you think I sell a movie?" And he said, "Oh, you'll have a sale within two years." And I said, "I got enough money to live six weeks." (*Laughs.*) He said, "Have you ever thought of writing for television?" And I said, "Television? No." And he said, "Well, what show do you like?" And I said, "There's a show, *Baa Baa Black Sheep*, and they've got it all screwed up. (*Laughs.*) I'm a former Marine and a pilot, and I could probably write that." So he sent my script over to the story editor of *Baa Baa Black Sheep*, a man named Ken Pettis, an older man. He was in his sixties then. So Ken calls me in and says, "I want you to meet our supervising producer, Phil DeGaire." I meet Phil and he says, "I like your writing. How about some stories?" So I pitched him three stories. He picked one and said, "I like that one, you've got a sale. Go write it." When I got home, I called my agent and said, "How much time do I have?" And he said, "How much time will it take you to write the script?" And I said, "Is a week OK?" And he said, "Yeah, a week's OK." So I write the script in a week. That week I see a truck pull up in front of my house with a little caravan behind it, and out comes my Uncle Paul and Aunt Mary, who I hadn't seen in ten years. Aunt Mary is still alive, she's in her nineties now. They had been retired and were traveling and they said my mom had told them I was there, so they just dropped in to see me. My uncle was Russian and he made jewelry. He made Russian Orthodox crosses (my mother was Russian Orthodox). And as he's leaving, he says, "Here Donnie," and he gives me a Russian Orthodox cross, which I still wear to this day, and he said, "This is going to bring you luck." I'll never forget that. He leaves and I sit down and finish the script, and sent it into Steve Cannell. And I'm thinking, Cannell's going to call me in and say, "How dare you take our money. What made you think you could write television?" And I get a call to go in and see him. In those days you only got half pay the first two scripts until you were a full member of the Writers Guild. So I get called to go into Steve Cannell's office. Grace, his secretary, tells me to go in. Steve was doing *The Rockford Files* at the time. So I walk into his office, and Steve gets this strange look 'cause here I am, this forty-one-year-old guy.

Longworth: He's expecting a twenty-one year old.

BELLISARIO: Yeah, he's expecting a twenty-one-year-old kid. And he said, "Where have you been?" And I said, "I've been sitting outside waiting for a half an hour." (*Both laugh.*)

Longworth: What an idiot you are. (*Both laugh.*)

BELLISARIO: He said, "No, I mean, where have you been *hiding*?" He picked up the script and said, "I'm shooting this just the way it is, word for word." Well, it was near the end of the season and he said, "How would you like to be my story editor?" And I said, "What's a story editor?" And he says, "Well, that's somebody you chain to a typewriter, and he turns out scripts." And I said, "I'd love to be a story editor." And he said, "If the show gets picked up, which we'll know in about six weeks, you're my story editor for next season. Meantime, I'm going to put the word out about you at Universal, and you're going to have a lot of work to do." And the next thing I know, I'm doing a *Switch*. I'm writing a *Delvecchio* for Bochco. I'm doing a *Kojak*, also a *Big Hawaii*. That show only lasted like thirteen episodes. So I did five scripts in a matter of two months. I made more money on that than I had made in advertising in a whole year. And I thought, "Oh, shit, I've found the candy store." When *Black Sheep* was renewed, Stephen made me story editor, and that lasted four episodes. The fifth episode he made me producer of the show, 'cause I had been doing this in commercials, I would edit and cast. I ended up directing the last show, and *Black Sheep* got canceled. Steve had done two pilots he was trying to get on, one was called *Boston and Kilbride* and the other was called *Gypsy Warriors*, both with Tom Selleck and Jim Whitmore, Jr. And Steve came in and said, "They like the *Gypsy Warriors* pilot and want to see a sample script." This was on a Friday, and he said, "Can you have me a script by Monday morning?" And I said, "Sure." So I sat there all weekend and wrote this script for *Gypsy Warrior*. There's a reason behind this story that I'll get to in a minute. They loved it, and he came back to me on Wednesday and said, "Can you turn me out another one by Monday?" I guess they didn't love it that much because they didn't pick up *Gypsy Warrior*. I get a call from Glen Larson, who says, "I hear your show wasn't picked up. How would you like to be supervising producer on *Battlestar Gallactica*, my new show?" I go over there, and after that Universal says, "How would you like to be executive producer of Jack Klugman's show?" I'm in the business two years, and they move me up to executive producer.

Longworth: Your Uncle Paul's cross must have worked.

BELLISARIO: (*Laughs.*) It sure did. Tom Selleck was to do a show called *Magnum* with Glen Larson. Glen wrote a script that Tom and everybody hated. It was about a private eye in the islands who had hang gliders with machine guns, and wristwatch decoders.

Longworth: Like James Bond?

BELLISARIO: It was James Bond, it was shoot 'em-up, blow 'em up. James Bond all the way. And Tom said to Charlie Engel, "I'll pound roofing nails before I make a show like this." So Tom says to Charlie, "There was a guy on *Black Sheep* who wrote two *Gypsy Warriors* scripts, and they were good. What's he doing?" And Engel calls me in, and Tom says, "I'll make the show with Don." So I went over to CBS and said, "What do you like about *Magnum* that Glen Larson wrote?" They said, "We like Tom Selleck as a private eye in Hawaii." And I said, "But what do you like about that script?" And they said, "We like Tom Selleck as a private eye in Hawaii." (*Both laugh.*) Well, I had been in development writing a show called *HH Flynn* about a private eye on Rodeo Drive who drove a red Ferrari that didn't belong to him. It belonged to the man who owned the shop that he rented his office from, and the shop was *Flowers to the Stars*. And it was this guy's Ferrari and he would let HH Flynn use it because he liked the kid, who was a Vietnam vet. And he liked him so much that HH Flynn lived in his guest house behind the walled estate in Bel Air, and he would drive his Ferrari through the gates, go into the guest house, throw on sneakers and Levi's and a shirt, and he'd jump in a jeep and drive down to Long Beach to a bar run by one of his teammates in Vietnam, Rick. He also had a buddy T. C. who flew helicopters out to the oil rigs off the coast here at San Pedro. And the three of them hung out.

Longworth: So basically you just had to fit them into your HH Flynn story.

BELLISARIO: What I did was, I took the *Magnum* title. I had wanted to use *HH Flynn,* but they said, "No, we like *Magnum,* sounds good, like a gun, *Magnum.* And I started writing this show about Thomas Magnum, which was really just HH Flynn converted. And I wrote the pilot, and had all the trouble with the Vietnam flashbacks, which we talked about earlier. It became a huge hit, and my star was forever cemented. I didn't want it there, I wanted it cemented in features.

Longworth: You were one of the first producers in a straight drama to break the fourth wall and allow Magnum to speak directly to the audience.

BELLISARIO: The network hated that at first. They said, "You can't do that, you're breaking the fourth wall," and I said, "Why can't I do it?" And they said, "Because you can't," and I said, "Why not?" I was directing the show and we put it into the titles, where I had Tom wink right into the camera. I was behind the camera when he did it, and Tom said, "We can't use that, can we?" And I said, "The hell we can't." And that became the signature wink. The other thing that became a signature (*laughs*) was when he was holding that girl in the ocean and looks down at her, and then looks up at the camera. (*Laughs.*) I had a reputation for being a tough producer. I would stand up for what I wanted, and you couldn't get by me or turn me around on it. I think obstinate is the word. (*Both laugh.*) What it really comes from is, when I was making that first show, I just didn't know how hard it was to have a successful TV series. I just had this attitude of "I can do it; it's going to be great. It's going to work." It's the same with *JAG.* Everybody's worried it's going to be canceled, it's the first season on CBS, and I said, "Just don't worry about it. The show's going to be on a long time."

Longworth: Speaking of *JAG,* let's take a "quantum leap" back to its inception.

BELLISARIO: I took it to Kerry [McCluggage] at Paramount, whom I had known for twenty years. I walked in and tossed the forty pages on his desk and said, "Read it," and I went out and got a coke and came back and flopped in the chair and drank the coke. Kerry read the forty pages and he said, "Go write the rest of it." So we took it out to all the networks. NBC said to me, "You can't make this pilot, it's too expensive," and I said, "Yes, I can. I'm going to make the pilot using footage from other films such as *Top Gun.*" And Paramount owned *Top Gun.* When I directed the *JAG* pilot, the Navy would not give me any cooperation. In fact, they were obstructionists. I had gone down to the *Lexington* in Corpus Christi, which was a museum ship. It was an old World War II–class carrier that was converted into a flight deck trainer, and it couldn't even handle an F-14. And the Navy was really being nasty. So I approached a rear admiral that I knew when he was a lieutenant commander while I was doing *Magnum* in Hawaii. And he said, "There's a misunderstanding. We didn't mean that we would try and stop you from making this show." So I shot it down there and put it together, and NBC—Don Ohlmeyer—said, "You can't make this as a series." I made the pilot for the budget, so I said, "Of course I can." Long story short, they [NBC] made eleven drama pilots that season. They picked up one—*JAG*. Then they called me in and Don said, he didn't like the female lead, Andrea Parker. She was a very attractive girl, I thought, and had a lot of heat with David James Elliot. She was great. But Don's minions said to me, "Don wants a blonde, good-looking, big casabas." (*Laughs*.) And I said, "No, I'm keeping Andie." And I was up in New York, and Don said to me, "Are you going to fall on your sword over this? Because you're the only pilot picked up out of eleven." So I went to Andie, and she graciously said to me, "Don't worry about it." And I said "Andie, here's my plan. I'll hire another girl, but I'm going to bring you back as a guest star. And I'm going to show NBC just how good you are and how wrong they are." So I go out and hire Tracey Needham, the perfect girl for what they wanted, and put her in the show. Meanwhile, Patrick Labyorteaux, who was to be my humor relief and who was in my pilot, I find out to my dismay was off to do a Fox comedy. And I said to him, "You're making a mistake, but I'll tell you what. When that thing goes under, you give me a call, and you'll be back on this show, which is going to go on and become a hit." And that's exactly what happened. Anyway, the guy who was playing the admiral went off to do a feature. So here I am having to introduce a new female lead, I've lost my sidekick, I've lost my admiral. And Don says to me, "If this is a cross between *Top Gun* and *A Few Good Men*, we want *Top Gun*. So I am making a show that I'm really not happy with. Now this is the ironic part. At the end of that year, I put Andie Parker in two episodes, and NBC admits to me, "Boy, were we wrong to take Andie out." They put her in *The Pretender* and they put *The Pretender* in our time slot and dropped *us*. (*Both laugh.*) Is that unbelievable? Now again, being optimistic, I'm saying, "They're not going to cancel us, this show's going to grow." And I get the word that we were canceled. And the way we get the word is, ABC and CBS call us and say, "We hear you're getting canceled. If you are, we want to talk to you." We were canceled on a Friday. ABC and CBS talked to us, and I was on an airplane flying to New York. I was on the air phone with Kerry McCluggage, who says, "Les Moonves he'll give us thirteen episodes, but he's got to know by four o'clock. Or we can hold out for more from ABC. What do you want to do?" And I said, "I think we take the thirteen and I'll make it go. You get the thirteen, I'll get the other nine." (*Both laugh*.) So Les surprised me by not putting us on the fall schedule. He put us on midseason. But it was great because Les said to me, "What do you want to do?" And I said, "I want to go back and make the show that I wanted to make in the first place. I wanted to make a show that had the big Navy toys. You'll see some action about every fourth show, but basically it's a courtroom and relationship series. I can't bring back Andie because she's now doing an NBC show, but let's get Patrick if he's available, and cast somebody *like* Andie Parker in that other key role. We'll also need a new admiral. I'll tell personal stories that are out of the headlines." And Les said "Go," and he's never said another word to me, and neither has anybody else.

Longworth: What a great story.

BELLISARIO: And the show has become extraordinarily successful, even against *Millionaire*. While it has kept us from being a top-ten show in the raw numbers, we have continued to grow in the key eighteen to forty-five numbers.

Longworth: One of the trades reported recently that audience sampling revealed people would watch *Millionaire*, then flip over and catch *JAG*, and that was actually helping your show because they had grown bored with *Millionaire*.

BELLISARIO: Yeah, we're getting a younger audience now.

Longworth: Since that time, has the vertical integration of Paramount, Viacom, and CBS taken pressure off of you? Do you get better support, better promotion?

BELLISARIO: No, not really. Maybe I do, but I still scream at them about support. (*Laughs*.)

Longworth: Really?

BELLISARIO: Well you *always* do, you're always screaming. I don't call Les very often. I bet I don't make two calls a year to him. I will say that Les, when he picked us up, really went to bat for us to the press, to the media, and pushed the show. But our show is successful and going along, and he brings in other *new* shows, and he pushes those. You get your amount [of support].

Longworth: *JAG*'s new success also coincides with the resurgence of dramas in general. Why do you think that the drama genre has come back so strongly?

BELLISARIO: The world is cyclical, my friend. (*Laughs*.) Everything goes in cycles. I remember when I was doing *Magnum*, they said "Sitcoms are dead." Then sitcoms started back with *The Cosby Show* which was against *Magnum*, and knocked us on our ass and shocked us. Sitcoms came roaring back and have been back for about fifteen years. Now the cycle is starting to go the other way, shifting again. I mean with this game show *Millionaire* and *Survivor*, God knows *where* this cycle's going to take us.

Longworth: Not to belabor the point, but how much does that bother you? Because if it weren't for the game shows and reality shows, there would be six or seven dramas in the top ten.

BELLISARIO: I'm very serious when I say to you, if *Millionaire* wasn't on against us, we would be a top-ten show every week, and probably a top-five show. It just came out of nowhere, and being on against it is just clobbering us.

Longworth: And these shows are dumbing down the audience.

BELLISARIO: Well it *is* dumbing down the audience, but then again the audience looks at that and what makes it successful is they say, "God, I could answer that! I could be the guy making that money."

Longworth: But, if it wasn't for *Millionaire* you would make more money based on ad revenues, right?

BELLISARIO: Absolutely, absolutely. But, hey, that's show biz.

Longworth: You spoke of a show about relationships earlier. We talked about the liberal bias against all things military. *JAG* is a relationship show, but when I think back on it, *Magnum* was a relationship show, as was *Quantum Leap*.

BELLISARIO: They're all relationship shows.

Longworth: And yet, people still paint you as Mr. Military Guy when who you *really* are is Mr. Relationship Guy.

BELLISARIO: I guess it's because of the style of shows that I do. I remember writing an episode of *Magnum* that, to this day, gives me more comments than anything. And I thought, in my humble opinion, that it was one of the best-written hours on television that year. It got absolutely no recognition. It just floored me. The entire episode was nothing but Magnum treading water for forty-eight hours, and flashing back to his relationship with his father. How his father always said, "Never give up." And I thought it was an incredible show. We filmed the whole thing in the Pacific, in dark, shark-infested waters. It was a bear to make. I received a letter from a woman who said her child had cancer. The child was eight or nine years old and at a cancer center for children, sort of a hospice, and the parents stayed in a hotel next door. It was a Thursday night and the beginning of a new season, and she and her family watched *Magnum*. And, at the end of that episode, everybody in their room was hugging their child and saying, "They would never give up, never give up." And, for years, I got letters from her, saying, "You're in our prayers because we never gave up, and our daughter is still alive." The last I heard, her daughter was eighteen years old.

Longworth: Well, you're a guy who has had to tread water before and you never gave up, so was that *Magnum* story sort of a reflection of your life?

BELLISARIO: Oh, I don't know.

Longworth: I mean, you are always optimistic and seem to have no fear of failure.

BELLISARIO: I think that's true. The older you get, the harder it is to keep going, but I keep at it, and I'm still at it. I mean Christ, I'm going to be sixty-five this year. I don't know anybody else my age in this business. I am active, hands-on, read every script, cast the shows, edit them, direct them, write them, work with the actors. I don't know of anybody in television doing that at my age.

Longworth: And you're still wearing the cross?

BELLISARIO: I'm still wearing the cross.

7

PAUL HAGGIS | subversive scribe

Paul Haggis. COURTESY OF PAUL HAGGIS.

TELEVISION CREDITS

1982	*Different Strokes* (NBC)
1983	*One Day at a Time* (CBS)
1984–87	*The Facts of Life* (NBC)

1987	*Sweet Surrender* (NBC)
1987–88	*The Tracey Ullman Show* (Fox)
1988–89	*thirtysomething* (ABC)
1990–92	*L.A. LAW* (NBC)
1993–2001	*Walker, Texas Ranger* (CBS)
1996	*Due South* (CBS)
1996–97	*EZ Streets* (CBS)
1997–98	*Michael Hayes* (CBS)
1999–	*Family Law* (CBS)

MW   MW   MW

In an episode of the 1960s cartoon *Dudley Do Right*, the narrator proclaims, "Canada was overrun by Canadians." Perhaps that is why young Paul Haggis (an avid fan of the *The Rocky and Bullwinkle Show*), eventually headed *Due South* to write cartoons (and much more) in glamorous Hollywood, U.S.A. Unlike his Saturday-morning heroes, though, Haggis is not the most animated human you will ever meet, but his wry sense of humor is right out of the Jay Ward playbook.

Like many Canadians, Haggis appreciates a good hat trick, so it is no surprise that he has made his mark as writer, producer, and director of both comedy and drama, where his offbeat approach to the former helped shape the development of three-dimensional characters for the latter.

Paul is opinionated, but not overbearing. He is confident, but not self-centered. And he never plays the blame game. He is a nice guy who has finished first.

Paul Haggis was born in London, Ontario, in 1954 to a good Catholic family. His father, who worked in road construction, and his mother (who passed away in 1999) also raised two daughters, Kathy and Joey. Early on, Paul's tastes in television and motion pictures tended toward the eclectic.

Longworth: You mentioned that your favorite show was *Rocky and Bullwinkle*, but what other TV programs did you watch, and did any of them have an influence on your writing?

HAGGIS: Well, a lot of television shows, from *Sky King* to *The Rockford Files*. And, anything with Lloyd Bridges in a wetsuit worked for me. (*Laughs.*)

Longworth: You're kind of strange, aren't you?

HAGGIS: Yeah, I'm pretty strange. (*Both laugh.*)

Longworth: Let me make a note of this. Haggis likes Lloyd Bridges in a wetsuit.

HAGGIS: And, I liked all of the cartoons that had a perverse edge. Not perverse by today's standards, but certainly by the standards of the 1950s and '60s. Really, I thought it was so hip. Even at a young age I knew that my parents were watching it and laughing for other reasons than I was, and I thought that was really cool.

Paul and his father also shared an interest in theater.

HAGGIS: My younger sister Kathy was in high school and she wanted to be an actress, but there was no place for her to work, so my dad decided to build a little theater. He found a Baptist church that had been converted into a discotheque called *Purgatory,* which had been gutted by fire. He went in there and said, "We're going to turn this into a little, hundred-seat theater." And we did, and I managed that, and wrote plays. We got a grant and had a professional theater company in there for a while, and it was a very cool experience. London, Ontario, was a small city, and we didn't get a lot of films that I wanted to see, so I started a little film society, and we'd just book all the films that I wanted to see—the Bergmans, the Godards, and the Pasolinis, things like that. We showed them Saturday after midnight and Sunday afternoons, then we'd strip things down, and put it back into a theater for the next day's play. Hitchcock and Godard were my two largest influences as far as film goes. I was just wowed by both of them. I loved good, solid entertainment, and with Hitchcock, I loved the suspense. And I loved the nonlinear storytelling that Godard would do, and these flights into—I don't know *where* he flew. (*Laughs.*) He flew into really strange territory, and he didn't have any navigation equipment.

For a while, Paul seemed to be flying without direction, as well.

HAGGIS: I went to several parochial schools, St. Thomas Moore, St. George's, and, Catholic Central High [where] I was suspended, I think seven times in my first year there. My parents didn't know what to do with me, so they sent me to a place called Ridley College, which, at that time, was the last bastion of British conservative thought in Canada. It was a private boarding school that still used the cane, literally, and I felt that one a few times. So they sent me there for a year, and that was a fabulous education because I learned how to subvert any system, and I *did.* It was great. I was the only kid at this school, and probably one of the few kids in Canada, who had a subscription to *Ramparts Magazine,* which, if you remember, was the magazine of the Black Panther Party. So imagine that coming into *this* school! I don't think there was a black face *anywhere*. The only "person of color" was the kid from Hong Kong who was my roommate. That was as close as it got. Anyway, it was a fabulous way of learning how to deal with corporate America. And the agreement was, if I survived a year at that school, I could go to any college I wanted. So I chose this little school called Muskoka Lakes College for my last year of high school. It was what we called a "free school" back in the '60s. The school had about thirty boys and it was sort of like, "Well, what do you feel like learning today?" They closed down after I left. (*Laughs.*) But I had a great teacher named Max Allen who was the first real intellectual I ever met. He talked about civil issues and art, and things I had never really experienced. And he really influenced me. Max also worked as a producer for CBC radio. He produced a show called *As it Happens*, which is the Canadian equivalent of *All Things Considered*. He was also the owner of a pornographic video theater (*both laugh*), which he opened in order to circumvent the Canadian pornography laws. He showed these movies on television screens rather than showing them projected, thereby openly subverting Ontario's very repressive censorship laws.

Longworth: Gives a whole new meaning to the phrase Canadian Mounted Police.

HAGGIS: Exactly. (*Laughs.*) He is a fascinating person. I would go into his office and listen to John Dean's Watergate testimony. He gave me copies of all the Nixon tapes.

Longworth: Now that was *real* pornography.

HAGGIS: (*Laughs.*) That's exactly what he would have said.

Longworth: This is a bit off point, but of all the Watergate figures, I only had respect for Gordon Liddy. He did the crime, did the time, and said, "Screw you, I'm not talking."

HAGGIS: That's the basis of one of my favorite books and favorite movies, *Prince of the City*. You've got the Treat Williams character, who's torn but does the right thing. The Jerry Orbach character then says, "Fuck 'em all, I'll never give up my friends." And you go, "Yeah, Jerry!" That was an influential piece of work for me because I found myself rooting for the villain. Same with Hitchcock, I think it was *Strangers on a Train*. He did a scene in which the villain, Bruno, was on his way to plant the lighter near the carousel in the park where the murder was supposed to have happened. He's got the hero's lighter, and he's going to plant it there, but he's running and bumps into somebody, and the lighter goes down the drain, through the grate in the catch basin, and he has to try and squeeze his fingers down to get this thing. I'm sitting in the audience, willing him to reach it. And I realized I was rooting for the bad guy, and that really formed a lot of what I do,[to try and] manipulate people to empathize with people they shouldn't.

Longworth: And that's why you ended up in the principal's office so often.

HAGGIS: Exactly, much too often. I think it was partly to do with trying to blow up bridges on Halloween with Molotov cocktails, and not doing a very good job because they were concrete bridges.

Longworth: So, in addition to being incorrigible, you also weren't very bright, either?

HAGGIS: No. (*Laughs.*)

Longworth: So, did you ever make it to college?

HAGGIS: I went to Fanshawe Community College for one year to study film, and found out that they didn't know what they were teaching. They just had a little bit of equipment, and let us run around with it. Then I studied art in a place called H. B. Beale, which was another technical school. I studied art and photography, and then went off to be a fashion photographer.

Now a full-fledged subversive, having majored in pornography, explosives, and photography, Haggis once again found a new, creative direction, thanks to his father's support.

HAGGIS: I worked road construction with my dad, and one day he said, "Construction. You're no damn good at it, are you?" And I said, "No, I'm really not." So he said, "You want to be a writer? Why don't you give it a shot in Hollywood?" At the time, he was paying me one hundred and fifty dollars a week to work for him in construction, and he said, "You go on down to Hollywood, and I'll give you the one hundred and fifty dollars a week for a year if I can afford it." And that "year" turned into three or four. If not for my mom and dad, I wouldn't be here because they believed in what I wanted to do. And they really believed in their kids following through with their dreams.

Paul's mother took constant delight in his work right up until her death in 1999. His father, meanwhile, continues to be an inspiration and a source of support, and works closely with Paul researching projects. He also served as a producer on Haggis's short-lived series, *EZ Streets*.

Haggis's career in television has, like his tastes in kid vid and films, tended toward the eclectic. After a stint as a writer for animated cartoons, he pulled tours of duty on sitcoms like *Different Strokes* and *The Facts of Life* before testing the drama waters with *thirtysomething* and *L.A. Law*. Paul also worked on the original *Tracey Ullman Show* and later tried his hand at a comedy pilot for CBS titled *City*. The show, starring Valerie Harper, lasted only one season. Apparently, America was not yet ready to embrace a show that posited Haggis's theory that all city bureaucrats were either corrupt or incompetent. He then went in a less subversive direction and co-created *Walker, Texas Ranger.* In so doing, Paul began a longstanding relationship with CBS.

In 1994 he created and produced the quirky dramedy *Due South,* about a Canadian Mountie on assignment in Chicago. Tim Brooks and Earle Marsh in *The Complete Directory to Prime Time Network and Cable TV Shows* commented that, "The producers made fun of American stereotypes of Canadians, and Canadian stereotypes of Americans, and managed to weave spoofs of almost every television genre into the stories." Despite the show's like ability, however, it only survived two seasons on CBS.

Next, Haggis created *EZ Streets,* a crime drama (starring *thirtysomething* veteran Ken Olin) whose title refers to the slums between E and Z Streets. Viewers for Quality Television's Dorothy Swanson called it "The most morally ambiguous quality drama ever offered on network television," and referred to it as "a mini art film." Following a two-hour premiere, however, *EZ Streets* aired only once more before CBS put in on the shelf. Then the network reintroduced the series, allowing six more episodes to air before calling it quits for good. Ironically, *Time* magazine had named *EZ Streets* "Best TV Show of the Year" on the very day the series was finally canceled. The few loyal viewers who watched *EZ Streets,* as well as most television critics, still recall the series with fondness and high praise, but its tone was just too dark for mainstream audiences.

At the Viewers for Quality Television's 1996 conference, Haggis said he wanted the audience to be able to understand the show but to also reach for it. He admitted that he "had a really good chance of failing at it. I wanted to do something that just terrified me, that I didn't know if I could succeed at. I always like to do something that I think I can fail at."

Even so, with both *Due South* and *EZ Streets* failing to score in the ratings, Haggis needed a hit, and what better way to guarantee one than by working with ex-*NYPD Blue* hunk David Caruso as the lead in a new drama. Unfortunately, Caruso's portrayal of *Michael Hayes* fell short with viewers, and the series struggled through its one and only season.

The new millennium was dawning, and in January of 1999 NBC's *Providence* (created by John Masius) signaled a new era in women's dramas. The door was wide open for Haggis and co-creator Anne Kenney to take us on a journey inside the world of *Family Law.* In its first two seasons on CBS, *Family Law* (starring Kathleen Quinlan, Dixie Carter, Julie Warner, Chris McDonald, and later Tony Danza) has been a solid performer, pulling respectable numbers against ABC's *Monday Night Football*. Paul Haggis at last had a hit on his hands.

With a reputation for creating critically acclaimed but short-lived dramas, Haggis's talents might have been written off by other networks, but not by CBS. CEO Les Moonves explains, "Paul is a very versatile guy. When you think of the different things that he has done, starting with *Due South*, and then he did maybe the best 'failed' show I've ever been involved in, *EZ Streets*, which was a show that I loved and unfortunately the public didn't embrace. It was a little too dark, a little too complex. And then, we were continually developing with Paul, and *Family Law* came out of sort of a middle ground. You know, 'let's come up with a show that can deal with complexity, yet is imminently commercial.' Paul wanted a hit as well. Paul is a terrific leader. He is a take-charge guy. He comes from a background that has a lot of comedy in it, which is one of the things that works about *Family Law*, is its great humor content. I think he also has a magnificent feel for casting, and I think you can see—it's an all-star team. In addition, he's a fine director. I think the good thing about Paul is, he is so good at so many different things. Once he is able to get focused on something, that's where the success is."

For Paul that success means producing *Family Law* while maintaining a normal home life with actress wife Deborah Rennard ("Sly" on *Dallas*), his three daughters, and a young son. In fact, Paul is outnumbered by women both at home and at work—so much so that, while participating in a seminar on "Women in Drama" for the Academy of Television Arts & Sciences, he joked, "I can't wait to do a 'guy's show' again. I'm *so* tired of asking myself, 'What do I think? What do I feel? What do I feel about what I am thinking? What do I think about what I am feeling?' My happiest moment was when I was doing *EZ Streets* and Ken Olin came to me and asked me this very intense question about how to play a particular scene. And I took a gun and put it in his hands, and I said, 'Try to act like a man!' and he said, 'Oh, I get that.' That's what I want to do." And Paul may get his wish. At press time, he has turned over the producing reins of *Family Law* to Steve Nathan and is developing new projects.

I spoke with Paul on many occasions, including during our "Women in Drama" event in Los Angeles, with the bulk of the interview taking place just prior to the start of *Family Law*'s second season.

Longworth: Thanks for agreeing to do the interview.

HAGGIS: Not at all.

Longworth: Actually, I have a confession to make. I'm not really writing another volume. I was just hoping to meet Kathleen Quinlan.

HAGGIS: (*Laughs.*) I would do the same.

Longworth: We'll get back to *Family Law* later, but first, talk about how you got your first big break in television.

HAGGIS: I was doing theater photography when I was twenty, something like that. And I had started to write some of the worst plays ever to be produced on the continent. (*Laughs.*) If you think my reviews are bad now, you should have seen what they wrote back then. I wrote a play that was supposed to be a comedy revue and it was supposed to run an hour an a half. And I directed it, of course. And, opening night it ran three and a half hours. It went on forever. Actors fell off the stage (*laughs*); it was humiliating.

Longworth: It sounds like you were inoculated early on against any kind of embarrassing experiences so that, when you hit the big time, you were prepared.

HAGGIS: Well, I don't know if I was inoculated, but certainly my nose was rubbed in it. I mean, I was chased out of the country for doing some of the worst plays. I had to come down here because America was the home of bad theater and television. Anyway, I was twenty-two or twenty-three, something like that, got married, and immediately had a baby. I was unemployed. I was working as a photographer doing those albums for churches and schools, which is like sixty seatings a minute, you know, shuffling families, taking the pictures, and getting them out. I started writing spec scripts for movies and television. My first was a *Welcome Back, Kotter* spec script. And I had written a movie script, a dark, psychological suspense thriller that was basically just no good. Finally, I think the first work I got was writing cartoons.

Longworth: You're making that up.

HAGGIS: No, no, no. I met a friend, a fellow writer called Michael Maurer, and he was trying to break into cartoons. He had written one and he said he knew that this Ruby Spears Company, which was like a smaller version of Hanna Barbera, was looking for some writers to do a series, and so we wrote a spec script for a series called *Dingbat and the Creeps* (*both laugh*), which was just coming on. So I wrote it, and they loved it! So they assigned us to write the entire series. I wrote every episode of *Dingbat and the Creeps* for a year, which was a series of three-minute, five-minute, and eleven-minute cartoons. So I wrote that, and I wrote *Scooby Doo, Plastic Man, Ritchie Rich*, everything I could get my hands on with Michael for the first year and a half. Then I finally realized I had to get out of it, because I had become successful at it.

And, not that I didn't want to be making good money, but if I kept doing it, I could see myself doing it for the rest of my life, so I wanted to get out and try other things. So, there was a Canadian series called *Hangin' In* that I heard about, and I sent them up a sample script. And they were impressed because I was a "Hollywood" writer and was living in Hollywood. I was a big deal. (*Laughs.*) So I met with them and I took Michael up with me and we wrote eight or ten of those. So I started to get my chops up, and then we sold a script to *Love Boat* because his father knew somebody over there. We got in and pitched them a bunch of stories, and they liked one of ours. It was fun. They completely rewrote it and it was totally fine because we did a very bad job. Then the next thing was *Three's Company;* we wrote an episode of that. And I decided to go on my own at that point.

Longworth: So now you've built up a bunch of credits.

HAGGIS: Well, two (*laughs*), but a bunch for *me* (*laughs*) because it was a Canadian show, it didn't count! (*Laughs.*)

Longworth: So you then moved from cartoons to sitcoms.

HAGGIS: I met a fellow at a writing class (I was taking a lot of writing classes) who had a contract to write a script for *One Day at a Time*, and he was writing with a partner, but his partner decided that he didn't want to write anymore. But they had been paid for the script, and this was a Thursday, and they had to get it done by Monday. And I said, "I'll write with you." And he said, "You don't understand. I can't give you credit." And I said, "I don't care." And he said, "Well, I can't give you money either," and I said, "Fine with me, I'll just write it with you." I looked around the room and he had an old chair in the corner from the Salvation Army, a real comfortable chair, and I said, "I'll take that chair." And he said "OK." (*Laughs.*) So I wrote the script, and I got the chair, and the chair is still in my bedroom, by the way. (*Laughs.*) It has been recovered since then. And they liked the script, and he said to them "Well, you understand, I wrote this with a guy named Paul Haggis." And so, they had me in and we were hired on staff for one of Norman Lear's other shows, I think it was *Different Strokes*. Norman has put me in every one of his bad shows he could find. (*Laughs.*) And so I did *Different Strokes*, and I was on staff at *One Day at a Time* for a year and then *The Facts of Life* for three or four years. I made it to executive producer of *The Facts of Life*. I think I was the only person who would accept the job, but I really learned how to edit and I learned a lot from Norman and his creative people there, and how to produce a show. So I was finally up to executive producer, and then at age thirty-one I went into Glen Padnick's office, who was the head of the company, and I said, "Let's do something different with *Facts of Life* this year. I'd like to try and make it funny." (*Laughs.*) And he didn't take that awfully well. (*Both laugh.*) And so, I went off and hired a new actress to play Mrs. Garrett, I hired Cloris Leachman. And I did two episodes, half of which was about a Winnebego teetering on a cliff with all of them in it, and I was immediately fired. (*Laughs.*) The network said, "What the hell have you let this man do?" I was out of control. So they fired me, and rightfully so. I never had a moment where I felt malice towards them at all. They were completely right to do so. Glen said "Listen, we'll pay you off with your contract." And I said, "I've only done two weeks' work, you can't pay me for the entire year, put me [on] another show." So I went to work on this other show called *Sweet Surrender*, which was Dana Delany's first show. She and I have remained close over the years. After that, I had been writing spec features all along, and my agent sent one of these over to Marshall Herskovitz and Ed Zwick at *thirtysomething*. And they called me up and said, "Come on over, we want to meet." They showed me the pilot they shot, and I thought, "Why in the hell would they want to meet with *me*?"

Longworth: 'Cause you'll work for a chair.

HAGGIS: Jesus, I was expensive by then (*laughs*) because after seven or eight years of this, your price goes up, especially in comedy. And so I went in there and I spent the entire meeting trying to talk them out of hiring me. I said, "You're making a big mistake. I don't know what I'm doing." And they had read everything I had written by then, plays and stuff, and said, "No, we really do think you *do* know what you're doing." And I said, "Well, you're making a mistake, but it's your business, so go for it." So they hired me, and I had a wonderful, wonderful time. I really learned how to write on their show. It was a great experience for me, because I went in there, I wasn't trying to be modest, I *didn't* know what I was doing. I tried my best, worked it through, and they really took the time to work with me and let me write my own scripts, but really gave me a lot of guidance. They also encouraged me to dig in and start telling stories that were personal where I was exploring myself.

Longworth: Ed and Marshall are great guys who have really contributed to the television landscape.

HAGGIS: Yeah, I learned a lot from them, and I can't say we've remained close, because you have so few people that you can actually call friends in this business, and that usually comes from geography. If you live within three blocks of them, you hang out with them. But I see Marshall and Ed all the time.

Longworth: But you don't get to watch *Once and Again* because you're busy?

HAGGIS: No, I *have* watched their show, and called Marshall up when it was first aired, and told him how terrific I thought it was. In fact, I complimented Ed last week on the show. I thought it was a great episode. And I complimented him on his ratings, too. (*Laughs.*) They're our competition, but a good show is a good show, and it's not their fault or mine that we're up against each other. And the reason one will succeed and one will fail, really, sometimes has nothing to do with quality.

Longworth: You, Marshall, Ed, John Masius, and others have sort of led us back to an era of quality drama. Why was America ripe for the transition from mindless sitcoms into hour dramas, and will the new era last?

HAGGIS: I don't think there *was* a transition. I think we've always had good television. It's much like when I went to Britain. I had been raised in Canada on British and American television, and there was very little Canadian programming that was any good. I just thought it was brilliant what the British did, and I watched it every night. I realized that there were two brilliant shows on, and the rest was just dreck. But we got to see those two in Canada, and we get to see the best of them here. I don't think that this is the golden age of television. I think we already had the golden age of television. (*Laughs.*) We forget that Paddy Chayefsky did some *pretty* good work back then, you know? (*Laughs.*) I think that a lot of the stuff we were raised on really reflected the times. And it's just that this is reflecting the era we're in currently. It's not that we have better shows or worse shows, it's just that they're a little more complex and a little more introspective perhaps, because that's what we happen to be going through right now. But there were always groundbreaking shows. I mean, some of the most fun [times] I've had in my life were on shows that really pressed the boundaries—*The Tracey Ullman Show*, when I wrote for that. I had so much fun. Just to work with those people, Jim Brooks and all the writers there. You couldn't say that Tracey's show was a huge success, it happened to be at Fox, and Fox didn't have anything to put on for a few years that would pull a bigger audience. But it was a terrific show. I think we'll always go through waves, we all go through situations where we start to believe that we are responsible for the things that are occurring around us. The good things, and not the bad things. And networks who are successful tend to say, "Well, *we* did this," and forget that it was the creative people, including their creative staff—the writers, producers, and directors that they brought in—who created those successes and who took risks to get them.

Longworth: You took some risks with *EZ Streets*. Brooks and Marsh in their *Complete Directory to Prime Time and Cable TV Shows* described *EZ Streets* by saying, "All of the principals were flawed with both good and bad sides."

HAGGIS: With *EZ Streets*, I had three black characters in the pilot. One was the corrupt mayor of the city, and the other two were internal affairs cops who had questionable morality, let's put it that way. But they believed Ken Olin's character was dirty, and they would do anything to prove that. I thought I was going to get killed over the mayor. I didn't get one complaint from the African American community. People loved it. Carl Lumbly, who played it brilliantly, fought to play the role because it showed a very real, very flawed human being, but it didn't fall into the stereotype of a flawed human being.

Longworth: But, my question is, are we lacking the traditional hero in prime-time TV who is *not* flawed, and who is accountable for his or her actions?

HAGGIS: Well, I think we have them, but they're in cartoons, and I think when kids are young they want to see, and you probably want them to see, "White hats and black hats." But by the time they get to about age ten, they start to figure out that the white hats are looking a little soiled, and that the black hats occasionally do good things. From that point on, although we love our heroes, we don't want them to be superheroes. Even when you look back at Christopher Reeve playing Superman, he played him as a flawed hero, and that's what made him endearing, that's what makes you a human being. So no, I don't think we've had perfect heroes for a long time, and that's a very good thing. I guess the cops in *Dragnet* were the last ones we thought of as just strictly good guys.

Longworth: Straight arrows, but with no personality.

HAGGIS: No personality and *boy*, I wouldn't want to run into those cops, would you? (*Laughs.*)

Longworth: No, but I think I have.

HAGGIS: They weren't human beings. There was no way you could deal with them, so I think you have to have flawed heroes and flawed villains.

Longworth: So why didn't *EZ Streets* make it?

HAGGIS: I think the plots were too complex. I think that people will accept flawed human beings. I mean, look at *The Sopranos*, talk about flawed, and it's a huge hit, at least on HBO. But there's a couple of reasons. CBS, Leslie Moonves, loved the project but had no place for it, and he was just taking over the network, and he put us on after *Touched by an Angel*, which was the only slot, the only place he could put us was on Sunday night.

Longworth: And that's a big leap from *Angel* to *EZ Streets*.

HAGGIS: Yeah (*laughs*), and we didn't keep much of that audience. (*Laughs.*) And so CBS was probably the wrong place for it, and we were on in the wrong time slot. And then the plot was so complex. Interesting, I thought, but very complex. You had to really, really watch it, and if you ever sneezed or, God forbid, went to the bathroom, you were lost. You missed a key piece of information and you were gone. And sometimes those key pieces of information were just a look; a look from this person or that person, and "oh my God, they're having a relationship!" (*Laughs.*)

Longworth: So why would you make such a complex show if you knew that most viewers wouldn't be able to follow it?"

HAGGIS: Well, I didn't know that, and I *don't* know that. I don't think it's necessarily true. I just didn't do it well. I think I made it too complex. I mean, if you were sitting in a movie theater watching, it would be just fine. It's dark, you're focused on the screen. And that's the medium you're dealing with. I just wasn't smart enough to think, "You know, when I watch TV, other things are going on. My kids are in the other room, there's noise outside, I have to get up, the phone rings." And so it's not that the people who go to the movies are smarter than people who stay at home and watch television.

Longworth: They're just more focused in the setting.

HAGGIS: Yes, in an hour you have to be a little clearer on the story you're telling.

Longworth: Steven Bochco told us at the Museum of Television & Radio in New York that he loves to screen television shows in settings like the museum theater because the room is dark, people are focused, and there are no commercial interruptions.

HAGGIS: And strangely enough, having been in those situations with screenings, I would think some of the stuff I have done, and some of the things others have done, I wouldn't *want* to sit in a darkened room and focus on it. Because when you really, really start to inspect it (*laughs*), it's not complex enough, but in the movie theater we've come to look for those nuances. We've come to expect a glance to mean something. And so, what works well in television *doesn't* work well in features necessarily. I was hoping to do the equivalent of what the British had done with some of their miniseries, and do it over twelve episodes or twenty-four episodes, with something that I really enjoyed watching. Like the shows I remember watching on PBS.

Longworth: Except your characters would all have good teeth.

HAGGIS: (*Laughs.*) That's true.

Longworth: Wouldn't it be better, though, if you and the network executives had to screen your TV shows on a small screen with forty different distractions going on in the room?

HAGGIS: And run commercials.

Longworth: Yeah.

HAGGIS: If I had watched the pilot with commercials, I would have made a lot of changes.

Longworth: So why don't more producers do that—watch a pilot in a room with the kids, let the dog soil the carpet, and have the phone ring.

HAGGIS: Well, we do but we do it too late. We do it when it's on the air. And by then, I mean, I watched *EZ Streets*, the two-hour pilot, when it was on the air, and it kept cutting to these commercials that would go on for five or six minutes, and I couldn't remember the last damn thing that happened. (*Laughs.*)

Longworth: And *you* wrote it!

HAGGIS: I wrote and directed the thing! (*Laughs.*) So you sit there and go, "Oh shit!" But I think also if it had been on a different network, on Fox or HBO, I mean, there are very good series that start off with nothing. You look at *Hill Street Blues*, you look at *Homicide,* but they had a network that could afford to believe in them, or couldn't afford not to.

Longworth: Let's talk about *Michael Hayes,* which, like *EZ Streets* didn't last very long. You mentioned time slots earlier as being a factor. Is it true that Bochco had a contractual agreement with David Caruso that would prevent David from appearing in any show that went up against *NYPD Blue?*

HAGGIS: That's true. I guess you can do anything, make any sort of agreement. Caruso wanted to get off the show, and Bochco had a contract with him. The producer has the right to say, "You can't develop television for anybody else for a certain period if you've got my money." So he [Bochco] was generous in allowing David to do television *at all.* (*Laughs.*)

Longworth: No, what he said was David could *repair* televisions, but he can't work in television. (*Both laugh.*) But let me turn it around on you. Granted you don't make the schedules, and even though you knew about the contractual agreement, you had no control over which night your show aired. So now *Michael Hayes* is on Tuesday night at 9 P.M., and you've got to be thinking, this is not the right place to be.

HAGGIS: You know, I so seldom think those things. It's probably why I'm not more successful.

Longworth: You *are* successful, that's why I'm asking you.

HAGGIS: (*Laughs.*) But at a certain point, you fight for what you believe in the way of support from the network. You fight for a time slot, if you're smart enough to *know* what the best time slot is, because sometimes you just don't know. I thought our time slot [for *Family Law*] was much better than *Judging Amy*'s. Well, guess what? I was wrong. (*Laughs.*) *Judging Amy* is just "heat" in that time slot because the female appeal was just lacking in that hour. And it's a good show, as well. So you never *really* know what's your best time slot, and even the networks with all their studies are just taking a guess at what will fit. So you do that, and then at some point, television becomes a very Zen experience. You have to deal with what you can control, and don't try to control what you can't. Because then you go nuts. And talk about being a control freak; if I was continually worried that we were in the wrong slot and was trying to manipulate that as well as trying to do a good show. You need a separate person to do that or just trust the network, and I just trust the network.

Longworth: Well, you sound as if you are at peace with yourself. I sense a calmness about you.

HAGGIS: You probably just caught me at a good moment. (*Both laugh.*)

Longworth: Tell me about *Due South*, a very interesting concept of a Canadian Mountie on assignment in Chicago. Wasn't that the first time TV had sort of a NAFTA deal going on between CBS and Canadian TV?

HAGGIS: It was the first and only time that a non-American show has been on prime-time on a major U.S. network. That's what CBS tells me.

Longworth: What were the advantages and disadvantages of that arrangement? I mean, this wasn't just a bicoastal production. You're dealing with two different countries. What were the pros and cons?

HAGGIS: The pro and the con was that I had to be in Canada to do it. I thought about trying to do it from a distance, but I just couldn't. I'm too hands-on. So I only did the first season, then turned it over to others for the subsequent two seasons. Being away from my family was the hardest thing.

Longworth: But what exactly brought you to *Due South*, and don't tell me you used to be a Mountie.

HAGGIS: Well, I'm a Canadian. And the idea came from Jeff Sagansky, who was running CBS at the time. He and the head of the Alliance, Robert Lantos, had a conversation. Robert wanted to break into the business down here, and was talking to Jeff, and said he wanted to do a show about a trapper, or a Mountie, or some Canadian. So Jeff called me up. I had had a deal with CBS for many years (basically they said, "Get Paul Haggis, and we'll talk about it"), so Jeff called and said, "I've got an idea for a show for you. A Mountie or a trapper comes to big city, USA." And I said, "Gee, thanks Jeff." (*Laughs.*) And I had just pitched something really dark and twisted. I wasn't into this Mountie or trapper, so I hung up the phone. I get so depressed when the networks pitch me these ideas. And then I started thinking, and said, "I could do something really cool and perverse with this. I could twist around all the archetypes and all the stereotypes, and make everyone think I'm doing one show when I'm actually doing *Rocky and Bullwinkle* (*laughs*), which is one of my favorite shows of all time. It could play to so many levels," and I thought that could be very cool. So I started studying Mounties and going and looking at all the archetypes of Mounties. I then started looking at stereotypes of how Americans view Canadians as really polite but boring people who spend their weekends clubbing seals, and how Canadians viewed Americans as being gunslingers, money grubbing, and imperialistic. And I said, "You know what? I could start a little border skirmish here." (*Both laugh.*) And so, I wrote the pilot and CBS liked it, and I took that slant on it. It *was* a little bit of a genre buster, because you weren't really sure what the show was. It was a straightforward, cop action show with humor and comedy, that, at its best, toyed with deeper and darker themes. And so we prepared to shoot the pilot and during preproduction we got a message from the RCMP [Royal Canadian Mounted Police] saying that they were not going to allow me to do it.

Longworth: No kidding?

HAGGIS: And I thanked them for their opinion. (*Laughs.*) And the Alliance said to me, "No, you don't understand. There's a law in Canada from 1896 in which the Royal Canadian Mounted Police has total control over anything that's said about them in the media in Canada." And I said, "What?" And they say, "This *isn't* America, it's a different country. And so you can't do this." And I said, "Oh yes I can. This is wonderful. Tell them I'm not changing a word. Give them my home address. Tell them to come and arrest me because it will make great headlines in *Variety*." (*Laughs.*) To be arrested for something this absurd would be fabulous. I would pay big money for them to do it. (*Both laugh.*) So Alliance freaked out. And I went ahead and I refused to change anything and I shot it exactly as it was. I actually only changed one thing. The RCMP claimed that their image was copyrighted, and they were licensing that image to Disney. (*Laughs.*) Now I would go up against the RCMP, but I didn't want to go up against Disney. (*Laughs.*) I mean, that's serious stuff. So I changed the uniform slightly. I had the belt go from left to right rather than right to left across his chest. And I put the badge on the hat (which they don't have) just to make it look a little different. And they continued to make threats. They sent me a thirty-two page list of changes they insisted I make. So I don't make *any* of the changes, I shoot the pilot, and Alliance is shitting in their pants the entire time. And after it airs and gets such a great response, the RCMP fires the guy who'd given me all the trouble.

Longworth: That's funny.

HAGGIS: Yeah, and over the course of the first three years, RCMP recruitment went up. The RCMP quickly realized that we were improving their image, especially since, at that time, they were mired in corruption scandals. And so they ended up asking me to come and speak up there, and asking the actors to represent them. It's hysterical. But at the same time, after the pilot aired I got tons of letters from Canadians. Schoolchildren would write in droves to tell me what a disservice I was doing to Canadians, and to the Canadian image, how I was perpetuating the myths about Canadians being polite, etc. And they were *really* objecting to the way that I was portraying them as naïve and polite, opening doors for women and such. *These* were the things they were *objecting* to! (*Laughs.*) Schoolteachers would have their entire class write in. They'd say that the scene in the airport where he gives away his cab, and he gives away his money to the stranger, is totally unrealistic. And I'd write back and say, "I did that when I came here myself from Canada. I *did* give my money away to strangers. I'm a sucker." (*Laughs.*)

Longworth: Maybe, but you've also given some great TV shows to strangers, and that brings us to your current series. I love *Family Law*. Does it surprise you that an old, married guy like me, nearing fifty, loves a show that is largely a woman's drama?

HAGGIS: Surprise me? Yes. I think it surprises me that *I* like it. (*Laughs.*) I'm not closing in on fifty yet, I am happily married, and even though I've gone through this experience [divorce] it's not *that* which attracts me to the show.

Longworth: So if you hadn't created it, you would still watch it.

HAGGIS: I hope so. There are a lot of great shows out there that I *don't* watch and would love to watch. I've never seen *The West Wing*. I hear it's great. A couple of others that I would really like to see and haven't seen because of our schedule. But even if I didn't produce *Family Law*, I think I would watch it, probably because of what we attempt to do on every show. I do the same thing over and over again, which is to pose questions to which there are no answers, or no *right* answers, and then argue both sides as if your life depended on them, as if you really desperately believed in both sides of an issue. And that puts you in really strange territory.

Longworth: But you mentioned earlier that it also came out of your own personal experience. Talk about that.

HAGGIS: I went through a long and painful divorce as did my ex-wife. And so, it was a nine-year divorce when it got finished, including custody and all that. It was very, very difficult for both of us and for the kids, as well, who are only now recovering from it. So, I'm in the middle of this, and my attorney said, "Oh boy, you should do something about *our* work—there's a lot of stories here." And I said, "Yeah, yeah." And so I sort of filed that in the back of my head. Well, I have these multiple series commitments with CBS, to do a series per year, and so I came up with what I thought was a really cool cop show, just from a different angle. I took it to them and they said "Oh, that is so good, [but)] we have cop shows already in development, so do a law show for us." And I said, "A law show?" There's so many good law shows, there's *The Practice* and *Law & Order,* and I got to thinking overnight, well, family law is an area where there's very little law, and it's more about the moral complexities of what appear to be very simple issues. And when I went back to pitch it to them, I said, "I'd like to do a woman's point of view."

Longworth: And they said?

HAGGIS: And they said, "Cool, do it!" So I went out and called my friend Anne Kenney, who I had written with on *L.A. Law* during their last season. She was one of the co-producers there, and I called her and said, "Do you want to do a show with me?" and she said, "Sure." I wanted to do it from a woman's point of view for several reasons. First, all of the law shows that were on air appeared to be very male-oriented. And even if there were female characters, the shows had a real male feel about them, other than *Ally McBeal,* which really isn't a law show.

Longworth: Well, we're not sure *what* it is.

HAGGIS: (*Laughs.*) So, I wanted to create a woman's law firm, or at least one that is largely female. I also felt it would be unfair, given my recent history, to tell a show from a man's point of view.

Longworth: Now why would you be that diplomatic and sensitive? I mean, if it were me, I'd jump right in there and say, "Here's my first ten episodes. Episode number one—'how I got screwed in my divorce,'" and so on.

HAGGIS: Well I think the horrible thing about being a writer is that you're constantly viewing things from opposing points of view, because you have to create heroes who are flawed, and you have to create villains who believe they're heroes. You need internal conflict to create an interesting plot. And so, I think you're destined to look at your life like that. You look at yourself as the hero you are and the villain you are. And so I would rather take the other side. If you had to bet who comes out of divorces better, men or women, the men usually do. So I thought it more interesting to do a show about the underdog, rather than the top dog.

Longworth: Before we leave the whole male/female thing, I want to tie that demographic issue into some things that were written about *Family Law*'s premiere. I'll mention a few criticisms and get you to comment. *Entertainment Weekly*, for example, savaged the show, at one point writing that the pilot of *Family Law* screams out "No males should watch." They also called it *First Wives Club* meets *Ally McBeal*. They went so far as to say it's an "anti-male series." They said that Kathleen "seems awkward in a role that one minute asks her to be vulnerable, and the next minute to be a male-basher." I think the critic missed the point. I mean, her character was going through a nasty divorce and she's *supposed* to be awkward, right?

HAGGIS: Yeah. I mean, I wanted to place that character at that point of imbalance, and then see which way she would fall and how she'd right herself. I love pushing characters to extremes. And to rip your clothes off in an office, one has to be fairly unbalanced. So, yes, you're absolutely right, she did seem awkward. When your life is being torn apart like that, it's hard to find things to grab on to, and you just try to grab on to anything you can, and usually you grab on to the wrong things. That's why, just because I was doing a show about women, I didn't want to treat them in some way that says, "She's a martyr, she's a saint, she's a Madonna." No, I want to show that she's falling apart, and she's not handling it very well.

Longworth: As far as the anti-male remark, I went back through all of the first season story lines, and the only men that get bashed in the series are scumbags who *happen* to be men, not just men in general. Would the critics have preferred that you have all positive male role models?

HAGGIS: I could be wrong about this, but I've spoken to a handful of critics from that time on, and I think a large majority of the people who had a real problem with it were men. And so, that made me very happy because . . . if I wasn't making *somebody* uneasy in this world, I would just be making pablum. If I have a choice, I would much rather make my sex uneasy, because we've had it pretty darn well. (*Laughs.*)

Longworth: Well, I've had uneasy sex myself (*both laugh*), but that's a whole other episode.

HAGGIS: Exactly. (*Laughs.*) That's next week. So I think these male critics were very threatened and I think they lashed out. I liked the pilot but thought I failed in a lot of ways. So, as to the merits of the show they can say whatever they want, but as far as the "male-bashing" thing, when I see someone say, "Don't watch unless you're a woman," I think for the most part these are men who are terrified or threatened by women, and don't know it.

Longworth: Interesting.

HAGGIS: Yeah, because they think, "My God, this is just silly," but every woman critic I've spoken to, they've said, "*What* male-bashing? We've had to put up with this for *years!* We've been stereotyped, we've been placed in roles that—if there was a term 'female-bashing' (which there isn't), then we could have used it hundreds of thousands of times in television and movies." But the first time you show a guy who is a real bastard (*laughs*) and the woman is getting jerked around, then it's "male-bashing."

Longworth: *TV Guide* also wrote of *Family Law,* "This unconventional vehicle hardly raises the bar on traditional law series." But again, it seems to me as if you've invented a new genre of law shows. So not only have you raised the bar, you've changed the bar.

HAGGIS: Oh, I don't think we've reinvented the genre. I've just stolen effectively. (*Laughs.*) When my last series, a cop show, came out and failed within the first four days, all the critics loved it.

Longworth: *EZ Streets.*

HAGGIS: Yeah, and in *Time* magazine, I was literally reading this review when Leslie [Moonves] canceled the show. *Time* magazine had called it "The best program of the year, one of the most profound crime dramas ever to be made." It was canceled as I was reading that article (*laughs*), and so I looked at that and said, "You know what? I've done something wrong." It's not like, "Well, I'm smart and these morons just didn't get it." No, I've done something wrong, I've made things too complex in many areas, and so you just couldn't follow the fucking thing. And so, what I want to do is try and put something more in a box, and then take one complexity, one area where I say, "OK, I'm going to make the stories themselves challenging. I'm not only going to challenge people's assumptions, I'm going to challenge their beliefs in things they hold dearest. But I'm going to put it into a box so they think I'm *not* going to do that." I wanted to put it into the box of a normal law show, something we've seen before many times, so that it's comfortable, so that the audience wouldn't be threatened by this format, and then deal with issues that make people squirm, or challenge them to think a little bit. Have them rooting for a person from the beginning, and say, "Well, I know who's the good person here and who's the bad person." And then, like a guy on a street corner running a shell game, I ask you to point to the good guy . . . and it's only *then* that you realize you chose the other person. We did an episode where Danni has a case, a woman comes into her office, she is divorced, and she had given up custody of her daughter at the time of the divorce with very limited visitation, and she wants to change that. And Danni says, "Well, you don't have to explain to me, I know why a woman would fight for custody." And the client says, "I don't think you understand. I wasn't a woman at the time. But that doesn't mean I want to give up being a father." And so we start out with this absurd notion that this woan still wants to be a good father, so, at the beginning, the audience goes, "This is ridiculous." Hopefully, if we've done our job by the end of the episode, they think like Danni, who says, "Every father should be just like you." (*Laughs.*) So you take it from one extreme, so that we look at America, our biases and our own personal bigotries, large and small, and then try and very covertly change that point of view. Not sociological, not another big, sweeping "I'm going to change society" way, but just get the people to view things a little differently. So what I would then do is say, "What makes me uncomfortable? What don't I believe in? What do I think is just nuts?" How do I make everybody believe that *that's* the right thing. (*Laughs.*) And then you would argue both sides as if your life depended on it. If I'm doing it right, you should change your mind about the character three or four times in the episode, hero/villain/hero/villain, and so forth. And so you'd come out to the end and go, "Well, it could go either way on this, and maybe I still believe what I did, but now I understand this character." They can still damn one, or damn them both, but that's how I decided to tell stories, twist the characters around in that way, rather than to take a plot and untwist it over twenty-two episodes.

Longworth: Do you also do what Dick Wolf does, which is to scan the headlines for ideas?

HAGGIS: Absolutely. I grab stuff from the *New York Times* all the time. [But] unlike *Law & Order*, we try not to just do the case. We try and be *inspired* by the case. We did the Jeremy Strohmeyer case, but we used it to argue, "Is it 'nurture or nature' that is responsible?" You have this adopted boy who went bad; is it because of his genes, and there's nothing you can do but feed him drugs that would *change* those genes? Or was it these very nice parents who somehow created this monster? Who's responsible? And so, in the lawsuit we posit, the parents of the dead girl are suing the parents of the killer, saying "You're responsible for this." And then, take that woman from having called her own son a "monster" all the way through to her realizing she loves her son, no matter what.

Longworth: OK, so you've decided on a story. At what point do you select a particular writer or determine how involved you're going to be in the process?

HAGGIS: Well, I'm very lucky that I've found a good group of writers that I want to work with. Over the first twelve episodes, I was all over every line of every script, and then at that point I started to give them more and more room. That's where we're at right now; I work in partnership with my other co-executive producer/writers. I work with them breaking the initial story or they break a story and bring it to me and tell me what the beats and the twists are, and how we're going to view it. Then, usually they write the script and do the rewrites, and then I'll read it and give my notes, and that's it. Other stories and issues about which I feel strongly, I'll take and write and then usually direct. I have another producer who supervises the stage and usually works with the directors, and then I'll usually take over again in post-production. When the director finishes his cut, I'll go through frame by frame and make sure that it's a show we'll be proud of. If there's a problem, you can do a lot in editing.

Longworth: Is it difficult for you, as a writer who knows what your vision is, to relinquish even a tiny bit of control and creative input over a story?

HAGGIS: I think I've been very successful this year. It was very hard on *EZ Streets.* I wrote or co-wrote every single episode. This year I'm starting to learn that in television, to survive, to make a good series, you have to find people you trust and then work with them to develop a unified vision, so that it's *our* show. That starts off as your vision, but fairly soon, with all the influences of the actors and directors, the other writers, if you're managing it well and trying to manage these things better, it becomes a unified vision that isn't *just* yours. And you only then have to correct it when it deviates from that vision.

Longworth: Dick Wolf and others have articulated their belief that a writer must have some miles on the odometer to be able to write good drama. Don't you have to employ writers of a certain age, who have experienced life to the extent that this vision deserves?

HAGGIS: I think the ideal writer is always *your* age. (*Laughs.*) But not in a way that people think. I remember when I was on *thirtysomething* all of our writers were in their thirties. I think the youngest was probably thirty, and Marshall and Ed were probably thirty-six or thirty-seven. I think I was thirty-five at the time. I remember at that time, a writer came in who was recommended for staff, and then she came in to meet Ed and Marshall. She was in her late forties, and there was *no* way she was going to get the job! I think it was because they believed that she didn't share a common reality, a common set of experiences unique to that generation. Now, it's preposterous to say that a woman in her forties can't remember back ten years (*laughs*), but when we were in our thirties we certainly believed that.

Longworth: The arrogance of the thirties.

HAGGIS: Yes, exactly. Now that we're in our forties and we start looking like we're between our forties and sixties, when you can't really tell the difference, I think we're probably a little more accepting of writers who are older. I *don't* know if we're that accepting of younger writers. (*Laughs.*) We're probably jealous of them. (*Laughs.*)

Longworth: So how young is your youngest writer on *Family Law?*

HAGGIS: The youngest writer is twenty-five, the first staff writer we ever hired.

Longworth: But how can that writer identify with what Dixie or Kathleen's characters are going through?

HAGGIS: I didn't ask myself that when I hired him. I think he can, because he wrote a good script. I would think he could probably more closely identify with experiences he has had with the other characters—Danni, etc.— but I would hate to think that he couldn't put himself in that person's life, because if *that's* true, then I couldn't possibly put myself in Kathleen's life.

Longworth: So you are more tolerant now than you were in your thirties?

HAGGIS: No question, because in our forties, we start to understand how deeply flawed we are. I think we can appreciate that concept in our thirties, so we revel in it, and wear those flaws as a badge. (*Laughs.*) I mean, if you watch *thirtysomething,* there is something very arrogant about it, in *all* those characters, but I think we were all arrogant in our thirties.

Longworth: Were there any story lines you've struggled with on *Family Law* because they were just too close to your own painful experiences?

HAGGIS: I've certainly struggled with a number of them, but, perversely, the ones that scared me the most are the ones I want to do immediately. And as soon as I get really scared, I know I've written something good. I think the second or third one we did scared the hell out of me, and that was the one about race and bigotry. The thought of me having to write an empathetic racist, someone who was a better father than a very liberal mother. Someone who could spout the most hideous things. And I had to sit there and come up with a really good reason for that, and had to co-opt the language of the African American community and their own complaints to use against them.

I talked to an African American male who drives a BMW to find out how often he'd been pulled over for "failing to signal" or some other bullshit excuse. And so, I had my white racist father character use that against the black step-father. He says, "It may not be fair, but that's life. My kids are going to have guns pointed at them because they are driving with a black man in a nice car." And you react and say, "But that's *my* argument! You can't steal my argument!" (*Laughs.*) And that thought made me so uncomfortable that I ended up not doing it right away. It still gives me shivers to think of it, really.

Longworth: That was a very effective opening sequence where the camera keeps moving around the table to everyone in such a way that the last thing you do is reveal the color of the stepfather's skin. That was brilliant.

HAGGIS: Thank you.

Longworth: John Wells and others have indicated that a good story-driven drama will always outlast a good character-driven drama, because in a character-driven drama you will eventually run out of original things for those characters to do. If that theory is correct, where does that put *Family Law,* which really does a good job at being both?

HAGGIS: I think we're story driven. We look at what the story is and then we say, "What's happening in our characters' personal lives?" Our stories are not driven by what is happening with our characters that week. We have an arc in which we say, we want Lynn to get in trouble, we want her husband to start asking her out again sometime between episode ten and fifteen. Or we have ideas that we want to see happen with her family. When Dixie had an estranged daughter in the story, that just came from Anne Kenney, who said, "What if Dixie has a daughter?" And I went, "Cool. I'll bet she hasn't spoken to her, etc., and we can do something with that." We introduced her, and then she goes and tries to meet her and finds out that she has a grandchild. That's interesting, but it came out of a story we were doing with this Jerry Strohmeyer case about responsibility in parents, and the line that Lynn had that says, "Do you ever feel sorry that you didn't have kids?" And Dixie says, "I regret it every day," and as soon as she said it, I said, "Cool, she has a kid." (*Laughs.*) She has a kid, she's hiding it. So really the character issues come out of plot. And we figure out what the plot is and then we say, "Well, how can we make this personal to the people in the office? How can it have a personal impact on their lives?" rather than starting with what's going on in their lives and somehow extrapolating new court cases that reflect that. It has to go the other way.

Longworth: Doing so many emotionally charged issues, I'm always curious what kind of feedback you drama producers receive, and I don't mean just fan mail. Can you tell that you've actually touched people and made a difference?

HAGGIS: Oh, yeah, we get quite a bit of mail. On the second episode we got a lot of mail from parents of Down's syndrome children. That was a really tough one. We had a Down's syndrome kid, Lynn needed his testimony in order to win, so she put him on the stand and nearly destroyed him. It was a show that dealt with the arrogance of the righteous and how far you'll go to win for a just cause. In the end, Lynn wins a big settlement and her client slaps her across the face for what she put her son through. We got a lot of mail on that, and all of it supportive and thanking us for it. The racism episode I expected just to get killed on. I expected that my African American friends would never speak to me again because I said hideous things. I mean, horrible, horrible things. All the fan mail we got was from African Americans. They loved it. They said, "Thank you. You're actually saying what people refuse to talk about." *They* know there's a problem with racism in this country. They *know* there are people like that out there. It's us, the nice, liberal white Americans who say, "Oh no, we're not like that." So it's like fighting a pillow, they feel they can't get to it, because no one will admit to it, or talk about it. And so *all* the fan mail was positive, and it was all from African Americans. That shocked me.

Longworth: Are you planning to do anything to subvert *Family Law?* You know, something so off-the-wall that will take the show down from the top to the bottom?

HAGGIS: Well, I think I would like to do that (*laughs*) because I *am* uncomfortable with success. I tend to be much happier when I'm failing. I like success, don't get me wrong, I really like it (*laughs*), but I don't think I actually earn it.

Longworth: You make your money the old-fashioned way, you subvert it.

HAGGIS: Exactly.

Longworth: Well, thanks for doing the interview.

HAGGIS: Gladly. I love to spend the time talking about myself. (*Laughs.*)

Longworth: I'll also need to get a photo of you for the book.

HAGGIS: Get it while I'm young. (*Both laugh.*)

8

BARBARA HALL | Author, Author

Barbara Hall. COURTESY OF BARBARA HALL.

TELEVISION CREDITS

1982–84	*Family Ties*(NBC)
1984–86	*Newhart* (CBS)
1987–88	*A Year in the Life* (NBC)

1988–89	*Moonlighting* (ABC)
1991–92	*Anything but Love* (CBS)
1991–93	*I'll Fly Away* (NBC)
1994–95	*Northern Exposure* (CBS)
1996–99	*Chicago Hope* (CBS)
1999–	*Judging Amy* (CBS)

〰〰 〰〰 〰〰

while participating in a panel discussion at the Academy of Television Arts & Sciences on the topic "Women in Drama," award-winning writer/producer Barbara Hall drew laughs when she confessed, "My family still has no idea what I'm doing . . . I've worked on so many different shows, they think I can't hold down a job."

Her family was right, of course, but in Barbara's case that is a compliment, because Hall's Hollywood job-hopping has included stops along the way at *Newhart, Moonlighting, I'll Fly Away,* and *Northern Exposure* before landing at *Judging Amy.* More importantly, wherever she has journeyed, critical acclaim has followed.

Barbara has paid her dues by writing and producing prime-time programs of one kind or another for more than twenty years, and her employment record reflects a woman whose talents have been, and continue to be, in demand. Hall is a gifted storyteller and a strong leader, qualities that come in handy when wearing two hats every day—one for writing, and one for showrunning. And she is acutely aware that those of her gender have not always had the opportunity to wear those hats. Interviewed by Susan Littwin for *Written By* magazine, Hall said, "Men have been in positions of power in television for a very long time, so you can't blame them for developing the shows they would like to see. I set out to write a show that I would like to watch. Women, for obvious reasons, are better at writing female characters and what women want to see. It took a while for . . . the network to understand that the female audience was really strong and would be loyal to shows that were custom made for them" (April 2000). In her mind, the lack of women writers and showrunners once slowed the progress of dramas about women, and vice versa. But all that has changed, thanks in part to the revolution of 1999 led by John Masius's *Providence.*

Not content to rest on her new plateau, however, Hall is also committed to improving, then monitoring, those sharing the perch with her. One example? Television's culpability in portraying and perpetuating unhealthy images for young women, something she was impassioned about while speaking at the "Women in Drama" event. "I think that trend in TV is just appalling, and I would never, ever work on a show where I had women starving in front of a nation," Hall said. "If those women were shooting heroin on TV every week, somebody would do something about it. But they're starving themselves to death in front of everybody including my daughter, and I could never be on a show like that, and allow that to happen. And I think the producers are accountable and should do something about it."

Hall also related the issue of health to that of overall success for women. "As someone who is behind the scenes, and one of a handful of women showrunners in television, if you're going to put that much effort into being thin and focusing constantly on how you look, and being hungry and exhausted from looking that way, you're not going to have the energy to do things like run corporations, or come up with television shows and get them on the air," she said. "It's a question of energy and how you want to spend it, and I think it's really important for women to know that. I don't think you can have big ideas and manage things if you're starving. How about just looking like a normal woman, and having some energy left over to do other things?"

Barbara's words are powerful, whether they appear in her seven novels, in a teleplay for *Judging Amy,* or in debating the role of television in shaping society. While this is an examination via the printed page, her words are particularly persuasive when heard in person. Her ability to communicate with conviction, humor, and poise is a telling experience for the intended receiver. I felt this while moderating "Women in Drama." Musical composer Pete Himmelman felt it over the phone. An accomplished songwriter, he had no intention of scoring a TV series but was hooked after only a few minutes talking with Barbara. "It all happened pretty quick after that. What can I say," he told *The Hollywood Reporter* (August 22, 2000). Of course, deep convictions and a power of persuasion are often misunderstood, particularly in Hollywood. Barbara told Susan Littwin, "You're always walking a fine line between being authoritative and being perceived as bitchy . . . if you're motivated by the work rather than ego, you can justify it and get away with it" (*Written By,* April 2000).

A woman with aristocratic beauty and an ability to be both wildly funny and deadly serious, Barbara, unlike the family members about whom she jokes, *does* know what she does for a living, and now, thankfully, so do we.

Barbara Hall was born in Chatham, Virginia, population twelve hundred. Her mother was a housewife and her father (now deceased) was general manager of a printing plant. Her older brother is now an Air Force chaplain, and her older sister, Karen, like Barbara, is a television writer. Both girls showed a talent for writing early on. "My parents were very frightened by the fact that we both wanted to be writers," Barbara recalls. "It's not as if we were surrounded in Chatham by success stories, people who planned to be writers and then became them. (*Laughs.*) They didn't encourage it so much. They wanted us to get our schoolwork and everything done first, and then if we had time to sit around and write stories, fine. They kind of tolerated it a little bit. Then I got a poem published when I was fourteen, and another one published when I was fifteen, and then I started publishing stuff in local magazines. When I started getting things published, they started to be more comfortable with it."

After high school, Chatham's leading poet traveled up the road to Harrisonburg, Virginia, to major in English at James Madison University. "I did absolutely every type of writing [there] except screenwriting or playwriting. I did journalism, creative writing, short stories, and poetry, but I never tried my hand at playwriting or screenwriting."

Graduating from James Madison in 1982, Barbara followed her big sister to the west coast to seek a career in television. "She was sort of a pioneering force in television years ago," Barbara says of Karen. "She was the first female staff writer on *M*A*S*H*, and the first female staff writer on *Hill Street Blues*. She did *Moonlighting* the first or second year, and I was there the last year. By the time I got to *Moonlighting*, I was coming off of *A Year in the Life*, a [Joshua Brand/John] Falsey show. It was kind of a coincidence that our paths crossed. She did a lot of TV movies, [such as] *The Women of Brewster Place* [and] *The Betty Ford Story*, and she just wrote a novel a couple of years ago that did really well. She also wrote an episode of *Judging Amy*. For years when she was writing drama, I was writing comedy. Then by the time I switched to drama, she had switched to comedy (*laughs*), so we never really had much of an opportunity to work together. Our paths just didn't cross very much."

Barbara's early comedy credits included penning an episode for *Family Ties* and spending a year working on *Newhart*. After *A Year in the Life* and *Moonlighting*, Hall crossed back into comedy with a brief stay as a co-producer on *Anything but Love*, then returned to the Brand/Falsey stable to work as a producer on both *I'll Fly Away* and *Northern Exposure* with good friend David Chase (*The Sopranos*). She then landed at *Chicago Hope* for two years as a consulting producer.

In 1997 her pilot for a new drama titled *The Doyles* was considered by ABC but never materialized into a series. The failed pilot, however, was anything but devastating for the talented Hall, who had maintained a career as a novelist since the early 1980s. Her books include: *Skeeball and the Secret of the Universe, Dreams, Dixie Storms, Fool's Hill, A Better Place, The House Across the Cove, Close to Home,* and *A Summons to New Orleans.* Hall's stories come from the heart and mostly from the South, and their publication proved that she was an author who could move with ease between two very diverse mediums. But in 1999 this southern girl was summoned back to television to rescue a pilot in distress, and ended up helping to craft a drama set in the North. CBS president Les Moonves recalled Barbara's beginnings with *Judging Amy.* "I first became aware of Barbara during my Lorimar, Warner Brothers days," he says. "We did *I'll Fly Away.* Barbara wrote probably the best scripts on that show. She won a Humanitas for it, and was so literate, so in touch with human feeling. A pure writer. *Judging Amy* was not her creation. It was a terrific concept, which Amy [Brenneman] had brought in the door. The original script just didn't do it. We were under an amazing time crunch, and we needed a script in, like, five days in order to give it a thumbs up or thumbs down. Barbara came in, and what she accomplished in five days was miraculous. We then shot four or five scenes from the [new] Barbara Hall script, and that was our pilot. It was sort of a fifteen-minute presentation. What Barbara really did was give us the impetus for the series. In other words, she gave us the feelings. She gave us the drama. I mean, it's a great lawyer show, but more importantly, it's a great family show. There are such well-drawn characters that are so fleshed out. There isn't a family in the world that doesn't relate to that situation."

Today, Barbara's TV family includes Brenneman and EMMY queen Tyne Daly, while her real-life family includes husband Paul Karon (also a native Virginian and a writer) and her nine-year-old daughter Faith, a photo of whom is seen during the open titles of *Judging Amy,* representing a young Amy. At first some critics panned the show. *TV Guide*'s Matt Roush called it "pandering melodrama" (October 30, 1999), and *Time* magazine lamented, "If this judge doesn't stop wearing her robe like a security blanket soon, she's going to try our patience." But it did not take long for *Judging Amy* to silence the critics and draw praise from all corners for its emotion and realism. *The Hollywood Reporter* raved that *Amy* "sizzles with plenty of crises and plenty of heart" (October 10, 2000). Howard Rosenberg of the *Los Angeles Times* heaped praise on Hall's work as well. Meanwhile, Caryn James of the *New York Times* called it one of the year's best dramas.

Judging Amy has gone on to be one of CBS's most solid performers, in terms of both ratings and revenues, and has won numerous awards. As Susan Littwin observed, "Success not only succeeds, it changes the rules" (*Written By*, April 2000). Barbara Hall, speaking at the "Women in Drama" event, concurred. "I think one of the best kept secrets about television is that there really isn't a rule book," she said. "They keep trying to create a rule book, and then every time a show like *Judging Amy* succeeds for reasons no one can understand (except the people behind it), all of the rules change. And I think that's true of all the shows represented here [*Providence, Family Law, Any Day Now, Once and Again*], and that's what I like about working in this industry as a woman. It's kind of a meritocracy, and if you can get out there and people respond to your show, then you've just rewritten the rules for everybody." But whether rewriting rules or penning novels or scripts, Barbara Hall is an author who cares deeply about her work and about the impact it may have on others, and she welcomes the responsibility that goes with it.

Hall, Brenneman, and Daly were among the panelists joining me for an evening of "Women in Drama" at the Television Academy in Los Angeles on November 2, 2000, but my primary interview with Barbara was conducted earlier that year.

Longworth: I finally got a copy of your novel, *Close to Home*, and I thought it was great.

HALL: Well, thank you.

Longworth: As a transplant to Virginia, my favorite part of the book was boycotting the Quality Mart.

HALL: (*Laughs.*)

Longworth: But my question is, would Barbara Hall shop at a Quality Mart?

HALL: (*Laughs.*) Well, you know what, I'm from Chatham, Virginia, and that was a town of like twelve hundred people and we shopped where something was available. Of course I shopped at Quality Mart. (*Both laugh.*) But I grew up in stores like that, so any chance I get, I go into them, actually, because I'm fascinated by them. Saturday night for us meant going to K-Mart. But what I was interested in was that I grew up in this small town where they would let nothing into the town. They wouldn't let a fast-food restaurant in, anything that tried to come into that town was summarily dismissed and run out of town. I just thought that was an interesting thing to try to write about.

Longworth: What was the name of that first poem you wrote as a kid?

HALL: (*Laughs.*) It was called *Goodbye*.

Longworth: What a great *start*.

HALL: (*Laughs.*)

Longworth: Do you remember any lines from it?

HALL: Oh God. No, actually I don't, but the next one I got published in a national magazine was called "Another Poem for You," and it was kind of a cute little poem. It was about, well, everything was about boyfriends when I was fourteen and fifteen. (*Laughs.*) It was a poem about how I couldn't write any poems except about this guy.

Longworth: Did you and your boyfriend neck in the Quality Mart parking lot?

HALL: Yeah, but the golf course is really where you go to neck, come on!

Longworth: I hadn't heard about the golf course.

HALL: Yeah, that's where you go.

Longworth: What TV shows did you like when you were growing up?

HALL: Ironically, I was never a kid or teenager who watched much television. I mean, I came to it late. But when I was real little I remember liking *The Rifleman, Wagon Train,* all those westerns. And then later I liked the trendy things, like *The Monkees, The Partridge Family.*

Longworth: But girls weren't supposed to like *The Rifleman.*

HALL: Oh really? I think I identified in some way.

Longworth: How could you as a woman possibly identify with a man who carried a repeating rifle.

HALL: I liked the idea that he was aggressive and took control of things. (*Both laugh.*) Not surprisingly, my first book was told from the point of view of a boy.

Longworth: I'm fascinated by your "adopted family" of Caron, Chase, Falsey, and Brand.

HALL: My TV Family.

Longworth: You could almost write a novel about this woman writer who was taken in by these four guys and they looked after her.

HALL: Right.

Longworth: So you were pretty lucky to fall into that "family"?

HALL: I was lucky to fall into the family, although I started writing when I was very young, and I didn't know better in a lot of cases, and one day I said to my agent, "I want to write for drama." I was a comedy writer at the time, and I didn't understand that that's a really difficult transition. And my agent was like, "Well, I'll try," but I didn't have a drama sample. What I had was a novel, and I was lucky in that Josh Brand is somebody who really likes novels and reads them and was willing to read that as a sample, because there are a lot of people who wouldn't have. So after that, he was willing to take a chance on me. I really responded to his work and to him as a person, and to John also, his partner at the time. And I remember, when they offered me the job they said, we think she's a good writer, we think we can make her a better writer. And that was absolutely what happened. I was just smart enough to learn from them, I wasn't in a big hurry to have my own show or anything like that. I always like to work with people that I can learn something from. In fact, the only time I'm *not* happy is when I'm not in that situation.

Longworth: What influence did each of these guys have on your career and its development? Let's start with Josh Brand, and John Falsey, the team who co-created *St. Elsewhere* and created *A Year in the Life, I'll Fly Away,* and *Northern Exposure.*

HALL: Well, from Josh and John I learned a lot. It was under their tutelage that I began to understand what storytelling was about. I'm talking about television storytelling, and what made a scene. They let me in on the whole process, watching dailies, editing, stuff like that, so I got to see from start to finish what it looks like when you write a scene that doesn't work and then have to go back to the typewriter and fix that. And by the way, it *was* a typewriter back then. They were great at motivating writers—they didn't want to rewrite people. They didn't feel like they had to pass everything through *their* typewriter. They wanted the writers to do it. And the greatest reward you get for that is they shoot your words. So they taught me how to motivate myself and become a self-starter. They were great at that.

Longworth: A good kind of discipline.

HALL: They were very hard on writers, by the way. They were like your toughest teacher in college.

Longworth: So they literally hired you based on which book?

HALL: A book called *Skeeball and the Secret of the Universe.*

Longworth: What about your relationship with Glenn Gordon Caron?

HALL: Well, it's interesting what happened with Glenn because, when I was at *Moonlighting,* Glenn wasn't there anymore. He had left. But he was one of the first persons I had met when I came to Los Angeles because we had the same agent. And he read the same book Josh Brand read and wanted to work with me. [He] gave me the pilot for *Moonlighting* and I read it and actually turned the job down because I was so intimidated by it. I said to my agent, "I don't think I can write this." Then, ironically, my sister went on to work there, and several years later when I had more confidence in myself as a writer I ended up there. Glenn has a certain vision and he knows how to execute that vision. And what I learned from writing at *Moonlighting*, even though he wasn't there, I was obviously trying to mimic what he did, so I learned everything about pace, and what you can get away with if you have the right people saying these words, and that you can really keep up the pace and you don't have to slow down for the audience. I also learned that writing for television can be kind of lyrical in a way.

Longworth: So your stint at *Moonlighting* was when?

HALL: 1988 or '89. Then I did about six months of another comedy, *Anything but Love*, the Jamie Lee Curtis show. After that I went back to drama, and then I went to development for a little while. Then, Josh Brand called me in one day out of the blue. Here's another great story. He called me up with this pilot he was doing called *Northern Exposure*, this weird little pilot. And he said, "I don't know what it is, but maybe you'd be interested in it." And I read it and loved it, but I was under contract at a studio and I couldn't leave.

Longworth: Which studio?

HALL: I was at Castle Rock. So that was a missed opportunity, and then the next time I heard from him, I was now out of my contract and he was doing *I'll Fly Away*, and that was such an obvious show for me to do, because, well, *you* know what it was [referring to our shared background as southerners growing up during the Civil Rights Movement]. So he called me up and gave me the pilot and I read it, and I called him and said, "I'm perfect for this show." And I made him laugh, 'cause it was like blowing your own horn. And that's where I met David Chase and started working with him.

Longworth: What did you learn from David?

HALL: David, you have to understand, became a friend of mine, so I have my *personal* feelings about David. I just adore him, I love him. But in terms of the person I worked with, there aren't enough words to explain how much I learned from him. I feel like I just learned everything *else* from David, you know? First of all, the most important thing I learned from him was fearlessness. He was absolutely fearless in his own writing, and he totally encouraged that from anyone working with him. I sort of lost my fear of making mistakes because it's easier to overstep the line and then pull it back than it is not to get there at all. And so, his writing inspired me. I would read a script by him, and I would just kind of be breathless, and I would want to do that. It was really just great. There's nothing like the mind of David Chase.

Longworth: I was immediately won over by him while working on my first book. What *is* so special about him?

HALL: He's totally uncompromising. He has a vision and he completely believes in his work, and he is really unswayed by outside opinion. You can't do a show like *The Sopranos* if you're going to spend even a second worrying about what people think, you just can't. He's also a great director. He has a vision so he knows what a scene is going to look like on the screen. He's just one of those wonderful people who had just a bad enough childhood (*laughs*) to make him great.

Longworth: Are you surprised that he's come to such great success this late in life?

HALL: Actually, I'm not surprised, I'm only pleased because back before people knew who David Chase was I went around saying, "David is the best writer in Hollywood, *period!*" Not just in TV. I would rather read a David Chase script than any movie script that came across my desk. And I was surprised that he had not been recognized for that, but I understood why it wasn't happening, and it was because David refused to ever compromise or take any stepping stones. He was offered other people's scripts to direct their movie and he wouldn't do that, and I would always say, "David, just do that, take that step," and he would say, "No, I don't want to direct a movie unless I wrote it." And if you're going to go that way, it just takes longer for the payoff, but then I think the payoff is bigger.

Longworth: You also mentioned comedy. You wrote for *Newhart* when?

HALL: 1983, right out of college.

Longworth: Did you at that time consider comedy to be your forte, or did you take the work just to break into the business?

HALL: No, I considered it my forte. I still think of myself as a comedy writer. I mean, obviously I know how to write drama, too, and I enjoy it, but I wouldn't be interested in doing strictly a dramatic show. If I couldn't do comedy I would get bored really quickly. My goal has always been to create a show and work on a show where I can combine those two things and use them to emphasize each other. And I think we really try to do that on *Judging Amy*, but, really, *I'll Fly Away* had a lot of humor in it. It's not a show that's remembered for humor.

Longworth: As I told David [Chase], that was one of my favorite shows.

HALL: Oh, thank you. But we strove for that. David encouraged that because I think he understood that one emphasizes the other.

Longworth: Many of the TV creators I have talked with are loathe to do a sitcom, yet are very humorous people. So that fits with your dream situation to be producing a drama with honest humor.

HALL: Uh-huh, and a lot of it, too. Not just sprinkled throughout, but aggressive humor.

Longworth: But not jokes.

HALL: Not jokes. Jokes are different.

Longworth: Is it harder to write jokes than it is to write humor?

HALL: I don't know that I would say harder, but I know that I'm not a joke writer. I know that's one of the reasons that I ultimately felt I needed to move away from comedy because that's not my strength and I didn't enjoy it, having to write a gag. It wasn't fun.

Longworth: From which do you derive more enjoyment, writing a TV drama like *Amy* or writing a novel?

HALL: Well, I don't know if enjoyment is the right word, and also, *Judging Amy* is a different situation, because I've had these two parallel careers for a long time. The way I always felt about it was, I enjoy doing TV, it's not my "soul" work (*laughs*), if you will. That's writing novels. *I'll Fly Away* felt like writing novels. It was the same process, that you could be just as challenging and introspective and all those things. So then I started having a hard time saying which I preferred because I was using similar muscles. I then spent a year just writing novels, and that pretty much decided it for me, that I would never do that, I just would never do that. Working in television is extremely stimulating, and I really like the pace of it. I love being around writers. And the part of me that ever wanted to pursue journalism likes TV for that reason, which is that you do something, and then you execute it, and then it's on the air.

Longworth: Right, and of course the deadlines are different between novels and television, but before we leave this discussion, what's the difference in the writing discipline between the two?

HALL: First of all, it's so much lonelier when you're writing a novel. Second, writing a novel is all about self-examination, even if you're not writing about yourself or your own experiences. It's about putting yourself in the mind of those characters and figuring out what is the absolute core of those people.

Longworth: Yeah, 'cause I wondered if you were Lydia, the heroine in your novel *Close to Home*.

HALL: Well, I always say I'm a little bit of everybody. It's like the Gestalt theory of dream interpretation. Everybody's *me*. But mainly I'm Lydia, yeah. I mean, I have more to do with her than anybody else. But in television you're writing about behavior. You're observing human behavior. You don't have to get into the interior lives of these characters. And so, they're different, and I'm interested in both [novels and TV].

Longworth: Which is easier to accept criticism of, novels or television shows?

HALL: TV shows, because that is just so much a part of the landscape. To take criticism and input and feedback from everybody from the actors and directors to, ultimately, the press. So you can't be thin-skinned about that. I don't *like* it, I don't like criticism (*laughs*), I never want to hear it again, but I remember when my first book came out, and the first review I got was not a good one. The ones that followed were all pretty good, but the very first review I got was not a good one, and I remember thinking, "No, you don't understand, this is *my* book." (*Laughs.*) "I wrote this book and it took me a long time, and I worked hard," and my first reaction was, "How can you say those things?" It was like I was wounded, it wasn't even anger (*laughs*), like someone had attacked your kid or your dog or something. But I have to say that working in television you have a Ph.D. in "Taking Criticism," and it's not something that bothers me much anymore. I can walk away from it, let me put it that way.

Longworth: As we move now to *Judging Amy,* and since we've been talking about critics, allow me to start out with a couple of quotes, one from *Entertainment Weekly,* and one from *TV Guide.* Both of these reviews appeared in late 1999, when *Amy* first premiered. *Entertainment Weekly* said, "Hard to believe a successful woman like Amy could be the jellyfish we saw in the rough cut, but maybe that's a signal that her character will grow." *TV Guide* wrote, "It's pandering melodrama. Even when the situations are provocative the resolutions tend toward the forgettably pat." Before you respond, it may help to get a sense of exactly when you were brought onto the show, and why. And, were you in fact brought in to fix the things these critics referred to?

HALL: First of all I noticed that you didn't quote from the *New York Times* review, which was very good (*laughs*), as were a lot of them, so yeah, you picked a couple of people who didn't call us as a winner, but there were a lot of really good reviews.

Longworth: So now that *Amy* has become such a mega-hit the critics who panned the show look stupid.

HALL: Well they *do* look stupid, and all the shows that *TV Guide* picked to win didn't succeed, pretty much across the board. And we just won the *TV Guide* Award, by the way (*laughs*), so it's like it's all irony. I'm married to a journalist, and I know what happens around the time that shows come out.

They have pretty much decided what shows they're going to like, and ours just wasn't on the agenda. Ours came out of nowhere. You're watching a hundred pilots, and it's really impossible to tell which work and which don't. Sometimes when I read what people have said about it, though, it's like they didn't see it. It's like they didn't actually watch the show.

Longworth: But what about the reference to the rough cut?

HALL: I have been with the project since the beginning. I was brought in at scripts level because the first draft that they did with the script was not what Amy and Connie wanted to do. So I was brought in to fix it, and I really think I was brought in for more of a female perspective. And then we shot a twenty-minute presentation, and the presentation was never meant to air 'cause you can't air a twenty-minute presentation. (*Laughs.*) So, some journalist saw that, I guess, but then I wrote a whole other pilot, and we shot a brand-new pilot with maybe two scenes from the original presentation in it. And then some journalists saw *that,* and it was hard to tell. I could never tell if people had seen the presentation, or if they had seen the pilot. It was kind of a confusing beginning, and I think one of the reasons people were confused by the show was that it came at the last minute. There was no buzz on it because it was like a Cinderella project, and as I said, it came in at the last minute. People didn't expect it to be on the air, and there it was, and they didn't know what to make of it. So that's my involvement.

Longworth: Of course you would bring a female perspective, but what was it specifically they thought you could contribute?

HALL: From what I understand, they wanted more humor and they wanted more of a perspective of a woman, and I was a single mother at the time, and that's what the pilot was about. They just didn't have a script they wanted to shoot, and no matter how much of a perspective Amy had on being a woman, she couldn't write the pilot. So I just came in there and wrote a brand-new pilot.

Longworth: For the viewer who notices credits, there seems to be a lot of names on screen in the category of "created by." There's Amy, Connie Tavel, John Tinker, Bill D'elia. What did each contribute to the project and what are their roles today?

HALL: John and Bill wrote a script, several versions of a script, which they ultimately did not use. However, they were obviously very much involved in developing the premise, the franchise, and the characters, and so that's why they got a "created by" credit. Amy and Connie basically shopped the idea around for months trying to find a writer and trying to make it all work, trying to put the package together. The other executive producer is my partner, Joe Stern, who physically produced the pilot; I mean he is also a very creative producer but he was strongly responsible for a lot of the casting.

Longworth: With *Amy* you were brought in to make someone else's vision work. Which kind of assignment do you prefer—that kind, or working on a show that you created from scratch?

HALL: I prefer creating things from scratch. In fact, I almost never do what I did. It's almost a rule that I have, that I won't do what I did on this show, which is come into a situation where other people have been involved, and other people have brought ideas to the table. My whole thing is I'm a writer, I have ideas, I don't want to piggyback on other people's ideas.

Longworth: But you did.

HALL: But the reason I did with this one was because, through some sort of magical coincidence, the story they were telling was basically my life. It was happening to *me* at that moment. A couple of years before, I had blown up my life by getting divorced at the age of thirty-five with a three year old. I had not moved in with my mother, but I had moved to another state and started over and kind of changed my profession a little bit. I had so much to say about that situation that I felt that here was an exception, that I would do this. And then, of course, I struck an agreement with everybody involved that I had to do *my* version of this. So it was kind of like starting from scratch. If I hadn't written the script, the pilot would not have gotten made; it was almost over, I wrote the script in five days. So I pretty much could do it on my own terms. They had nothing to lose by letting me do that.

Longworth: In your novel *Close to Home*, Lydia's friend tells her that "Hamilton is your way of apologizing for dropping out of law school." It's a commentary on how we often marry too soon and for the wrong reasons. You mentioned that Amy's story was *your* life, so were you trying to put a lot of your own emotion into the show, and has that been tough to do?

HALL: One of the things that I really get tired of seeing in movies and televison is women as victims, and women having a hard time coping with things like divorce and being a single mother. I mean, come on, give me a break. Women have been coping with this stuff since the beginning of time. Women are really good at coping. And also, you never see on television [drama] women with a sense of humor, and that really bugs me. And the way that I got through my own personal tragedies, which are really just learning experiences or transitions, is through humor and by refusing to believe that I had destroyed my life or my daughter's life by getting a divorce, because I felt

I was moving on to a healthier place. I really wanted to show that sometimes, when you have to make huge transitions, they're for good and healthy reasons. It's not because your life is falling apart. It's about moving on, and that doesn't mean it's not hard. And so I was very passionate about that subject and that's what I really wanted to bring to the show.

Longworth: Is there any story line that you would absolutely stay away from?

HALL: As odd as it sounds, I don't like to do issues. If they arise in the context of the show (and naturally they do because we're doing a show about a courtroom), then it has to be balanced and it has to be realistic, and it has to be personalized, it can't be generic. So, I like to stay away from trying to tell people how to live, for the most part. (*Laughs.*) And that's hard in a show where you're doing a judge. I try to focus on human behavior and not so much lecturing, and putting out messages. I don't want to do that.

Longworth: Do you bring stories from home? Do things that your daughter, Faith, says to you end up in the dialogue of *Amy?*

HALL: Absolutely. Sometimes, though, I have to dial it back because my daughter is incredibly precocious. I would put literal lines of dialogue into the scripts and people would say, "No kid talks like that." And I say, "Come live at my house for a while." And of course that's not fair, because you have to believe the kid dramatically. It's no fair saying, "Well, *my* daughter talks like that." (*Laughs.*) My daughter is real unusual. She grew up with a smart-ass mother. (*Laughs.*)

Longworth: On a couple of episodes, we noticed that Amy seemed preoccupied with sex or the lack thereof. Then on one of the promos, the editing is such that we're led to believe Judge Amy is going to have sex with her male assistant. Of course, the scene in question turns out to be a dream sequence. Is that something that you and the network designed in order to spike the ratings for that episode?

HALL: I oversee all the stories, they all come from me or are approved by me, but I'm not involved in the promo at all. In fact, I'd rather they hadn't teased that stuff. I would rather people just sit down and have the organic experience of watching it. But at the same time, I understand what they're up against. They have to get people to watch the show. They told me they were going to tease that, and I just said, "Don't reveal the kiss," that's all. "Tease it, but don't show them kissing in a promo." So it was sort of a combination of me and them.

Longworth: Speaking of relationships, there is an unwritten rule in television that, if the lead character is single, he or she had better remain single because if they get married, that destroys the chemistry of the show. Will that "rule" continue to hold even with all of the strong, unmarried, female leads on TV these days?

HALL: I think that anything you do to dramatically change the premise of your show can injure it. When you start out with couples that *aren't* together because there's a lot of sexual tension between them, once you get them together and relieve the sexual tension, you've dramatically changed the premise of your show. Therefore, if you start out with a married couple, that's fine because that's what your show is, and you know how to go from there and develop it and make it interesting. I just think it's a case of you have to be careful when you decide to change the entire premise of your show. So it's not really an unwritten rule, but you have to think carefully before taking a big leap like that. I made a decision that I wanted to do a full season without giving Amy a boyfriend, for a couple of reasons. One is I wanted everybody to get to know her first, and then you get invested in who she's going to go out with; the other [reason] is, we've done an entire series of a single woman who has something on her mind other than getting a man. Out of the first twenty-two shows, we'll only have done two episodes where she even talks about sex and wanting to have sex. So that was important to me because I didn't want anyone to label this as a sort of a "girlie" show.

Longworth: Prior to *Providence* coming on the scene in January of 1999, it seemed that the networks were losing women baby boomers. Now, with your show and others, those women are back. In an *Entertainment Weekly* article you indicated that the audience was always there, and if we had *had* more female producers there would have been more female-oriented dramas. So, are you saying that if there had been ten Barbara Halls in the business a decade ago, there wouldn't have been such a dearth of quality dramas in the 1990s?

HALL: Well, it's not just that it's me. I did four pilots before this show that didn't even get on the air, so it's not like I can't fail or miss the mark. *Judging Amy* happened at a time where—yeah, obviously I had a story I was passionate about telling, which was about single motherhood and working in a male-dominated profession, which she also does and I do. So I had a lot of passion going into this, but I also had a lot of fearlessness because I pretty much decided that if I couldn't make things work in television, I was going to do something else. If I couldn't get my own show on the air, I was going to concentrate on writing novels or something. So I brought a certain amount of fearlessness to it simply because of where I was emotionally and intellectually about my career. And I think it was a combination of being a woman, wanting to tell the story, and being kind of uppity about it. And kind of saying "no" a lot. "*No*, this is the story I want to tell. *No*, I don't want to change this. I don't want to back off. This is the character I want to try and portray." So I think it's a combination of more women getting involved in the workplace, and also women *and* men getting a little bit more fearless about what they want to do.

Longworth: Everyone now recognizes that you're a big success in television, but I'm always fascinated to examine the failures or what didn't work for people like yourself along the way. Tell me about the pilots that never made it to air.

HALL: Well, they were all about powerful women in male-dominated professions. The first one was with Kelly Lynch, and it was called *On the Line* (NBC), and it was about a female FBI supervisor. The reason that show didn't get on the air is because I was developing for the *ER* time slot, so a lot of shows didn't get on the air that year. (*Laughs.*) The next year I did kind of a quirky *Moonlighting*-type, male/female, *Adam's Rib* kind of thing. Well, not really, but it had kind of that comedy/drama mix, and it was about a female U.S. attorney working with a scuzzy defense attorney who's been brought into the prosecutor's office to teach her some of the tricks of the trade. It was developed during the O. J. Simpson trial, and I was thinking, "God, the prosecuting attorneys need to learn how to be more like the defense attorneys if they're going to win cases." (*Laughs.*)

Longworth: And what was that called?

HALL: It was called *The Legal Limit.* That was with Vincent Spano and Kelly Rutherford. And that didn't get on the air because—I can't remember why. It was for NBC. Then the next thing I did was for ABC, which I produced about an Irish working-class family.

Longworth: Was that *The Doyles?*

HALL: Yeah. And that came really close to getting on the air. That was on and off the schedule like eight times. And then the next thing I did was this [*Judging Amy*], and it got on the air. And I don't know why. (*Laughs.*)

Longworth: I like *Judging Amy* and *Family Law.* Am I in the minority, or do you have a lot of male viewers?

HALL: We *do* have men watching. I can't give you the breakdown. Obviously we're strongest among females. I check in with the website every now and then, and I read the fan mail, and I get feedback from friends, and a lot of men watch the show, and I think partially because they're interested in the franchise. It's basically a courtroom drama. It's like 50 percent courtroom drama, 50 percent single mother's personal life. And I think they find that compelling, and I think they like Amy for some reason. I mean, it's not necessarily because she's a babe, because there are a lot of babes on TV that men watch. And obviously there aren't *all* women behind the scenes here. We have men writers, men directors, men producers, and so we always hoped it would be a show that men and women could watch together and be equally interested in. We weren't trying to single out women necessarily.

Longworth: Other than your own personal experiences, where do you find the stories for *Judging Amy?*

HALL: We have researchers on staff and they come up with a lot of good ideas and they just kind of type up synopses of stories in the paper, and we go through and pick them out. That's sometimes how it works. Other times— for example, we were just doing a courtroom story about the date-rape drug, and that's just something I wanted to do because I'm very involved in the rape-treatment center out here in Santa Monica. So sometimes I'll just say, "I want to do a story about this date-rape drug," and I'll just figure out a way to do it. It doesn't necessarily come from the news. So it's a combination of both. Sometimes I have my own personal issues that I want to examine and look at, and I just find a way to do them, and sometimes we take them right out of the paper.

Longworth: In *TV Creators,* volume one, I made the observation that the average person can spend an hour reading a novel and after putting it down can tell you who the author is, but that same person can spend an hour watching a TV drama and couldn't tell you who wrote it if her life depended on it. Will that ever change, so that there is an equal status between novelists and screenwriters?

HALL: It's a really interesting question, particularly because television is *so* writer driven, so much more than movies. Your theory almost works better in television than movies these days because it's just a writer-driven medium. But, first of all, it *has* already changed a lot. I remember when my sister first started talking about writing for TV. I had no idea what that was. Nobody did. It was like, "You mean the actors don't make it up? What do you mean write for TV?" (*Laughs.*) Somebody *does* that? And when I was growing up, there was no such thing at all as the celebrity TV showrunner. There was no David Kelley. And now everybody knows who David Kelley is. Everybody knows who Steven Bochco is. And maybe everybody knows who Dick Wolf is and who Chris Carter is, and there are some celebrity showrunners now. So the concept of writer/showrunner is at least in existence; people can understand the concept. So I think, yeah, I think it's going to continue to grow, and people are going to continue to look at TV and realize that there are *authors* behind these things. Shows like *The Sopranos* certainly helps that, because watching those shows is like reading novels. It's like installments of Mark Twain–type stories.

Longworth: Do you work eighty hours a day, or do you and Faith have time together?

HALL: Well, I'm really good at delegating, and I think you have to be—well you don't *have* to be, you can work yourself into an early grave, but I just don't want to do that. I have a lot of people around me I trust, and I just don't get into what they do. I trust them to do their job well. I don't micromanage. I don't have to oversee every little detail. So, to answer that question, I work at home often when I'm writing, so I'm able to be around her. I take her to school every day, and I'm home by dinner time every night. We do a lot of different things. We have some sort of unusual interests. We're both into yoga. We'll do yoga together. We're both into music, and I play the guitar and sing, and stuff like that. And we also read together. We do a lot of things like that, and sometimes I'll just take off a day and go to the movies. So I find that the higher up I am in my job, to the point where now I'm basically the boss, the more time I get to spend with her. As long as I get the job done and the show is going well, and it is, then I can just continue to do what I'm doing and give myself some time off here and there because I have *certainly* put in those hideous hours.

Longworth: I think I know the answer to this, but what's your favorite TV show other than *Amy?*

HALL: Oh, it's *The Sopranos*. (*Laughs.*)

Longworth: Now that's what a lot of writers tell me.

HALL: I'm addicted to *The Sopranos*. I think that I would be even if I didn't know David. But I'm able to call David up every now and then and just say, "It's so amazing, I'm such a huge fan of this show." And it's so rare to be able to actually call that person up and say, "I loved that episode," and get the inside scoop on it. (*Laughs.*)

Longworth: Do you plan to spend any time at the Quality Mart over the next year or so?

HALL: (*Laughs.*) You know, Quality Mart is based on the Value City chains. Did you know that?

Longworth: No.

HALL: It's in Danville, Virginia, where my mother lives.

Longworth: I spent a year in Danville one night.

HALL: Did you? I spent many long nights in Danville. (*Laughs.*) So whenever I would go home, my mother would take me out there. It was like this huge discount store, and I'm fascinated with that whole thing. So if I ever get back there, you can bet I'll be at the "Quality Mart."

Longworth: You're a celebrity, though, so I don't know if you can go into just *any* Quality Mart.

HALL: I think it's really important to continue to go to Quality Mart no matter how big you get. (*Laughs.*) It's spiritually important. (*Both laugh.*)

9

JOSS WHEDON | Feminist

Joss Whedon. COURTESY OF TWENTIETH CENTURY FOX.

TELEVISION CREDITS

1989–90	*Roseanne* (ABC)
1990–91	*Parenthood* (NBC)
1997–2001	*Buffy the Vampire Slayer* (WB)
2001–	*Buffy the Vampire Slayer* (UPN)

| 1999– | *Angel* (WB) |
| 2002– | *Firefly* (Fox) |

ʌʌʌ ʌʌʌ ʌʌʌ

"**Even** a man who is pure at heart and says his prayers by night, may become a wolf when the wolfbane blooms, and the autumn moon is bright." Those lyrical strains from Curt Siodmak's 1941 classic screenplay *The Wolf Man* describe the tormented lycanthrope Larry Talbot. But they might also apply to Buffy the Vampire Slayer's one-time heart throb, Angel, who, because of his conflicted nature, is more akin to a werewolf than to a Dracula-like figure.

Still, while vampires and wolf men can sometimes be sympathetic characters, Buffy's pal Willow observed that "Men can be jerks, dead *or* alive." Translation? It is a man's world out there, and that is why the world needs Buffy, an empowered woman who fights not just her own battles but also those of others—all the while protecting the meek against any adversary, regardless of its manifestation.

So, what radical feminist invented this superchick? None other than Joss Whedon, a yuppie-era scribe with a love of Gothic horror films and a passion for arming the disenfranchised against the modern horrors and villains that confront us every day. Thus, Whedon's TV tandem of *Buffy the Vampire Slayer* and *Angel* works on a number of levels. Both breakthrough dramas appeal to horror fans of all ages. They appeal to girls looking for a strong role model. They appeal to young men with an eye for beautiful slayers and young women with an eye on hunky vampires. Finally, they appeal to anyone who knows what it is like to be a victim and how good it feels (albeit vicariously) to exact a pound of flesh from a bossy bully or a bullying boss.

Joss Whedon is a mild-mannered, highly imaginative man whose talents are as varied as the demographics of his programs and as diverse as his mix of genres. Whedon is a writer, producer, and director, whose work is a veritable smorgasbord of drama, comedy, action, science fiction, and romance. Says former WB executive Susanne Daniels, "Joss has a genius mind like television has never seen. I think *Buffy* is that rare combination of humor and suspense. It makes you laugh and makes you scared at the same time, which is very difficult to achieve, in a way that these scary movies like *Scream* haven't achieved, because they rely very much on gimmicks, and parody, and extreme violence."

Marti Noxon, Whedon's co-executive producer on *Buffy*, told *TV Guide*, "[Joss] is a student of creating mythologies to get to the heart of real emotional matters" (February 10, 2001). Perhaps through writing and presenting prime-time parables on social equality, Whedon has created a mythology that has transcended the 3:4 aspect ratio and given society a lesson in tolerance and respect. The best part is that Whedon's mythologies are also fun. And, as Mary Poppins (herself an empowered female) said, "A spoonful of sugar helps the medicine go down." Thanks to Whedon, we twenty-first century males are learning to take our medicine with less and less resistence.

Joss Whedon was born into a family of letters in 1964. His grandfather and his father wrote episodic television, with the former contributing to such shows as *Leave it to Beaver* and *The Donna Reed Show* and the latter composing dialogue for *Alice* and *Benson*. His mother, a teacher, also wrote. Growing up in Manhattan, Joss had two older brothers. His family later expanded following his parents' divorce when he was just nine years old. With both his mom and dad remarrying, Joss would gain two half brothers and a stepsister. Prior to the amicable breakup of his parents, Joss was influenced greatly by his father's creative spirit. "I think my father's best work was probably done at our dinner table," Joss says laughing. "It was great to live around a writer, and my mother also wrote in her spare time, so the sound of typewriters was probably the most comforting sound in the world to me. I loved that. And while I really enjoyed all of the funny things my dad was working on, it was really just being *around* someone who was that funny. And all of his friends were comedy writers. So the house was constantly filled with these very sweet, erudite, intelligent guys just trying to crack jokes—my father's friends, my mother's friends, teachers, drama people. It just had a great air to it, and what you wanted to do is to go into that room and make those guys laugh."

After the divorce, Joss lived with his mother and came to respect her strength and independence. For ten years Whedon attended Riverdale, the same school where his mother taught. But a change in venue was in store for Joss. "She was going on sabbatical to England, and since I couldn't stay in New York, and since she didn't think there were actual schools in California (*laughs*), she suggested that I go to boarding school in England," Joss recalls. "By incredible happenstance, and I stress that because I in no way earned it, I ended up at the best school in the country (Winchester), and when my family returned to America, I stayed on there for two more years."

While attending Riverdale, Whedon had been both bullied and ignored, but at Winchester he enjoyed his role as an outsider. "I wouldn't trade it for the world, and I wouldn't wish it on a dog," he says laughing. "This was a six-hundred-year-old, all-male school where you have to wear a suit and a straw hat to class every day. Not long on fun, also 'chickless' in the extreme, and I don't mean Michael, I mean, *lack* of women. (*Laughs.*) When I left there I found out how much they hated us [Americans]. Every Fourth of July I walked around saying, "We won, we won!" (*Laughs.*)

Joss the Yank also went on to win a diploma from Winchester, *and* with a special guest in attendance. "There was no prom, and the only reason we had a celebration was that the Queen came for the school's six hundredth anniversary."

Whedon left England, but he would eventually return to the world of old Gothic architecture, and the Brits would love him for it. While attending Wesleyan University, Whedon became more focused on his future. "I said, 'Film is what interests me. Film is what I'm going to study. I'm going to give up my drawing, I'm going to give up acting. I'm going to give up all the other stuff that I've done and just focus on one thing, making movies.'" Upon receiving a degree in film studies and literature from Wesleyan, Joss moved to Los Angeles in hopes of catching a break. "I got out here with nary a dime, and thought I could perhaps write a spec TV script, and maybe sell it and get enough money to get myself started," Joss says. "That was the first time I had ever sat down and said, 'I'm going to write something, and try to be a writer.' And it was like, 'Where have you been all my life?' And then I realized that I just never loved anything as much, and *will* never love anything as much as writing. The first time I sat down just to write, just to create a script, was extraordinary."

In the meantime, Whedon took a job in a video store to support himself, but the experience would later pay huge dividends in helping him devise a title for what would become his signature project. After penning several spec scripts, Joss landed his first steady job in show biz, working for the ABC hit comedy, *Roseanne.* "I thought it was the best show on TV, and it was the last spec I wrote," he recalls. "I sort of knew the format of a script, I knew generally how they looked because I had read a lot of them that my father did. So I knew the structure, and my father, when he read my stuff, was extraordinarily supportive, which was a big, nervous moment for me. He showed it to his agency, where I still am, or they might have shown it to him. I'm not sure who read it first, but obviously they wouldn't have read it, or it would have been harder to have them read it, if it had not been for my father."

Staff positions on *Roseanne* and *Parenthood* followed. But the idea for *Buffy* had been brewing for some time. While still working on *Roseanne*, Whedon began scripting and pitching the Slayer concept but found no takers. Joss was back to writing specs and hoping for his first film deal. "I wrote a spec called *Suspension*," Joss says. "It was a rip-off of *Die Hard*, where terrorists take over a bridge. Loads of fun. (*Laughs*.) Having then written *Suspension* and *Buffy*, I got a lot of comedy pitches, and I was like, 'I want to write hard action. I want to write big summer movies because so many of them suck.' (*Laughs*.) Seeing my two scripts, Jorge Saralege at Fox asked again if I was interested in trying to revive the *Alien* franchise, because he had seen me write action, and he had seen a woman hero in those two different scripts, so he just thought I had the right qualifications."

In addition to writing *Alien Resurrection* (1997), Joss had also penned *Speed* (1994) and *Toy Story* (1995). But it was his earlier screenplay for *Buffy the Vampire Slayer*, which was made into a movie in 1992, that would lead him to a rendezvous with the medium in which the Whedons had worked for generations. Says Joss, "Without Fran Kuzui there would have been no movie. She produced it and put it together. She directed it. She made it her own. As a creator, every writer will think of themselves as that. It's frustrating, because I have a very specific vision when I write, directorially speaking, about everything, about camera angles. Somebody said that mine was the first script they had ever read by a wannabe costume designer, because I was very specific about the way things should look, and feel, and be. And, inevitably, my vision was not going to be the same as Fran's. She was interested in making more a sort of head-on comedy, and I wanted to make an action horror movie that was funny. And we had different sensibilities."

Five years later, Whedon, who had already followed in his father's footsteps as a television writer, would now also create and produce his own series, the vehicle for which would be the saga of his old, familiar teenage vampire vigilante. Susanne Daniels, former president of the WB network, recalls the beginning of *Buffy*'s TV incarnation. "When the network first started out, we were in a position where writers weren't really coming to us," Daniels recalls. "For the most part, we were going to them. At the time we were pitching two things, teenage female superheroes, and a contemporary version of *The Nightstalker*. And so, when Joss walked in and told us he was going to do *Buffy* the movie as a TV series, he immediately responded to the two things we were looking for. I didn't have a lot of drama experience then, and that really worked to our advantage (*laughs*), so we didn't know enough to say, 'You don't buy a drama series based on a failed movie.' (*Laughs*.) We just did it. And we loved Joss's work. I was very familiar with the movie version of *Buffy* and familiar with what I felt were the flaws. Joss really had worked out so many improvements and acknowledged those flaws, and how he was going to make the show stronger and better, and it was just very appealing to us for all of those reasons."

Disappointed with the campy tone of the movie, Whedon was determined to make TV's *Buffy* more three dimensional. Joss wrote and directed a twenty-four minute presentation pilot. *Buffy the Vampire Slayer* premiered in March of 1997 and soon became one of the fledgling WB's biggest and most reliable hits. Like Brenda Hampton's *7th Heaven* and Kevin Williamson's *Dawson's Creek*, *Buffy the Vampire Slayer* would help the WB to balance its programming with a mix of dramas that could attract more broad-based demographics. *Buffy* was also an instant hit with critics. *TV Guide*'s Matt Roush proclaimed *Buffy* to be "smart, with unfailingly glib dialogue" (January 2, 1999), while Frederick Szebin wrote in *Cinefantastique* magazine that "*Buffy* may have finally kicked asunder that tired cliché of the screaming maiden in distress" (October 1999). *Time* noted that the show was a "postfeminist parable on the challenge of balancing one's personal and work life." And David Graeber, assistant professor of anthropology at Yale University, wrote, "Joss is responsible for subverting the message of the horror genre . . . and making it a form of empowerment for women" (*Entertainment Weekly*, April 2000).

Of course, there have been some bumps in the road. *Buffy* is, after all, a drama that contains more violence than some action hours, and that's something that Congressional crusaders have been critical of as they suggested a link between television drama and real-life crime. In a February 2000 interview with *Dreamworks* magazine, *Buffy* star Sarah Michele Gellar weighed in, "I just got back from Europe where they have the same TV shows and movies, yet this problem really only exists in *our* country. So how can we blame entertainment?" Still, there are unfortunate extremes with any issue. In the spring of 1999, on the heels of the Columbine High School shootings, Joss (who once described his relationship with the WB for *Cinescape*'s Edward Gross by saying [November 1997] "they let me get away with murder" [from *Terror Television* by John Kenneth Muir]) was directed by the WB to reschedule and make changes to remaining episodes containing particularly violent themes or scenes. Susanne Daniels defends her decision. "I didn't want to overreact, but it seemed important for us and for our affiliates to feel like we were responding, not just to the Columbine families, but to all of the families in America who were affected by it and have been affected by local shootings," she says. "And even though Joss's show, that episode, works so clearly on a level of fantasy and is not at all realistic, even despite that, I now believe that we did absolutely the right thing, without a doubt . . . I was proud of that decision."

But despite mounting pressures from politicians, Whedon and the WB launched a *Buffy* spin-off, starring a two-hundred-and-forty-four-year-old vampire given to violence in the name of protecting the innocent. *Angel* premiered in the fall of 1999 and, like its mother-ship series, met with rave reviews. Ken Tucker of *Entertainment Weekly* called it "fully satisfying across a whole range of emotions." And *TV Guide* wrote, "We are intrigued by the deft blend of classic film noir and hip, horror allegory" (September 11, 1999). The magazine's Matt Roush later proclaimed *Angel* to be "The best of this season's spin-offs" (November 13, 1999). John Kenneth Muir in his book *Terror Television* deemed *Angel* to be a "darker, more adult version of *Buffy*, one that labors on the idea of redemption."

Ironically, it was the maturing of Whedon's cast and audience that became a sticking point during the embattled licensing negotiations of 2001. *Buffy* had helped the WB broaden its viewer base. In fact, the show has consistently increased its numbers across every demographic category. From 1999 to 2000, for example, the series saw a 100 percent jump in men, eighteen to thirty-four years old, with significant gains among both males and females in the eighteen- to forty-nine-year-old demographic. However, Jamie Kellner (a former WB executive who later became CEO of Turner Broadcasting, a division of AOL, as a result of the AOL/Time Warner mega-merger) suggested that *Buffy*, which is produced by 20th Century Fox, had an aging audience base. But faced with rising production costs, Whedon entertained offers to move his franchise from the WB. Whedon told *Entertainment Weekly*, "The idea that *Buffy* viewers are getting too old now is a spurious argument for not paying for a show that has as much to do with the WB being the WB as anything else" (March 23, 2001). Eventually the battle was won by UPN, which outbid the WB. Much like baseball's Curt Flood, who tested the waters of free agency, Whedon became one of the first TV creators forced to deal with the impact of vertical integration. (Newscorp, the parent of 20th Century Fox, was negotiating a dual ownership of UPN *with* Viacom, the parent of CBS.) But regardless of its home base, *Buffy* will continue to be a marketing phenomenon. The series has generated comic books, magazines, novels, dolls, trading cards, videos, and a huge following on the Internet. Hollywood insiders may finally even be succumbing to the fandom frenzy. Perennially locked out of Emmy contention, Whedon snagged his first nomination, for writing the December 1999 episode

"Hush," in which a supernatural "force" robs the main characters of their ability to speak. It was a brilliantly crafted script, replete with imaginative nonverbal communication, and should have netted its author a gold statue.

Rich, successful, and happily married, Joss the aging feminist is growing a bit more comfortable with his lifestyle—but not so much so as to lose his edge. His mind is still teeming with innovative stories that continue to slay us each week.

To my relief and surprise, he agreed to be interviewed in broad daylight.

Longworth: First of all, how can I be sure that I'm really talking to Joss Whedon and not some otherworldly imposter?

WHEDON: There is nothing even remotely supernatural about me, it's all just a bunch of fakery. Why do you think I'd be so desperate to make shows about it, if I thought it was real? (*Both laugh.*) We'd never come near it.

Longworth: As a writer, does it offend you that my all-time favorite *Buffy* episode, "Hush," contained the least amount of dialogue?

WHEDON: Not at all. That was actually one of the best experiences I've ever had as a writer because it forced me to think through things differently. Writing is not about the number of words. Very often there should be fewer than there are, although I love words. I love the sounds of words. I love syllables. I love the whole deal. Sometimes you gotta shut up. (*Both laugh.*) Particularly me.

Longworth: You seem to enjoy nonverbal humor. I'm thinking, for example, when Lindsay points to a sign near a broken elevator that reads, "In case of emergency use stairs." There's another one where Seth is on his way to a party, and someone asks him who he is going as, and he points to his name tag that says "God." This kind of nonverbal humor threads its way through your work. It's seamless, and yet there are no spoken words.

WHEDON: The thing has to work visually. It all has to be in concert. This show, because it's a fantasy show obviously we knew it was going to rely on visuals to a great extent, but creating visual humor is much more difficult to do because so much of TV is just radio with faces.

Longworth: And so much of what kids are exposed to is manic and frantic, whether on TV, the Internet, or in video games, whereas you offer up a more intelligent product with moments of nonverbal communication.

WHEDON: Ultimately, if it's not working on that level, you're not going to make it scary by talking about it. And while you can make a lot of jokes, what differentiates it from a sitcom is by really embodying it "filmically" so that it's visually funny and so that the frame is working, and it's not just standing there.

Longworth: Since you brought up jokes, let me ask you about your father and grandfather, who both wrote comedy. What is the difference in writing comedy for a sitcom like *Roseanne,* which is *supposed* to be funny, and writing comedy for a *Buffy* or *Angel* series, which is a drama?

WHEDON: Well, in a way *Roseanne* would be easier to write because you don't have to write blocking. But the thing about *Buffy* is you don't have to make a joke, you don't have to make dense, wall-to-wall jokes. But if there aren't a couple of jokes on a page, I still get nervous. I'll never get over that.

Longworth: Why?

WHEDON: Because when a joke works, I know it. I can hear the audience laugh, and I still watch the show with a bunch of people. I still watch it with people who haven't worked on it, so I can see when they laugh, and when they get scared, and when they think it's ridiculous, and when they cry, and all that good stuff. And that's the fun. So it's very hard for me *not* to make a joke, because I know that a laugh is a surefire reaction, whereas if you're playing something more dramatic, I don't know if they liked it till it's over *(laughs)* because they'll just sit there, and that's very nerve racking.

Longworth: OK, so I know that you have written some funny lines for *Buffy* and that you did *Toy Story,* but your writing career veered off a hundred and eighty degrees from the sort of things that your grandfather and dad wrote. I don't recall either of them writing horror, Gothic, sci-fi screenplays, for example.

WHEDON: My grandfather did write *Island at the Top of the World,* possibly David Hartman's finest movie. *(Both laugh.)* But yeah, I'm very much attracted to the dramatic, and though I enjoy half-hour [shows] I don't see myself working in there much because the shows that really move me are always dramatic. In fact, my father wrote a script for *United States,* a very short-lived show. The script never aired, and it was one of my favorite things I ever read because it was one of those early attempts at a dramedy that everybody said wouldn't work, around the time of *Slap Maxwell.* And to read something that was very serious and very moving and very personal, and not schtick, schtick, schtick, not only was it very gratifying, but when the jokes hit, they hit ten times as hard because you were in the middle of something dramatic. That to me is the essence of what I'm interested in. It's something you see in the Hong Kong films that [Quentin] Tarantino has followed. You don't *know* what kind of scene you're in. Something can be very funny and then suddenly very terrifying—very exciting, and suddenly very ridiculous. I think that's what life is like, that's what interests me. But ultimately, while humor is definitely the voice that I'm the most comfortable with, drama is the structure that will always attract me.

Longworth: You mentioned your affection for half hours, and that your father dabbled in dramedy. Why is it that producers won't do half-hour dramas anymore?

WHEDON: You know I think certain things get locked down, format wise. Even though sometimes I think, "God, if my show were only a half hour long!" (*Laughs.*) But if somebody's going to give me a half an hour more to talk, I'm going to do it. Also, there is a very big difference in terms of visual information and telling a story. Every "hour guy" is going to say, "We're making a little movie every week." In our case, God help us, they're not that little.

Longworth: But suppose the network said you had to do "Buffy" as a half hour?

WHEDON: It was originally supposed to be a half hour, *Power Rangers*–type afternoon adventure with some comedy. That was what they first approached me with, and I developed it as a half-hour drama. Now I knew that it would be funny, but I thought that you could also really get into the characters, and, actually, it was my agent, Chris Harbert, he said, "This is an hour. You have too much. With all the action and suspense you want to create in a half hour, you're never going to get a chance to get into the character, and that's what's interesting and that's what you're interested in." And an hour gives us time to do all of that. Yes, you could do all of that in a half an hour, there is no reason why you *couldn't* have a half-hour drama except structurally people would be like, "Oh, what will we pair it with? What will we do?" But if you're going to give me an hour, I'm going to take an hour.

Longworth: You could have a *Buffy/Angel* hour, though.

WHEDON: But I have a *Buffy/Angel two* hours. (*Both laugh.*) It's like I produce a movie every week, and the fact [is] that I may die at any moment.

Longworth: Well, we don't want anything to happen to you. What's your diet like when you're working, by the way?

WHEDON: Sometimes it's good, and sometimes it's bad. I'm actually getting better at living during these shows. The first year I was sick constantly. And this year I didn't get sick once. Two shows, no sickness. I'm a god. Except having to go into the hospital, but that's different; it was my appendix, not exhaustion. But you learn to live the life of nothing but your shows.

Longworth: Well, let's see if anything about those shows is autobiographical. Did things happen to you at Riverdale or Winchester, for example, that in any way made writing *Buffy* somewhat cathartic for you?

WHEDON: Oh yeah. When I devised the show, it was very different from the movie. The movie had "the girl you think is going to get killed turns out to be a superhero," that type of thing. That's enough for a movie but it's not enough for a show. And the show was, "High school is a horror movie." And there are not a lot of people I know who don't relate to that. I sold the show with *Invisible Girl* as part of my pitch, and that was the girl who was just so unremarkable that she had gradually disappeared. That was based on, when I was fifteen I actually drew a picture of myself becoming transparent.

Longworth: That's kind of sad.

WHEDON: It was, because I felt myself feeling extraordinarily alienated.

Longworth: Did you save that picture?

WHEDON: You know, I think it's somewhere in my closet. I mean it was really a cartoon. But it was very specific, and when you're able to be that it is very gratifying, because even though the show had a lot of problems, [was] very difficult to write, the filming didn't go that well, and every now and then we get a kid watching it who, you can tell on their face that "this has happened to me."

Longworth: But I think most of us have experienced some of that unless you were the star football player.

WHEDON: But part of the point of the show is that even if you were the star football player, there comes a point in every human's life where they realize that they are alone in their mind, and they can't help but feel alienated. That's why anybody can relate to the show.

Longworth: What was the first time you remember writing stories, and when did you realize this was something you wanted to do in earnest?

WHEDON: Sort of always, and never. I always wrote things. Stories, poems, songs, plays, comic books. Whatever came to mind. And I always sort of vaguely associated writing with my life, in that I thought I could make movies. I always assumed making them meant writing them, but I never really thought about that. I thought about directing, and when we studied film we really didn't study writing at all. I was doing various things, but I wasn't doing any heavy writing and I never studied at all. I never thought of myself as definitely becoming a writer. I tried to write several novels as a kid, and I'd usually get to page twelve. (*Both laugh.*)

Longworth: So even sitting around the dinner table with your father, you still didn't make that connection early on?

WHEDON: Not specifically. I mean, I knew I wanted to do something that wasn't a real job, because I just can't do it. I'm pathetic that way. I knew

I wanted to be an artist. I loved drawing, I loved singing, I loved acting, I love every kind of art that there is. So I had never really narrowed it down, and it wasn't like I was slaving away. I did write a couple of screenplays when I was a kid, but I always thought that was just part of the process. I didn't think of myself as a writer. And then I got out of college, and I swore that I wasn't going to write for TV because I had actually not been raised on American TV much. I was more into the sort of highbrow British stuff that my mother watched. I was a PBS kid.

Longworth: That's weird. Your father is writing all of these shows on commercial television, and your mother wants you to watch PBS.

WHEDON: Well, you know, my father and my mother are divorced, and I was living with my mother, but, no, actually they got along splendidly. But yeah, we weren't a huge TV family. And my father, one of the things about working in television is that you never have time to watch any. So my father wasn't an avid TV watcher either. He would enjoy himself, there were things we watched, but it wasn't like we all sat down.

Longworth: What *did* you like to watch on television when you were growing up?

WHEDON: The things that made an impression were all like *Masterpiece Theatre*, Monty Python, and the BBC Shakespeares.

Longworth: I think that college students and young people breaking into the business could benefit from hearing how you actually picked up work. You did *Roseanne*, then the films *Speed, Alien Resurrection*, and *Toy Story*. How do you get those kinds of jobs? Do you wait by the telephone until someone calls your agent and says, "Hey, I loved *Speed*; can he write *Toy Story?*"

WHEDON: Basically I'm never satisfied with where I am. I always want to be doing more, I always want to be doing the next thing. So when I was on *Roseanne*, I started to write *Buffy* (the film) because I wanted to make movies also. And then, when it was clear that there was no more for me to do on *Roseanne*, I sort of got shut out by the producers, I quit. *Buffy* went around, I got a job on *Parenthood* that lasted half a season, that show disappeared, and I sort of backed off from TV at that point. But *Buffy* had gone around, and I then also wrote a spec *Die Hard* rip-off called *Suspension*, about terrorists taking a bridge. Loads of fun. (*Laughs.*) The person who told me to write *Suspension*, Jorge Saralege, I had pitched it to him as a joke while we were having lunch. He was pitching me a movie about a dog, and I think it later became a movie about a pig. (*Both laugh.*) And I told him how little I wanted to be pitched another dog movie, and I told him my funny *Die Hard* rip-off, and he said, "Write it, don't pitch it. Just go and write it. You will never be pitched another dog movie again."

Longworth: Very prophetic.

WHEDON: He was smart. But anyway, while we were working on a treatment of *Alien* together, he was also in charge of *Speed*, and production was coming up, and he needed someone. So he set me up with Walter Parks and Laurie McDonald.

Longworth: So it really *is* all about connections?

WHEDON: Well, it's in doing good work. If I get the job done for somebody, they're going to think of me for somebody else. I hear the word "connections," and I think it doesn't matter how you write. I believe I had a very easy start. I didn't work as a production assistant, I didn't work in the industry at all until I worked as a writer. And I had the advantage of my father, who told me, "When somebody tells you to get a job as a production assistant, don't do it. Hold out, and you're going to be employed as a writer."

Longworth: Really?

WHEDON: Yeah, it was beautiful because he was the guy that I wanted to be like.

Longworth: So how did you get the idea for creating the character of Buffy?

WHEDON: It basically came through my love of horror movies and having seen all of the ones that had been made (*laughs*) and seeing the trend of the blonde girl who always got killed, like P. J. Soles in *Halloween*, who was cute, had sex, was bouncy and frivolous, always got her ass killed. I just felt really bad for her. I thought, I want to see the movie where she walks into a dark alley, a monster attacks her, and she just wails on him. And a lot of that came from me, as well, because I have been mugged a lot of times.

Longworth: Seriously?

WHEDON: Yeah. Four times. I've been picked on, I was the little brother, not somebody anybody ever took seriously, so, in a weird way, I identified with this extremely pretty, blonde, frivolous person who was the polar opposite of myself. Nobody ever expected she could take care of herself, or turn around and become a superhero. And not just a superhero, but a hero in the classical sense. To me that's extraordinarily gratifying, and I think it is to other people, too, because everybody thinks of themselves as something more significant than the world believed.

Longworth: You spoke earlier about how the TV series was originally slated to be sort of an afternoon kids' show, but prior to that, while writing the screenplay for *Buffy*, did you think it could ever be a great TV series one day?

WHEDON: No, I really didn't. I thought this could be an icon. I thought, in a very small way, this movie was designed, even with the title, to be one of those movies picked off the video shelf because it had a funny title. This was around the time they were making, *Revenge of the Killer Bimbos*, or whatever, and that bothered me.

Longworth: I missed that one.

WHEDON: Well, maybe it was *Attack of the Killer Bimbos*, I can't remember. (*Both laugh.*) But titles like that leap out at me because I *want* them to have their revenge because everybody's been calling them bimbos. But these movies weren't really about that, they were "T&A" fests. So I wanted to make a movie that would grab you in that same way. That juxtaposition of something very frivolous versus something very serious. *Buffy the Vampire Slayer* was actually a good, responsible, feminist, exciting, enjoyable movie, and not just a titty bash.

Longworth: Every episode of *Buffy* jumps between genres. One minute there's high drama, the next there's comedy, then science fiction. How would you, then, categorize the show?

WHEDON: As an action, comedy, romance, horror, musical. (*Both laugh.*) It is a hodgepodge. Structurally it is a drama. We break it like a drama. Everything is about the momentum of the storytelling, whether the story is somewhat farcical, or straight-ahead action, or horror. So, if I had to choose one, I'd choose drama. If I had chosen comedy, who knows, maybe we'd have an Emmy. (*Both laugh.*)

Longworth: Ouch!

WHEDON: No, I very much doubt that would happen in any category. (*Both laugh.*) But that question did come up after *Ally McBeal* did that, and they were the first ones [in drama] to call themselves a comedy. But I can't anymore. It gets so schizophrenic at this point that drama sort of covers everything. But comedy/horror/drama/action, those are the big four.

Longworth: OK, since you brought it up, what *about* the Emmys? Sarah Michelle Gellar was quoted as saying that Emmy voters don't consider the WB to be a real network. Do you agree with her assessment, and, if so, is that prejudice likely to abate any time soon?

WHEDON: I don't know. Sarah knows a great deal more about these things than I do. And when I don't understand what's happening, I'll go to her and ask, "What does this mean?" She's the insider. She knows all the awards. She knows all the machinations of the studios, and things like that. But I don't have a clue.

Longworth: She is empowered.

WHEDON: (*Laughs.*) Dangerously so. She's absolutely the expert. And she's very much in charge of her career, which I admire. There's a lot of confluence between her and the young Buffster. She may well be right. I've heard people say nice things about how we should get an award, and I work so very hard on this show that, of course, in my heart, I believe it, but I never expected that we would. You know, I think the Academy has proved itself kind of stodgy in the last couple of years. Not to say that we should be getting it. I watched the first *Sopranos* and was like, "Give it to *these* guys, Oh my God!" I watch *The West Wing* and say, "Give it to these guys!" There's great shows out there. I'm not like, "Oh those stodgy voters, they don't get how great we are, blah, blah, blah," because the fact that I'm *ever* having a conversation about the Emmys in regards to a show called *Buffy the Vampire Slayer* means that something's gone horribly right (*both laugh*), so the critical understanding of this show has been so gratifying. The fact that the critics got it and appreciated it from day one, and the rabid, almost insane fan base is great. Anything else is just gravy. The thing, though, about the show that I think holds it back is the wacky title. It's not serious drama if you have a wacky title. One of the things that TV is about is comfort, is knowing exactly where you are. I know what's going to happen when I tune in to a particular show. With *Buffy* we'll do French farce one week and *Medea* the next week. We try very hard structurally not to fall into a pattern either, so there's not a shoot-out in a warehouse every episode. Buffy will appear in the film at some point, but, at the same time, I'm very much committed to keeping the audience off their feet. It's sort of antithetical to what TV is devised to do. Not that there aren't surprising and delightful shows out there, but not to have that particular comfort level would throw people to a certain extent. It's like when we decide what show to send to the Academy voters, it's always a big question. Do we send the drama, the comedy, the horror show?

Longworth: I'm a big fan of the old Universal horror films principally because of the Gothic mood they struck. Not a lot of gore or violence. And I think that's what draws me to your two shows. I feel that this Gothic tone is going to thread its way through the episodes regardless of the story line. Do you work hard to make sure you are maintaining that tone?

WHEDON: Ultimately this was designed as a horror that is funny and exciting, so visually we want to keep those rich blacks, we want to keep that suspense. It's never been a gorefest because the one thing that leaves me really cold in a horror movie is excessive gore. I think I'm just a wuss, really, but that's the fact. We've pushed it sometimes, because when something horrible is happening it's sometimes better if it looks really painful, rather than sort of blithe. But, yeah, I'm much more interested in the suspense and the implied, in the unseen.

Longworth: But while you do the violence thing tastefully, you have pushed the envelope with some of the sexual scenes and innuendo. Like the episode where Buffy's imposter says to Buffy, "Oh, so Willow's not driving stick anymore?"—referring to Willow's lesbian tendencies.

WHEDON: I loved that. (*Laughs.*)

Longworth: And then, to go back to the "Hush" episode, where Buffy, who can't speak, is trying to gesture to her friends how they might drive a wooden stake through the villain's heart. The hand motion that she used to gesture resembled the international symbol for male masturbation. Has the WB Standards and Practices office ever rapped your knuckles?

WHEDON: We go back and forth. We have our episodes, but we have a pretty good relationship with them. I mean, it's always handled politely. I'm not one of these guys who says, "Fuck the network, fuck these executives." Obviously they have a different agenda than we do, and I respect that, and they let us get away with murder, so it works out nicely. But things like that [Buffy's gesture], they're pretty harmless, you know? It's not going to disturb a four year old that somebody made a gesture with his hand, because that four year old categorically can't understand. "Willow's not driving stick anymore" is going to go over the heads of everybody it needs to go over the heads of. Ultimately, because it's a show about teenagers and young adults, and because it's a horror show, there's going to be a heightened emotion and, particularly, a heightened sexuality that's inevitable. Because that's part of that time of your life, and because it's dealing with fantasy and horror. Your best dreams and your worst nightmares are going to come out of that.

Longworth: Did you support or oppose the network's decision to reschedule the famous prom episode in the wake of the Columbine shootings?

WHEDON: It wasn't actually the prom episode. They rescheduled two episodes. One was about a kid bringing a gun to school (episode number eighteen) that was supposed to air three days after Columbine, and I absolutely supported that because, let's say we came down against it. Any comment on the situation *after* that horror would have been offensively trite. So that was not a problem. They then started making us make cuts in the last show. We had to cut down explosions when it turned out that the kids had been trying to bomb the place, but the people hadn't known right away. And Xander trying to blow up the school had to go. And then they said they were going to reschedule episode number twenty-two, the season finale, as well. At that point, I got a little, well, I was not crazy about that situation, but I understood it. They were worried because there was violence at the graduation. Now admittedly it was crossbows against a sixty-foot snake, but, still, had there been any violent incident at a graduation, [after that] there would have been a very bad taste in everyone's mouth.

Longworth: OK, let's suppose the network hadn't changed a thing, and a violent incident had occurred in real life following the broadcast of your show. What's your responsibility as a producer, or do you feel a certain obligation toward young people and how your product may influence them?

WHEDON: I have always felt an enormous obligation, I mean, since I was a kid. Since I was writing stories alone in my room that nobody else was going to read, I worried about how much I needed to mix what my political beliefs were with the story I wanted to tell. How much I needed to protect good role models, how much I needed to make a statement, and how much I needed just to dig to some dark place and write whatever the hell I wanted. That's a huge part of it. I've thought about this a lot, particularly when I've been confronted by it, by events like this. To an extent, I think we have a grave responsibility. I think it would be belittling our audience to say that if we poke a stick in somebody's eye on the show they're all going to go do it, because they're a little more intelligent than that. But you absolutely have to think about what it will mean. At the same time, I feel strongly, and I've only come to realize this in the last few months, that we have a responsibility to be irresponsible. As storytellers, I've always been very offended by the whole, "lets rewrite all the fairytales" where the three little pigs settle their differences with the wolf by talking about their feelings.

Longworth: So that makes you very conflicted on this broad issue of responsibility versus creative latitude, doesn't it?

WHEDON: Well, it does, and it doesn't because ultimately, stories come from violence, they come from sex. They come from death. They come from the dark places that everybody has to go to, kind of wants to, or doesn't, but needs to deal with. If you raise a kid to think everything is sunshine and flowers, they're going to get into the real world and die. And ultimately, to access these base emotions, to go to these strange places, to deal with sexuality, to deal with horror and death, is what people need and it's the reason that we tell these stories. That's the reason fairy tales are so creepy (*laughs*), because we need to encapsulate these things, to inoculate ourselves against them, so that when we're confronted by the genuine horror that is day-to-day life we don't go insane.

Longworth: Do you ever attempt to moralize on an issue? For example, Buffy's first sexual encounter with Angel, which went badly in the aftermath. Was that your way of sending a message to young people to say, "You better abstain?"

WHEDON: Absolutely not. When I say we have a responsibility to be irresponsible, I'm not just talking about, "Oh, I'm trying to help kids deal with the world." I'm talking about the process of telling a story. These stories come from this place, and I think that stories are sacred. I think that creating narrative is a basic human function. It's why we remember some things and not everything. It's why everybody's version of the same event is different. Everybody creates narrative all the time. I think it's a really important function. And it has to come from this base place to be pure, to be art, to be anything other than a polemic. So I'm not just talking about "Well, I've got to help kids deal with their problems by showing them scary stuff." I mean, I've got to fulfill that human need for scary stuff, and sexy stuff, and racy stuff, and wrong stuff, and disturbing stuff. Because I think that's what storytelling is. Now, am I saying that sex is bad? Unfortunately, because it's a horror show everything that happens is bad. (*Both laugh.*) Everything that can go bad, will. Buffy's gonna drink beer, and it's going to turn her into a caveman. Now, I've been to college, and that's what happens. (*Both laugh.*) But we sort of undercut that specifically at the end of the show when Xander said, "And what have we learned about beer?" And Buffy says, "Foamy." I don't want to make a reactionary statement. I don't want to say, "Never have sex." I don't want to say, "Quick, go have it now." I want to say, "Some people have it. Everybody thinks about it. Here's how we deal with it." The thing with Angel wasn't, "Don't sleep with your boyfriend." Giles very clearly comes out and says, "I think you were rash, but I know you loved him and he loved you, and I'm not going to upbraid you for that." That wasn't about that. It was about what happens when you sleep with a guy and he stops calling you. What happens if you give him what he wants, and he starts treating you like shit. It was about the emotion of it. And that's a very real, emotional thing that everybody goes through. You consummate a relationship, and it disappears out from under you, and it happens to both sexes.

Longworth: I know you talked about being mugged and identifying with women, but why *are* you so good at writing for women and at understanding and empowering your female characters?

WHEDON: I've struggled with my ability to write women. My whole life I've wanted to make sure that I didn't idealize them, that I just didn't sort of scratch the surface. And sometimes I don't get it right. When I don't understand, I go to Marti Noxon, one of our female writers, and ask, "What did *you* go through?" But I have always been interested in feminism, partially because I was raised by a very strong woman, and partially because being small and fragile, and not taken seriously by anybody, I could identify with the way I perceived women were being treated once I got out of my house, where they were treated like equals. Gender and feminism has just always been a big area of study for me. It's what I concentrated on in film. And I think the other side of that is I'm a fella. One of the reasons why I was always able to do well in my feminine studies is that I never came from a knee-jerk, lesbian separatist, sort of perspective. I understand the motivation of the man with the murderous gaze, of the animal, of the terrible objectifying male, 'cause (*laugh*) I'm him. So it was very easy for me to sort of get into the mind set of, shall we say, the enemy.

Longworth: What kind of feedback or letters does the show get from young people? And I don't mean fan letters like, "I love your hair."

WHEDON: I know, but I have *really* great hair. (*Both laugh.*) I have great hair, just less and less of it. You know, we *do* get letters where people say the show has really helped them.

Longworth: So do you feel as though you've actually helped kids in dealing with life's situations?

WHEDON: I really do. I've had so many people say, and that includes people on my writing staff, "This [character] wasn't around when I was little. I needed this person to look up to and identify with." Creating Buffy is about creating not just a character who can take care of herself, but a world that accepts that. She's surrounded by men who not only don't mind that she takes charge in a situation, but find it kind of sexy. So in a way, it's kind of utopian, this group of people. But it's how I was until I went to a place where they didn't grow any. Most of my best friends were girls, and I'm very comfortable with them.

Longworth: Everyone assumes that the demos for your shows are thirteen to twenty, but what's the truth?

WHEDON: They charted it in our second year, and the median viewer age is twenty-six. There are young kids watching it, but I consider it as a college kind of show. The thing about it is, a lot of teen shows are all about, "Look at the crazy, bumbling grown-up." And we have some of those, some authority figures that we hate because I'll never get over that (*both laugh*), but the show is not designed to be exclusive to anyone. I was raised by teachers, so I had a very different idea of school than most of the kids around me. I tended to see the school as the way it functioned. I saw how tired my teacher was, 'cause I'd come home with my mom and she'd be more exhausted than I was. And the character of Giles is there to give that perspective.

Longworth: OK, so we know you can write for women, and young people, and vampires, and teachers, but let's suppose the studio came to you tomorrow and asked you to write a movie about senior citizens. Are you so ensconced in your genre that you either couldn't or wouldn't take the assignment?

WHEDON: Sometimes I'm like, "Oh my God, I just want to work with Abe Vigoda. Get me away from these fucking teenagers." (*Both laugh.*) Especially because at the WB there's a rotation of actors you just go, "Oh my God, I'm so sick of this world." But then, I *tend* toward stories about adolescents. I tend toward young-adult fiction, toward that moment in life. I'm interested in that. Yeah, I definitely want to tell other stories. I want to tell stories about grown-ups, and, to an extent that's what *Angel* is. Here's a guy who's living with decisions he's made, and so he's like a recovering alcoholic. What he's going through is not an adolescent experience. It's much more of a middle-age experience. But absolutely, sometimes I just want to run as far from here as I possibly can. It may be that as far as I can get is half a block (*both laugh*), but this to me isn't a teen show in the sense of, say, four years of giggling by the locker and "Will he ask me out," even though that's part of the human experience of it. The show exists on a much bigger level, and it deals with so much of life. She's changing so much, going to college. And what I have in store for her next year is so different from what happened last year that I don't feel stuck.

Longworth: You mentioned *Angel,* and as you know, some critics have said that the spin-off is better than the original. Do you agree with that assessment, or is it like being the parent of two kids, and—

WHEDON: It's basically like saying, "Girls, girls, you're *both* pretty."

Longworth: But when you raise a second child, you're automatically benefitting from your experiences in raising the first.

WHEDON: Oh yeah. But you know, you learn every day the exact same lesson. Every story we break, halfway through the story we're like, "Well, what if this was actually about Buffy? What if we cared about what Buffy was going through? That might make it better. Let's try that!" I mean, it's incredible how stupid you can be and how everything is a lesson. The same thing with *Angel*. *Buffy* to me is my first child. It's a phenomenon that says more about what I want to say about the world than anything I've ever worked on.

Angel has the potential to be that, too, and is starting to. But you look at the first scene in *Angel*, there's the blonde woman in the alley, and here comes Angel to save her. And I thought, "Oh my God, have I just betrayed everything I believe in by doing this scene?" But *Angel* works at a different level. *Angel* is about something else. But in terms of just creating an icon that I know exists in the endless sort of fantasy lives of young people, in a way that there hadn't been one that did before, or that's what *Buffy* is, I don't think I'm ever going to match that.

Longworth: I've talked at length with producers who have had multiple shows on the air at once, so I'll ask you the same question I asked of them. Do you feel that either of your dramas suffer because you're stretching yourself too thin?

WHEDON: Yes, a little bit. A little bit. I work really hard, not just on both shows, but to surround myself with really smart people who can get a great deal done without me. But yeah, there have been things in *Buffy* where I was like, "I could have spent a little more time tweaking that scene. I could have edited that for a little more excitement." You know, the extra yard that I could have gone. I see it inevitably. I'm still working as hard on *Buffy* as I possibly can, and doing as much on *Angel* as well, and I'm very pleased with the quality of the show. I think the problems we've had on *Buffy* have not been a question of my involvement so much as we're throwing a lot of new stuff up against the wall, and you never know what's going to stick.

Longworth: Is it hard to let go and entrust other writers with your creations?

WHEDON: No. When we came into it, I hired a staff. It took me four years to get a really, really solid staff. If I don't like something, if it's not right, I'll rewrite it. And I've rewritten a dozen scripts from the words, "fade in" on this show. I've written half or three-quarters of the scripts. Now I have a staff where that's happening much, much less, because they are really solid. If somebody else is getting it right and is embodying what the show should be, I don't need to do it. I've worked for producers who need to do every goddamn thing, no matter what. If you turn in a perfectly good script, they're going to rewrite it anyway, just so they could be the one to have written it. I do not like to create work for myself, and if somebody is getting it right, I like them to know it. So I'll never rewrite anything that I don't have to.

Longworth: In doing two shows at once you must have to be a disciplined person. Describe that discipline.

WHEDON: You know, I am incredibly *un*disciplined. I'm very lazy. I'm a big procrastinator. I happen to love doing this, which makes it easier. And, sometimes I can stay up all night if I have to, because I have no choice. Any discipline that I have comes from my desire to make the shows as good as I possibly can before I let them go. I reach a level of exhaustion, and this year I only reached it sooner, 'cause I had two shows going. But ultimately, how disciplined I am doesn't matter because I have this huge amount of work to do, and I get scripts in late, and it's not great in that sense. But I don't really have the opportunity to be as lazy as I really am because the show just doesn't allow it. I've often said that everyone who does movies should be forced to work in television for two reasons. One, the story actually matters, and two, you have to get it done. I think movies get sort of mired in this place of, "Well, we can do anything we want. We don't know what the fuck we're doing." (*Both laugh.*) In TV you have to tell the story, and you have to bring them back next week. And it has great discipline in terms of structure, in terms of meaning, in terms of what matters, and it's got to be done by tomorrow.

Longworth: Has writing become a chore for you, or is it still fun?

WHEDON: It is the most fun I'm ever going to have. I love to write. I love it. I mean, there's nothing in the world I like better, and that includes sex, probably because I'm so very bad at it. (*Both laugh.*) It's the greatest peace. When I'm *in* a scene, and it's just me and the character, that's it, that's where I want to live my life. I've heard about guys who find it strenuous and painful and horrible, and I scratch my noggin. I don't get it. I definitely get tired of rewriting, something that I'm not creating from whole cloth is tough. So every now and then I have to drum up the enthusiasm to write this exposition scene. It's a real drag. But, ultimately, the moment I break into a scene, the moment I figure out what it is, I'm there, I'm loving it.

Longworth: What, if anything, do you watch on TV when you have free time? I know you said you like *The West Wing*.

WHEDON: That's pretty much it. *The Simpsons* is starting to lose me. It's starting to happen, but, Jesus, it was only the best goddamn show on TV for ten years. But *The West Wing* I don't miss, and, quite frankly, I watch *Buffy*.

Longworth: How will you keep *Buffy* and *Angel* from getting stale after they've been on for a decade?

WHEDON: By dying of exhaustion.

Longworth: Are you going to know when to get out?

WHEDON: Maybe. Is the network? Is the studio? Are the actors? Who knows. It's clear to me that, even if I were to walk away, the show would continue to exist beyond me, which is the beauty and the horror of it. I do think this show will stop either before or soon after it starts getting stale. I don't think anybody wants that. I don't think the audience would put up with it. I don't think the actors would, either. It's hard for them to stay at the challenge, to come at it with the same joy that I do when I'm writing it. After seven years, some of it can be even harder.

Longworth: You mention the network, but your shows have a tremendous fan base on the Internet now. Stephen King tried his hand at a direct-to-Internet book. In that same vein, do you ever see a point where you or any producer would be able to bypass networks and make a good living taking your creations directly to the Internet?

WHEDON: Very possibly. Who the hell knows what's going to be possible in five years? Clearly, things are getting more spread out. Clearly, the TV and the computer are edging closer together, and I expect them to meld sometime within the next ten years for sure. And there's fifty-seven channels and all that good stuff. It's definitely possible. I'm not a great pioneer of technology and new thinking. I'm not a great independent maverick, either. I've always thought of myself as kind of a company man. I hope that I'm doing something original. I hope I'm pushing the envelope a little bit. I've always wanted to work with the studios doing great big hit shows and big summer movies. I love those things, and I always want to maintain a good relationship with the people I work with. I have a network that lets me put on a rather strange show.

Longworth: Speaking of strange shows filled with vampires and demons. You once said that everyone has demons. What are your demons?

WHEDON: Whoo, doggie! (*Laughs.*) Some of them I can't even describe. Generally, I'm a very depressive kind of person, and I think the world is a horrible, scary place where you die. And human interaction is kind of meaningless, and that's why I so desperately enjoy narrative, which provides me with that experience. So, if I'm not writing, I'm pretty much just not fun to be around. There's a sense of failure and mortality, and depression over, "Is my nose really going to look like this for the rest of my life?" (*Both laugh.*) I can be a real bummer.

Longworth: Your characters sometimes hang around graveyards, so I'll ask the obvious question. What's going to be inscribed on your tombstone?

WHEDON: If I'm lucky? (*Pauses.*) "He was getting better." Whatever I do, I just want to get better at it. I just want to keep trying, because I think of narrative and everything I do, whatever form it takes, as this sort of great, vast library that can be explored, that you'll never, ever see all of, but that you can just try and see as much of it as you can. I've learned more *this* year writing *Buffy* than I probably have in three years before, doing shows like "Hush," where everybody shut up for three acts. Writing "The Restless," which is the season finale, which took place entirely in dreams and is basically a forty-minute poem. The fact that I'm working in year four of a show that is giving me completely new challenges without becoming completely silly, self referential, and pointless, is a great thing.

Longworth: Well, not to belabor the point, but, again, "Hush" I believe will stand as one of the single greatest episodes in series drama. So you *are* getting better. Oh, say, before I let you get away, I need your advice on something. Can a vampire be repelled or killed over the telephone?

WHEDON: (*Laughs.*)

Longworth: The reason I ask is that I'm so damn tired of these telemarketers calling me.

WHEDON: A lot of them *have* risen from the grave, but I don't think so. Not unless you say, "Hey, look, sun's coming out!" (*Both laugh.*)

Longworth: Well, thanks for spending time with me.

WHEDON: There's just one more thing that I want to say about "Hush," because you've got me started on it, and something I've never gotten to talk about is this. The great thing about that episode was, I knew I wanted to do it silent, because I was starting to devolve into sort of a hack TV director, and I wanted to push myself visually. But what it became about was the way language interferes with communication. The amazing thing about it was, when you're writing about that, every word is on theme. Every single thing that happens in that show inevitably is about communication. And that was the most pure experience of language I ever had, was just writing the first act. People were using words wrong, somebody who needs to communicate because they're too busy talking, all that stuff. People just talking around the point. It all became so centrally thematic. That's never happened before. That was really *cool!*

Longworth: Of course, it's ironic that you and I have spent so much time verbalizing about a basically nonverbal episode. Shouldn't we be gesturing about it instead?

WHEDON: No, not on the phone. It's like killing vampires; it's harder over the phone. (*Both laugh.*)

10

CLIFTON CAMPBELL | Imagineer

Clifton Campbell. COURTESY OF CLIFTON CAMPBELL.

TELEVISION CREDITS

1986–87	*Crime Story* (NBC)
1987–90	*21 Jump Street* (Fox)
	Wiseguy (CBS)
	UnSub (NBC)

1993–95	*SeaQuest DSV* (NBC)
1997	*Moloney* (CBS)
1998–2000	*Profiler* (NBC)
2001	*Ms. Tree* (pilot)
2002	*McKinley* (USA)

МΛΛ МΛΛ МΛΛ

In the annals of literature there have been many biographical accounts that chronicled personal tales of suffering by some of our greatest novelists, poets, and playwrights. Poe, Wilde, Hemingway—all turned personal pain into passionate prose, and with great success, at least in terms of their eventual critical acclaim. In like manner, modern-day television scribes are not immune from human frailties, personal tragedies, and the slings and arrows of outrageous fortune. Reviewing volume one of *TV Creators*, Paula Bernstein remarked on the "emotional turmoil that often drives good TV" (*Variety*, February 12, 2001). In that regard, then, it would seem that Clifton Campbell has been working at a distinct disadvantage.

Cliff was not raised in a dysfunctional family. He has not been in rehab for alcohol or drugs. He does not suffer a gambling addiction, and he has never had a blowout with the network brass. Former boss Stephen J. Cannell says of Campbell, "He's a really nice guy, a very quiet guy. He was not one of these guys standing out in the hall telling jokes, but he had a great sense of humor. He was a good, hard worker."

Of course, it is quite possible that Cliff has faced adversity in his life, but you would never know it from talking with him. What you *would* come to know is that he is a disciplined writer, a respected producer, a devoted husband, and a loving father. Somehow, though, Campbell has managed to "overcome" his lack of personal drama in order to write some of the darkest scenes in the history of episodic television.

Much like Tom Fontana, who was the product of a loving family, then educated by Jesuits before going on to create the profane prison drama *OZ*, Cliff Campbell has also made the leap from being a normal guy to writing about abnormal characters and situations. His speciality is creating contract murderers and serial killers. "It's about imagination," says Cannell. "It's about abstract thought, and it's about putting your head someplace where it isn't normal. It's like acting, in a way. It's very similar to doing improv, where you have to take on the clothing of the character. But if you're dealing with darkness, and Clifton is very good at dealing with dark characters, you have to go there, you have to be it."

Like the novelist who writes travelogues but has never left his backyard, Cliff writes with expertise about things he can only imagine, and that is a tribute to his skill. Numerous "how-to" books have instructed budding artists to "write what you know." Fortunately Campbell never heeded that advice. In his world, writing is all about exploring what he does *not* know. In short, when it comes to writing television drama, Cliff's imagination is his greatest asset and his best friend.

Clifton Campbell was born in Hialeah, Florida, in 1957 to Fred and Joyce Campbell. Fred worked for Eastern Airlines in the printing services department, and Joyce was employed as a secretary at Winn Dixie. They had three children in addition to Cliff. Mark, the oldest, is now in real estate. Bonnie is a social worker, and Brenda, the baby of the family, is a therapist. "There is a twelve-year spread between us," says Cliff. "Brenda was the "oops" baby. My brother, Mark, and my sister Bonnie and myself are within five years of each other, so we remember knocking each other's heads in." (*Laughs.*)

Early on, Cliff was enthralled by cartoons and dreamed of one day writing his own comic strip. Like most children of the 1950s, he was a product of television; as a result he was inspired to try his hand at acting. But early into his college career at Florida State University, he realized that his desire to manipulate the roar of the crowd was not best served through the smell of greasepaint. He gave up acting and turned to writing. Campbell graduated from FSU and immediately moved to Chicago to try his hand at writing for the theater. His work as a playwright landed him a writing assignment on the NBC series *Crime Story*, a period cop drama produced by Michael Mann and set in Chicago of the early 1960s.

Campbell then signed a three-year contract to write for television mogul Stephen Cannell, who recalled, "We got him [Campbell] originally, actually I think Patrick Hasburgh found him, and he had been writing plays. We read some of his plays and thought they were terrific, and we brought him in. He was very good with character, that is in mining the second and third levels of characters, which, in hour television is a very hard thing to do. Generally what Clifton brought was good dialogue and a good, deep sense of character, and that came from his playwriting. He was a real good dialogue man."

Campbell's first assignment for Cannell was with *21 Jump Street*, which starred Johnny Depp as one of a team of young cops who go undercover to fight crime in Los Angeles high schools. He then served as producer on Cannell's CBS series *Wiseguy*, the story of an undercover agent who infiltrates a noted mob family. The series was recognized for its superb writing and Campbell himself netted both Emmy and Golden Globe nominations. Robert Thompson, in his book *Prime Time, Prime Movers*, commented on the quality of the show. "Like Bochco's *Hill Street Blues* and Don Bellisario's *Magnum P.I.*, *Wiseguy* was a network series capable of offering dramatic moments that were competitive with the theatrical releases offered as counter programming by HBO and Showtime."

In 1989 Cannell assigned Cliff to a new series for NBC titled, *UnSub* (Unknown Subjects), which dealt with a special law-enforcement unit dedicated to tracking down serial killers.

Campbell then went from *UnSub* to a real sub, serving as executive producer on Steven Spielberg's *SeaQuest DSV*, a big-budget drama set twenty-five years in the future. *TV Guide's* Jeff Jarvis reported that at a press preview, critics joked that *SeaQuest* "looked leaky before it left port" and referred to it as "Voyage to the Bottom of the Ratings" (October 9, 1993). Despite its high production values, superb special effects, and a premiere audience of more than thirty million viewers, *SeaQuest* struggled to stay afloat.

Campbell jumped ship to return to a life of crime, serving as co-executive producer of *Moloney*, a cop drama about a police psychiatrist. Cliff won the 1997 Angel Award for his work on the show, which was canceled after just one season.

He then joined the *Profiler* team as executive producer and shepherded the transition from one female lead to another. In its first season, *Profiler* had ranked a dismal ninetieth overall, but during Campbell's tenure the show continued to hold on to an important demographic group; as *TV Guide* noted, "its distinctive film noir look and its unique casting of a woman at the center of a crime series has made it a favorite among eighteen to forty-nine year olds" (September 5, 1998). At the start of the fourth season, Jamie Luner (*Melrose Place*) signed on to take the reins from Ally Walker. Both characters appeared together in several transition episodes, and afterward Luner even pulled double duty on a two-hour crossover with *Pretender*. The joint venture was not unexpected, since NBC had begun promoting its lineup of *The Others*, *Pretender*, and *Profiler* as its "Saturday Night Thrillogy." While *The Others* struggled to find an audience in it first and only season, *Profiler* and *Pretender* maintained steady numbers with key demographic groups. But something was rotten at 30 Rock. NBC jumped into the ring with World Wrestling Federation

CEO Vince McMahon and became a 50 percent owner of the XFL (Extreme Football League). The network announced that XFL games would be broadcast on Saturday nights, and the handwriting was on the wall. The "Thrillogy" was murdered to make way for the new "sport." Garth Ancier, former NBC executive (now executive vice president of Turner Broadcasting) opposed the deal and was forced to justify the move from quality drama to faux football. *Profiler* was pretty good, but *Profiler* was not *Law & Order*. It was not the level of *The West Wing*, or *ER* . . . it was sort of a marginal-performing show for us. It was certainly pretty good, but pretty good is not cutting it anymore." Unfortunately, NBC, seeking to raise its standards to a level on par with *ER*, ended up sending its Saturday night schedule into cardiac arret. In the first three weeks of the new XFL, ratings dropped drastically. The first game drew 15.7 million viewers, but that number fell to 6.5 million in the second week (*Broadcasting & Cable*, February 19, 2001). By the third broadcast, "wrestle football" had put a sleeper hold on audiences, netting only a 3.8 rating—well below the 4.5 guaranteed to advertisers (*Broadcasting & Cable*, February 26, 2001). By late March, XFL dropped below 2.0, with the lowest rating of any prime-time show in the history of television. Suddenly "pretty good" was looking better and better, but it was too late. *Pretender* signed a deal with TNT for a series of TV movies, and the *Profiler* crew scattered to other assignments.

As some sort of vindication, *Profiler* has met with extraordinary success in syndication, attracting the highest concentration of women twenty-five to fifty-four among all off-network hours and leading all new off-network shows among women eighteen to forty-nine.

Profiler Samantha Waters once proclaimed "failure is not an option." And so it was for Clifton Campbell, who did not sink into a deep depression or gloat over XFL's fumble and his show's subsequent success in reruns. He simply went right back to work, writing for other series (such as *Law & Order: SVU*) and then creating his own.

As this book goes to press, Cliff is working on two projects for USA. *Ms. Tree*, a one-hour action project based on a comic book series, and *McKinley*, a sort of "*CSI* in the wilderness." I spoke with Cliff on many occasions in 2000 and 2001, with the first interview taking place prior to cancellation of *Profiler* and subsequent interviews afterward, both by telephone and in person.

Longworth: (*March 30, 2000*) How's *Profiler* doing?

CAMPBELL: It looks good. The transition from Ally to Jamie Luner has worked out well. People are very responsive to her character and her take on that character. It looks good, but it's going to go down to the wire because we've got to see what NBC has developed. And, of course, the news that they just acquired the rights to XFL is probably going to have some sort of significance in the pickup, but we look pretty good at this point.

Longworth: Well, speaking of football, here in Virginia we still haven't gotten over VPI losing to Florida State in the '99 national championship game. So before we go any further with this interview, I have to know. As a Florida State University grad, are you one of those obnoxious Seminole fans who continues to rub it in?

CAMPBELL: (*Laughs.*) Ah, the Hokies. Well, I wouldn't call me obnoxious, but I love college football. We had a great program when I was there, and I was pretty excited about that.

Longworth: You guys really bend the rules.

CAMPBELL: No, it's just that we recruit right out of prison. (*Both laugh.*) That's the easiest thing to do.

Longworth: OK, so we know you like football. What were your favorite TV shows growing up?

CAMPBELL: I loved *Gilligan's Island,* I liked *Star Trek.* I loved *Green Acres.* I thought, when they broke the fourth wall, you know, when the main title credits would appear in the waffle batter, I used to get a kick out of that.

Longworth: But as I've gone back and studied *Profiler* episodes, I didn't see any *Green Acres* influence.

CAMPBELL: It's real subliminal. (*Both laugh.*) It's like subliminal flashes. Every now and then you'll see a blonde New Yorker running around, going, "Oliver, Oliver!" (*Both laugh.*) Just a couple of frames of that.

Longworth: But did any show you used to watch as a kid actually have an influence on your getting into the business?

CAMPBELL: It must have on some level; I did watch a lot of television as a kid. *The Wild, Wild West* was probably one of my all-time favorite shows, and *Mission Impossible.* So, presumably at an early age the four-act structure was pounded into me on an unconscious level.

Longworth: Like many other noted TV creators, you started out writing for theater. At what point, at what age did you know you liked writing, that you had a flair for it?

CAMPBELL: I started in theater as an actor, and I was pretty awful, but it was a great way to get laid. (*Both laugh.*) But I guess it was around nineteen or twenty when I was exposed to material, and to the opportunity to either make the material either come to life, or lay like a dead duck, that I thought that I had an opportunity to develop some writing. I guess it had always been there, I didn't quite know. I always wanted to be a cartoonist when I was a kid, and this is sort of like the transition into that. Cartoon strips have beginnings, middles, and ends, and somewhere in the back of my head I developed that as I matured, and I wrote my first play when I was in college when I was nineteen.

Longworth: What was the title?

CAMPBELL: It was called *Checkers*.

Longworth: It wasn't about Nixon's dog, was it?

CAMPBELL: It was not. In fact, that was the opening line in the review that I got when it was produced.

Longworth: What did it say?

CAMPBELL: I think it said something like, "*Checkers* is a pretty strange name for a play unless it was about Richard Nixon's dog." (*Laugh.*)

Longworth: So then, what was the play really about?

CAMPBELL: *Checkers* was a metaphor for these four people whose lives are sort of intertwined in this house, and it was a real dysfunctional single mom, and her son, using the kid to befriend a man she wanted to get close to.

Longworth: What was your major?

CAMPBELL: Playwriting.

Longworth: Do you *need* a degree in your hand, or could you personally have done the same thing without it? And, what value did the college experience have for you?

CAMPBELL: Well, other than the life experiences of that time in your life, I don't think anybody can teach you how to write. You're either born a writer or you're not. You learn how to tap it, and control it, and really develop a work ethic towards that end, because writing by nature, I think, is the act of daydreaming. So you just have to channel it, and figure out that there's a structure you have to adhere to, not so much that you have to choke the story to death, but audiences are used to a beginning, a middle, and an end. I don't think you need a degree for that, and I certainly could have found my way into this business without the college experience. I probably couldn't have balanced the checkbook or learned how to live on my own, which are really the experiences that I got from college.

Longworth: Degree or not, writing dialogue is difficult, is it not?

CAMPBELL: Well, I guess you either have an ear for it or not. And when I say you're either born a writer or you're not, that's the intuition of motivation and character development, and how it manifests itself in expression is something that maybe you're born with. Structure is something that you can learn.

Longworth: But dialogue for plays and television isn't like real speech.

CAMPBELL: Again, I think you need to expose yourself to a lot of other writers and not just in novels, but in plays, and screenplays, and poetry. It certainly helps to have come from a big family and to have been the shy kid who kind of listened to what was going on around him. I mean, there isn't a better education than a life experience and one full of a diverse group of humans that will enlighten you to their way of thinking.

Longworth: Were there particular novelists or playwrights, family members that helped get you going?

CAMPBELL: Yeah, my all-time favorite playwright [is] Harold Pinter. I love his work, but there's no story going on in a Pinter play. It's all language, and it's so layered and dense, and yet simple that, at a very early age, about the time I came across Steely Dan and their lyrics, I said, "You know what? There's another way to express yourself. You don't just have to say it like it is. You can sort of sneak around and make your point that way," and hopefully someone will wake up in the middle of the night and go, "God! That's what he meant." (*Both laugh.*) And that would be the best of all victories.

Longworth: How did you get from college to television?

CAMPBELL: Right after graduating Florida State, I moved to Chicago. This was 1980, when, at that time, the regional theater scene in Chicago was really busting at the seams, with Gary Sinese and John Malkovich, at the Steppenwolf and all those places. It was a great time to be a playwright because you could get your work read, and you could get real powerful, unknown actors to help develop material and hear how right or wrong you were about something. It was a great move. I got stuff produced fairly quickly. In fact, *Checkers,* after having been developed and produced in college, was my first professional play. And, a play I had written after that had gotten some really good reviews, and they were shooting a pilot to *Crime Story,* which was an NBC series back in '85, I think. Michael Mann read the review and went to see an actor in the play. And I get a call a few days later saying he wanted to meet me. So I ended up getting hired to write *Crime Story.*

Longworth: How involved were you with *Crime Story?*

CAMPBELL: Of the first thirteen episodes, I wrote three. I was a staff writer, and there were a couple of story editors. The first order was filmed in Chicago. The overall story arc of the series then moved to Las Vegas, and I was offered to move to Las Vegas, but I didn't want to do that. I had recently gotten married, and for a lot of reasons it didn't make sense for me. So I passed on that opportunity, but it gave me a handful of other options.

Longworth: Were there any special challenges that you faced in writing a show set back in the 1960s?

CAMPBELL: Well, Chicago is still of the '60s in a lot of ways. It helped that I moved from a warm, sunny climate to a city that had been around forever and was really like everybody's big brother. I got into the lure of Chicago when I first got there. I loved to read about it and to listen to people's stories. I really felt kind of frozen in time. Even though I was only five or six at the time that this story line was unfolding, it wasn't that difficult to conceive.

Longworth: Did you go immediately from that to *21 Jump Street*?

CAMPBELL: I did. I signed a three-year deal with [Stephen] Cannell, and I was doing *Jump Street* at the time. I started with him in 1986. By then I was a story editor, then I went to executive story editor.

Longworth: How much of a hands-on writer is a story editor?

CAMPBELL: The answer back then was very hands-on. That's not the case these days.

Longworth: Why?

CAMPBELL: The original staff for *21 Jump Street* [created by Stephen J. Cannell and Patrick Hasburgh, who was the executive producer], involved a writer/producer and then three story editors like myself—you know, "baby writers," basically. Stephen let Patrick put his own staff together and we did everything under his aegis and under his watchful eye, but I didn't know that I was having a really hands-off experience [where he was concerned]. I thought, "Well, I'm a story editor, so I'm supposed to write every other episode, and do notes, and do everything." I haven't had that experience since then. [On *Profiler*] we bring in story editors and they hammer out stories and throw out ideas and put out first drafts, and if they're good, we give notes, and we keep going back and forth. But the other showrunners that I talk to say, "No, it doesn't seem to be the same as when we were story editors," and we all act like we're a bunch of old men.

Longworth: So which do you think is the better system? Do you wax nostalgic about the old days, or do you believe it's OK the way things are today?

CAMPBELL: It's OK the way it is today. I think it also has to do with the show, the tenor of the show, whoever the figurehead is, and the creator therein, and what they feel they can get out of somebody. And listen, if somebody is a baby writer and has never written anything and gets the show, they can start writing episodes immediately. Things today tend to get overworked. It starts with a staff writer, goes up to a story editor, gets rewritten by a producer, then is rewritten by an executive producer. You lose a little spontaneity and freshness, but that's just what you have to do because of the constraints of time. Sometimes you just get the right group of humans and the right talent together, and it's a nice, well-oiled machine; [like] with *Wiseguy* there were only the four of us, and we just had a blast. It was a great show to write, and everybody was sort of on equal footing, ideawise.

Longworth: Wasn't that show a little ahead of its time? Do you think if you had brought it to air a year ago it would have been a big hit like *The Sopranos?*

CAMPBELL: Well, if we could have been on HBO and been more irascible, yeah, we could have pushed even further. I think we pushed about as far as the network would permit at that time.

Longworth: I don't know if you've read the reviews of the CBS series *Falcone,* but, for example, *TV Guide* advised viewers not to compare it with *The Sopranos* but to compare it against *Wiseguy,* and if they do *Falcone* would still come up short, because it didn't have the same texture as did *Wiseguy.*

CAMPBELL: Well, the source of pride we all felt for that show was for a lot of reasons, not the least of which was it was a cop show where Vinnie never pulled a gun. We're not even sure he *had* one. We know he had one somewhere (*laughs*), but it wasn't about that. It was about the personalities and the complex human emotions behind being a rat, and befriending people for the sake of ratting on them, and how you really felt about that. Hopefully we were just testing the moral boundaries of right and wrong, and any great show is going to do that, whether it's a medical drama or a sitcom. It was just a really nicely conceived series. And Cannell, God bless him, had enough confidence in the franchise that he created to just let the writers continue to challenge those boundaries. He gave us free rein.

Longworth: I want to come back to that in a moment, but let me ask you something about the boundaries of *21 Jump Street.* As I remember, you would end up the show with a public-service announcement where one of the young guys like Johnny Depp would do a message about some issue. Whose idea was that?

CAMPBELL: That was Patrick Hasburgh's idea.

Longworth: That seemed like a pretty innovative thing to do. Given the current climate of violence in America and politicians drawing a link between television and youth violence, do you think if more dramas had followed Patrick's lead things would have been better now? Or do you think TV has no impact on violent behavior?

CAMPBELL: That's a big question. It's impossible for me to separate the tragedy that we see going on around us from popular culture, which television is obviously a big part of. But in terms of the public-service announcements, we got some remarkable letters from kids who were in trouble. And quite often those toll-free telephone numbers we ran at the end of episodes specifically involving abuse, it was sort of frightening how much response they got, but it was satisfying in that kids were crying out for help, and the show might have given them at least a band-aid on their feelings or a place to be heard. I can't imagine anything like that would work in any real significant way with a *Dawson's Creek*–type of show that kids are watching now, by virtue of the fact that the story lines on *Dawson's Creek* are probably perpetuating them becoming adults ahead of time.

Longworth: Do you see that as a problem?

CAMPBELL: Well, I don't know if I see that as a problem, I just don't think that the running of a PSA at the end of it would necessarily have the same impact today.

Longworth: Did you ever save any of those letters you received from kids?

CAMPBELL: I'll bet they're somewhere. Patrick and the staff, we were invited at the time to Mayor Bradley's office because of the response we had gotten from one particular episode. Patrick had even gotten a letter from the President.

Longworth: Earlier you spoke of shooting in Chicago before *Crime Story* moved to Las Vegas. And *21 Jump Street* was shot in Canada. We always hear producers and studios talk about saving money by moving out of Hollywood, but can you put a number on the savings? Specifically, give me an example of how much money you can save on one episode.

CAMPBELL: It's about 30 to 35 percent, and that depends on your budget. It would make a lot of sense to shoot *any* drama in Vancouver; if you felt like the show's going to have a nice long, healthy run, you would automatically go up there. The problem is a lot of actors don't want to relocate there, and you can't get your order without the right cast, and you end up starting in Los Angeles and *wishing* you were in Vancouver. Unless you're David Duchovny and you decide to get married and move back to L.A. and the show has to move with you. But yeah, it's about 30 percent, and that fluctuates with the strong dollar.

Longworth: Did you know at the time you wrote *Jump Street* that Johnny Depp was going to be a breakout talent?

CAMPBELL: You couldn't help but know, 'cause as an actor he would never go for the obvious choice. He would take chances, he would turn things on its side. He was a very agreeable person. A very sweet, giving guy who'd do exactly what he wanted, and obviously that was a lot of fun to write for, but you could tell that he wasn't just going to go down the middle with anything. Also, he was just such a neat guy to be with, you just knew there was something special about him.

Longworth: Of course you had had experience as an actor, too. Does that help you in writing for actors?

CAMPBELL: Having been an actor?

Longworth: Yes.

CAMPBELL: Well, I wasn't much of an actor. (*Laughs.*)

Longworth: OK, so you were a *bad* actor, so you can still answer the question. (*Both laugh.*)

CAMPBELL: Well, I suppose, just because I remember struggling with scenes of dialogue that I couldn't make work internally, I'm very conscious about what actors say. I try to be both honest with the story and honest with the character, which are sometimes in conflict, and that's partially because of those experiences that I had as an actor. I really didn't do that much acting. I did enough to know that I'm not good at it, and that someone who really *is* good at it I have a tremendous amount of respect for.

Longworth: Before we leave *Jump Street,* is it more difficult for an adult to write dialogue and stories for young people than it is writing for people your age or older? Does that make any difference at all?

CAMPBELL: Well, I believe that writers make the voices of their characters regardless of their age. I mean, Kevin Williamson [*Dawson's Creek*] obviously has the teenage patter down pat. No, I think a good, solid writer can get into their characters, which means finding their voices. I've got a nine-year-old daughter, a thirteen-year-old stepson, and a fifteen-year-old stepdaughter, and I listen to them and try and involve myself as much as I can in their world, (a) because I love them, and (b) because it may come in handy some day, and it usually does.

Longworth: *21 Jump Street* also went into syndication with new episodes. Did you stay with it or move on to *Wiseguy?*

CAMPBELL: I did *Jump Street* for two years, then I went over to *Wiseguy* for two years.

Longworth: How did you land the job on *Wiseguy?*

CAMPBELL: David Burke was one of the executive producers on *Wiseguy,* and we were all in the same building. I was doing *Jump Street* and David had signed on to do *Wiseguy.* He had been a story editor on *Crime Story,* and that's where I first met him. We used to give each other grief. After doing two seasons on *Jump Street*, I was getting a little tired of that, and I really loved *Wiseguy*. David was very helpful in making that happen.

Longworth: In looking at the stories you have written, whether it's a cop gone undercover, or someone good posing as a bad guy, or young cops posing as high school criminals, or a cop who's also a psychiatrist, it seems like you're attracted to writing about conflicted characters. Is that a conscious decision, or am I making too much of that?

CAMPBELL: You might be making too much of it, but the meat and potatoes of the shows that I've done have fallen into the genre where it's basically the good-versus-evil story line.

Longworth: But your characters are also very torn. They're having to live two lives at once or deal with two sets of feelings at once.

CAMPBELL: Yeah, I think that's kind of what I am still saying. I think every good show that involves a police story line is going to have that, because the best cops have to be a little demented because of who they're chasing, and the fact that they have probably left their families in tatters in the pursuit of these monsters. There's something both noble and a little left of center about that. I did a show called *Moloney* with Peter Strauss that was only on for one season (he was a police psychiatrist), and he had the same dilemmas. By virtue of getting close to someone you are betraying them because everything they say, and every emotion they allow you to see, you're going to use against them.

Longworth: Stephen Cannell remarked on your imagination and ability to use abstract thinking to create dark characters. Now, since you have never been or lived with a serial killer, how do you summon that ability to imagine and create abnormal characters from your very normal existence?

CAMPBELL: Well, anybody who claims that their life is normal, I would be suspicious of from the beginning (*laughs*); they're generally hiding something. Although, sure, I think I had a fairly normal upbringing, but that's also kind of a blank canvas and an opportunity with that safety net emotionally to be able to delve into the dark side. I think I've always sort of done that on some level, growing up, coming from a decent, honest, hardworking family that gave me freedom to be a kid and explore, and that didn't stop with my schoolwork. It extended into my personal life. I grew up in Miami, and that was a pretty funky town to grow up in the late '70s.

Longworth: So your hero was Don Johnson?

CAMPBELL: (*Laughs.*) I wouldn't say my hero was Don Johnson, no. But that's a big drug culture. I wasn't big into the drug culture myself, but I had a lot of friends who were. I lost friends, both to the prison system and to the grim reaper. I always felt safe enough to mourn that situation, and to wonder why it would happen to kids I was shooting marbles with and playing football with just a few years earlier. So, I've never considered myself all that nice a guy, but if Stephen thinks I'm a nice guy, I'll take it. (*Laughs.*) He's one of the nicest guys I know.

Longworth: But there's a perception that one has to suffer in order to create. So since you haven't had any Edgar Allan Poe hardships to call upon, how can you imagine dark characters and disturbing story lines?

CAMPBELL: Given that you already have examples of other people in this business who have had hardships that had to be overcome, I don't necessarily *have* one of those. Part of me is sort of envious of people like Steven Gaghan, who wrote *Traffic,* who had a difficult upbringing and addictions, because I don't have that place to mine.

Longworth: That's a weird thing to be envious of.

CAMPBELL: Well, it *is* a weird thing to be envious of, although you have to appreciate the perception that was born from those periods in his life. And I'm not really envious, because I think I can get there like any writer can get there if they have a fertile imagination, and if they're comfortable enough with themselves that they can let those sides of them develop.

Longworth: OK, so if you're a good writer, you can imagine dark characters, but how can you make those characters three dimensional and not just caricatures?

CAMPBELL: I still think it's the degree to which you trust your emotional stability, and the desire to go into those dark places and to continue to turn over rocks, and continue to confound your expectations about a character, that flushes that character out and makes him three dimensional. Turn a character on his head and [imagine] what's the least likely thing a character would do? Explore that a little bit. Put it into situations that you are writing, and see what you come up with.

Longworth: So then character development is character development, no matter what?

CAMPBELL: I think so. I mean, I've never been a fourteen-year-old pregnant teenager with a drug addiction, but I think I could write a scene about that. I have a niece who, unfortunately, has a very powerful drug addiction and has given up two children, and I can put myself in her place. Not really, but I certainly think if I sit and think about the unfortunate set of circumstances that led to my niece's addiction I can emotionally track that, and I think I could exhibit it on the page.

Longworth: But in that case, at least your niece provides a benchmark for your character development.

CAMPBELL: Yeah, you need a bullet copy of a tragedy that is the character's life, and that is sort of your blueprint. Then you track it emotionally through each scene and make sure that your language is evocative of that tragedy in your life.

Longworth: *SeaQuest DSV* was probably the exception to what we've been discussing in terms of character development. Nothing too dark or deep, but let me just spend a moment on it. The show *looked* fantastic. It was like watching a big-screen film adventure that just happened to be on a small screen in my living room. Why didn't it catch on with audiences?

CAMPBELL: You know what? That's a tragedy as far as I'm concerned because it could have been and should have been the new *Star Trek*, it should have had a ten-year run. My perspective is that it was neither fish nor fowl. It struggled early on because, creatively, the show was supposed to be set in the future when there was supposed to be no conflict on this planet. Well, that's a problem. (*Laughs.*) People have to be arguing or it's not drama. Everybody can't be on the same page of every issue. And Roy Scheider really signed on to play Jacques Cousteau. He wanted to be more the scientist than in the military, and as the pressure from outside sources came to develop and create conflict, Roy got more and more unhappy, and it didn't feel like the show he had signed on to do. You can't hide that kind of thing from an audience, you know? You try and balance the magical, the science-fiction aspects of the show with the constraints of drama, which dictates a little conflict, and it's going to show, it's going to read. We couldn't do the magic seaweed episode every week, and in that first season, which I wasn't a part of, it went from being Jacques Cousteau to being real far to the left science fiction, and the audience went, "Whoa, what's going on here? We've got mermaids and aliens when we were exploring the underwater library." It was confusing for an audience member. And the network, feeling that it had had some success at the end of that first season with the much more promotable science-fiction aspect of the show, went with that full bore in season two. Roy just believed that it wasn't the show that he had signed on to do, and he felt uncomfortable in the role.

Longworth: So what was the chronology on your involvement?

CAMPBELL: I went with *SeaQuest* in their second season, 1994 I think. And I did it for two seasons.

Longworth: Now, on to *Profiler*. First, let's give credit where credit is due. When people watch the screen, they see several key names. They see Cynthia Saunders, they see Steven Kronish's name, your name. What did each person contribute to the series?

CAMPBELL: Cynthia wrote the pilot episode and is the creator of the show. I believe she was on staff for the first initial network order of thirteen episodes, I presume as writer/producer. But she wasn't on for the back order of nine, and she hasn't been around since then. I've never met Cynthia. She gave us a great platform, obviously, and some very compelling characters.

Longworth: What about Steven? What's the relationship there?

CAMPBELL: Steve is the guy who was brought in to take over the show, and he brought me in to help run it. We first worked together on *Wiseguy*, and while we were doing *Wiseguy* Cannell got the opportunity to do a short-order series called *UnSub* (short for *Unknown Subject*), which is what the FBI calls serial killers. *UnSub* really was *Profiler*. It starred David Soul and Kent McCord. It was about a special task force dedicated to the pursuit and identification of serial killers and other offenders of violent crime.

Longworth: That wasn't around too long, was it?

CAMPBELL: It wasn't. It was a short order for eight. We kind of knew what it was going to be. And when I look back on that, they just let us really have our way. It was very violent, and not just violent, but with the depiction of character, they let us really get into some things. We had some real crazies on that show, and we spent a lot of time on it. We had great relationships because of *Wiseguy*. Kevin Spacey did an episode of *UnSub* and he was great. We'd give him a small role and he'd turn it into something big, which is something he's good at. (*Laughs.*)

Longworth: Tom Fontana and I were talking about the episode of *Homicide* where they killed off a bunch of characters because they thought it was going to be their last episode. It was real bloody, and the overnight ratings came out and the show had great numbers. It was the exception to Barry Levinson's rule in terms of violence on the show, but it was a big hit. Do you ever have the sense that, if you put more blood and guts and gore into *Profiler*, that you would do better in the ratings?

CAMPBELL: Well, we look at our competition on Saturday nights at ten o'clock, and *Walker, Texas Ranger* is leading the pack, and has for many years, and is a fairly violent show. I'm not "dissing" that show, I haven't really seen much of it, but their bread and butter is the action part of it.

Longworth: So you're counterprogramming with *Profiler*?

CAMPBELL: Right. And *Profiler* is a pretty dark show, and you can overdo that stuff real easy. But in a lot of ways it's scarier because we stay away from the real graphic nature of it. But the emotional fallout for the families of victims, and even our characters as they get too close, I think is probably depiction enough for anybody.

Longworth: As some of our other TV creators have noted, story-driven dramas last longer than character-driven dramas. How would you describe *Profiler* in that regard, because it seems that you cross over and do both very well?

CAMPBELL: Well, I think that's true. One of the original paradigms of the show was that the stories had to stand on their own, but like any good show that a writer wraps their brain around, you want to go home with those characters every week. You want to know what they're about and what makes them tick and why, for God's sakes, they would do this kind of thing week after week. It's a pretty dark, oppressive world they live in, and we can't just skip over the surface of it. They've got to live it, or they can't do their job. I'm certainly not Dick Wolf or John Wells, but I agree that stories have to win the day, and if you tell a great story, everybody's going to watch. But over the course of fifty years that television has been around, there have been a lot of series that have survived simply because the characters were so wonderful.

Longworth: Where do you get story ideas from? Do you watch the headlines, or do the ideas come from your head most of the time?

CAMPBELL: Well, they're all sort of inspired by articles we read. We've got a couple of technicians who were former FBI agents who have helped conceive story lines. There's lots of material out there about serial killers. The difficulty for us becomes we can't show too much. And the biggest thing we can't do is link sex with violence, and everybody knows serial killers kill primarily because of the sexual thrill.

Longworth: But why can't you do that?

CAMPBELL: We can't glorify sex and violence together. We can deal with sex, we can deal with violence, but the motivation behind the violence can never be for sexual gratification, which is tough, because that's what serial killers are all about. So we get real story lines or real articles, and we kind of twist it around to find out what the root cause or motivation is. For instance, how did this character become this monster, because he or she certainly doesn't *think* they're a monster. It's just the hand that they've been dealt, and how they're trying to survive and beat back their own demons.

Longworth: Do those constraints handcuff you, or does it even bother you anymore?

CAMPBELL: At this point it doesn't bother us, but it was frustrating in the beginning. But then, if we didn't have that hurdle to get over, we may not have conceived some really interesting killers. And our better shows really are ones with killers who have such a unique and complex psychology that our characters can profile them for four acts. So I think we've been able to not only live with, but live better, because of the constraints.

Longworth: *Profiler* and *Pretender* did cross over episodes. Why didn't you ever do a crossover with *Law & Order?*

CAMPBELL: Well, we asked to do that, and we did the crossover with *Pretender,* but we certainly had more in common with *Law & Order,* because *Pretender,* even tonally, is different. But they've [NBC] never been interested in that. They like the "Thrillogy" block they've got for Saturday night, and thought that we would all be best served if we could keep it within the family.

Longworth: The strong female dramatic lead has made a comeback in the new millennium. You were there before the trend took hold again. You weathered the teen shows and the mindless sitcoms. Why is America now ready to accept a mature woman as a lead in a drama series?

CAMPBELL: Because they are fascinating characters. Their struggles are our struggles. I think, as the baby-boomer generation continues to push forward to retirement, we're looking at the reflection of our own lives. And we've seen men go through those struggles [on TV] and now we're having an opportunity to see really successful professional women go through those same struggles, with the added pressure of single motherhood. I think viewers find that fascinating, how actresses can juggle all that, because anybody who has kids and has ever taken a swipe at rearing them singlehandedly can only appreciate the struggles they're going through.

Longworth: (*May 26, 2000.*) We now know that *Profiler* was not renewed for a fifth season. Were you surprised that NBC axed its entire "Saturday Night Thrillogy" in order to do a deal with the World Wrestling Federation for broadcasting XFL games?

CAMPBELL: It wasn't entirely unexpected. As a person in the "hour" business, I was frankly glad that there was only a minimal fallout from the alternative-programming craze, such as the XFL. Obviously we took a direct hit with that directive, but there could have been more. There was going to be across the board, with all five or six networks, a complete overhaul embracing that kind of programming. But really, except for the XFL that was sort of it. It wasn't as if any of the shows on Saturday night failed, but NBC felt they had to try a new direction.

Longworth: I'm thinking of Aaron Sorkin's *Sports Night,* Glenn Gordon Caron's *Now and Again,* and *Profiler* as examples of outstanding dramas that deserved a longer run. Why can't programs with niche audiences survive these days?

CAMPBELL: Well, the networks need to have a little more patience. I don't know what kind of pressures the programmers are under, I just know the laws of nature dictate that if you give a show ample time to start showing some legs, and that's been the cry of showrunners for ages, you've got to give a show a chance.

Longworth: Why not stay in production and just go to another network or to cable?

CAMPBELL: There had been some talk about that because the show had sold well in syndication. But there would be so many contracts that would have to be honored above the line that, financially, it probably would be difficult to ratchet the show back as many notches as you would have to in order to afford it and still maintain the quality.

Longworth: Even though you're making lots of money in syndication, it still hurts not to be renewed.

CAMPBELL: We had a big farewell dinner, me and Steve Kronish. The advertisers were very disappointed that NBC wasn't bringing the show back. They felt that the "Thrillogy" was easy to sell because they had a trademark. They questioned the wisdom, and, according to accounts I've read, there was confusion if not concern on the advertisers' part.

Longworth: Well, not to pour salt in the wound, but for most of the last season I saw fewer and fewer promos for *Profiler.* There seemed to be a concerted effort not to single out your show for promotion.

CAMPBELL: Well, historically that's been the case. It's always been explained to us that since they [NBC] are an owner, they kind of know what to expect in terms of performance. They had partners in those other two shows in the "Thrillogy" [*Pretender* and *The Others*], and they sort of had to appease the partners to some extent. Every week we'd watch *The West Wing* and *Law & Order* and say, "Where's the promo for *Profiler?*" And then they would promo us, and we'd get a nice hit, and it showed. We would invariably get a nice number that Saturday. The network knows, but they're just having to serve a lot of masters.

Longworth: It's just like in *your* household, where you have to serve two masters. And just so my segue makes sense, I'll ask you if your daughter is allowed to watch *Profiler.*

CAMPBELL: No, that's too dark for her.

Longworth: At what point would she be ready to watch it?

CAMPBELL: I would say by twelve is OK. I mean, we've really had to sand down the darkness and the rough edges, so I think twelve years old is OK. Anything younger than that it can be a little bit disturbing.

Longworth: Are you a good dad?

CAMPBELL: I like to think so.

Longworth: What do you guys do together?

CAMPBELL: My daughter loves to roller skate and she loves this place called the Clay Café. She loves pottery, so she and I do that.

Longworth: What kind of pottery does she make?

CAMPBELL: She loves to make bud vases. My house is littered with bud vases. (*Both laugh.*) But we don't have any buds in Los Angeles. (*Laughs.*)

Longworth: Does she paint them for you?

CAMPBELL: Oh yeah, she has a lot of creative energy and we've found some wonderful places for her to exhibit it.

Longworth: Now back to *your* creative energy. Do you have some other projects in mind that you've always wanted to pursue?

CAMPBELL: I've always got a new play in the typewriter, spec features, and that kind of thing. Development season comes once a year, and every now and then a new idea springs to mind. I'm working on a pilot tentatively titled *Ms. Tree,* which is loosely based on a comic-book series.

Longworth: But you've pretty much hung up your playwriting spurs while you're doing television?

CAMPBELL: It's been here and there, but not nearly as much as I would like. The hours are pretty long, and when hiatus rolls around, probably the last thing I want to do is sit down and write, but I always manage to kick out a new play every year.

Longworth: What is your writing routine like, except for the days when you're being bothered by me. (*Both laugh.*) In other words, how many hours do you try to write each day, and when you're in production, how long does it take you to write an hour script?

CAMPBELL: Well, I wake up dead to the world in the morning, so I need to work out. I do the stationary bike and the weights for about an hour. Then I need to get three or four hours of quiet in the morning when I write. That's difficult, obviously, when you're in production, but if I start early enough, then I sort of resurface around 10:30 or eleven A.M. and get on to the showrunning responsibilities. But I need a good three or four hours in the morning fresh.

Longworth: Alright, let's say you get your three hours in before noon. Typically, how far along are you in terms of completing the script?

CAMPBELL: Sometimes it takes three or four hours just to write the teaser because you're not quite sure what the tone and the pace of this particular hour is going to be. At the opposite end, I've written act four in an hour. I don't know why that is. Let's say it takes a week to write a script, five to seven days to write a script. I'll take half that time to write act one, just because of everything that you're setting up. You have to have an understanding about every character's point of view, and where he wants to start off, and the impression you want to leave with the audience, and the promises you want to make. Then, fulfilling those promises gets easier the deeper into the piece you get. And, again, generally act four takes a day.

Longworth: Does writing continue to be fun, or is it a chore when you're on deadline?

CAMPBELL: I enjoy it always. I hate the first couple of days because it's like, "Oh, I'm the worst writer. They're going to find out I'm a fraud, and I can't write worth a shit." For the first couple of days until you're confident that the material is holding up, it's not much fun. But by the end, you can't wait to hand it in and you're jazzed again. So my overall impression after the end of each season is that I can't wait to get back to next season.

Longworth: Syd Field has talked about how, in the truest sense of the definition, that directors, producers, cameramen are not, per se, artists because what they do is a collaborative process. On the other hand, someone who paints, or sculpts, or writes a TV script *is* an artist because he or she creates alone. Do you agree?

CAMPBELL: Yeah, I do agree with that, the same way that anybody who throws pots for a living is an artist. If you're creating something from someplace inside you, and it has a personal point of view and a personal message, and it makes you feel good and satisfied to have done it, then you are an artist. I've always found, with television in particular, that a lot of the reward comes with simply getting the job done because it's such a demanding occupation. As you grow as a showrunner, then you get to express yourself creatively in a lot of other ways, not just on the printed page but with postproduction, editing, casting, walking a director through a script. These are all opportunities to exhibit that creative side of you.

Longworth: So you *are* an artist?

CAMPBELL: Yeah, I guess, by definition. Certainly I feel a little funny about that word since television is more of a popular art and the original derivative art form. But yeah, I suppose by the definition I just gave you, that makes me an artist.

Longworth: If you were hiding out and no one could locate you, and a profiler was asked to do a report on you, what could she tell us that would help us to understand you better?

CAMPBELL: I guess I'm a very private person, which is why I write and don't act. I enjoy spending time with my daughter and my new family. I'd like to think that I'm going to be in this business, or at least going to write until the day I die. So I feel like there's always something to be done to that end, traveling, getting to know new people, being available for things even if they're painful. Or, the profiler might just reveal where I go to drink every day. (*Both laugh.*)

Longworth: Are you planning to do any crime stories involving Florida State football players?

CAMPBELL: Well, we've kicked around the idea of doing a show involving a professional athlete, because the crimes could be occurring in different cities, and we're not sure how or why the killer is moving from place to place. We plan to have a slaughter in Virginia where these Hokie football players and fans are all lined [up] prostrated, having been killed by Bobby Bowden and his fine group. (*Both laugh.*)

Longworth: You're a dark and disturbed person, even for a Seminole.

11

JOHN MCNAMARA | "Fugitive" Phile

John McNamara. COURTESY OF JOHN MCNAMARA.

TELEVISION CREDITS

1993–94	*The Adventures of Brisco County, Jr.* (Fox)
1994–97	*Lois & Clark* (ABC)

1996	*Profit* (Fox)
1997	*Spy Game* (ABC)
1998–99	*Vengeance Unlimited* (ABC)
2000–2001	*The Fugitive* (CBS)

MWV MWV MWV

It is normal to reminisce about our favorite TV shows from childhood, but few of us ever act upon those remembrances. John McNamara is the exception.

As a boy John liked *The Adventures of Superman,* so as an adult he ended up producing *Lois & Clark.* He also loved *The Fugitive*—so much so that he found a way to update the series for the new millennium.

There is probably some deep, symmetrical meaning in McNamara's pursuit to make old dramas new again, but for anyone who likes good television it is sufficient just to sit back and enjoy the fruits of his labor; with John, it is a labor of love.

John McNamara was born in 1962 in Ann Arbor, Michigan. His father (now deceased) was an attorney and a law professor. His mother is an artist and also sells a line of clothing. John has two younger sisters, Molly and Maggie, the latter of whom is a half sister from his father's second marriage. "I grew up in kind of a bifurcated home that I think in some ways was probably a perfect environment for somebody who would end up doing what I was doing for a living," John says. "My father was a very business-oriented, methodical, logical person who dealt with the realities of life as they played out in the courtroom. My mother was and is a very emotional, mercurial, extremely talented, very passionate artist. And, in a way, I'm probably a result of both of their natures."

Asked to describe his family's favorite interests and activities, John laughed as he told me, "We argued a lot." McNamara became a child of divorce, but he was also a product of television. "I would have to say that TV, for good or ill, is probably the biggest influence on my life," he says. "We were a typical middle-class family up to and even through my parents' divorce. We would see the same movies other kids saw . . . but there weren't really kids' movies then the way there are today. Kids' movies then were a kind of a ghetto of *Godzilla, Planet of the Apes,* and crappy Disney films. So I think movies had much less of an influence on me. Television was just *it!* Even D-level television, like *Ultra Man* and *Rocket Robin Hood* or the original *Batman* with Adam West. And, of course, *Superman* with George Reeves."

Somewhere along the way, though, John discovered that he had a talent for more than just watching what others wrote. "My dad read in the local paper that someone was having a short-story writing contest," John recalls. "There were categories by age, like 'best kid's story,' 'best high school story.' And he sort of nudged me to do something. I had dabbled in writing and was actually going to be a cartoonist, a comic-book artist, but I was color blind and was limited in how far I could go. (*Laughs.*) It was literally on the heels of that, of going, 'Gosh, I can't be a comic-book artist now. I can't be the next Jack Kirby, so what am I going to do?' So that's when my Dad said, 'Why don't you try writing a short story?' I sort of just sat down, and this thing came out, and it was not based on anything that ever happened to me. It was a political thriller set in Washington, D.C. I don't even know how I thought of it, probably watching *Seven Days in May* and going, 'Oh, I can do that.' I think it was called "The Washington Decision." I was also very influenced by Robert Ludlum at the time. So I popped it out, and sent it in. I had no expectation that it was going to do anything. And the next thing I knew, it had won the contest, and I got a check for, like, a hundred dollars. That was big money in 1976. I was fourteen, so that was big dough."

John's college career began in his home state, but he soon relocated to New York City. "I went to the University of Michigan and pretty much failed everything due to lack of interest in the curriculum," he says. "I don't know, I felt like I was ready to be a writer, I was ready to make a living at it. Besides, what would I need to know any of *this* crap for? So, midway through the year, without telling anybody, I put in a transfer application to NYU, and I was accepted. I thought, 'Well, at least NYU was focused on writing, and they had a dramatic-writing program that was very specifically about learning to be a writer.'"

By age nineteen McNamara had written and produced his first play; then in 1982 he wrote an ABC Afterschool Special. That led to a short stint on the *New Love, American Style* and then to a string of what McNamara refers to as "fluffy" TV movies for Disney. John was making money, but, to his way of thinking, not much headway. "I had this feeling of dissatisfaction that I would write something, and just give it to somebody else, and they would cast it, and hire a director, and do all of the other stuff," he says. "And they would change what I wrote, oft by necessity. I got this nagging sense that 'Gosh, I'm only doing half of my job.' And it got bad enough in the early 1990s to where I was still doing a combination of TV movies that I was selling, then walking away from, and/or feature films that I was selling, and nobody was making. My career, by my own power, kind of came to a halt, and I stopped working for about a year and a half."

Then John landed his first prime-time assignment, but only as a result of not being able to sell his own project. "This is why failure is sometimes a good benefactor, almost like an angel looking out for you," John says. "My movie career, such as it was, just ground to a halt, and I had no interest in reinvigorating it or reinventing it. I was pretty much out of dough and I sat down with David Greenwalt one day in 1992, and we very naïvely said to each other, 'If we were ever going to do a TV series of our own (and neither of us had worked on a TV series at that point), what would we do?' And we basically concocted an idea, which ultimately became *Profit*. The idea was, what would happen if the most morally bankrupt person who ever lived came into a corporation? The answer to that question was, if he made money, he would eventually take over and become one of the most heralded men of his century, because that's the nature of corporations. They don't reward anything other than profit. So we sat down and began to build this world. I think our naïveté was very helpful to us. That, and the fact that neither of us was really working. So we were pitching the show around town, and everybody hated it, except for Kim LeMasters, who was then the president of [Stephen] Cannell's company. Kim loved it, and he optioned it for, I think, two thousand dollars. We developed it with him, took it out, and we were promptly rejected by everybody in town until the last day that pitch season was open. We walked in and pitched it to Bob Greenblatt at Fox. It took an hour for the pitch, and I thought it had been a disaster. I walked out, and thought, 'I've got to find something else to do for a living.' And the next day (election day, 1992) Dave called me up and said, 'They bought it!' We wrote it, turned it in, and it quietly became one of those scripts that everybody in town was trading back and forth. They were reading it saying, 'You've got to read this thing, it's unbelievable. It's a guy who basically fucks his mother, kills his father, and sleeps in a box.' In my mind, I thought the [scenario] was no big deal, but in television (*laughs*) it was a hugely new way to approach drama, so even though no one picked it up it got me a lot of job offers. Bob revived *Profit* in 1994, the pilot was finally produced in 1995, and the series went on the air in the spring of '96. But during the time we were waiting for *Profit* to be picked up, I landed a writing position on *The Adventures of Brisco County, Jr.* Carlton Cuse had read *Profit* and liked it, so he called me in. We had one meeting, and the next thing I knew, I was a story editor and I didn't even know what that was."

Audiences did not know quite what to make of *Brisco*, with its mix of fantasy, humor, and action set in the old West. But McNamara's experience as a story editor landed him a job as producer on *Lois & Clark* in 1995. Three years later, Fox resurrected and fast-tracked John's earlier project, *Profit,* but the lack of a protagonist with any redeeming qualities was a disturbing turnoff to viewers, and the series was canceled after only four episodes. That opened the door for *Spy Game,* an offbeat comedy that John co-produced with Sam and Ivan Raimi. *Spy Game* premiered on ABC in March of 1997 and only lasted through July. Tim Brooks and Earle Marsh in their *Complete Directory to Prime Time and Cable TV Shows* describe *Spy Game* as a "cartoonish series [that] soon went the way of the out-of-work spies it lampooned." Nevertheless, McNamara recalls the show with fondness. "It was fun. I got into that show for all the right reasons. I love spy shows, and I thought, 'Why couldn't I do a spy show?' I had worked on a western and a superhero show. And I thought, 'Well, couldn't we have just as much fun bringing back something that would have some of the feeling of *I Spy* and *The Avengers?'* The fact is, it took us too long to figure out what the show was. By the time we figured it out, I think the audience and the network had grown equally restless with the lack of cohesion. I think we really hit our stride by episode eight, but by that time we were gone."

The next year, McNamara co-created a tongue-in-cheek version of *The Equalizer* titled *Vengeance Unlimited* and starring Michael Madsen. Most critics missed the point of the humor, and most people with TV sets missed it all together. *Vengeance* was gone by February 1999.

But once again "failure was a good benefactor" for McNamara. Working under the Warner Brothers banner, he resurrected a project that he had pitched much earlier: a remake of *The Fugitive.* CBS president Les Moonves recalled the beginning. "Before I was at CBS, when I was at Warner Brothers, the one show that I wanted to revive was *The Fugitive.* I really believe *The Fugitive* is the best concept ever thought up for a television show. It combines every element that you would want in a hit show. At that point in time they [Arnold and Anne Kopelson] were doing the feature film, so obviously they couldn't allow the TV rights to be taken up. Then the film was a huge success, so I went to my boss at the time, Bob Daly, and I asked him again. He said, 'Unfortunately for you, they're talking about doing a sequel.' What they ended up doing was *U.S. Marshals.* I then came to CBS about five years ago and last year they brought this project out. So Johnny Mac [Moonves's nickname for McNamara] was attached to the project. He and I had known each other for quite a while, and the truth of the matter is, we had been talking for a long time about it. He had worked under Bob Singer on *Lois & Clark,* and Bob is my best friend in the world and a top-notch producer. Bob had always said to me, 'You know McNamara? He's going to be a superstar. He's a great writer. He also has good leadership abilities.' He has the right amount of cockiness without being an idiot about it, and with creators and showrunners, you have to be a very talented person, but you also have to have the skill of being a leader. There are a lot of terrific writers in television. There are *not* a lot of terrific showrunners. It's unusual because a lot of times you'll find a writer who's a great writer but he's just meant to be behind the typewriter. A showrunner needs to be in charge of the crew, in charge of the cast, in charge of dealing with the network, dealing with the studio, dealing with a hundred different things. And McNamara, its only a question of time 'til he hits."

Roy Huggins, who created *The Fugitive* nearly forty years before John's TV revival, also has high praise for McNamara. "He's a very good writer, and he has learned to be a very good producer. He's also a helluva salesman. From what I hear, it was John who got the deal with CBS, and that's quite a commendation—a man who can write and come up with stories, and then go to the network and sell them on doing it his way. That's pretty good."

The Fugitive was a hit with critics, industry watchers, and overseas buyers before the pilot was ever broadcast. Advertisers even voted it as the show most likely to succeed. Ken Tucker of *Entertainment Weekly* proclaimed, "Rather than being a rip-off, this *Fugitive* is a real grabber" (October 13, 2000). Tucker's reference was to the classic original starring David Jansen, whose final episode registered the highest rating (a seventy-two share) of all time, a record that held until *Dallas* resolved "Who Shot J. R.?" Roy Huggins's formula was simple, and, CBS hoped, timeless. McNamara was realizing a dream of bringing his all-time favorite TV show back to the small screen. But the young man from Michigan also had some concerns, which he shared with *TV Guide*'s Mark Schwed. "The question is how do you stay a fugitive in the age of satellite tracking? How do you stay a fugitive in the age of the Internet . . . [but] the hardest part about writing *The Fugitive* is to be absolutely true to Roy Huggins's original concept [which] is: He wants to stay, but he has to run" (October 7, 2000). CBS's Les Moonves was impressed with McNamara's resolve. "I commend John," Moonves said. "Most guys would have said, 'I want nothing to do with the original. I want to come up with a hundred original ideas myself.' Instead [John] says, 'Gee, there were some good scripts there. It's not to say we should shoot them verbatim, but give me a germ of an idea or the one or two liner to jump off from.' What a great thing to have . . . it says a lot about John. It says that his ego is absolutely in the right place."

Moonves gave McNamara's *Fugitive* unprecedented promotion, including hefty spot schedules inside *Survivor*, the network's trendsetting reality/game show. But audiences did not respond as had been expected, and although the series was greenlit for an entire season, critics and media analysts began to rethink their earlier assessments. Allison Hope Weiner wrote, "*The Fugitive*'s Dr. Richard Kimble has a foe even deadlier than his one-armed quarry: Nielsen" (*Entertainment Weekly*, January 12, 2001). And an anonymous media analyst told *Entertainment Weekly*'s Ray Richmond, "Viewers must feel like *The Fugitive* is yesterday's news, been there, done that. I mean, how many guys named Richard Kimble can you give a crap about in a lifetime?" McNamara jokingly commented to Allison Hope Weiner, "It's like being stuck on Normandy Beach. I've been there before with a really good show [*The Adventures of Brisco County, Jr.*] and it's brutal. You're fighting for numbers because not a lot of people are watching TV."

Despite *The Fugitive*'s cancellation, though, John McNamara will, no doubt, manage to hold our interest with one riveting story or another. And, like Dr. Richard Kimble, his resourcefulness will always keep him one step ahead of everyone else. I spoke with John during the first season of *The Fugitive* and later met with him in Los Angeles.

Longworth: Your production company is called McNamara Paper Products. What does that mean?

MCNAMARA: It's a joke. Our motto is "We make scripts so you don't have to." (*Both laugh.*) So that's why it's Paper Products, 'cause we just manufacture scripts.

Longworth: When did it begin?

MCNAMARA: I think I formed the company around 1996. The first company I had was with David Greenwalt. We did *Profit* together, and then he went to Twentieth [Century Fox] and I went to Warner Brothers. And when I signed my first deal with Warners, it was nice. They give you a production-company credit and let you hire a couple of people to work with you.

Longworth: You mentioned Warner Brothers Television. There seems to be a trend lately there toward nurturing and supporting above-the-line talent. They've inked long-term deals with you, Wells, Sorkin. Does the security of a multi-year deal take away your creative edge? Does it remove the pressure of unemployment, because even if something is canceled you know you're still in the game? Or, on the other hand, does it give you an empowered sense of self-confidence and security that actually makes your work better?

MCNAMARA: I think, like anything else, you've got to be acutely aware of the dangers of both. There's a danger to having your entire livelihood rely on whether the numbers for the next episode, or the dailies of the next episode, or the next script you write, if that's going to impact your ability to pay a mortgage. I think you can make really stupid, cowardly decisions if that's true. By the same token, if you have a big, fat, soft overall deal, there can be a tendency to say, "Well, geez, I'll get to the office around eleven, I'll have lunch at one, I'll get back at three, I'll have a martini and go home." So somewhere between the two, between the edgy fear that *not* having an overall deal can potentially create, and at the other end, the sort of soft "I'm the King" feeling of having an overall deal, in the middle lies what being a showrunner is really about. You've got to show up every day, you've got to work really hard. You've got to constantly juggle twenty to twenty-five different elements of production, preproduction, and postproduction every single day. And most of all, you've got to love what you do and not do it for the money.

Longworth: So that's the common denominator?

MCNAMARA: Yeah, that's essentially why you get into it. You hopefully get into it not because you wanted to be rich or even moderately comfortable. You hopefully started writing because you had something you wanted to say and you wanted a large forum in which to say it. And a lot of showrunners, what's interesting is that they primarily think of themselves as writers. I think that that's the thing that separates the television business from, say, the movie business. The movie business, from what little I understand of it, is more or less driven by concept and stars. And you're chasing a combination of those two elements. In television you're chasing what the next great story is to illuminate this concept, so essentially television shows are conceptually driven, there's no question about that; but what keeps them alive, what is essentially the lifeblood of television, is great stories every week.

Longworth: OK, writing is the lifeblood, but 2000 and 2001 were fraught with strikes and threats of strikes and, so, when there's a strike by the Writers Guild, are you a writer, or are you the producer, with responsibilities to deliver a product?

MCNAMARA: If push comes to shove, I'm a writer. That may not be the most politically astute thing for me to say in print, but essentially I feel that I'm primarily sought after and paid because, not only do I write OK, but I can also work with other writers and get good work out of them.

Longworth: But in a strike situation, *The Fugitive*, for example, would have to shut down. And unlike other industries where management can take over some of the production process, in this case you *are* management, yet you're saying you would assume the mantle of writer.

MCNAMARA: Listen. Whether or not there's a strike, my feeling is, be ahead on scripts, be ahead on scripts. Work as long as you can. So I want to be ahead on scripts regardless of whether or not there's a strike. So let's say a strike were to hit. As an executive producer, if there's a finished script and it requires no more writing, it is my job under a contract to Warner Brothers to produce that script. I can cast it. I can hire a director. I can visit the set. I can complain about the craft service. I can edit it, and I can put music on it and broadcast it. But I will not write during a writers' strike.

Longworth: OK, let me get back on track. And forgive me for rambling, but I'm old. By the way, you probably never lose your train of thought. You're younger than I am.

MCNAMARA: I'm thirty-eight.

Longworth: (*Groans.*) Yeah, well, I thought I detected a tone of confidence and energy in your voice.

MCNAMARA: Oh please, that's completely created by a Diet Coke I had a few minutes ago. (*Both laugh.*) It has nothing to do with confidence.

Longworth: Getting back to the issue of long-term deals with a studio and how that can be a very good thing—

MCNAMARA: Or, a very bad thing. It really depends on your attitude about it. I'm not saying it's the only way to go or the best way to go. I'm saying that I seem to be able to function pretty well within it. And a couple of guys I know function pretty well within it.

Longworth: You learned both creativity and discipline from your parents. Do you get that same kind of nurturing in the studio system?

MCNAMARA: Yeah, what I got from my mother, father, and stepmother helped me deal with both fantasy and the real world. I think my job now is 50 percent fantasizing about something, and then as soon as the fantasy reaches a zenith and it's ready to go, the second half of my job—and in some ways the *harder* part—is to then execute it. To cast it, to get a good director to interpret it, to get good editors to cut it together; all for a very specific budget, which does not change from week to week.

Longworth: Is it kind of a drag, when you're as creative as you are, to say "Gee, I've written this great script, and I have this great vision, and I'm excited about my work, and, oh yeah, now I've got to spend five hours doing paperwork and other business functions." Does that ever bring the creative side down? And because of that, are you glad you have your father's genes to be able to handle the discipline side of the business?

MCNAMARA: I am glad that I grew up in a household where dealing with the real world was very much a valued thing. You were valued if you could deal well with other people. You were valued in my household if you could be logical, make an argument as to why you wanted something. My dad was a very challenging guy. He loved a good argument. As a law professor, not unlike the character of Kingsfield in *The Paper Chase,* he believed in the Socratic method of education, which is to constantly question and re-question. So, in a sense, *answers* don't become as important as the process by which you *seek* the answers. That's a very highfalootin' way of saying there are days I get up and see my schedule is everything *but* writing, and I get really depressed. So, yes, that's the short answer. However, once I had to write episode one of *The Fugitive,* when the deadlines happened to fall over the Fourth of July weekend, and it was one of these *rare* Fourth of July weekends that was, I think, five days long. And I spent every damn day of it writing alone in my house while talking to friends on the phone who were off having these fantastic vacations all over the world, or were just enjoying a typically beautiful southern California holiday. Meanwhile, I was literally in this kind of hellish pit, trying to figure out how to get Richard Kimble away from the one-armed man. And I'm thinking to myself, "I just hate this, I loathe my own inadequacies as a writer." I would put on the television set and what would be playing? *A Few Good Men.* And I know Aaron [Sorkin]. I've known Aaron for ten years, and I'm going, "I can't write that well," and I flip the channel and there's fucking *The West Wing,* and I'm like, "goddamn it!" And then I'll flip over and there's David Milch and Bochco, and I seem to have been assaulted all weekend by my own insecurities. They visited me like demons.

Longworth: *(Laughing.)* Well, if it's any consolation, Sorkin told me that he wished he could be Paul Attanasio.

MCNAMARA: Paul's writing is just superb. I have a lot of friends who work in various capacities in the industry, and we all trade scripts with each other, and we all say, "Oh my god, you've got to read this pilot or that pilot." And the hot pilots go around. And one of the best pilot of last year was *Gideon's Crossing.* And it was in no small part due to the fact that the writing was just *so* good.

Longworth: Now let me understand something. You guys, the TV creators, will read each other's pilots?

MCNAMARA: Well, yeah. I can't speak for anybody but myself, but I have a lot of friends who are executives, both at the studio and at the network. You always stay in contact with them even when you're not working with each other. And very often you'll say, "Oh man, what's going on with that new Sorkin thing? I want to get ahold of that." Or, "What's going on with the new Wells thing?" Either you'll get a script or you'll get a cut, and it's part of [the] ecosystem out here. I like to always know what everybody else is up to. Probably there's a certain amount of masochism in it, to be perfectly honest.

Longworth: Would you and other showrunners give each other input, or does that cross the line?

MCNAMARA: Well, it very much depends. I don't have that kind of relationship with Aaron. We're casual acquaintances, but I'd be terrified to give Aaron a script. (*Laughs.*)

Longworth: But what if someone you admired offered you bad advice? Suppose they read your script and said, "In episode two of *The Fugitive*, just let Kimble and the one-armed man become friends."

MCNAMARA: Listen, I've been pitched dumber ideas. (*Both laugh.*) But I have a close circle of friends, like David Greenwalt. We co-created *Profit*, and he's now running *Angel* and is one of the executive producers of *Buffy the Vampire Slayer*. With David and me, our friendship predates our working relationship. We've known each other for almost fifteen years. So David and I very often will trade scripts. I think I've given David probably every first draft of every script I've ever written since first knowing him. And it just so happens that David is also a showrunner, but first and foremost he's my friend, and then we were business and writing partners, and now we are friends who rarely see each other because we both work these horrible hours at these crushing jobs. But it really very much depends upon the nature of your relationship. In most cases I would say that my relationship with most showrunners is too casual for me to impose myself on them. And then probably—we all think of each other as incredibly busy, you know? So we don't—unless there was some huge problem, we wouldn't say, "Hey, could you read this?" Or, "Could you take a whack at this scene?"

Longworth: You mentioned Aaron Sorkin. Comment on his writing style.

MCNAMARA: Every time I read something he writes, every time I see something he's written, I hear specifically the way he speaks. He accesses something very direct within him that very few writers can do. On the page he sounds like himself and that's amazing, because he's tremendously entertaining and verbal as a person, and he's tremendously entertaining and verbal as a writer. And he has the most perfect rhythm of anybody writing television today. His rhythm almost sounds like music underneath the words. I have no idea how he does it. I can't do it. I'm very glad that people don't ask me to do it (*both laugh*) or I would have a very frustrating life. I genuinely find him to be so sharp and so brilliant and so fun to be around. I don't see him much anymore, but we have a friend in common, Timothy Busfield, who was in my first play and now he's on *The West Wing*.

Longworth: Now, was that the play you had produced when you were nineteen?

MCNAMARA: Yeah, it was called *Present Tense.*

Longworth: What was it about?

MCNAMARA: It was about an extremely neurotic high school student who is constantly besieged by his inner insecurities. So basically it's the story of my life. (*Both laugh.*)

Longworth: Then *and* now?

MCNAMARA: Yeah.

Longworth: So you're still an insecure high school person?

MCNAMARA: Basically. I think we're all insecure high school people who, if we're lucky, get stock options. (*Both laugh.*) That's about as good as it gets, if nothing inside changes. My favorite show of last season, *Freaks and Geeks,* is by a writer by the name of Paul Feig. That was the best show I've seen—well, probably since *The West Wing* pilot. It was just amazing because what Paul Feig and Judd Apatow did in that show is, they showed you exactly what high school *felt* like. And in watching it as a thirty-eight year old I realized very strongly, I have *not* changed. (*Laughs.*) I am still that guy who can't get his locker open. I am still that guy who fears being beaten up by bigger guys.

Longworth: And for some people that was not a comedic time of life.

MCNAMARA: Oh God, no. Watching *Freaks and Geeks* I used to grab a pillow on my couch, roll over and scream into it, and that's very embarrassing if there are other people around. (*Laughs.*) Again, that's what gets me excited about writing sometimes, the notion that a guy like Paul Feig can write something that feels so natural that it looks like it's just unraveling organically. All these little details of time, place, texture, and characterization are so seamlessly perfect.

Longworth: Your buddy Aaron Sorkin told me that for him, theater was the guiding influence even as a child.

MCNAMARA: Which is why Aaron is probably a better writer. (*Both laugh.*) He was probably reading Marlowe and Wilde and I couldn't wait to see if Batman got away from the Riddler. (*Both laugh.*) If anything delineates me from Aaron that would be it. But no, I got into theater in high school but I realized in retrospect it was simply, and I hate to sound mercenary, but it was kind of the only thing you could write and have performed within the budgetary constraints of being a teenager. It was really cheap to put on a play. There was no videotape back then. Film didn't have synced sound the way it does now. If I was a teenager now, I'd probably be making high-def video movies that I'd be editing on my Mac, and trying to do the next *Blair Witch*. But back then I liked theater. In high school I saw a lot of musicals and a lot of plays and was exposed to Kauffman and Hart, and Noel Coward, and Steven Sondheim, and Rogers and Hart. I think I was interested in getting my stuff said by other people, by actors. I mean, that was my primary goal for whatever reason. I had written short stories and I had had some minor success in high school, winning writing contests.

Longworth: You were really into this then?

MCNAMARA: It was a real basic form of expression for me. But there was something about wanting to collaborate. I found that writing fiction, while immensely satisfying, could also be immensely anticlimactic as an experience for me because it felt half finished. You finish the writing part, you look at the set type, make your last edits, and then as you pointed out earlier, you'd wait anywhere from three weeks to nine months. And then it's published, and people kind of go, "Oh, it's published."

Longworth: It makes you wonder why we get excited about the birth of a baby. You know that it's in there for nine months, then it comes out, and—

MCNAMARA: But with the birth of a baby there's more of a similarity to theater or a movie opening. There is a huge, calamitous, almost violent crescendo that doesn't happen in publishing.

Longworth: Except for Salman Rushdie.

MCNAMARA: Yeah, that was pretty calamitous.

Longworth: Your mother set you on a path to writing by exposing you to good literature.

MCNAMARA: Yeah. She was the first person I ever knew to read Jim Harrison. She gave me a short story when I was seventeen from *Esquire* magazine and said, "This guy's really good." Harrison wrote *Legends of the Fall*. He has probably become one of my favorite writers. Whereas my dad and I both loved Michael Crichton. I love all kinds of books. I like a really good "beachy" bestseller, and I like kind of more esoteric stuff like Jim Harrison and James Salter. I think, again, it's the influence of my two parents, because they both had very strong opinions and exerted spheres of influence on me. Very often when you see my reading list for a weekend it's exactly half bestsellers and half European writers or Buddhist texts.

Longworth: You talk about your reading list, but the perception about you showrunner types is that you never have any free time to yourself.

MCNAMARA: Steven Bochco gave me very, very good advice not too long ago. He said, "Make an effort to get home at a decent hour every night." And I said, "Why?" And he said, "Because if you stay late at the office every night you're going to be behind schedule. If you go home at a decent hour, you'll *still* be behind schedule, but you'll be home." (*Both laugh.*) That's very Bochco. Very, very good advice.

Longworth: You said that you went to NYU to learn to be a writer, but can you really learn to write in a "Learn to Write" class?

MCNAMARA: No. You can't learn it and you can't teach it. All you can do is practice it and get better and receive good advice on things, some of which you should take, and some of which you should ignore. Even good advice should sometimes be ignored because it's not right for you. You can teach technique. You can teach what is good story structure. The rules of that can be taught in the same way that you can take somebody who has a talent for painting and teach them the rules of shape and dark and light. And then if you're brilliant, if you're Picasso, you throw all those rules out. If you're equally brilliant, you're Andrew Wyeth or Norman Rockwell, and you live and die by those rules, but you create something unique *from* those rules. But it begins with, I think, an understanding of the history of writing. You've got to read Shakespeare because you've got to realize not only what great writing is, but what great versatility in writing is.

Longworth: Shakespeare would have been a good television writer, wouldn't he?

MCNAMARA: Unbelievable. First of all, he was a complete whore. He would do anything for money, and he would adapt to the attitudes of whoever was in power. And he wrote every genre equally well.

Longworth: And he wrote for the guys down front drinking beer and scratching their crotches so they would understand it, too, so he would have had, like, a forty share.

MCNAMARA: Oh yeah, he would have been Bochco, David Kelley, Paddy Chayefsky, Roy Huggins, and Stephen Cannell all rolled into one.

Longworth: Are you saying all those guys are whores?

MCNAMARA: No, those guys are too rich to be whores. (*Both laugh.*)

What they did prior to being rich is their own business. (*Laughs.*) Those guys *hire* whores. (*Laughs.*) I mean that only metaphorically. (*Both laugh.*) But there is a key to surviving television—a certain adaptability and versatility. One of the things I really admire about Bochco's career, I admire the shows where he's tried and failed. I loved *Cop Rock.* I think *Cop Rock* is just awesome because they just went balls to the walls. A lot of guys get power, but very few guys attain power and keep trying new things. Bochco does.

Longworth: What have *you* learned from failures in television?

MCNAMARA: You only learn one thing. You learn to not fear it. You learn to not break into a cold sweat at the thought of it. You learn that your life will go on, and your creativity is not based on success, that your creativity is based more on how you spend your days. If you spend your days excited and creatively challenged, those are good days. What the world thinks of it—you don't have any power over that. You might put a show out there that you are absolutely convinced is going to be a bomb and it ends up being a huge hit, and vice versa. The only thing to remember, in life as in work: most things fail. They just do, by nature. I think it has something to do with gravity. (*Both laugh.*) I think gravity is this thing that holds things together, but it also pulls things down. And when you look at a guy like a Bochco, not to keep waxing about him, but if we have royalty in television, he is the emperor. Bochco is a guy who found a way to subvert a lot of the gravitational rules that existed in TV. He basically broke the sound barrier with *Hill Street Blues.*

Longworth: You're saying Bochco is the Chuck Yeager of TV?

MCNAMARA: Again, this is going to sound like he and I are sharing a condo in Venice (*laughs*), and I *don't* know him very well, so this is all said with admiration at a distance. But he was Chuck Yeager and Einstein, because he both *created* the theorem and then he acted it out. He had the balls to say, "This is what we're going to do every week." And I remember being in college when *Hill Street* was on, and I was just dazzled by it. You had never seen anything like it. And it got better every week. Back then that was *The Sopranos.* Everything stopped for *Hill Street.*

Longworth: You mentioned college, so before we go any further tell me what happened in your life between the time you left school and the time you got your first big break in the business.

MCNAMARA: A lot of little things, which at the time probably seemed random.

Longworth: You know this is exactly why the Bible never wrote about Jesus during his wilderness years.

MCNAMARA: Yeah, it was probably pretty embarrassing and pretty dull. (*Both laugh.*) I had a play produced while I was at NYU, and that got me my foot in the door in television with an agent. I came to California, and I spent about a year just drifting and not working. In that year I had also sold a couple of children's books to Delacourt Press. Barely anybody knew they existed, but they both had really long shelf lives and I got kind of nice regular royalties. So I got this sort of base income where I could just barely afford to eat, live in an apartment, and not get a job. I sort of stumbled into screenwriting. I had never really intended to be a screenwriter as my primary means of making a living, but it just happened.

Longworth: So is it your theory that writing is writing, that is, if you can write great children's stories, you can write great television shows?

MCNAMARA: No, because the one thing about writing for television or writing screenplays is that you've got to be able to write dialogue. And written dialogue and spoken dialogue are two different things. If you read the dialogue in most books, it stinks, in terms of actually being able to say it out loud. Even in something like *The Great Gatsby*, which I think is maybe the greatest book of the twentieth century, *that* dialogue is unsayable by human beings. It's just too perfect. It shimmers too much. The adjectives are too precisely chosen, which is why Fitzgerald was not a great screenwriter, by his own measure. He cared too much about every single word and every single comma, and, ultimately, whether you write dialogue like Aaron Sorkin writes, which really is heightened, or dialogue like I write, in which people can barely finish sentences—it's something that ultimately has to sit in an actor's mouth and be comfortable there. I think you can learn technique about it, but you either know it or you don't. It's like telling a joke. You've got the rhythm to tell a joke or you don't. It comes from some genetic, experiential place.

Longworth: OK, so you go to work on *Brisco County, Jr.* Describe your responsibilities.

MCNAMARA: I just did what I was told. I was the lowest form of life on that show. I was one click above a typist, at least for the first half of the season. I mean, I was barely able to keep from getting fired, my first script was so bad. Carlton Cuse, Jeffrey Boam, and David Simkins, who had all collaborated on the pilot together, none of them had ever done television before. So they didn't have a pre-set notion of what this should or shouldn't be. When I came into it, probably one of my primary functions was as a kind of student of TV history. So when we'd be in these story meetings if I couldn't think of something original to say, which was quite often (*laughs*), I would say, "Well you know, I watched an episode of *Maverick* last night, and you can go more comedic here. I mean *Maverick* was forty years ago and they did some pretty amazing shit back then." And everybody would go, "What do you mean you're watching *Maverick*? That's so old." And I said, "Yeah, but I went to the Warner Brothers vault and I got the original tapes and I watched some of them." And I said, "I think we can push this a little harder. Here, watch this scene with James Garner." And, sure enough, Roy Huggins, back *then* was breaking the fourth wall. He was inverting the nature of what a western hero was in the 1950s. Roy, along with Steve Bochco, was one of the guys who created a kind of quantum leap in both form and content.

Longworth: And yet, nobody ever followed Roy's lead with the *Maverick* form.

MCNAMARA: Right, nobody did. Roy did the same thing with *Rockford Files*. Roy and Steve Cannell took a very staid, tried-and-true form and they just flipped it on its back and sliced it open. It was great. With *Brisco*, we just didn't have the luck to be a hit. I think a lot of that is both timing and time slot, many factors. We were correct, and I was the smallest part of the "we," in the notion that an audience was probably ready to have a trans-genre form. To have science fiction, comedy, and a western all mixed together. Because what we were thinking was [that] our audience sort of grew up with all three. They grew up with *Lethal Weapon,* and they grew up with *Star Trek,* and they grew up with *The Wild, Wild West.* And so this would be really cool. When the show really found its voice, and that's generally anywhere from ten to fifteen episodes into a typical first-season show, I think objectively looking back on it, it was one of the best TV series of its season, if only because it would always surprise you. It was just audacious. There were jokes we made that were so low, you couldn't believe they were happening in a western.

Longworth: You mentioned Roy Huggins. How well do you know him?

MCNAMARA: Now I know him very well. I only met him after we had sold *The Fugitive* to CBS, and after we had hammered out the deal for him and me and Arnold and Anne to bring *The Fugitive* back. I met him at a lunch afterwards, and then he was involved as a consultant. I call him "Tom Hagen," he's sort of the consigliare. But, God, he's bright and fun to talk to. He's very loquacious and he's really funny.

Longworth: Were you a big fan of *The Fugitive?*

MCNAMARA: Yeah, I watched every single episode. I didn't watch it growing up because I was too young, but it started to rerun quite heavily in the '70s and the early '80s, and I never missed it. I became really obsessed with it. When it came out on tape, I made my friends watch it.

Longworth: Did you ever envision that you would be doing this when you were watching that?

MCNAMARA: No, I mean, how could you? Back in 1990 I had heard that there was going to be a movie. Then I actually met with Arnold Kopelson to write the movie.

Longworth: And?

MCNAMARA: Well, such was the nature of my incredible screenwriting career, that I was not hired. (*Both laugh.*) I even made it very clear that I would do it for free. Arnold claims that he wanted to hire me except that I was under contract elsewhere, and that is true. But the fact of the matter is, if you really want something in Hollywood, you get it. And the fact is he had every screenwriter in Hollywood wanting to write that thing. He had the top, top A-list guys.

Longworth: *Could* you have written the movie at that point in your career?

MCNAMARA: No, I would have fucked it up. (*Both laugh.*) I would have fucked it up and also would have been very bitter about the fact that I didn't have final control over it. So that's a perfect example of you never really know when you should or shouldn't get what you want. That's why you should never be upset when you don't get something you want because you just never know.

Longworth: But that's tough to do, though.

MCNAMARA: But the only way you can build that kind of perspective is by living and trying to learn. I mean, Arnold and I now laugh about that, which is so great.

Longworth: It's a bizarre story. Sounds like you made it up.

MCNAMARA: No, no. 1991. I get a call from my agent, and this is the valley of what had been a career that did not have a lot of hills. (*Both laugh.*) You know? I get the call that Arnold Kopelson, the Academy Award producer of *Platoon* wants to do a Gulf War movie. My initial response was, "Well, who the hell would want to see a Gulf War movie? It's a bunch of guys throwing sticks at fighter jets." It did not seem like a war that had any real conflict. There was not a lot of opposition to us.

Longworth: Just like making a movie about Grenada.

MCNAMARA: Yeah. Little did you know that a guy like David Russell could turn it into *Three Kings*. He and John Ridley are brilliant because they took what I think is undramatic material and made it dramatic. But be that as it may, *I* said "No way," and my agent said, "You should meet this guy, he's doing *The Fugitive*," which my agent knew I was quite obsessed with. I said, "OK, I'll meet with him on the Gulf War thing." So I walk into his house, which to quote Raymond Chandler from *The Big Sleep*, "was smaller than the Chrysler building and maybe had fewer windows than the Empire State building." That's Arnold's house: huge. And I said, "I have no interest in writing your Gulf War movie. I just wanted to get in here and pitch you *The Fugitive*." He had had a couple of scripts written for him, and I had read all of them, and I pitched him my take on it, and he said to me in his inimitable fashion, "You're hired. When can you start?" And I said, "Three months," and he goes, "No, can't do it. I need you now." And I said, "You can't wait?" And he said, "Nope." And that was it, that was pretty much the end of the meeting. We did not see each other again until 1999, at which point I had initiated the idea of bringing it back as a series because I was under contract to Warner Brothers. I very much wanted Arnold and Roy both involved. I felt as if there was a real lineage from Roy to Arnold to me.

Longworth: It's like watching the evolution of the Yankee franchise from Ruth to Gehrig to Dimaggio to Mantle. And what's more, you probably made television history by producing a weekly series which was based on a film, which was based on a weekly series.

MCNAMARA: Yeah. I was nailed by a reporter not long ago who said this has never been done before. And I said, "No, no, this has been done, and you're going to feel really dumb when I tell you . . . it's *Star Trek*. *Star Trek* was a series. Then it was a series of huge movies. And then it was *four* TV series again." There are some ideas that warrant this kind of re-examination every generation or so. Or even every seven or eight years. They speak to something central within us that to *not* do them becomes the stupid thing. To *not* do them because, "Oh, I'm afraid it will fail, or I'll be the fellow who ruined this billion-dollar franchise, is stupid." *The Fugitive* is a good story.

Longworth: But given that a lot of people loved the movie and are skeptical about another series, didn't that concern you at all?

MCNAMARA: Here's the thing I know, that I'm not arrogant about, but I am extremely conscious of. No one loves *The Fugitive* more than I do. Maybe Roy, maybe Arnold. Maybe a few people who were attached to the movie or the series. But no one knows it better than me, no one loves it more than I do. No one is more passionate about how to do it. I didn't come at this as a piece of business. This was not like, "Oh gee, I need to get a show on the air." When I went in to pitch my boss at Warner Brothers, I was very sure that this was a good idea. But I was not only sure that *The Fugitive* itself was a great idea—anybody can tell you that *The Fugitive* is one of the best ideas for a TV series ever—I was very sure for the same reason that it was the right time to bring it back, and that I knew exactly how to do it.

Longworth: So you, not Roy or Arnold, were the impetus for pitching the series?

MCNAMARA: It was me. I've been under contract to Warner Brothers now since 1993, when I started on *Brisco*. And every year, they gave me more and more freedom and money to develop my own stuff. I've had a very fruitful relationship with this company under its many leaders. Leslie Moonves was my boss for a while. Tony Jonas was my boss for a while. Peter Roth is now my boss. And I get along well with every executive on the lot. We just have fun and we make fun, interesting television together. Not always successful, but we always kind of push the boundaries. (*McNamara is interrupted by a telephone call.*) My director [is on the line and] wants to talk to me about this new episode.

Longworth: Do you want to stop and pick back up on Monday?

MCNAMARA: No! Forget it! I'm too important. (*Both laugh.*) Aaron Sorkin wouldn't take that call! (*Laughs.*) But anyway, a couple of years ago I went into a network, and the network pitched *me* an idea. And the idea was basically a rip-off of *The Fugitive*. I remember very specifically the moment I walked out with my immediate boss, Steve Perlman, V.P. of drama, and I said to Steve, "You know, *we* [Warner Brothers] own *The Fugitive*. Why don't we just do *The Fugitive*?" Steve looked at me like, "Well, that's a pretty good idea." We pitched it to the management of Warner Brothers, who did not want to do it at that time, for a variety of reasons involving the sequel, *U.S. Marshals*, and thinking it's not viable to bring it back so soon after the movie. And so I let it go, and I went on and did *Vengeance Unlimited*. The Warner management changed, and I went in to see Peter Roth, my new boss, and I said, "*The Fugitive*," and Peter got this look that I can only describe as half "Oh my God, this is so great" and half "Oh my God, we can't do this. It's too audacious." (*Laughs.*) I said, "Peter, I don't have any other ideas. This is it, man. I'm out of ideas." I wasn't, but I just kept bugging him. And I think there was a certain initial response from everybody like, "Well, who's *this* guy? This is *The Fugitive*, we should give this to somebody who'd had a hit." I'm sure that was discussed at some point. I'm equally certain that Peter Roth said, "It's got to be a guy who loves it. And for all his lack of commercial success, McNamara *does* love it. He does have a vision of how to do it." I kept saying to everybody involved, "We can't punk out. The first ten minutes have got to blow your mind. The rest of it should be very good drama, but the first ten minutes have got to exceed every expectation. We can't let any one element be left unspectacular." And, in Arnold Kopelson I had the perfect partner, because no one says "No" to Arnold. Arnold is a bull.

Longworth: You could have taken the easy way out and rehashed scenes from the movie, like adapting the train-wreck footage. Why didn't you?

MCNAMARA: It was discussed very briefly at the beginning. I was the most adamantly opposed to it, probably for reasons of pride, but I also knew that we live in an age where people don't see movies just once, they see movies five, six, seven, eight times. I *loved* the movie, so I've seen it fifteen times. If I was to watch the pilot of *The Fugitive* and I hadn't worked on it, and I saw Tim Daly jumping off the same bus with the same train, I'd flip the channel. And I'd say, "What do I need this for? I can go watch the movie with Harrison Ford." In other words, we owe it to the audience, to the guy playing Richard Kimble, to ourselves, to reinvigorate this franchise. To create it fresh.

Longworth: My wife and I sat down and watched your pilot in a dark room, big screen, turned off the telephones, and it was great. Now here's the rub. Do you think all of this planning and creativity on your part are diminished by the way people normally have to watch TV, complete with distractions and commercial interruptions?

MCNAMARA: My job is to make all the details great because I want the show to be watched ten and twenty years from now. I want it to hold up and withstand the test of time. That's my job. But ultimately, if that quality is diminished because the picture's not that great, because they're broadcasting it on cable and the cable stinks, and the sound specs are reduced, and the color is a little washed out, and there's all these commercials, I can't control that.

Longworth: The original *Fugitive* TV series was more about a good samaritanism than anything else. Now in this age of O. J. and cynicism over courts and police and politics, how can the Richard Kimble good-guy saga still be riveting television?

MCNAMARA: Cynicism is like a tide. It comes in and it rolls out. I mean, we're not living in the first cynical age that has ever hit the world. I think living in Rome during the last of the Caesars was probably a pretty cynical time. I think the Elizabethan Age makes our age look kind of sunny and holistic by comparison. You can go to many, many epochs of time that were cynical, but the story of the lone stranger who comes to help is timeless. It's just something we like. The Count of Monte Cristo, or Shane, it's there.

JOHN MCNAMARA | 263

Longworth: OK, but if we love Richard Kimble, why didn't we take to *Vengeance Unlimited?*

MCNAMARA: I think *Vengeance Unlimited* was misperceived. It probably was, to a certain extent, my fault. I thought that everybody got that it was a comedy. Starting with the title, which was so ridiculously over the top, I thought, "Well, no one's going to take this thing seriously." It was intended to always be a black comedy. Ken Tucker, the guy from *Entertainment Weekly,* came around later and re-reviewed it and said, "Oh, I get it," because the audience was writing him letters saying, "Hey Ken, it's *funny.* Madsen's *playing* it like a comedy, it's being *written* like a comedy."

Longworth: But with Kimble, there's pure good samaritanism.

MCNAMARA: It's not a curve ball. It's a fast ball down the middle. There were moments when I was writing the pilot when I said to myself, "Shouldn't Kimble be more smart aleck, or more self referential, or maybe he should be twenty-three instead of thirty-six? Maybe he should be a medical student?" I played with a lot of different ideas of how to reinterpret it. And at the end of the day I said, "Look, the material is the material. It is the story of a very, very sincere guy who suffers a huge loss, who is trying to cope with that loss." One thing I like about the story is that all three of the main characters—Kimble, the one-armed man, and Gerard—are all guys dealing with failure. Every week Richard Kimble fails to get the one-armed man, every week Gerard fails to get Kimble, every week the one-armed man fails to shake Richard Kimble loose from him. You have Kimble making these small, minor victories, but he can't stop to appreciate them or even reflect upon them.

Longworth: But can today's audiences understand where you're going with this?

MCNAMARA: I don't know. On any project I think sort of narcissistically about what I would like, and sometimes I'm right, and more often than not I'm wrong.

Longworth: Let me go back to other shows you've worked on. We skipped over *Lois & Clark.* Was that fun to do?

MCNAMARA: Oh my God. The best job. My boss was a guy named Bob Singer. He did *Midnight Caller, Reasonable Doubts* and actually, he and I used to talk about *The Fugitive* constantly, just as fans. Because of Bob, *Lois & Clark* was the first time I began to see my career as being something that could be really fulfilling and really fun. *Lois & Clark* helped me define the kind of producer I wanted to be. I wanted to do things that were smart. I wanted to do TV shows that I might have watched as a kid or fully appreciated as an adult.

Lois & Clark was for me a perfect kind of splice. From day one I just knew how to write that show. I knew Superman like I know my own big toe.

Longworth: That seems to be important to you, to really have an affection for and a knowledge of what you're doing?

MCNAMARA: Oh yeah. That's why I was so unhappy being a screenwriter; I didn't like a lot of the stuff that I got assigned. I didn't like what was done with it, and I suddenly found that in television, if you had great affection and you could couple that with a certain amount of skill, people respected that and they left you alone. My experience in television has been mostly one of autonomy. I never sought to be autonomous, but I care greatly about what I write. I don't think I'm the best writer in Hollywood, but I do work really, really hard, and I never write anything that is remotely insincere. I never write stuff just to get the job done.

Longworth: You speak fondly of *Lois & Clark*. Do you still have that same level of enthusiasm today?

MCNAMARA: Writing has gotten harder for me as I've gotten older. Writing used to be purely enjoyable, and as I've gotten older writing has gotten harder, and I think one of the reasons is I have, in my life, exorcized a lot of my demons. Back in the '90s, I basically put all my demons, of which I had many, into my writing. It was a relief to get them out through fantasy. To be able to give voice to them. To stop dreaming about them. The fact is *now* I don't have as many of *those* kinds of demons. And so, the writing becomes much more about subtler things. *The Fugitive* is really much more subtle in its execution than *Profit* was.

Longworth: Speaking of *Profit*, and looking back on the short-lived shows that you worked on, did you ever begin to question your ability to write and create something marketable or think that maybe it was time to leave television and go back to writing plays and short stories?

MCNAMARA: No, because Steven Bochco claims that the only reason I'm indifferent to success is because I never *had* any. (*Both laugh.*) He said to me, "When you have success, you won't be so indifferent anymore, you'll want more of it."

Longworth: That's funny.

MCNAMARA: Maybe, but for now I remain kind of indifferent to whether anything is successful. I only care about, do I like it? Is it good by my own standards? Am I collaborating well with other people in the studio, the other writers, the actors? Are we all on the same page, moving in the same direction? And, finally, what do I feel like when I get up every day and go to the office? Do I feel good? Am I enjoying this? Am I playing my best game? Have I created an environment in which everybody is pushing themselves to play *their* best game, because I don't think you play your best game unless there's a certain enjoyment. And every show is different. There's not a right way or a wrong way to run a show. I consider myself to be like the coach of a team. If I was coaching a professional sports team, one of the things I would want to create is a space in which the athletes can do their best and enjoy doing their best.

Longworth: Anything you regret?

MCNAMARA: Look, you don't feel *good* about the fact that your stuff is in the red, but by the same token, I've never gone over budget; I produce responsibly. I try to be a collaborator with both the networks and the studios without ever compromising what I want to do. I've never done anything I don't want to do.

Longworth: Speaking of collaborating, describe your relationship with your writing staff.

MCNAMARA: Well, I don't rewrite others if I can help it. That's the last resort for me. Again, every showrunner is different and every show is different. On *Profit* David and I sort of *had* to write everything. We understood it and it was hard to explain to other writers. *Vengeance,* I did some rewriting. But mostly I would nudge the writers and cajole them.

Longworth: Are you the one who breaks the stories, though?

MCNAMARA: I break the stories with the writers, absolutely. And I keep sending them back. I'll say, "Do it again," or, "Let's go over it again. This is good, this is bad." That continues through the process of writing the script. I want the writers to be able to come into my office and be excited about their ideas. I tend to like writers around me who are strong and proud of their work, who would be pissed off if I rewrote it, but who won't quit. I want them to be defensive in a good way about their work.

Longworth: If there were no credits on screen, how would someone know they had just watched a John McNamara show? What is the McNamara style?

MCNAMARA: Boy, I don't know. I think probably, it's that I always want to make the audience a partner in the scene with me. And that's a very conscious way of writing, stylistically. It's writing as if the audience is already in on the joke. For instance, on *The Fugitive,* irony is at the center of every single scene. People say to Richard Kimble, "How come you can't stick around?" And he doesn't say anything. Because the audience is going, "*Hello!* He's a fugitive!" (*Both laugh.*) Or, on *Profit* characters would say to him, "You're the nicest person I've ever met," and the audience would be going, "No, he's not!"

On *Lois & Clark,* Lois would say to Superman, "Why can't we be together? I love you so much." And Superman says, "I've got to go return a videotape." So I think probably, if there's some continuous thread in all this work, while it's certainly all over the map in terms of genres, there's a level of irony, of recognizing that the audience is not passive. And that probably comes from my having started writing in theater. You're very aware in theater that the audience is a silent partner. Their laughter becomes part of the rhythm of the play. Their tears become part of the rhythm of the play. So I don't consider myself to be smarter than them, and I don't consider myself to be better than them. But I also don't let them lead. I lead, but I want them kind of in step with me, and I think that forms the nature of the scenes I write.

Longworth: We started out by talking about your long-term deal with Warner Brothers and it occurs to us that most writers and producers don't enjoy the luxury of job security. Secondly, a lot of those same people are concerned about the trend in realty TV, which provides almost zero jobs for writers and artisans of drama. Do you share their concerns and fears, and as Clinton said, do you "feel their pain," or do you see this realty trend as nothing more than a short-lived fad that will pass?

MCNAMARA: I think all things pass. I mean, that's the wonder of living in the world and being old enough to have actually experienced the 1970s, '80s, and '90s. I remember in college hearing about Brandon Tartikoff giving a speech at the University of Michigan. At that time Brandon said, "Sitcoms are dead." There were headlines in the trades, "Sitcoms are dead." Well, guess what? A year later *The Cosby Show* came on. And Brandon was quoted as saying, "Sitcoms aren't dead, they just have to be funny." I remember when I went through a period where I was under contract to Disney and I was primarily known as a light-comedy guy. If I was ever going to do a series, it was going to be a light, eight o'clock, one-hour show. Well, Disney basically said, "One-hour drama is dead, we're cutting loose every one-hour drama deal." And they cut me loose, and I sat around with all my friends and said, "Oh my God, one hours are dead." Well, shit, *thirtysomething* came on the air, and then *Moonlighting* came on the air, and *NYPD Blue* came on the air. And one-hour dramas were back.

Longworth: But what's happening now is somewhat historic. Today, the current crop of reality game shows has taken over schedules, and even in the 1950s game shows didn't keep *Playhouse 90* off the air, and writers weren't being driven out of work. So this makes it a little bit more scary for writers and people who are normally employed on hour dramas and half-hour sitcoms.

MCNAMARA: Listen, I think there's always going to be some reason to be scared, and there's always going to be some reason to think that whatever it is we're doing is going to be displaced. I remember going through this in the early '90s, when there were so many *Datelines, 20/20s.*

Longworth: I stand corrected.

MCNAMARA: But I don't mean to correct you because one thing you said was true. *Dateline* was never a phenomenon. *Survivor* and *Who Wants to Be a Millionaire* are like these tsunamis. But the thing about a tsunami, in nature, is that it has a short life. It's huge, but it's short-lived.

Longworth: If Dr. Richard Kimble were to compete on *Survivor*, wouldn't he be able to kick everyone's ass?

MCNAMARA: Absolutely, there's no question.

Longworth: Les Moonves at CBS has been a big supporter of yours over the years. That must make you feel good.

MCNAMARA: He's just great. I say that without reservation. God, does that guy love TV. He was my first boss at Warners in 1993, and he chased *The Fugitive.* At one point I thought I was going to be physically tackled in the office.

Longworth: So Les should actually be playing the Gerard role himself?

MCNAMARA: Les would be the scariest cop chasing you that you could possibly imagine. (*Both laugh.*) He would never stop. He'd find you in your car, he'd find you at the dentist. You do not want this guy for an enemy (*laughs*), but you sure want him for an ally.

Longworth: Well, since we talked about reality game shows earlier, I'll end by asking you if *you* are a survivor?

MCNAMARA: I guess I am. I've survived gigantic failures and seemed to have kept working. And not because I ever promise to deliver ratings bonanzas. I think I keep working because I deliver good shows. I learned long ago I can control the quality of my work, but I can't control what happens in the marketplace. I've chosen to work with people who value quality more than immediate success. I've always picked good partners and healthy ecosystems. I'm protective not only of *what* I write, but where and with whom. I love what I do too much.

⋙ 12 ⋘

AARON SPELLING | Prime-Time perennial

Aaron Spelling. PHOTO BY HARRY LANGDON PHOTOGRAPHY ©
COURTESY OF AARON SPELLING.

TELEVISION CREDITS

1959–60	*Johnny Ringo* (CBS)
1959–61	*The Dupont Show* (CBS)

1961–63	*The Dick Powell Show* (NBC)
1962–63	*The Lloyd Bridges Show* (CBS)
1963–66	*Burke's Law* (ABC)
1965–66	*Honey West* (ABC)
1965–66	*The Smothers Brothers Show* (CBS)
1967–69	*The Guns of Will Sonnett* (ABC)
1967–68	*The Danny Thomas Hour* (NBC)
1967	*Rango* (ABC)
1968–72	*The Mod Squad* (ABC)
1969–70	*The New People* (ABC)
1970–71	*The Silent Force* (ABC)
1970–71	*The Most Deadly Game* (ABC)
1972–76	*The Rookies* (ABC)
1974	*Chopper One* (ABC)
1975–79	*Starsky & Hutch* (ABC)
1975–76	*S.W.A.T.* (ABC)
1976–80	*Family* (ABC)
1976–81	*Charlie's Angels* (ABC)
1977–86	*The Love Boat* (ABC)
1977	*The San Pedro Beach Bums* (ABC)
1978–84	*Fantasy Island* (ABC)
1978–81	*Vega$* (ABC)
1979–84	*Hart to Hart* (ABC)
1980	*B.A.D. Cats* (ABC)
1981	*Aloha Paradise* (ABC)
1981–89	*Dynasty* (ABC)
1981–82	*Strike Force* (ABC)
1982–86	*T. J. Hooker* (ABC)
1982–85	*Matt Houston* (ABC)
1983	*At Ease* (ABC)
1983–88	*Hotel* (ABC)
1984–85	*Glitter* (ABC)
1984–85	*Finder of Lost Loves* (ABC)
1985	*MacGruder & Loud* (ABC)
1985	*Hollywood Beat* (ABC)
1985–87	*Dynasty II: The Colbys* (ABC)
1986	*Life with Lucy* (ABC)
1988–89	*Heartbeat* (ABC)

1989	*Nightingales* (NBC)
1990–2000	*Beverly Hills 90210* (Fox)
1992	*Hearts Are Wild* (CBS)
1992–99	*Melrose Place* (Fox)
1992–93	*The Heights* (Fox)
1992	*The Round Table* (NBC)
1992–	*2000 Malibu Road* (CBS)
1994	*Winnetka Road* (NBC)
1994–95	*Burke's Law* (CBS)
1994–95	*Madman of the People* (NBC)
1994–95	*Models, Inc.* (Fox)
1994	*Heaven Help Us* (syndicated)
1994–95	*Robin's Hoods* (syndicated)
1995	*University Hospital* (syndicated)
1996	*Savannah* (WB)
1996	*Malibu Shores* (NBC)
1996	*Kindred: The Embraced* (Fox)
1996–	*7th Heaven* (WB)
1996–	*Charmed* (WB)
1996–	*Any Day Now* (Lifetime)
1998–99	*Love Boat: The Next Wave* (UPN)
2000	*Titans* (NBC)
2001	*All Souls* (UPN)
2001	*Deep* (WB)

〰〰 〰〰 〰〰

Britannica defines a "perennial" as being "present at all seasons, constant . . . continuing without interruption," a definition that, had it been accompanied by an illustration, surely would have depicted the face of Aaron Spelling. That's because, more than anyone else in the history of dramatic television, Spelling has endured year after year and done so with unprecedented success. Moreover, his longevity is not just rare, it is unbelievable, especially in an industry that lives and dies by the Nielsens. Network executives swear by the numbers, as do advertisers and syndicators. But with apologies to Shakespeare, if "numbers (not the play) are the thing," then consider these: Aaron Spelling has created or produced prime-time dramas in six consecutive decades. During a nineteen-year span, from the late 1960s to the late '80s, one or more of his shows finished in the top thirty, and that was an era in which a thirtieth-ranked program attracted a larger audience than a number-one show does today. On two occasions, Spelling had four different dramas ranked in the same season, and at six different times his creations were top-five finishers. He has had at least one drama on the air every year since 1968—save for 1990, when he was rebuilding the Spelling dynasty into a new mod squad of groundbreaking youth programming. He has created or produced more than sixty prime-time dramas and seldom has he had fewer than two shows on air at the same time. In 1984 alone, his company produced nine prime-time dramas at once.

The late Leonard H. Goldenson, former chairman of ABC, commented in his book *Beating the Odds* that "Aaron has produced more film than anybody in the history of motion pictures or television." And Goldenson was an expert on Spelling. During most of the 1970s and '80s Aaron had an exclusive agreement with ABC, and his output was so prolific that broadcast executives jokingly referred to the network as the Aaron Broadcasting Company. In *Inside Prime Time*, Todd Gitlin noted that Spelling was guaranteed two pilots per year with one guaranteed to go to series, as well as a number of TV movies. Goldenson also wrote that, "Aaron became virtually an extension of our programming department. If we made a mistake with a show and it flopped, he could create a replacement, and have it ready within five or six weeks. I don't know anyone else who can move that fast and that well. Aaron became our secret weapon when we began to depend on a second season. He was a tower of strength."

Spelling's numbers, in terms of both output and ratings, kept ABC competitive for most of two decades; however, numbers serve only to quantify success, not to qualify it. To do that we must inventory Spelling's extraordinary and innate abilities.

First, Spelling was the original TV psychic. Today's late-night, 900-number hucksters can't hold a scented candle to Aaron's ability to read an audience. The late Brandon Tartikoff once said of Spelling, "There hasn't been a decade when Aaron didn't figure out what the American public really wanted and give it to them before someone else did" (Spelling and Jefferson Graham, *A Prime Time Life*).

Second, Spelling is an innovator. As did Henry Ford with the Model T, Ray Krok with fast food, and Bill Gates with software, Aaron Spelling understands the principle of supply and demand, as well as when and how to market his product. Gitlin observed that "Spelling had an eye for trends," while Robert Thompson and David Marc in their book *Prime Time, Prime Movers* called Spelling "both an innovator and an imitator," and noted, "Spelling can go with the flow, or change the course of a river." Certainly the debate about whether television itself is a reflection of society or a catalyst for change has raged for years and will likely never be resolved; however, given the nature of our industry, a producer like Spelling must be able to facilitate both sides of that debate. Therefore, the river metaphor should not be construed as a criticism of Spelling's creativity.

Third, Aaron is still a teenager at heart. Throughout his career he has showcased young talent in groundbreaking roles, so that as he grew into senior citizen status it is not surprising that his programs continued to get younger as he got older. The man who gave us *The Love Boat* on ABC is just as comfortable developing a series for the youth-oriented webs, like WB, Fox, or UPN.

Fourth, Spelling is a master of process. He is a micromanager who knows how to nurture without hovering. In an article for *Entertainment Weekly*, Kristin Baldwin reported, "He approves every story concept, makes notes on every script, and has final cut on each episode. Not to mention keeping tabs on wardrobe and hair, even requiring actors to notify him before changing their [hair] do's." And Nancy Miller (creator, *Any Day Now*) said of her boss, "His casting ability is unparalleled, as is his knowledge about the business. He is like a figurehead; he comes in when you need him, but he isn't intrusive."

Fifth, Aaron Spelling is an agent for social change and a champion of diversity. Most of his dramas have featured strong women, a trait which up until recently was an exception to the rule of prime-time television. He also wrote substantive parts for minorities as well as for older actors. But perhaps most importantly, he has, over the years, nurtured and promoted a family of women producers who otherwise might have languished in a sea of male-dominated writing staffs. Brenda Hampton, creator of *7th Heaven*, said of Spelling, "He absolutely does not discriminate because of age, race, or gender. It's all about the work. Can you do the work? And I think that he's great at recognizing who can do it." Nancy Miller's explanation goes a bit deeper. "Aaron has always been fair, and he's always been open," she says. "I don't know if it goes back to his background as a little Jewish boy growing up in Texas, and feeling not part of the 'club.'"

In fact, it is that exclusionary upbringing that not only accounts for Aaron's treatment of his fellow man, but also explains the genesis of his development as a passionate and compassionate storyteller, an ability he formed early on, thanks in part to a childhood that would have given Dickens pause.

Aaron Spelling was born in Dallas in 1928 to an ethnically diverse parentage. He was the youngest of five children who were crammed into a tiny house on Browder Street. For a boy of Jewish heritage growing up in the heart of Texas, life was, to say the least, difficult, and he encountered severe prejudice at an early age. Jack Condon and David Hofstede in their book, *"Charlie's Angels" Casebook,* noted that Aaron learned to entertain anti-Semitic bullies by telling them stories. Unfortunately, the stories did not always diffuse the violent encounters. Appearing at an evening given in his honor by the Academy of Television Arts & Sciences (October 2000), Spelling recalled, "I went to the most bigoted school in Dallas, and I got my butt kicked every day. So my mom would walk me to school, and the kids would throw rocks at her. I had a nervous breakdown at age nine." Clearly Aaron's mother was courageous, and his father, a hardworking immigrant tailor, was supportive, but it was another strong woman who helped young Spelling survive the bigotry and bullying by nurturing his love of, and innate talent for, writing. Again, speaking to Academy members in Los Angeles, Spelling said, "When I was ten, my teacher, Mrs. Jones, took an interest in me. She said, 'If you write two book reports for me, I'll promote you.' I gave her thirty-seven. She said, 'Have you ever thought of being a writer?' She then gave me an assignment, directing me to write a sentence that had meaning to me. So I wrote, 'Dog Spelled Backwards Is God.' Mrs. Jones sent me a book to read every year until the day she died."

Aaron's education was put on hold while he served a brief hitch in the Air Force, where, ironically, he would develop a fear of flying. Reportedly a plane he was scheduled to board ended up crashing. As a result, he sticks to ground transportation exclusively.

After his military tour Aaron attended Southern Methodist University, where he majored in theater and even won the coveted Eugene O'Neil Award for his one-act plays. After college he tried his luck on the Great White Way, but decided after only a few months to head for Hollywood. He set out in an eight-year-old Plymouth with two hundred dollars in his pocket. The money was a gift from his father. "It was all he had," Spelling confessed to the Academy of Television Arts & Sciences audience. Initially Aaron supported himself by acting. One of his mentors, Jack Webb, hired the gangly youth to appear in a half dozen episodes of *Dragnet*. Then, after appearing in numerous TV shows and prompted by his first wife, actress Carolyn Jones (*The Addams*

Family), Spelling abandoned acting and returned to writing. Webb purchased a script from Aaron just so the rookie could snag a writing credit. Then Aaron went to work for another mentor, Dick Powell, founder of Four Star Productions. Under the aegis of Four Star, Spelling created his first TV show, a western titled *Johnny Ringo*. Though it lasted only one season, the show was well received by critics and is still acknowledged for its forward-thinking messages. Gary Yoggy, in his book *Riding the Video Range*, noted that "Among the topics covered by the series was that of mistreatment of various ethnic immigrant minorities." Spelling's message of tolerance was, given his background, not surprising, and his *Ringo* scripts set him on a career path as a producer. Following Powell's death, Aaron formed his own company, producing a number of series during the mid to late 1960s including *Honey West* and *The Mod Squad*. *Honey West* broke new ground for women in action roles, while *The Mod Squad* was, according to Robert Thompson, a "repackaged version of *Johnny Ringo*, featuring the rehabilitated criminal as a lawman." In *The Mod Squad* the lawmen were three hip misfits out to make a difference.

Spelling then teamed with Leonard Goldberg; together they co-produced nine series from 1972 to 1979, beginning with *The Rookies* and including *Starsky & Hutch*. On an E! Entertainment Channel special titled *The King of Prime Time*, Spelling explained the significance of his first buddy drama. "It was the first love affair between two men, and I mean that in the best essence of the word," he said. "They were not lovers, but they were so bonded. They had fights with each other, but they dearly loved each other. I think it was a relationship that hasn't been equaled in television."

In 1976 Spelling Goldberg produced *Charlie's Angels,* and, in a stroke of master showmanship and marketing genius (Joan Collins in her book *Second Act* called Spelling the "P. T. Barnum of television"), Aaron made a broad-based audience embrace his drama about three lady detectives. Todd Gitlin noted, "Aaron Spelling appealed at once to elements of the new feminism and its conservative opposition. The Angels were skilled working women and sex objects at the same time." With his Midas touch now firmly established, Spelling began churning out one hit after another. He closed out the '70s with *The Love Boat, Fantasy Island,* and *Hart to Hart*. To many baby boomers, *Charlie's Angels* was and always will be Spelling's signature show. It influenced hairstyles and fashions, and proved that women could carry a hit series. But as those same boomers aged into the Reagan era of junk bonds and materialism, Spelling answered with another influential drama. *Dynasty* was also Spelling's counter to the *Dallas* craze, and it launched an entire cottage industry of prime-time soaps, including *Hotel, Glitter,* and the *Dynasty* spin-off, *The Colbys.*

The 1980s brought Spelling more money than the Carringtons and Colbys could have amassed in a lifetime. But Spelling's wealth afforded him the luxury of experimentation. Years earlier he had produced *Family* with famed director Mike Nichols, a drama in which the characters could address everyday issues and problems, ranging from dating to breast cancer. In the 1980s Spelling would produce a number of TV movies as a forum for the continuation of that kind of issues-oriented television. *The Best Little Girl in the World* was the first teleplay to tackle anorexia nervosa among teenage girls; *Day One* questioned the morality of atomic weapons; while *And the Band Played On* (dropped by NBC then picked up by HBO) challenged the United States government to step up its fight against the AIDS virus.

Both *Day One* and *Band* were honored with Emmys. As the 1980s came to a close, however, the perennial showman found himself without a series on air for the first time in nearly twenty years. But to paraphrase Tartikoff's words, it did not take long for Aaron to figure out what the public wanted. The fledgling Fox Network was entering its third season, and, just as Goldenson had called upon Spelling to make ABC competitive in the 1970s and '80s, Barry Diller approached the legendary producer to buoy Fox and develop a show about high school. The result was *Beverly Hills 90210.* Premiering in the winter of 1990, the hip drama got off to a shaky start, but by the second season had doubled its audience, attracting a fifty-two share of all teens watching television. Former Fox president Peter Chernin admitted that "90210 was instrumental in broadening the network." Spelling and Fox followed in 1992 with the spin-off series *Melrose Place,* which featured slightly older hunks and hunkettes, hunkered down in an Los Angeles garden apartment. *Entertainment Weekly* called it, "The most mindlessly entertaining apartment complex in TV history." But for all of their "mindlessness," both youth-oriented dramas allocated a significant amount of time to addressing social issues, and audiences responded. *Melrose Place* lasted for seven seasons, while *90210* spanned the decade with a ten-year run.

Spelling offered up a variety of programs throughout the 1990s, including an attempt to boost the new WB Network with *Savannah,* an old-fashioned soap. And, no longer bound by exclusive deals as he had been a generation before, Spelling was free to peddle his independent wares to the highest bidder. A *Burke's Law* revival showed up on CBS. *Models, Inc.* (a *Melrose* spin-off) went to Fox, and Nancy Miller's *Roundtable* held court at NBC.

But by the end of the decade, merger mania and vertical integration were beginning to rule television. One by one, all of the major broadcasting companies were being folded into larger corporations, and independent production studios were falling by the wayside as networks preferred to purchase (and air) programs that were produced by one of their own subsidiaries. But "Spelling the Perennial" survived those trends and rode into the new millennium sporting an eclectic mix of dramas for several different broadcasters. *7th Heaven*, Aaron's updated version of *Family*, became a staple for the WB, as did Connie Burge's *Charmed*, a supernatural sister series featuring three witches and led by *90210* veteran Shannon Doherty. *Any Day Now*, Nancy Miller's show about race relations, became Lifetime's highest-rated drama, and *Titans*, a *Dynasty*-type sudsier landed at NBC. Like other Spelling serials before it, *Titans* was pure camp, and, given time to find an audience, might have enjoyed a long run. In its premiere episode *Titans* improved its time slot by 37 percent over the previous season when *Dateline* had expanded to Wednesdays. Nevertheless, *Titans* was canceled after only a few airings. Former WB and NBC executive Garth Ancier, who championed Spelling's late-1990s entries, had recruited the producer to develop *Titans.* He commented on Aaron's durability and success. "Aaron Spelling is one of these producers who has this wonderful commercial sense to him," Ancier said. "I've done all these shows with him, and I know his tastes quite well. He's also marvelous at manipulating film and casting . . . I think what's really interesting about Aaron, and it's a good example for producers, is he's really been terrific at mentoring terrific writers, and then steering them on how to make shows work, and then providing the support and organization on how to make the shows terrific."

Now, well into the twenty-first century, Spelling is still making shows terrific and continues to develop new programs. He also continues to be devoted to his wife, Candy, and their two children, Tori and Randy. It is fitting that both kids are actors; after all, acting is how their dad started out. With a little care and nurturing, they might also grow into producers. Who knows? By the year 2059, perhaps they will shoot a remake of *Johnny Ringo.* If so, you can count on Aaron being there for a cameo and to make script notes.

Spelling told moderator Leeza Gibbons at the Academy of Television Arts & Sciences event, "Follow your dream. Even if you only get a small piece of your dream, that's better than living in a world of harsh reality." Aaron Spelling has followed his dream, and year after year he has made our harsh reality a bit more bearable as a result.

I spoke with the legendary producer on two occasions in the summer of 2000, prior to the cancellation of *Titans*.

Longworth: The first thing I have to mention is that Brenda Hampton [creator of *7ᵗʰ Heaven*] told me that if it hadn't been for you, she wouldn't be a mother. So you have a lot of explaining to do, young man! (*Both laugh.*)

SPELLING: No, she just means, well, I was supportive of her efforts to go to Vietnam to adopt a child. And she went through hell with it, and I supported her any way I could—not monetarily, Brenda doesn't accept things like that—but giving her time off to do it, and calling people when I thought I could help her.

Longworth: She said you were great.

SPELLING: She's terrific.

Longworth: Well, let's talk about your role as an employer. You've always been supportive of your work family. Is that something that grew out of your early experiences? What was your model for that kind of nurturing role?

SPELLING: Oh, God, my first job was writing host spots for *Zane Grey Theater* for one hundred and twenty-five dollars a week. And Dick Powell kind of adopted me, bought my first script, and said, "Someday you'll be producing this show." And I did, and I produced five shows for him at one time. And it's having a mentor, that's what it's really all about, is having a mentor, somebody you can learn from. Somebody who knows the problems of being poor from Texas. I never asked for a raise, but Dick was continually giving me raises because he had heard how I had grown up in Texas in a six thousand dollar house with wall-to-wall people, one bathroom. The house, by the way, was fully furnished for six thousand dollars.

Longworth: Brenda also told me that, at the time you helped her, she was brand new, hadn't even turned in her first script. You didn't know her very well, and you still helped her.

SPELLING: Having been an actor, and a bad one (*both laugh*), and a writer (I never wanted to produce), I love actors and actresses and writers. And I try to make them a member of our family. We're not run like a big studio. I mean, God Almighty, I can't tell you how many times the *90210* kids have been over to my house to shoot pool and have dinner. We're family, and I feel the same way about writers. If I create a show, I never take credit for the creation. I give it to the writer.

Longworth: Well, not to get off track, but in defense of your acting, I saw a film the other day with Phil Carey and Martha Hyer, where you were a kooky sidekick and got shot at the end.

SPELLING: I usually got shot at the end. (*Both laugh.*) My greatest success was doing *I Love Lucy* where I danced with a young lady who weighed about one hundred and ninety pounds. (*Laughs.*)

Longworth: OK, we'll forget the acting for a moment. Let's talk about producing. You know, a lot of media pundits used to refer to *Charlie's Angels* as a show for men and *Love Boat* as a show for women. But here's my problem. My wife loved *Charlie's Angels,* and here I am pushing fifty and I liked *The Love Boat.* Does that surprise you?

SPELLING: No, not at all. But first I must tell you I have socks older than you. (*Both laugh.*) Number two, I think *Charlie's Angels* was for men *and* women, because it was really campy. I kept saying to everybody, and I may have put this in my book, but we had a big press thing and somebody stood up and said, "I don't believe the reality of this show," and I said, "You take three of the most beautiful young ladies in the country, graduated from the police academy, were given jobs parking cars, typing, and checking meters, and they worked for a voice over the telephone for a man they never met. He was paying them four hundred dollars a week, and they were wearing five thousand dollar Nolan Miller gowns, you missed the camp of the show." (*Both laugh.*)

Longworth: But what about *The Love Boat?*

SPELLING: I had more fun with *Love Boat* than anything, I guess. But I think *Love Boat* was appealing to men *and* women. I think both those shows were. But I would have thought more women would have watched *Love Boat* than *Charlie's Angels,* and we were shocked at the female audience on *Love Boat* because, you know, I don't have to tell you how many times we shot everybody in the swimming pool with bikinis. That was for you, the guys. (*Both laugh.*)

Longworth: But why do Spelling shows have such widespread appeal in general?

SPELLING: I'll tell you something, maybe I've said it before, I don't remember. All the tour buses that come in front of our house, you know that little place that my wife built? I still can't find my room, OK? (*Both laugh.*) I go out to the buses and I talk to them. And I ask, "What do you like?" I don't mention my show, I just ask, "What do you like to watch?" And since I don't fly, we catch trains everywhere, and I talk to the people on the train, and they tell me what they like. Some industry folks say, "First you must please the network that's buying the show." That's not true. First you have to please your audience, then the network will buy shows from you. And I still believe that. They built my house, that audience of mine. I still love them, and I answer every fan letter I get. They send me money to autograph a picture for them, and I would never accept money for that, but I'm thrilled by it.

Longworth: But a modern-day media analyst would say that your method of audience feedback is not very scientific.

SPELLING: (*Laughs.*) I don't know. All I can tell you is I think when you go to do shows, from *And the Band Played On* to doing *90210* and *Charlie's Angels*, I'm interested in everything. I want to give them what they want, not what *I* love.

Longworth: And you not only love your shows, you also have an extraordinary ability to process every detail about them. Brenda Hampton told me that she can pitch six episodes of *7th Heaven* with a total of thirty different story lines to you at one meeting, and you can then comment to her on how the comic runner in episode two plays into the subtext of episode five. Do you have a steel-trap mind or something?

SPELLING: Well, I'm proud to tell you that senility has not set in yet, and I'm not on Viagra. (*Both laugh.*) But when you deal with a talent like Brenda, there are only minor things that I would suggest. I love working with her, she is so bright, and the credit for that show should go to her. I'm thrilled to have my name on it as a producer with her, but the entire credit of that show should go to her.

Longworth: Going back to your acting days for a moment. Does your experience as an actor help your creative process when writing a show like *Johnny Ringo* or producing a series like *Charmed?* Does it help to remember back to those days as an actor when you're being creative, or does that not have anything to do with it?

SPELLING: No, that has a lot to do with it, 'cause you say, "How would an actor play this?" Always write for the actor, don't write for yourself. Once a character is created, as an actor I know what I would have said if I were that actor. Even as a bad actor, I know that. (*Laughs.*) And I love actors. I study actors. I went to a charity affair last week and I rushed over to a guy and said, "I've never met you, but I'm one of your biggest fans in the world, and I'm embarrassed. But my name is," and he interrupted me and said, "Oh, like I don't know your name, Aaron!" And that was Dustin Hoffman. That was a big thrill to me. (*Both laugh.*)

Longworth: Where are you most creative, if you had to pick a place? In the mansion? At the office? Alone? In a staff meeting?

SPELLING: I would say in the office. I do a new thing now, though. I work out of the house on Fridays and I take my assistant with me to the house, so we can go to my office. I don't think Candy has found that office yet. (*Both laugh.*) But I can get some work done without all the phone calls in the office, without at least twenty-five of our one hundred and fifty employees calling with questions. I hate the business end, but I love the creative end. I really care about the script and the concept. Concept first, then script, then casting. When actors come in to read for us, they put them on tape for me so I can see what the camera thinks of them. You can't just sit in my office as we do for the first interview and think that you can learn everything about this actor. Usually they're reading from the pages they just got, and second of all you don't get a chance to see the feeling in their eyes, and that tells everything.

Longworth: Nancy Miller [*Any Day Now*] said that you have an uncanny ability when it comes to casting. I'm thinking back on all of the actresses that you've made famous, and once again, it occurs to me that perhaps your experience as an actor gives you an edge in selecting people.

SPELLING: I hope so. Did I tell you the story about Bette Davis?

Longworth: No.

SPELLING: OK, well I once wrote a half-hour comedy pilot, which I shouldn't have done. I wrote it with a buddy of mine from Texas. I don't know a damn thing about comedy and I don't do comedy. But we were reading actors for our show, and Bette said, "Aaron, don't just listen to them, look to the *windows*." So I turned to look out the windows of my office that we were sitting in. And she said, "No, not those windows, you idiot! Their *eyes*. When they're acting for you, it's their eyes. If what you see in their eyes is a reflection of yourself, that's a mirror, that's not a window, but if you can see the drama within those eyes, then you're going to the soul of the actor." And I looked at those windows, man! (*Laughs.*)

Longworth: One of those actors, Thomas Calabro from *Melrose Place* said, "Mr. Spelling is known more for beautiful people than [for] great actors." Do you agree with that?

SPELLING: It depends on the show you're doing. If you're doing *Charlie's Angels*, obviously they have to be beautiful, but, my God, we've done so many series that I think they were all beautiful actors. If you're looking for the lead in a western, he should be tough, not beautiful. But, by the way, I thought Thomas Calabro was beautiful, so screw him! (*Both laugh.*)

Longworth: Well, that's what he was saying, that he was good looking but not much of an actor.

SPELLING: Well, the truth is, he's a helluva actor, and he's *not* beautiful, and you can tell him I said that. (*Both laugh.*) You can print that.

AARON SPELLING | 281

Longworth: You mentioned the many different types of series you've produced. It seems that you've always been able to redefine yourself, always able to adapt. It seems that, no matter what direction someone or society spins you in, you always come out going in the right direction. Where does that resourcefulness and determination come from?

SPELLING: You're very nice to say that, but I think if you're going to do something you haven't done before, you better do a lot of research on what it is, and look at shows similar to it that were successful, and what in that show made it work. We do *7th Heaven*, which I love, but I also did a show years ago called *Family.* And I found out what an audience wanted in a family show. They wanted to have faith in that family. I'm not talking about religious faith, but they wanted a good father and a good mother who were capable of coping with their kids and directing them correctly. And that's what it's all about, I think. We're doing a pilot for Paramount that may not sell called *All Souls Hospital.* It's about a haunted hospital. Let me tell you, though, I've never been in a haunted hospital. (*Both laugh.*)

Longworth: Speaking of *Family*, the critics at that time said the show was a "distinct departure from the Spelling style," and I'm thinking to myself, aren't all Spelling shows about relationships?

SPELLING: Boy, I hope so; my God, what else is there? What else is there? If the characters on the show aren't relatable, and if your characters don't relate to each other, whether that be love or hate, what is your show about? I don't think everybody has to *love* everybody on a show. With Heather Locklear, she was the lady that you love to hate on *Melrose Place.* She could be bitchy and she could fire somebody, she could want to buy this company and she'd go to any length to do it, including sleeping with somebody to get it. But then we gave her scenes where somebody couldn't pay the rent in her apartment building, and she let them stay. She paid for the funeral of one of the kids' parents when the kid had no money. Way back when, ABC said to me, "You can't have a gay character on *Dynasty.* Now there are shows like *Will & Grace* that have fun with gay characters. But when we started they said, "You'll see how the audience is going to tune out." No, they didn't. And I can quote you the greatest line, I wish I had written it. In an episode of *Dynasty*, Blake [John Forsythe] could never accept his son as being gay, but when he went to visit his son and his son's lover, before he left, Blake shook hands with the lover and said to his son, "I'm happy now. I see someone loves you as much as I do." Now for a father to say that to a gay son when he had fought the gayness forever shows that he had learned something from his gay son.

And I think that those are the things that matter. Those are important things. We have a sign up here that says when you do issues, and God knows we did forty-one issues on *90210* alone, "Don't preach, *teach.*" Say things in a way that young people understand them. The other great line I liked, there was a PTA meeting on *90210*, and Donna's mother was leading the charge on not selling condoms at the high school. And Donna asked if she could speak, and her mother said, "No," and Mr. Walsh said, "Let her talk." So Donna says, "Mom, if you have a swiming pool in your backyard, shouldn't you teach your kid how to swim?" Now you know what? That's better than saying, "Condoms are essential because of social diseases, etc." You know what I'm saying? That would have been preaching. But here, saying it like a kid had more effect. I can't tell you how many tons of letters we got with that one line. Chuck Rosin wrote it, I didn't. Gee, how did I remember Chuck wrote it? You're affecting me, Jim. (*Both laugh.*)

Longworth: We were speaking earlier of the old Four Star [Productions] shows under the aegis of your mentor, Dick Powell. You've worked under a number of different systems, including the independent studio like Four Star. You've worked under the network system, too, and under the corporate banner of Viacom. Which is better for creative people to work under, the old-style independent studios or the networks?

SPELLING: You think I'm going to say this because I'm worried about selling a pilot, but I don't mind working with networks. I don't mind them telling me what kind of show they need instead of my pitching eighteen ideas that maybe they don't have any interest in. I've been very lucky. Once we sell a show, they have a trust in me that I deeply appreciate. They don't tell us what to do. They don't give us notes on every script, on every day's dailies. They just don't do that, and I appreciate that a lot. But no, I wouldn't want to go back to the old days. I do resent some of these new trends where ABC is only buying shows from Disney. Come on. Disney owns ABC, give me a break.

Longworth: That concerns you, doesn't it?

SPELLING: It concerns me a lot. I think it's unfair, 'cause that means you could have the greatest show in the world, but they're not going to buy it 'cause we don't belong to Disney. I think that's going to happen more and more, but I hope it doesn't happen.

Longworth: You've had so many successes, but you've also had low moments. What does it feel like when you have a show canceled?

SPELLING: It's strange. I don't care what the show is, I don't care how you try, you feel like *you've* failed, and you feel a certain animosity toward the network for not giving it more of a chance. And it's not easy to live with. I mean, they're pointing a finger to the press and saying, "He failed." And it's hard, I don't care how many shows you have on.

Longworth: You never get over it.

SPELLING: No. But I'll tell you one thing. When David Kelley failed with *Snoops*, I never heard it mentioned anywhere. Isn't that weird?

Longworth: Speaking of high failure rates, nearly every producer I've interviewed has been somewhat critical of the pilot system. Now, as I understand it, you did three different pilots for *The Love Boat*.

SPELLING: Well, they weren't pilots actually, I'll tell you the truth. The same thing happened with *Fantasy Island*. No, that's not true. We did three *Fantasy Island* movies for television, and out of the clear blue sky they called and said we'd like to turn it into a series. And we had already shot the third one, so we had to divide it into two segments. On *Love Boat* I didn't do three different pilots. Doug Cramer owned *Love Boat* at the time, and he did two pilots that didn't sell. I loved the idea and I went to the network, and this was after Doug joined my company, and I said, "God, I'd like us to get a chance at another pilot." And they said, "OK, but give us a piece of casting so we could go back to New York." And it was their idea to come up with Gavin McLeod, who had been so successful in the *Mary Tyler Moore Show*. So I invited Gavin to my house and we talked, and he loved the idea. ABC gave us so little money, whereas Doug had shot both of his pilots on the ship and everything. You know where we shot ours?

Longworth: No.

SPELLING: The *Queen Mary*, docked in the harbor here. (*Both laugh.*) We used a lot of stock shots. And then who knew—that started nine years of the shows. But I had a lot of fun with that.

Longworth: But it's tough to get past the first season so you can go on to nine seasons. Even for a producer of your status, it seems that, today, there's more pressure from the networks to succeed immediately than there used to be. Is that true?

SPELLING: There's a *lot* of pressure. But I must say one thing. When I started there were three networks, ABC, CBS, and NBC. Now we have those three, but we have Fox, WB, UPN, so we have three more outlets. That's important. Instead of three, we have six now. And that helps, but boy, do they move fast, holy cow!

Longworth: In 1990 after *Dynasty* stopped production, it was another twelve months before *Beverly Hills 90210* burst onto the scene. So even though you were already wealthy and successful at that time, did you begin to doubt yourself at all?

SPELLING: When *Dynasty* was canceled, *Variety* came out with a big headline, "Spelling's Dynasty Dead." But "Dynasty" was not in quotation marks. And that really hurt me. I mean, that was like saying, "Well *he's* through." And then of course we got *90210* on the air, but they never retracted it. (*Laughs.*)

Longworth: Someone once asked you why you didn't just retire after *Dynasty* ended. And I think you replied, "Work chases away the nightmares of Browder Street."

SPELLING: That's true. But you know me, I love doing it. Everything is a challenge. It's like if you strike out in a game, you still want to go up to bat again, don't you? And that's what it was to me. I was making fifty thousand dollars a year at Four Star, which was more money than I had ever heard of in my life. I called my dad at that point and asked him to retire. He was a tailor at Sears & Roebuck. He retired and passed away six months later. You gotta keep active.

Longworth: You also said you were kind of like a hooker who just can't seem to retire.

SPELLING: No, what I really said (*laughs*) and I never should have said it. I said, "I was like a hooker on Saturday night. I just want one more." (*Both laugh.*) Don't you tell your wife I said that. (*Laughs.*) Hey, why don't *you* retire? You just going to keep writing books the rest of your life?

Longworth: Don't call *me* a hooker.

SPELLING: You're like me. You're like the hooker who just wants one more. (*Laughs.*)

Longworth: OK, since we're speaking of hookers, have you ever had to prostitute your talent or principles to appease a boss or a network?

SPELLING: No. Even with Dick Powell, no. Did I ever tell you the Sammy Davis, Jr. story?

Longworth: No.

SPELLING: I was writing *Zane Grey* for Dick Powell after I got promoted from writing the host spots, and we had a show that we were producing with Sammy Davis. Dick Powell had introduced me to him, and I went to see him perform, and loved him, and I wanted to use him. He played the first African American deputy on TV. And Dick Powell played the sheriff. The two characters did not get along, so we approached bigotry and discussed it, and in the end, they got to be very close friends. Dick's character was walking down the street, and there was a heavy (who was white) about to kill him by shooting Dick in the back, and Sammy Davis killed the white guy, saving the sheriff's life. Dick Powell called me to his office, and I'll never forget the sponsor, Lorillard, and he had them on the phone, and they said, "You cannot do a show where a black man kills a white man." And I was furious, and I said, "But wait a minute! He's saving the lead character's life." They said, "You cannot have a black man shoot a white man." So I said, "OK, I quit, Dick." And Dick said, "If I'm going to lose 'Skinny' or a sponsor, I'll lose the sponsor." And I said, "Wait, Dick, I have an idea." Over the weekend, I wrote a show called "Buffalo Soldiers," and we had a scene where Sammy was leading an all-black troop to meet with the Indians to try and get peace. And the Indian said, "Why do you hate us? The white man hates you as much as he hates us." You know, the sponsor left that in? (*Both laugh.*) Dick and I just clapped hands, there weren't high fives in those days. And we said, "We won! We said something more important than shooting the guy on the street."

Longworth: So we know that you never compromised your principles in those days. But you mention in your book that your first wife, Carolyn Jones, advised you not to ever write anything that you didn't produce. And you decided to heed that advice. Of course, when she said that, back in the '50s, you weren't financially secure.

SPELLING: Hardly.

Longworth: So wasn't that kind of tough to stick to that principle in the days when you needed a buck?

SPELLING: I wish I could tell you what show upset me so much. I had created something, and they put another producer on the show, and the show bombed. And I took her advice. But you also have to understand that she felt I could make twice as much money producing what I write (*laughs*), and she was right. Mostly she wanted me to stop acting. That was the big thing.

Longworth: Why?

SPELLING: 'Cause I was *terrible*! (*Both laugh.*)

Longworth: But that's because you always played some kooky guy.

SPELLING: Except one time. And the big thing that made her say, "You're never going to act again" was that I was cast in four weeks in *Kismet*. And she was good friends with the director, Vincent Minelli. And she came on the set while Vincent was directing me. And for four weeks I walked around wearing sackcloth and going, "Alms for the love of Allah!"

Longworth: (*Laughs.*)

SPELLING: Why are you laughing? That was a very huge part. I did that one line fifty thousand times. Then I heard laughter behind the camera, and Carolyn had surprised me by visiting the set. And she waited, it was my last shot of the day, and she whispered to me, "You're never going to act again. Stick to your writing." (*Both laugh.*) Best advice I ever got, by the way.

Longworth: Speaking of smart women, we spoke earlier about some of the great ladies who are producers on your shows, Nancy Miller [*Any Day Now*], Brenda Hampton [*7th Heaven*], Connie Burge [*Charmed*]. I'd like to say that there are dozens and dozens of women showrunners of dramas, but the reality is there are still only a handful. Why have you always been so supportive of women producers?

SPELLING: You're not going to like my answer, but since I'm a guy, and I'm an executive producer along with them, isn't it better to get a woman's viewpoint on a show? I mean, Jim, that's not hard to figure out, is it? Man plus women equal both side of a coin (*both laugh*), and I love working with women producers. Brenda and Nancy especially are just brilliant. And Connie worked on *Savannah* with us, then created *Charmed*.

Longworth: But you sort of nurture that brilliance. You had Connie in your family, then you let her come up with another show. It's sort of the same thing that Dick Powell did at Four Star and Grant Tinker did at MTM, and you don't see that too often in other companies.

SPELLING: No. And also, thinking back to *Charlie's Angels*, there were no shows that starred women in those days. The networks, all of them, said, "Women can't carry a show." What a stupid phrase. Do you see a lot of men producers on *Touched by an Angel*? Do you see a lot of male stars on *Touched by an Angel*? You don't know how hard it was for us to sell *Charlie's Angels*, you don't know. 'Cause, again, everybody said, "Women can't carry a show (drama). And we'd say, "Well, we have a man, John Forsythe," and they'd say, "Yeah, but he's just a voice over the telephone." Forgive us, we thought that was a clever idea.

Longworth: You've also cast some pretty empowered leading ladies: Anne Francis in *Honey West*, Stephanie Powers in *Hart to Hart*. And now, empowered leading ladies are making a comeback in television drama. Are you glad to see that trend?

SPELLING: Oh yeah. The lady on *Providence* is marvelous, and the ladies on *ER* are marvelous. It's about time, isn't it? I remember when we did a miniseries, six episodes of *200 Malibu Road,* and the network said, "You really want to go with this young kid named Drew Barrymore?" I said, "Yeah, she's OK." And I used Hillary Swank in thirteen episodes of *90210*.

Longworth: Yeah, you've had sort of a proving ground for talent. Didn't you cast Sharon Stone in a couple of series?

SPELLING: Yeah, we did a pilot with Sharon Stone [*Mr. and Mrs. Ryan*] that I loved. She was a detective working with a male detective in her own agency. ABC said she wasn't sexy enough. (*Both laugh.*) I think they've probably changed their minds a thousand times by now.

Longworth: ABC said that Sharon Stone was not sexy enough?

SPELLING: Was not sexy enough.

Longworth: That's unbelievable.

SPELLING: No, nothing's unbelievable in television.

Longworth: But going back to your comment about how tough it is for women showrunners to get a show sold. Is that because it's still such a good old white boys' industry?

SPELLING: Yeah, but it's getting better. Susanne Daniels at Warner Brothers, Karey Burke at NBC. The head of ABC now is a woman. And I remember working with a woman who is very talented, everybody was pushing her around at the network. Her name is Marcie Carsey. She was running drama at ABC when I was there, and, at the time, ABC had problems with Stephanie Powers in *Hart to Hart*. Thank God for Marcie Carsey.

Longworth: First Sharon Stone wasn't sexy enough. What was ABC's problem with Stephanie Powers?

SPELLING: It was probably because she was a woman, but it would be silly to do *Hart to Hart* with two guys. (*Both laugh.*)

Longworth: Well, you have always been an innovator when it comes to women in drama, but didn't you also innovate an experimental format? The program was *The New People* and it was forty-five minutes long.

SPELLING: It wasn't my fault. One of my dearest friends came to work for me out here when I had an appendicitis attack, and he was in from Mississippi, and he became my driver because I couldn't drive, and then my roommate for years, and still one of my closest friends. He's done a few movies like *48 Hours*. It was Larry Gordon. And we created *The New People*. We had a commitment to the network, and they had a variety show that led in to *The New People*. *The New People* was about an airplane carrying visiting students from Asia and it crashes, killing the pilot. The college students land on this island in the South Pacific, and they found this strange little town where the atomic bomb had been tested. Then it was abandoned after we bombed Japan, and no planes ever came around, so these kids have no chance of getting off the island. And they had to elect a mayor, a sheriff, they were *The New People*. I loved that show. So ABC was loving it too, but they had no spot for it. So it was the network who made the variety show forty-five minutes and us forty-five minutes.

Longworth: So the format was not by your design?

SPELLING: No. As a matter of fact, if you want to know how stupid I was, I agreed to do it. How about the fact that you can't sell a forty-five minute show in foreign syndication? (*Laughs.*) 'Cause in those days with the forty-five minute show you only had about thirty-eight minutes of story. The rest is commercial.

Longworth: Everyone is so hung up on hour dramas these days, but I remember asking David Kelley and Steven Bochco at the Museum of Television & Radio why there weren't more half-hour dramas being produced, and they all sort of looked at me funny. But my point was that *Johnny Ringo* was a drama, so was *The Rifleman*. *Dragnet* was a drama. So I'll ask you. Why can't half-hour dramas work anymore?

SPELLING: I got to be honest with you, I don't know that they *can't* work. And you know something, you've given me an idea. I'm going to get people to start writing some half-hour dramas. I think it's a great idea. Who said the half-hour drama can't work? You just listed some of them. And you want to know what? Sometimes an hour gets stretched out, 'cause it has so little story line. It's like panning to get through an hour.

Longworth: Most of today's producers will tell you that you can't develop a story in a half hour, but I remember being really moved by some of the story lines on *The Rifleman*.

SPELLING: Well God, most of the Four Star dramas were a half hour. They worked then, why can't they work now? You've given me a great idea. Thank you. I'll send you one percent of nothing. (*Both laugh.*)

Longworth: Let's talk about the influence of television on society. Now, we all know that your shows started a lot of fashion trends with Nolan Miller's gowns and so forth, but let's talk about another kind of influence. You're always careful not to influence with violence. Did you make a decision early on in your career that you didn't want to do a lot of blood-and-guts type shows?

SPELLING: I think even stronger now than it was when I first started. On *90210*, we did a show on rape. We did four shows about guns, where in one, a little kid was playing with a gun he found in his father's unlocked drawer, and he shot and killed himself. That was way before Columbine. We did a show about one of the kids carrying a gun on campus, and he was going to kill the guy who beat him out for the football team. We did that way before Columbine. I think instead of violence, let's do things on the show where, we don't have to preach, but we can teach. We can certainly say things. We did shows about AIDS. We did shows on the use of condoms. We did two shows about manic depression in kids. People say, "Well, kids don't get manic depressive." Really? Excuse me? Again, that was way before Columbine, and you don't think *those* boys weren't manic depressive?

Longworth: What's different about writing good scripts that are youth oriented now, versus when you produced *The Mod Squad?* Do kids have the same concerns and same issues that they've always had? Or is it more difficult to write to youth issues these days?

SPELLING: Well, it's not more difficult to write, but there *are* more issues. When I was growing up, when my friends were growing up, the big problem was getting passing grades in school. Now it's divorced parents, abusive parents, guns at school. It's so many things they have on their minds today. Drive-by shootings. Good God, out here, every night when I watch the news at eleven o'clock, there's been another drive-by shooting.

Longworth: Speaking of the way things have changed, are you at all concerned that critics and audiences will compare *Titans* to *Dynasty,* and how do you know it's the right time to come back with an adult, prime-time soap opera?

SPELLING: Well, there *has* been one on the air, and now, since *Melrose Place* is gone and *90210* is gone, and *Party of Five* is gone, I just thought it was time. It's not *Dynasty* at all. *Dynasty* mostly dealt with older people like John Forsythe, and Joan Collins, and Linda Evans, but we have five young people on *Titans. Dynasty* took place in one house, they owned oil fields, there's none of that here. Does it take place in a wealthy surrounding? Yeah. I found out with *Dynasty* that viewers love to know that rich people have problems. And they love to laugh at rich people and the stupid things they're doing.

Longworth: On most of your programs, you take people on fantasy trips. You let viewers live vicariously through wealthy folks. What about the *Millionaire* craze? Some say it's a fantasy, too, but with it being broadcast four nights a week, it's occupying air time that could be filled with four quality dramas. Does that trend toward game shows concern you?

SPELLING: I hate how other networks have tried to emulate the game show, and none of them have worked. But I think these things have a life all their own, and I don't think they last a long time. I gotta tell you I was very proud when I got the ratings back on the two-hour *90210*. How about this for competition? We had an hour of *Millionaire* against us and the closing hour of *Jesus* against us. We beat them all.

Longworth: You beat "*Jesus* and Regis" on the same night.

SPELLING: (*Laughs.*) That's funny that you said that.

Longworth: And you beat both of them.

SPELLING: Not only beat them, but our numbers were astronomic.

Longworth: I don't think that's such a good thing, though. I mean, a Jewish man who beats up on *Jesus*.

SPELLING: I watched ten minutes of that miniseries, and I hated that they cast someone as Jesus. If you're going to do a movie about Jesus, do a story about the people he helped. Who are we going to depict next, God? (*Laughs.*) You know what? You couldn't have paid me a billion dollars to do that show because I thought it was disgraceful depicting Jesus. But that's me. I guess I'm wrong.

Longworth: People talk about you as wearing many, many hats.

SPELLING: I don't *own* a hat, Jim. (*Both laugh.*) I got a Dodger baseball cap.

Longworth: I don't care what you say, you should have been in comedy. I don't know what your problem is.

SPELLING: I don't know either.

Longworth: Finally, I do have a bone to pick with you.

SPELLING: Yeah?

Longworth: My favorite TV western movie was *Yuma* with Clint Walker, which your company did.

SPELLING: I remember that, Jim. (*Both laugh.*)

Longworth: Good for you. (*Both laugh.*) My question is, why didn't that turn out to be a series, because I thought it was great.

SPELLING: That was really weird. We shot it in Arizona, I remember Candy coming with me before the kids. And I loved it. I think Clint at that time was interested in doing the series, but most all of the networks said, "We have enough series." They didn't have enough games shows, or stupid comedies. If I see one more show about young people making love when they're sixteen years old, I'm going to throw up.

Longworth: Why aren't there any westerns on TV these days?

SPELLING: I think a good western would do a tremendous audience, especially if it was on Saturday night. I think that a western would do great.

Longworth: And you could play the kooky sidekick.

SPELLING: Yeah, I'd say, "I ain't got no money a'tal!" (*Both laugh.*)

Longworth: So If we *could* get a western series on the air, you would play the kooky sidekick?

SPELLING: Damn right. (*Both laugh.*)

Longworth: Do you have the trick gun from *Johnny Ringo?*

SPELLING: I think that the trick gun was captured by a bigger name than me, Dick Powell. He wanted that gun.

Longworth: Did that gun really work?

SPELLING: Hell, no! You had to put in an offstage "bang." (*Both laugh.*)

Longworth: So you're admitting that you're pretty much of a fake?

SPELLING: God, yeah, Jim. But I'm only telling you. Don't ruin my career. I mean, come on. If people find out, no matter what it is, they'll say, "Produced by Tori Spelling," they'll forget my first name.

Longworth: Well, thanks for doing this.

SPELLING: Hey, I enjoyed it.

Longworth: I'll be out in Los Angeles in November.

SPELLING: Try and drop by and say hello, would you?

Longworth: I'll be moderating a panel for the Television Academy, and—

SPELLING: Oh, well, *excuse* me! (*Both laugh.*)

Longworth: Well, you can't be in it because it's about "Women in Drama."

SPELLING: OK, but I can be a drag queen. (*Both laugh.*) Hey, I'm doing something for the Television Academy, too.

Longworth: That's right. They're going to honor you for an entire night in October.

SPELLING: But you and women, you can't be too bad. (*Both laugh.*) Good God, they should honor *me* and women. (*Laughs.*)

Longworth: Well, let's work on a half-hour drama.

SPELLING: I will, and we'll work on a western, too. Call me when you get time, buddy.

Longworth: OK, but all I *have* is time right now because of this horse injury.

SPELLING: I heard about your accident. What happened?

Longworth: I was walking one of our race horses, and—

SPELLING: You have race horses?

Longworth: Standardbreds for harness racing.

SPELLING: Oh God, the happiest days that Candy and I had, we owned some horses at Hollywood Park, and do you know that was the only time I could relax, just going there. I *love* horse racing, I love horse racing.

Longworth: They're great, just don't ever make the mistake of getting between a stallion and a mare who's in season. That's what I did.

SPELLING: And what happened?

Longworth: I was walking him and when he turned to see the mare, he and his twelve hundred pounds spun me around, then he stomped his hoof to impress his girlfriend. When he did, he crushed my knee.

SPELLING: Well then, you've learned that "sex is violent." (*Both laugh.*) You tell your wife I told you that. Now doesn't that prove that I can't write comedy? (*Both laugh.*)

Longworth: OK, so you *are* a comedian, but humor me for one last, serious question. Let's suppose we were burying a time capsule for the planet earth, and there was only room enough in the capsule for one listing by each person's name. What would your phrase say?

SPELLING: I've said many times that my tombstone is going to read, "He did *Charlie's Angels* and was Tori Spelling's father." (*Both laugh.*) That's it for me.

Longworth: But you know what I mean. You're a writer, producer, actor . . .

SPELLING: Well, if you let me have *three* words in the time capsule, I would like it to say I was known for "Candy, Tori, and Randy." They're what I care about more than anything, including television. If, God forbid, anything happened to any of them, I'd just quit, period. I don't know what I would do. But they're the three most important things to me.

⋙ 13 ⋘

AFTERWORD | Terrorism and Television Drama

On September 11, 2001, this second volume of *TV Creators* was undergoing final editorial scrutiny by my friends at Syracuse University Press. Anticipating their imminent feedback, I fully expected to make a few last minute changes. I even planned on penning an afterword for purposes of reporting on more recent developments in the television industry, such as new studies on TV violence. Never, however, did I imagine that these pages would be devoted to commenting on the effect that one particular hour of real life violence would have on so many people, and on the drama genre for which this book was intended to examine.

On that September morning, nineteen Islamic extremists took possession of four commercial passenger jets, intending to use the planes as giant missles against various American landmarks. Three of the jets hit their mark—one at the Pentagon, and two at the World Trade Center's twin towers. Another was diverted by a handful of heroic passengers and crashed into a remote Pennsylvania field. The attacks happened in almost rapid succession. Within about an hour, the twin towers had collapsed. Within about an hour, nearly five thousand innocent people had lost their lives. Within about an hour, life in America had changed forever.

Initially there was shock and disbelief, followed by anger and sorrow as our country slipped into mourning. It was this unprecedented mix of emotions that sent TV programming executives scrambling.

As expected, all of the major networks offered uninterrupted coverage of the tragic events, which spanned most of the week following that fateful Tuesday morning. With each passing day, the webs sustained mounting losses in ad revenue: an economic problem that paled in comparison with the loss of life sustained in New York and here in Virginia, but a problem nonetheless.

In the weeks and months ahead, networks would announce cumulative and projected losses in the billions of dollars, and there was talk of cutbacks including ABC's threat of permanently dropping all Saturday night programming. And, by November, both Fox and Columbia Tri Star had announced the demise of their TV movie and TV program divisions respectively. But in the short term, as programmers prepared to resume regular schedules and reshuffle fall premieres, another dilemma arose. It would, many believed, be necessary to reevaluate the *content* of certain drama episodes that, in fiction, closely mirrored the real life terrorism of September 11.

Some season premieres were not just delayed, but taken out of their normal rotation. CBS, for example, put a hold on their pilot for *The Agency* because the CIA-based drama contained references to Osama bin Laden, the suspected mastermind behind the September attacks. Another episode which dealt with an anthrax scare in Washington, D.C. was shelved because U.S. citizens, including government workers in and around Washington, had in real life suddenly become victims of that very same type of bioterrorism. The premiere of *24*, FOX's innovative new series that occurs in real time (twenty four episodes represent a single twenty-four hour day), was moved from September to November because its primary story line focused on an assassination plot. And Dick Wolf, famous for his *Law & Order* crossovers, had planned a miniseries of sorts, featuring all three of his franchise dramas including newcomer *Law & Order: Criminal Intent*. But that big event was cancelled altogether because it dealt with terrorism in New York City.

Meanwhile, the EMMYs were rescheduled not once but twice: first out of respect for a period of national mourning, then because the U.S. had just begun its air strikes on Afghanistan, and America was put on alert for possible retaliation by the terrorist cells still operating here. The awards show finally made it to air on November 4, but with a much more reserved tone than ever before.

Everyone, it seemed, wanted to be respectful and politically correct. When prime-time programming finally resumed, some producers prepared special materials either in honor of or due to the September 11 attacks. Wolf augmented his trademark "In the criminal justice system" teaser opening with a tribute to the public safety officials of New York City who had given their lives helping others. Aaron Sorkin, meanwhile, went one better. He and his crew produced an entire episode of *The West Wing* that dealt with a suspected Islamic terrorist who might have infiltrated the White House staff. It was a combination passion play and social lecture. Titled "Isaac and Ishmael," it taught us about pluralism and prejudice, the latter of which had supposedly begun with the birth of the Biblical title characters, and the former of which was in danger of extinction unless calmer heads prevailed. At the start of the hour, cast members announced that this special episode would not be part of the third season; rather, it was a stand-alone effort from which "all profits" would be donated to charities for families of victims from the terrorists attacks. But Scott Brown and Lynette Rice observed, "Since when are there proceeds from an individual TV episode?" Warner Brothers explained that "the money will come from a yet-to-be calculated share of cable residuals, international sales, and broadcast syndication fees," to which Brown and Rice replied, "That means the charities won't be seeing the dough until at least 2004" (*Entertainment Weekly*, Oct. 19, 2001). Yet despite the philanthropic controversy, Sorkin's groundbreaking installment was significant. Ken Tucker noted, "While most of network television is busy erasing any image or line that might carry an allusion to September 11, Sorkin was the first TV series creator to address terrorism directly in prime-time entertainment."

But it was Sorkin's boss, John Wells, who contributed perhaps the most memorable episodic presentations in the aftermath of 9/11. Broadcast in three parts, *Third Watch* first offered a two-hour special, entitled "In their Own Words," in which actual New York City police, firefighters, and EMS personnel told of their personal experiences during that fateful day. Then in the following two weeks, *Third Watch* resumed its regular production with bookend episodes: one that was set just prior to the terrorist attacks, and the other that dealt with events immediately afterward. The Wells trilogy was educational and inspiring, and it provided a unique mix of fictional drama with that of the tragic, non-fictional kind.

Not surprisingly, so-called "reality" programs took a hit in the ratings and in the public psyche. An *America Online/Entertainment Weekly* poll (Nov. 2, 2001) revealed that only eight percent of TV viewers were interested in watching reality games. Comedies, news, and dramas were the runaway favorites at forty-eight percent, twenty-two percent, and twenty percent respectively. And an October 10 poll by Interactive Media claimed that eighty-three percent of Americans are "less interested" in reality programming since the attacks

(*Entertainment Weekly*, Nov. 2, 2001). Predictions by TV veterans Aaron Spelling, Roy Huggins, and Glenn Gordon Caron about the life span of reality programs were starting to come true, only much earlier than originally expected.

In the weeks and months that followed, industry experts, including leading drama showrunners, weighed in on what had happened and how our reactions had affected life in general and television in particular. Marshall Herskovitz (*thirtysomething, Once & Again*), in commenting on sacrifices made by Hollywood, told *US Weekly*, "They're emotional decisions based on feelings of the people making them. And they are acting accordingly, at a huge financial loss." Later, Herskovitz's partner Ed Zwick, Aaron Sorkin, and others appeared before a Policy Forum at Occidental College in late October to discuss America's new preoccupation. Zwick said, "We have treated death in a way that's irrelevant in movies, and I think now that denial has been broken." Sorkin added, "Everything changed that day (September 11). Among the lesser casualties was the fact that what we writers and directors do became instantly irrelevant." But Zwick took issue with Sorkin's assessment, saying, "I don't think what art does is irrelevant. It attempts to help us organize our experiences. I think that people can learn as much from art as they can from the editorial page." Zwick is somewhat of an expert on that matter, having coproduced *Special Bulletin* for NBC in 1983, a TV movie that, for the first time, forced viewers to think about nuclear terrorism within our own shores. Thirty years ago, a similar sentiment was articulated by former FCC Chairman Newton Minow in his foreword to *The Emmy Awards: A Pictorial History* (Michael and Parish, 1970). Once charging that television was a vast wasteland, Minow noted that "entertainment has also played a role in easing the mounting tensions of a population that lives on the edge of an atomic precipice."

On December 7, 1941, after having learned of the attack on Pearl Harbor, young Don Bellisario (Creator of *Magnum P.I.* and *JAG*) was frightened when he saw the look on his father's face. "What are we going to do?" asked the elder Bellisario. Without losing a beat, Don's mother said, "We're going to the movies just as we had planned." The threat of an attack from Japanese bombers was as real to them then as exploding airplanes and anthrax are to us today, but Americans of the 1940s turned out in record numbers to laugh at Abbott and Costello, and they immersed themselves in radio and film dramas. Nearly sixty years later, and only weeks after Sept. 11, Bellisario's hit series *JAG* scored its second-highest ratings ever among younger viewers who were, not surprisingly, awash in patriotism. Don's mother had inspired in him a sense of resolve and normalcy in times of crisis, and today he and his fellow television dramatists are teaching a whole new generation those same values during difficult times. TV Creators, it seems, are always there when we need them, and boy do we need them now.

Appendixes
Selected Bibliography
Index

Appendix

TV Creators of the New Millennium (Producers with Dramas on Air since 2000)

CREATOR/PRODUCER	PROGRAM	NETWORK OR CABLE
Tammy ADER	*Strong Medicine*	Lifetime
Chris ABBOTT	*Diagnosis Murder*	CBS
J. J. ABRAMS	*Alias*	ABC
	Felicity	WB
Steven ANTIN	*The Young Americans*	WB
Paul ATTANASIO	*Gideon's Crossing*	ABC
Alan BALL	*Six Feet Under*	HBO
Paris BARCLAY	*City of Angels*	CBS
Jon BECKERMAN	*Ed*	NBC
Michael Frost BECKNER	*The Agency*	CBS
Donald BELLISARIO	*JAG*	CBS
	First Monday	CBS
Peter BERG	*Wonderland*	ABC
Rick BERMAN	*Enterprise*	UPN
	Star Trek: Voyager	UPN
Chris BRANCATO	*First Wave*	Sci-fi
Steven BOCHCO	*N.Y.P.D. Blue*	ABC
	Philly	ABC
	City of Angels	CBS
Rick BRAGA	*Enterprise*	UPN
Amy BRENNEMAN	*Judging Amy*	CBS
Connie BURGE	*Charmed*	WB
Rob BURNETT	*Ed*	NBC
Glenn Gordon CARON	*Now and Again*	CBS
James CAMERON	*Dark Angel*	FOX
Clifton CAMPBELL	*Profiler*	NBC

CREATOR / PRODUCER	PROGRAM	NETWORK OR CABLE
Chris CARTER	*The X-Files*	FOX
	The Lone Gunmen	FOX
	Millennium	FOX
	Harsh Realm	FOX
David CASSIDY	*Cover Me*	USA
David CHASE	*The Sopranos*	HBO
Michael CHERNUCHIN	*Bull*	TNT
Robert COCHRAN	*24*	FOX
Michael CRICHTON	*ER*	NBC
Carlton CUSE	*Nash Bridges*	CBS
Ann DONAHUE	*CSI: Crime Scene Investigation*	CBS
Charles EGLEE	*Dark Angel*	FOX
Tom FONTANA	*OZ*	HBO
	The Beat	UPN
Alex GANZA	*Wolf Lake*	CBS
Alfred GEOGH	*Smallville*	WB
Terry GEORGE	*The District*	CBS
Jonathan GLASSNER	*Stargate SG-1*	Showtime/Sci-Fi
Lee GOLDBERG	*Martial Law*	CBS
Whoopi GOLDBERG	*Strong Medicine*	Lifetime
Jill GORDON	*First Years*	ABC
F. Gary GRAY	*The Badland*	FOX
Barbara HALL	*Judging Amy*	CBS
Paul HAGGIS	*Family Law*	CBS
	Walker, Texas Ranger	CBS
Brenda HAMPTON	*7th Heaven*	WB
	Safe Harbor	WB
Felicia HENDERSON	*Soul Food*	Showtime
Marshall HERSKOVITZ	*Once & Again*	ABC
Charles HOLLAND	*Soul Food*	Showtime
David HOLLANDER	*The Guardian*	CBS
Silvio HORTA	*The Chronicle*	Sci-Fi
Roy HUGGINS	*The Fugitive*	CBS
Jason KATIMUS	*Roswell*	WB/UPN
Evan KATZ	*Special Unit 2*	UPN
Rick KELLARD	*Wolf Lake*	CBS
David E. KELLEY	*Boston Public*	FOX
	The Practice	ABC
	Snoops	ABC

CREATOR/PRODUCER	PROGRAM	NETWORK OR CABLE
David KEMPER	*Farscape*	Sci-Fi
Chris KEYSER	*Time of Your Life*	FOX
Tim KRING	*Crossing Jordan*	NBC
Steve KRONISH	*Profiler*	NBC
Roger KUMBLE	*Manchester Prep*	FOX
David Alan JOHNSON	*Doc*	PAX
Gary JOHNSON	*Doc*	PAX
Mimi LEDER	*John Doe*	FOX
Deborah Joy LeVINE	*The Division*	Lifetime
Jim LEONARD	*Thieves*	ABC
Dennis LEONI	*Resurrection Blvd.*	Showtime
Barry LEVINSON	*Homicide: Life on the Street*	NBC
	OZ	HBO
	The Beat	UPN
Amy LIPPMAN	*Time of Your Life*	FOX
Sidney LUMET	*100 Center Street*	A&E
John MASIUS	*Providence*	NBC
John McNAMARA	*The Fugitive*	CBS
John McPHERSON	*Seven Days*	UPN
Jeff MELVOIN	*Early Edition*	CBS
Carol MENDELSOHN	*CSI: Crime Scene Investigation*	CBS
David MILCH	*N.Y.P.D. Blue*	ABC
	Big Apple	CBS
Miles MILLER	*Smallville*	WB
Nancy MILLER	*Any Day Now*	Lifetime
Ryan MURPHY	*Popular*	WB
Aaron NORRIS	*Walker, Texas Ranger*	CBS
Chuck NORRIS	*Walker, Texas Ranger*	CBS
Amy Sherman-PALLADINO	*Gilmore Girls*	WB
Jim PARRIOTT	*Emma Brody*	FOX
Wolfgang PETERSEN	*. The Agency*	CBS
Michael PILLER	*Stephen King's The Dead Zone*	UPN
Charles PRATT, Jr.	*Titans*	NBC
Dawn PRESTWICH	*The Education of Max Bickford*	CBS
Bill RABKIN	*Martial Law*	CBS
Kario SALEM	*The Beast*	NBC
Cynthia SAUNDERS	*Profiler*	NBC
Shane SALERNO	*UC: Undercover*	NBC

CREATOR/PRODUCER	PROGRAM	NETWORK OR CABLE
Joel SILVER	*The Strip*	UPN
	Freedom	UPN
Douglas SCHWARTZ	*Sheena*	Syndicated
Steven SEARS	*Sheena*	Syndicated
Fred SILVERMAN	*Diagnosis Murder*	CBS
David SIMKINS	*Freaky Links*	FOX
P. K. SIMONDS	*Party of Five*	FOX
Barry SONNENFELD	*Secret Agent Man*	UPN
Aaron SORKIN	*The West Wing*	NBC
Aaron SPELLING	*Any Day Now*	Lifetime
	Beverly Hills 90210	FOX
	Charmed	WB
	7th Heaven	WB
	Titans	NBC
Darren STAR	*The $treet*	FOX
	Grosse Point	WB
Beth SULLIVAN	*The Ponderosa*	PAX
Joel SURNOW	*24*	FOX
Connie TAVEL	*Judging Amy*	CBS
John TINKER	*Chicago Hope*	CBS
	Judging Amy	CBS
Tommy THOMPSON	*Freaky Links*	FOX
Hans TOBEASON	*Freedom*	UPN
Stephen TOLKIN	*Kate Brasher*	CBS
Craig VAN SICKLE	*The Pretender*	NBC
Joss WHEDON	*Angel*	WB
	Buffy the Vampire Slayer	WB/UPN
	Firefly	FOX
Mike WHITE	*Pasadena*	FOX
Christian WILLIAMS	*Hercules*	Syndicated
Martha WILLIAMSON	*Touched By An Angel*	CBS
	Promised Land	CBS
Kevin WILLIAMSON	*Dawson's Creek*	WB
	Wasteland	ABC
John WIRTH	*The District*	CBS
John WELLS	*ER*	NBC
	Citizen Baines	CBS
	The West Wing	NBC
	Third Watch	NBC

CREATOR/PRODUCER	PROGRAM	NETWORK OR CABLE
Dick WOLF	*Law & Order*	NBC
	Law & Order Special Victims Unit	NBC
	Law & Order Criminal Intent	NBC
	Deadline	NBC
Lydia WOODWARD	*ER*	NBC
	Citizen Baines	NBC
	Presidio Med	CBS
Brad WRIGHT	*Stargate SG-1*	Showtime/Sci-Fi
Nicole YORKIN	*The Education of Max Bickford*	CBS
Sacret YOUNG	*Level 9*	UPN
Anthony ZUIKER	*CSI: Crime Scene Investigation*	CBS
Ed ZWICK	*Once & Again*	ABC

selected bibliography

Alley, Robert, and Horace Newcomb. *The Producer's Medium*. New York: Oxford Univ. Press, 1983.

Altschuler, Glen C., and David Grossvogel. *Changing Channels: America in TV Guide*. Chicago: Univ. of Illinois Press, 1992.

Anderson, Christopher. *Hollywood TV: The Studio System in the Fifties*. Austin: Univ. of Texas Press, 1994.

Anderson, Joan, and Robin Wilkins. *Getting Unplugged*. New York: John Wiley and Sons, 1998.

Auletta, Ken. *Three Blind Mice: How the TV Networks Lost Their Way*. New York: Random House, 1986.

Baker, William F., and George Dessart. *Down the Tube: An Inside Account of the Failure of American Television*. New York: Basic Books, 1998.

Bianculli, David. *Teleliteracy: Taking Television Seriously*. New York: Touchstone, 1992.

Boddy, William. *Fifties Television*. Chicago: Univ. of Illinois Press, 1990.

Bogle, Donald. *Prime Time Blues: African Americans on Network Television*. New York: Farrar, Straus, and Giroux, 2001.

Brinkley, Joel. *Defining Vision: The Battle for the Future of Television*. Orlando, Fla.: Harcourt Brace, 1997.

Brooks, Tim, and Earle Marsh. *The Complete Directory to Prime Time Network and Cable TV Shows*. New York: Ballantine Books, 1999.

Chunovic, Louis. *One Foot on the Floor: The Curious Evolution of Sex on Television*. New York: TV Books, 2000.

Collins, Joan. *Second Act*. New York: St. Martin's Press, 1996.

Condon, Jack, and David Hofstede. *"Charlie's Angels" Casebook*. Beverly Hills, Calif.: Pomegranate Press, 2000.

Courrier, Kevin, and Susan Green. *"Law & Order": The Unofficial Companion*. Los Angeles: Renaissance Books, 1998.

D'acci, Julie. *Defining Women: Television and the Case of "Cagney & Lacey."* Chapel Hill: Univ. of North Carolina Press, 1994.

Deane, Bill. *Following "The Fugitive."* Jefferson, N.C.: McFarland, 1996.

Dubowski, Cathy, and Mark Dubowski. *"7ᵗʰ Heaven": Four Years with the Camden Family*. New York: Harper Collins, 2000.

Erickson, Hal. *Syndicated Television, the First Forty Years, 1947–1987*. Jefferson, N.C.: McFarland, 1989.

Feuer, Jane. *Seeing Through the Eighties*. Durham, N.C.: Duke Univ. Press, 1995.

Feuer, Jane, Paul Kerr, and Tise Vahimagi. *MTM: Quality Television*. London: British Film Institute, 1984.

Fulton, Roger, and John Betancourt. *The Sci-Fi Channel Encyclopedia of TV Science Fiction*. New York: Warner Books, 1997.

Gitlin, Todd. *Inside Prime Time*. New York: Pantheon, 1983.

Goldberg, Lee. *Unsold Television Pilots*. Jefferson, N.C.: McFarland, 1990.

———. *Television Series Revivals*. Jefferson, N.C.: McFarland, 1993.

Golden, Christopher, and Nancy Holder. *"Buffy the Vampire Slayer": The Watcher's Guide*. New York: Pocket Books, 1998.

Goldenson, Leonard, and Martin Wolf. *Beating the Odds*. New York: Scribner's, 1991.

Gottfried, Martin. *Balancing Act: The Authorized Biography of Angela Lansbury*. Boston: Little, Brown, 1999.

Gray, Herman. *Watching Race: Television and the Struggle for Blackness*. Minneapolis: Univ. of Minnesota Press, 1995.

Harolovich, Mary Beth, and Lauren Rabinovitz. *Television, History, and American Culture: Feminist Critical Essays*. Durham, N.C.: Duke Univ. Press, 1999.

Hawes, William. *American Television Drama*. Birmingham: Univ. of Alabama Press, 1986.

———. *Live Television Drama*. Jefferson, N.C.: McFarland, 2001.

Hill, George H., and Sylvia Saverson Hill. *Blacks on Television*. Metuchen, N.J.: Scarecrow Press, 1983.

Kalat, David P. *"Homicide: Life on the Street," the Unofficial Companion*. Los Angeles: Renaissance Books, 1998.

Kindem, Gorham. *The Live Television Generation of Hollywood*. Jefferson, N.C.: McFarland, 1994.

Lentz, Harris. *Television Westerns Episode Guide*. Jefferson, N.C.: McFarland, 1997.

Levinson, Barry. *"Avalon," "Tin Men," and "Diner": Three Screenplays by Barry Levinson*. New York: Atlantic Monthly Press, 1990.

Levinson, Richard, and William Link. *Stay Tuned*. New York: St. Martin's Press, 1981.

———. *Off Camera*. New York: Plume, 1986.

Longworth, James L., Jr. *TV Creators: Conversations with America's Top Producers of Television Drama*, vol. one. Syracuse, N.Y.: Syracuse Univ. Press, 2000.

Marc, David, and Robert J. Thompson. *Prime Time, Prime Movers*. Syracuse, N.Y.: Syracuse Univ. Press, 1995.

Marill, Alvin H. *Movies Made for Television, 1964–1986*. New York: Baseline, 1987.

Martindale, David. *Television Detective Shows of the 1970s*. Jefferson, N.C.: McFarland, 1991.

Meehan, Diana M. *Ladies of the Evening*. Metuchen, N.J.: Scarecrow Press, 1983.

Michael, Paul and James Robert Parish. *The Emmy Awards: A Pictorial History*. New York: Crown Publishers, 1970.

Milch, David, and Detective Bill Clark. *True Blue: The Real Stories Behind "NYPD Blue."* New York: William Morrow, 1995.

Morris, Bruce B. *Prime Time Network Serials.* Jefferson, N.C.: McFarland, 1997.

Muir, John Kenneth. *Terror Television.* Jefferson, N.C.: McFarland, 2000.

Nelson, Robin. *TV Drama in Transition: Forms, Values, and Cultural Change.* New York: St. Martin's Press, 1997.

New York Times. *The Sopranos.* New York: Pocket Books, 1999.

O'Dell, Cary. *Women Pioneers in Television.* Jefferson, N.C.: McFarland, 1997.

O'Neil, Thomas. *The Emmys.* New York: Perigee, 1998.

Owen, Rob. *Gen X TV.* Syracuse, N.Y.: Syracuse Univ. Press, 1997.

Paisner, Daniel. *Horizontal Hold: The Making and Breaking of a Network Television Pilot.* New York: Birch Lane Press, 1992.

Paley, William S. *As It Happened.* New York: Doubleday, 1979.

Paper, Lewis. *Empire: William S. Paley and the Making of CBS.* New York: St. Martin's Press, 1987.

Pourroy, Janine. *Behind the Scenes at "ER."* New York: Ballantine Books, 1995.

Press, Andrea. *Women Watching Television.* Philadelphia: Univ. of Pennsylvania Press, 1991.

Proctor, Mel. *The Official Fan's Guide to "The Fugitive."* Stanford, Calif.: Longmeadow Press, 1995.

Shepherd, Cybill. *Cybill Disobedience.* New York: Harper Collins, 2000.

Skutch, Ira. *The Days of Live: Television's Golden Age, as Seen by Twenty-one Directors Guild of America Members.* Metuchen, N.J.: Scarecrow Press, 1998.

Smith, Sally Bedell. *Up the Tube: Prime Time in the Silverman Years.* New York: Viking Press, 1981.

———. *In All His Glory: The Life of William S. Paley.* New York: Simon and Schuster, 1990.

Spelling, Aaron, and Jefferson Graham. *A Prime Time Life.* New York: St. Martin's Press, 1995.

Spigel, Lynn. *Make Room for TV: Television and Family Ideas in Post War America.* Chicago: Univ. of Chicago Press, 1992.

Stagg, Evelyn, and Frank Stagg. *Woman in the World of Jesus.* Philadelphia: Westminster Press, 1978.

Stark, Steven D. *Glued to the Set.* New York: Delta, 1997.

Stempel, Tom. *Storytellers to the Nation: A History of American Television Writing.* Syracuse, N.Y.: Syracuse Univ. Press, 1992.

Sumser, John. *Morality and Social Order in Television Crime Drama.* Jefferson, N.C.: McFarland, 1996.

Swanson, Dorothy Collins. *The Story of Viewers for Quality Television.* Syracuse, N.Y.: Syracuse Univ. Press, 2001.

Tartikoff, Brandon, and Charles Leerhsen. *The Last Great Ride.* New York: Turtle Bay Books, 1992.

Terrace, Vincent. *Television Character and Story Facts.* Jefferson, N.C.: McFarland, 1993.

————. *Experimental Television, Test Films, Pilots, and Trial Series.* Jefferson, N.C.: McFarland, 1997.

Thompson, Robert J. *Television's Second Golden Age.* New York: Continuum, 1996.

Tinker, Grant, and Bud Rukeyser. *Tinker in Television: From General Sarnoff to General Electric.* New York: Simon and Schuster, 1994.

West, Richard. *Television Westerns.* Jefferson, N.C.: McFarland, 1987.

Wild, David. *The Showrunners.* New York: Harper Collins, 1999.

Wilk, Max. *The Golden Age of Television: Notes from the Survivors.* Chicago: Silver Spring Press, 1999.

Williamson, Martha, and Robin Sheets. *Touched by an Angel.* Grand Rapids, Mich.: Zondervan Publishing House, 1997.

Woolley, Lynn, Robert W. Malsbary, and Robert G. Strange, Jr. *Warner Brothers Television.* Jefferson, N.C.: McFarland, 1985.

Yoggy, Gary. *Back in the Saddle.* Jefferson, N.C.: McFarland, 1998.

Index